DOUBLE FOLD

DOUBLE FOLD

Libraries and the Assault on Paper

Nicholson Baker

RANDOM HOUSE
NEW YORK

 Published in the United States by Random House, Inc., New York, and simultaneously in Canada by Random House of Canada Limited, Toronto.

Parts of this book were originally published in *The New Yorker.*

Library of Congress Cataloging-in-Publication Data

Baker, Nicholson.
Double fold : libraries and the assault on paper / Nicholson Baker.
p. cm.
Includes bibliographical references.
ISBN 0-375-50444-3
1. Libraries—United States—Special collections—Newspapers. 2. Newspaper and periodical libraries—United States. 3. Newspapers—Conservation and restoration. 4. Paper—Preservation—United States. I. Title.

Z695.655 .B35 2001
025.2'832—dc21 00-059171

Random House website address: www.atrandom.com

Printed in the United States of America on acid-free paper

9876543

First Edition

BOOK DESIGN BY MERCEDES EVERETT

To my son, Elias

Preface

In 1993, I decided to write some essays on trifling topics—movie projectors, fingernail clippers, punctuation, and the history of the word "lumber." Deborah Garrison, then an editor at *The New Yorker,* called to ask if I wanted to review a soon-to-be published history of the world. Perhaps I should have written the review; instead, I suggested a brief, cheerful piece about the appeal of card catalogs. I began talking to librarians around the country, and I found out that card catalogs were being thrown out everywhere. I grew less cheerful, and the essay grew longer.

When it was published in 1994, I became known in the library world as a critic (and, to some, as a crank and a Luddite), and as a result, librarians at the San Francisco Public Library thought of me two years later when they wanted to tell someone what had happened in their institution: administrators had sent a few hundred thousand books to a landfill after they discovered that a new library building was too small to hold them. I gave a speech on this subject in the auditorium of the new building, and I published an article about it in *The New Yorker.* There was a local fuss, the head of the library eventually lost his job (over deficits, not book dumping), and I found myself described as a "library activist."

In the midst of the controversy, a man named Blackbeard told a reporter that he had a story for me. He wouldn't reveal any details to the reporter (who was Nina Siegal, of the San Francisco *Bay Guardian*); I was supposed to call him. I didn't make the call right away, though, because the squabble over the San Francisco Public Library was sufficiently distracting, and because my family and I were packing to spend a year in England. Some weeks later, going through some papers, I found the name, Bill Blackbeard, and his number, which I dialed. Blackbeard had a formal, slightly breathless way of talking; he was obviously intelligent, perhaps a little Ancient Marinerian in the way that lifelong collectors can be. He had edited collections of comic strips (early *Popeye, Terry and the Pirates, Krazy Kat*), and he ran something called the San Francisco Academy of Comic Art—a one-man curatorship, apparently—which owned, he said, a very large number of ex-library newspaper volumes, including one-of-a-kind runs of the great early Hearst papers. Some of what Blackbeard told me I couldn't quite comprehend: that the Library of Congress, the purported library of last resort, had replaced most of its enormous collection of late-nineteenth- and twentieth-century newspapers with microfilm, and that research libraries were relying on what he called "fraudulent" scientific studies when they justified the discarding of books and newspapers on the basis of diagnosed states of acidity and embrittlement. I said that it all sounded extremely interesting and that maybe he should write about it himself; I thanked him and hung up. I was tired of finding fault with libraries; in theory, I loved libraries.

Almost two years later, I thought of Blackbeard again, and I decided to pay him a visit. He had by this time sold his newspaper collection, which filled six tractor trailers, to Ohio State University, and he had moved to Santa Cruz, where his wife liked to surf. He was in his early seventies, fit, clean shaven, wearing a nubbly gold sweater and a baseball hat turned backward. One room of his very small house was filled with dime novels and old science-fiction magazines in white boxes. In his youth, he'd written for *Weird Tales;* he'd driven armored vehicles in the

Eighty-ninth Cavalry Reconnaissance Squadron in the Second World War; and in 1967, filled with an ambition to write a history of the American comic strip, he'd discovered that libraries were getting rid of their newspaper collections. The San Francisco Public Library had, Blackbeard said, an "incredible treasure trove." Staff members told him that they would love to have him take it away, but unfortunately he was a private citizen—the library's charter permitted the transfer of material only to a non-profit organization. "I became a non-profit organization so fast you couldn't believe it," Blackbeard told me. Soon he had acquired a bound run of William Randolph Hearst's New York *American,* which the Hearst Corporation had donated to the Los Angeles Public Library (the library kept the custom-made burnished mahogany shelves), and another *American* run from the Stanford University Libraries. He went around the country picking up newspaper volumes, which he called "files," a usage that confused me at first. Sometimes he cut the comic strips or Sunday sections out and sold the remains to dealers; sometimes he kept the volumes whole. "When I suddenly discovered that I could have any of them that I wanted, I just went off my rocker. It was the most wonderful thing in the world." Blackbeard also told me about a test that librarians were using on paper, in which they folded the corner of a page back and forth until it broke.

Not long after I visited Blackbeard, I moved with my family from California to southern Maine. I sat in my new office, surrounded by boxes of books, staring out the window at a valley filled with young trees. There were several off-white nests of webworms clinging like the ends of Q-tips to some of the trees' upper branches. I looked at the webworm nests, and I thought, Why not find out what's happened to the newspapers? Why not learn more about the fold test? I called *The New Yorker* and asked Deborah Garrison if she could stand another article about libraries. She said yes, and I went to work. I learned about pyrophoric compounds, mummy wrappings, oversewing, artificial-aging ovens, redox blemishes, and a group called the

Council on Library Resources, founded by Verner Clapp. I became familiar with the efforts of a woman named Patricia Battin, and I watched a movie, *Slow Fires.* I began moaning and typing things like "Oh, my friends, it's worse than you think." I realized that I had something that was longer than a magazine article.

Then, four fifths of the way through writing this book, I found out that one of the last remaining collections of American wood-pulp newspapers would be cut to pieces unless I started a non-profit corporation—just as Blackbeard had—and raised the money to save it. I sent out letters and grant applications; then I resumed work on the manuscript. And that's how *Double Fold*—so named in honor of the brittleness test that Bill Blackbeard first told me about—came to be written.

This isn't an impartial piece of reporting. I've tried not to misrepresent those whose views differ from my own, but I make no secret of my disagreement; at times, a dormant prosecutorial urge awoke in me, for we have lost things that we can never get back. I must also say, though, that the Library of Congress, the British Library, and the other illustrious institutions herein held up for criticism, employ a great many book-respecting people who may not know of, or approve of, what their superiors or their forebears have done.

The following people read the manuscript, or parts of it, and made useful suggestions: Nicolas Barker, Viscountess Eccles, David McKitterick, Paul Needham, Randy Silverman, Thomas Tanselle, and Peter Waters—which is not to imply that they agree with everything I say. Many others were helpful in various ways, including Marty Asher, Ann Godoff, Melanie Jackson, Cressida Leyshon, Timothy Mennel, Charline Parsons, Susanna Porter, David Remnick, and Sasha Smith. I'm grateful to my parents and my parents-in-law, and, most of all, to my beloved wife, Margaret.

Contents

DOUBLE FOLD

CHAPTER 1

Overseas Disposal

The British Library's newspaper collection occupies several buildings in Colindale, north of London, near a former Royal Air Force base that is now a museum of aviation. On October 20, 1940, a German airplane—possibly mistaking the library complex for an aircraft-manufacturing plant—dropped a bomb on it. Ten thousand volumes of Irish and English papers were destroyed; fifteen thousand more were damaged. Unscathed, however, was a very large foreign-newspaper collection, including many American titles: thousands of fifteen-pound brick-thick folios bound in marbled boards, their pages stamped in red with the British Museum's crown-and-lion symbol of curatorial responsibility.

Bombs spared the American papers, but recent managerial policy has not—most were sold off in a blind auction in the fall of 1999. One of the library's treasures was a seventy-year run, in about eight hundred volumes, of Joseph Pulitzer's exuberantly polychromatic newspaper, the New York *World*. Pulitzer discovered that illustrations sold the news; in the 1890s, he began printing four-color Sunday supplements and splash-panel cartoons. The more maps, murder-scene diagrams, ultra-wide front-page political cartoons, fashion sketches, needlepoint patterns, children's puzzles, and comics that Pulitzer published, the higher the *World*'s sales climbed; by the mid-nineties, its circulation was the largest of any paper in the country. William Randolph Hearst moved to New York in 1895 and copied Pulitzer's innovations and poached his staff, and the war between the two men created modern privacy-probing, muckraking, glamour-smitten journalism. A million people a day once read Pulitzer's *World;* now an original set is a good deal rarer than a Shakespeare First Folio or the Gutenberg Bible.

Besides the *World,* the British Library also possessed one of the last sweeping runs of the sumptuous *Chicago Tribune*—about 1,300 volumes, reaching from 1888 to 1958, complete with bonus four-color art supplements on heavy stock from the 1890s ("This Paper is Not Complete Without the Color Illustration" says the box on the masthead); extravagant layouts of illustrated fiction; elaborately hand-lettered ornamental headlines; and decades of page-one political cartoons by John T. McCutcheon. The British Library owned, as well, an enormous set of the *San Francisco Chronicle* (one of perhaps two that are left, the second owned by the Chronicle Publishing Company itself and inaccessible to scholars), which in its heyday was filled with gorgeously drippy art-nouveau graphics. And the library owned a monster accumulation of what one could argue is the best newspaper in U.S. history, the New York *Herald Tribune,* along with its two tributaries, Horace Greeley's anti-slavery *Tribune* and James Gordon Bennett's initially pro-slavery *Herald*. The *Herald Tribune* set carries all the way through to 1966, when the paper itself died—it, too, may be the last surviving long run anywhere. And there was a goodly stretch of *The New York Times* on the British Library's shelves (1915 through 1958), with Al Hirschfeld drawings and hundreds of luminously fine-grained, sepia-tinted "Rotogravure Picture Sections" bound in place.

All these newspapers have been very well cared for over the years—the volumes I was allowed to examine in September 1999 were in lovely shape. The pictorial sections, but for their unfamiliar turn-of-the-century artwork, looked and felt as if they had peeled off a Hoe cylinder press day before yesterday.

But then, wood-pulp newspapers of fifty and a hundred years ago are, contrary to incessant library propaganda, often surprisingly well preserved. Everyone knows that newsprint, if left in the sun, quickly turns yellow and brittle (a connective wood ingredient called lignin, which newsprint contains in abundance, reacts with sunlight), but rolls of microfilm—and floppies and DVDs—don't do well in the sun, either; so far, many of the old volumes seem to be doing a better job of holding their original images than the miniature plastic reproductions of them that libraries have seen fit to put in their places over the years. Binding is very important. The stitching together of fifteen (or thirty or sixty) single issues of a paper into one large, heavy book does much to keep the sheets sound; the margins often become brown and flaky, since moist, warm air reacts with the acidic compounds in the paper and weakens it, and the binding glues can stop working; but a little deeper inside the flatland of the tightly closed folio, the sheer weight of the text-block squeezes out most of the air. The effect is roughly equivalent to vacuum-sealing the inner expanses of the pages: the paper suffers much less impairment as a result.

Many librarians, however, have managed to convince themselves, and us, that if a newspaper was printed after 1870 or so, it will inevitably self-destruct or "turn to dust" any minute, soon, in a matter of a few years—1870 being the all-important date after which, in American newsprint mills, papermaking pulps consisting of cooked rags gradually began to give way to pulps made of stone-ground wood. But "soon" is a meaningless word in the context of a substance with a life as long as that of the printed page—indeed, it is a word that allows for all sorts of abuses. Early on, fledgling microfilm companies fed the fear of impermanence with confident mispredictions. Charles Z. Case, an executive at Recordak, Kodak's microfilm subsidiary, wrote in 1936: "Since the adoption of wood-sulphite paper for newspaper printing, a newspaper file has had a life of from 5 to 40 years depending on the quality of the paper, the conditions of storage, and the degree of use." Had Case's forecast held true, the volume of the *Chicago Tribune* for July 1911 that lies open before me as I type (to an influenza-inspired illustrated section on "A New Theory of Baby Rearing") would have expired at least half a century ago. Thomas Martin, chief of the manuscript division of the Library of Congress in the thirties, agreed with the Recordak salesman: "Old wood-pulp files which have only a few years' duration remaining in them should be photographed on film as soon as satisfactory results can be obtained. In such cases we really have no choice but to make or take film copies, the original will soon crumble into dust."

But the originals didn't crumble into dust. Keyes Metcalf, a microfilm pioneer and the director of the libraries at Harvard, in 1941 predicted that the "total space requirements" of research libraries "will be reduced by paper disintegration." Then five, ten, twenty years went by, and the paper—even the supposedly ephemeral newsprint—was still there. So librarians began getting rid of it anyway. If you destroy the physical evidence, nobody will know how skewed your predictions were.

Vilified though it may be, ground-wood pulp is one of the great inventions of the late nineteenth century: it gave us cheap paper, and cheap paper transformed the news. "All that it is necessary for a man to do on going into a paper-mill is to take off his shirt, hand it to the devil who officiates at one extremity, and have it come out 'Robinson Crusoe' at the other," wrote the founder of the New York *Sun* in 1837. But there were never enough shirts, and in 1854 rag shortages lifted the price of newsprint to alarming heights. The arrival of the brothers Pagenstecher, who in the eighteen-sixties imported a German machine that shredded logs to pulp by jamming their ends against a circular, water-cooled grinding stone, brought prices way down—from twelve cents a pound in 1870, to seven cents a pound in 1880, to less than two cents a pound in 1900. The drop gave Pulitzer and Hearst the plentiful page space to sell big ads, and allowed their creations to flower into the gaudy painted ladies they had become by the first decade of the twentieth century.

There's no question that wood pulps are in general weaker than rag pulps; and old newsprint, especially, tears easily, and it can become exceedingly fragile if it is stored, say, on the cement floor of a library basement, near heating pipes, for a few decades. But the degree of fragility varies from title to title and run to run, and many fragile things (old quilts, old clocks, astrolabes, dried botanical specimens, Egyptian glass, daguerreotypes, early computers) are deemed worth preserving despite, or even because of, their fragility. The most delicate volume I've come across (a month of the Detroit *Evening News* from 1892), though the pages were mostly detached, and though it shed flurries of marginal flakes when I moved it around, could nonetheless be page-turned and read with a modicum of care—there was an interesting article, with two accompanying etchings, about a city shelter for "homeless wanderers." (Sinners slept on wooden bunks without bedding, while the newly converted got cots with mattresses, and a reading room.)

Old newsprint is very acidic—and so? Our agitation over the acid in paper is not rational. Just because a given page has a low pH (a pH of 7 is neutral, below that is acidic) doesn't mean that it can't be read. There are five-hundred-year-old book papers that remain strong and flexible despite pH levels under five, a fact which has led one conservation scientist to conclude that "the acidity of the paper alone is not necessarily indicative of the state of permanence of paper." It is difficult, in fact, to get a meaningful measure of how alkaline or acidic a paper actually is, since chemicals on the surface behave differently than those held within; the standard scientific tests (which often rely on a blender) don't discriminate. It's true that, all things being equal, pH-neutral paper seems to keep its properties longer than paper that is made with acid-containing or acid-forming additives; scientists have been making this observation, on and off, for more than eighty years. But saying that one substance is stronger than another is not the same as saying that the weaker substance is on the verge of self-destruction. A stainless-steel chair may be more durable than a wooden one, but the wooden one isn't necessarily going to collapse the next time you take a seat.

Can't scientists foretell with a fair degree of certainty how long a newspaper collection of a given age will last? No, they can't; there has never been a long-term study that attempted to plot an actual loss-of-strength curve for samples of naturally aging newsprint, or indeed for samples of any paper. Years ago, William K. Wilson, a paper scientist, began such a study at the National Bureau of Standards. For three decades he recorded the degradative changes undergone by a set of commercial book papers; then somebody decided to clean out the green filing cabinet in which the papers were stored—end of experiment. "That raised my blood pressure a little," Wilson told me.

In the absence of real long-term data, predictions have relied on methodologically shaky "artificial aging" (or "accelerated aging") experiments, in which you bake a paper sample in a laboratory oven for a week or two and then belabor it with standardized tests. With your test results in hand, you can, by applying a bit of chemist's legerdemain called the Arrhenius equation, come up with what appears be a reasonable estimate of the number of years the sample will last at shirtsleeve temperatures. But the results of these sorts of divinatory calculations, invoked with head-shaking gravity by library administrators, have been uniformly wrong, and they are now viewed with skepticism by many paper scientists. The authors of the *ASTM Standards,* for example, write that the use of the Arrhenius equation to predict the life expectancy of paper is "an interesting academic exercise, but the uncertainty of extrapolation is too great for this approach to be taken very seriously"; William Wilson points out that you can't predict how long an egg will last in the carton by putting it in boiling water for five minutes. Paper has a complex and as yet ill-charted chemistry, with many different molecular and mechanical processes under way concurrently; one Swedish researcher wrote that it is a "naive hope" to think that we can estimate "the life length of books by means of accelerated aging tests and [the] Arrhenius approach."

In a way, however, all surviving newspaper collections, in and out of libraries, are taking part in an immense self-guided experiment in natural aging—an experiment that confutes the doctrine of newsprint's imminent disintegration. Peter Waters, former head of the conservation lab at the Library of Congress, told me that he sees no reason why old ground-wood pulp paper can't hold its textual freight for "a hell of a long time" if it is properly stored. He notes that most of the cellulose-sundering chemical reactions that can happen to a book or newspaper volume seem to take place in the first decade or so of its life; fifty years of handling paper (Waters is a master bookbinder) have taught him that the rate at which paper loses strength decreases significantly over time—the curve of observed decay levels out. There is a very good chance, then, that a volume of the New York *World* that is doing okay at age ninety will be in pretty much the same shape when it is a hundred and eighty, assuming someone is willing to take decent care of it.

The British Library's papers had escaped the Blitz and the agenbite of their own acidity, but their keepers craved the space they occupied. English law requires that the library preserve British newspapers in the original but makes no such stipulation for foreign papers, and in 1996 the library quietly announced its intent to rid itself of about sixty thousand volumes—almost all the non-Commonwealth papers printed after 1850 for which they had bought microfilm copies. (The microfilm, much of it shot in the United States decades ago, is of varying quality—some good, some not good, all on high-contrast black-and-white stock, which wasn't designed to reproduce the intermediate shades of photographs.) The announcement appeared as an inside article in the newspaper library's newsletter; it was written up not long after as a short wire-service story— "British Library Giving Away Historic Newspapers."

In 1997 the library selected for discard more than seventy-five runs of Western European papers and periodicals, from France, Belgium, Germany, Austria, Greece, Italy, Portugal, Spain, the Netherlands, and Switzerland. They were able to place a number of these titles with national and university libraries;

others they planned to sell or throw away. (I first found out about these developments in 1999; library officials still have not provided an accounting of where everything went.) Baylor University in Texas asked for, and got, eight runs of important French and Italian papers from the 1850s on, some of which will become part of their renowned Armstrong Browning collection, since Robert and Elizabeth Barrett Browning likely would have read those papers in their expatriate years.

Very few people knew any of this was going on. Although I interviewed a number of American newspaper librarians and dealers, I heard nothing of it; and even well-connected heads of libraries within England—such as David McKitterick, librarian of Trinity College, Cambridge, who serves on an advisory board of the British Library—were not informed of the "overseas disposals project," and learned of it only late in 1999, when word began to get out. McKitterick objects to the "very quiet way" in which the deaccessioning was handled (at the very least, other British libraries should have had a better-advertised chance at the papers, he says), and he is troubled by what is on the lists; he mentions, for instance, the newspapers of pre-Revolutionary Russia, Nazi Germany, and occupied France. "I've now talked to a number of scholars about this," McKitterick told me, "and they're absolutely furious. When you replace a broadsheet newspaper with microfilm, you effectively kill stone dead much of what it meant at its time. Film can't deal adequately with illustrations—and yet they were discarding the great French illustrated papers of the early twentieth century."

But library administrators had other things to think about than illustration and scholarship. "Increasing pressure on the storage facilities at the Colindale site" was the justification for their desperate act. One of the finest libraries in the world was unable or unwilling to buy, build, retrofit, or lease a ten-thousand-square-foot warehouse anywhere in England that could hold their unique international collection.

With Western Europe taken care of, having freed up thousands of linear meters of shelf space without any political trouble, the British Library then moved on to papers from Eastern Europe, South America, and the U.S.A. They sent out notices of availability to the Library of Congress and the American Antiquarian Society, of Worcester, Massachusetts. The Library of Congress rejected everything, but the American Antiquarian Society, which owns a famous collection of early papers (bound in black with gold trim), took several titles, mainly covering the era of the Civil War and immediately afterward. "The redcoats are coming!" librarians there said, shelving the red-spined British volumes next to their black ones. Richard Bland College in Petersburg, Virginia, claimed several nineteenth-century runs. John Blair, head of the history department, says he would have taken more of the British Library's collection if his college had had more space; Blair remembers working as a stock boy in a large Massachusetts library in the fifties and hauling home dozens of unwanted newspaper volumes. "They just junked them," he said; he has used them for years in his classes. Blair likened the clearing out of newspaper collections to the overeager tearing up of track as the railroads went into decline. "Now maybe they regret losing some of those rights-of-way," he said.

No other libraries expressed interest in the huge remaining mass of U.S. material. The plan, blessed by the British Library's board, was to offer to dealers whatever libraries left unclaimed; anything dealers didn't want was to be thrown away: "Material for which we cannot find a home will be offered to dealers for sale, or as a last resort sent for pulping." Brian Lang, the director of the British Library, reiterated this plan in a letter to me: "The intention is that runs of newspapers for which no bids have been received will be pulped."

CHAPTER 2

Original Keepsakes

I didn't want the newspapers to be dispersed by dealers or "pulped" (awful word), so I hastily formed a non-profit corporation called the American Newspaper Repository, and, when it was clear that the auction was going to go forward whether I liked it or not, I submitted bids. A dealer from Williamsport, Pennsylvania, Timothy Hughes Rare and Early Newspapers, also bid on the papers, as it turned out. Hughes owns a medium-sized, pale blue warehouse, tidily kept, filled with rows of industrial shelving; on the shelves rest about eighteen thousand newspaper volumes. He is an undemonstrative man with a small mustache, honest in his business dealings, who was formerly on the board of the Little League Museum in South Williamsport. His usual practice is to "disbind" the newspapers—that is, cut them out of their chronological context with a utility knife (you can hear the binding strings pop softly as the blade travels down the inner gutter of the volume)—and sell the eye-catching headline issues (Al Capone, the *Lusitania,* Bonnie and Clyde, Amelia Earhart) or issues containing primordial Coke ads or Thomas Nast illustrations, shrink-wrapped against white cardboard, at paper shows (where buyers gather to look over vintage postcards, baseball cards, posters, and other ephemera) or through his printed catalog or website. His father, jolly and self-effacing, is a retired sharpener of band-saw blades, as was his grandfather; now his father and his brother, along with an amiable ex-schoolteacher named Marc, are employees of the company, filling orders, moving pallets of incoming volumes around with a forklift, writing catalog copy, and gradually working down the inventory, almost all of which came from libraries.

If American libraries had been doing the job we paid them to do, and innocently trusted that they were doing, over the past five decades—if they had been taking reasonable care of our communal newspaper collections rather than stacking them in all the wrong places, and finally selling them to book-breakers or dumping them in the trash outright (an employee of one Southern library recently rescued from a Dumpster, and successfully resold to a dealer, a run of *Harper's Weekly* worth ten thousand dollars)—then the British Library's decision to auction off millions of pages of urban life, although it would mark a low point of cultural husbandry, would not have been such a potentially disastrous loss to future historians. Fifty years ago, after all, there were bound sets, even double sets, of all the major metropolitan dailies safely stored in libraries around the United States.

But that is no longer true. The Library of Congress and the New York Public Library once owned Pulitzer's New York *World* complete, for instance, and Harvard University, the University of Chicago, the Chicago Public Library, and the Chicago Tribune Company once owned sets of the *Chicago Tribune.* They don't now. ("I'm sorry to say and appalled to say that they were tossed," an employee of the reference department of the *Chicago Tribune* said to me. "It was before my time.") At Columbia University (whose school of journalism Pulitzer founded), at the New York Public Library, and at the Library of Congress, you can flip through memoirs, biographies, scholarly studies, and original holograph letters of Joseph Pulitzer, works that describe his innovations in graphic design and recount his public squabble with Hearst over *The Yellow Kid,* a popular color cartoon that first appeared in the *World* in the 1890s—a squabble that begat the term "yellow journalism." But the *World* itself, the half-million-page masterpiece in the service of which Pulitzer stormed and swore and finally went blind, was slapdashedly microfilmed in monochrome and thrown out by the New York Public Library, probably in the early fifties. Columbia said good-bye to its *World* at some point thereafter; the New-York Historical Society did so around 1990. The University of Chicago library, under the direction of micro-madman Herman Fussler (former lead librarian and information specialist for the Manhattan Project), produced a bad copy of the *Chicago Tribune* in the fifties as well. The Library of Congress was quick to clear its shelves of the *World* and most of the *Chicago Tribune* and replace them with copies of the NYPL's and the University of Chicago's microfilm; and copies of that very same mid-century microfilm—edge-blurred, dark, gappy, with text cut off of some pages, faded to the point of illegibility on others—will now have to serve for patrons of the British Library, too.

All the major newspaper repositories—the Center for Research Libraries in Chicago, for instance, and the State Historical Society of Wisconsin, both of which once had collections of national importance—have long since bet the farm on film and given away, sold, or thrown out most of their original volumes published after 1880 or so. Nearly all major university libraries, state libraries, and large public libraries have done the same. Even the great American Antiquarian Society, having decided some years ago to narrow its focus to publications before 1876, is arranging with Timothy Hughes to swap long runs of some small-town papers—the Fitchburg (Massachusetts) *Sentinel* from 1888 on, for example—for older titles that they want.

The Kansas State Historical Society, founded by a group of newspaper editors in 1875, had, until a few years ago, an unusually fine out-of-state newspaper assemblage, including a pre-Civil War file of the New York *Tribune,* a long run of the Boston *Investigator,* and a large number of otherwise impossible-to-find Western and territorial papers. Then the society put up a new building that was smaller than it should have been and, in 1997, had an auction. One observer told me that the lots that Kansas ended up selling were so unusual, so valuable, that a group of buyers got together ahead of time to divvy things up, so that the bidding wouldn't go completely insane. It was "once-in-a-lifetime stuff," this observer said. The next step, according to Patricia Michaelis, the director of the library and archives division, was to dispose of most of the society's comprehensive collection of original Kansas papers printed after 1875, offering them first to institutions and then throwing out the leavings. Michaelis believes that the original papers are doomed anyway: "They're just inherently going to crumble apart, no matter what you do to them, because of the acid content." About half of the people who use the library come for the newspaper collection. Do they like the microfilm? Michaelis laughed. "Well, it's the only option we give them."

At another midwestern historical society, out in a pole barn, a collection was stacked twelve feet high and twenty feet wide near rows of shaft-drive bicycles and the disassembled pieces of a nineteenth-century machine shop. There were thousands of volumes of local papers and a run of *The New York Times.* Shawn Godwin, an employee of the society at the time, wrote me that this "cube of history" was made to disappear by order of the head archivist: the volumes were chainsawed in half and fed into the steam engine that powered a vintage sawmill exhibit. "I asked one of the more sympathetic assistant directors if it would be possible to sneak a few of the volumes away," Godwin writes. "He indicated if I was discreet and did not make a big deal about it it might be okay." Godwin saved a small stack and tried to avoid looking at the column of smoke rising from the sawmill.

The cleanout continues. Since the mid-eighties, the vast U.S. Newspaper Program, a government project whose aims are to catalog as many newspapers in the country as possible (a worthy goal) and to microfilm those local papers that were passed over in earlier decades, has given libraries about forty-five million dollars in so-called preservation money—and zero dollars for storage space. The National Endowment for the Humanities, which pays for the U.S. Newspaper Program (and funds a related enterprise, the Brittle Books Program), makes no requirement that libraries actually preserve, in the physical sense of "reshelve," their originals after they have been sent out for federally funded filming. The effect of all this NEH microfilm money has been to trigger a last huge surge of discarding, as libraries use federal preservation grants to solve their local space problems. Not since the monk-harassments of sixteenth-century England has a government tolerated, indeed stimulated, the methodical eradication of so much primary-source material.

Surely this material is all available on the Web by now, or will be soon? In time, eighty or a hundred years of a great urban paper could well become the source for a historical database of richness and utility. But at the moment, the scanning and storing and indexing of hundreds of thousands of pages of tiny type, along with halftone photos and color illustrations, would be a fearsomely expensive job; and even if money were limitless, there would remain the formidable technical challenge of achieving acceptable levels of resolution using digital cameras for formats as large as those of a newspaper spread. Nor will high-quality digital facsimiles of our major papers ever exist unless we decide right now to do a much better job of holding on to the originals—even the mangy ones with crumbly edges. You can't digitize something that has been sold off piecemeal or thrown away, after all; and attempts to scan the page-images of newspapers from old microfilm have not worked well—and will never work well—because the microfilm itself is often at the squint-to-make-it-out level. HarpWeek, a venture that offers a digital copy of *Harper's Weekly* on the Web, spent tens of thousands of dollars trying to scan the available microfilm, but they found that thirty percent of the resultant images were bad. Now they're working from two original sets of the journal, both of which they've cut out of their bindings in order to set the loose pages flat on the scanner.

Amid the general devastation, there are some librarians of courage and foresight whose accomplishments are as yet unsung. The Boston Public Library, owing to the belief of Charles Longley—the recently retired curator of microtexts and newspapers—that his institution's accumulated newspaper files are "part of the City's own heritage and the Library would be remiss in not retaining them," not only has held on to all its existing collections but has continued to lay away all the recent output of Boston and selected Massachusetts papers, wrapped in brown paper, right up through the present; and the library has taken ownership of important sets of bound Boston newspapers once owned by Harvard and other libraries in the region as well. Longley was lucky: his views were shared by the city's longtime librarian, the late Philip McNiff; often a change of administration proves fatal to a great collection.

At Ohio State, a librarian named Lucy Caswell, who wears quiet silk scarves and directs the Cartoon Research Library, is almost single-handedly attempting to rebuild a bound-volume collection of national scope—buying back for scholarly use material offered by dealers and collectors, most notably the lifetime harvest of Bill Blackbeard and his San Francisco Academy of Comic Art.

Several years ago, Caswell bought some volumes of the *Chicago Tribune* (from a dealer, who bought them from another dealer); two of them, one from 1899 and one from 1914, were out on a trolley at the Cartoon Research Library when I visited—four-inch-thick buckram-backed bulwarks, with heavy pull-straps triple-riveted to the binding in order to assist the frowning researcher in hauling their massiveness from the shelf. Their exteriors are scuffed and battered, but they are things of beauty nonetheless; they made me think of Mickey's book of broom-awakening spells in *Fantasia*. I opened the volume from 1914. The inside boards displayed the seal of Harvard University, and below it I read:

FROM THE BEQUEST OF
ICHABOD TUCKER
[Class of 1791]
OF SALEM, MASS.

The paper wasn't crumbling—it was easily turned and read. I called Harvard's microform department and asked if they had the *Chicago Tribune* on paper from 1899 and 1914, just to be sure that the Ohio volumes weren't from a duplicate set that they had sold. A sincere-sounding reference woman in the microforms department said, "Oh, we would never have hard copies going back that far—they just don't keep." They don't keep, kiddo, if you don't keep them.

Aside from what Lucy Caswell and Charles Longley have been able to save, the annihilation of once accessible collections of major daily papers of the late nineteenth and twentieth centuries is pretty close to total. Some state libraries—Pennsylvania's, for instance, in Harrisburg—reached back further than the 1870s or 1880s as they designed their disposal programs, and used 1850 as a draconian dump-after date. "Pennsylvania was the first state to undertake statewide microfilming and destruction of its newspaper files," Bill Blackbeard told me. "They did an extraordinarily, brutally thorough job of it. Unfortunately, some of the earliest color Sunday comic strips were printed in Philadelphia newspapers. So I never have gotten to see very many of those." The State Library of Pennsylvania did not keep its original bound set of *The Philadelphia Inquirer,* and neither did the Free Library of Philadelphia—a librarian there wrote me that wood-pulp newsprint "falls apart." Bell and Howell Information and Learning (formerly University Microfilms) will, however, sell the whole *Inquirer* to you on spools of archival polyester, encased in little white cardboard boxes, for $621,515.

Bell and Howell/UMI now owns microfilm negatives for most of the big papers in the country; and, to the extent that there are no originals left to scan when scanning resolution improves, its "master" microfilm (some of it inherited from now defunct filming labs and of poor quality) will perforce become the basis for any future digital versions of old newspapers, access to which the company will also control. Bell and Howell has successfully privatized our past: whether we like it or not, they possess a near monopoly on the reproduction rights for the chief primary sources of twentieth-century history.

Where did all the spurned papers go? Many were thrown out—and continue to be thrown out as statewide filming projects progress—but a colossal residue rests at a company called Historic Newspaper Archives, Inc., the biggest name in the birth-date business. If you call Hammacher Schlemmer, say, or Potpourri, or the Miles Kimball catalog, to order an "original keepsake newspaper" from the day a loved one was born, Historic Newspaper Archives will fill your order. In the company's twenty-five thousand square feet of warehouse space in Rahway, New Jersey, innumerable partially gutted volumes wait in lugubrious disorder on tall industrial shelves and stacked in four-foot piles and on pallets. I paid a visit one winter afternoon. The Christmas rush was over, and the place was very quiet. Torn sheets, sticking out from damaged volumes overhead, slapped and fluttered in a warm breeze that came from refrigerator-sized heaters mounted on the ceiling. When an order came in for a particular date, a worker would pull out a volume of the Lewiston *Evening Journal,* say (once of Bowdoin College), slice out the issue, neaten the rough edges using a large electric machine called a guillotine (adorned on one side with photos of swimsuit models), and slip it in a clear vinyl sleeve for shipping. Every order comes with a "certificate of authenticity" printed in florid script.

Not everything was on shelves—some were piled three pallets high against the wall; and the University of Maryland's large collection, a recent arrival, occupied about a thousand square feet of floor near the loading dock. The *Herald Tribune* set that the Historic Newspaper Archive is gradually dismembering is bound in pale-blue cloth and is in very good condition (where it hasn't gone under the knife, that is); its bookplates announce that it was the gift of Mrs. Ogden Reid, who owned and ran the *Tribune,* more or less, in the forties and fifties. It is a multi-edition file: five editions for each day are separately bound. I would guess that this was at one time the *Herald Tribune*'s own corporate-historical set; Mrs. Reid no doubt believed that she was ensuring its careful continuance by donating it to a library. Hy Gordon, the no-nonsense general manager of the archives, told me that he believes he got his *Herald Tribunes* from the New York Public Library. Gordon sold me one volume from the set, for February 1–15, 1934 (including rotogravure sections and color cartoons by Rea Irwin) at a discounted price of three hundred dollars plus shipping.

(The NYPL divested themselves of their *Tribune* run, but it must be commended for keeping a huge cobbled-together set of *The New York Times,* from 1851 right up through 1985, several decades of which exist in a special rag-paper library edition. They will let you read from it in room 315, where they serve "semi-rare" material under supervision. The run has some gaping holes—for instance, there are no volumes at all for the years from 1915 through 1925. And no research library, I believe, has saved the *Times* in paper over the past decade: the paper now prints thousands of color photographs a year, but you wouldn't know that from the film.)

I told Hy Gordon that I thought some librarians had exaggerated the severity of newsprint's deterioration. "Oh yeah, yeah, it doesn't fall apart," he agreed. "The ends might crack, but that's all. The newspaper's still fine."

I said I was distressed that so many libraries were getting rid of their bound newspapers.

"Don't be distressed," he said. "There are a lot of things more important in life."

Are there really? More important than the fact that this country has strip-mined a hundred and twenty years of its history? I'm not so sure. The Historic Newspaper Archives owns what is now probably the largest "collection" of post-1880 U.S. papers anywhere in the country, or the world, for that matter—a ghastly anti-library. They own it in order to destroy it. "Here are rare and original newspapers with assured value many from the Library of Congress," says the Archives' sales brochure—all for sale for $39.50 an issue. I saw identifying bookplates or spine-markings from the New York State Library, the New York Public Library, Brown University, the San Francisco Public Library, Yale, the Wisconsin Historical Society Library, the American Antiquarian Society, and many others. A now mutilated run of the New York *World* has this bookplate:

Presented to
THE NEW-YORK HISTORICAL SOCIETY
by
THOMAS W. DEWART
former President of The Sun
and by
ROY W. HOWARD
President and Editor of the
New York World-Telegram and The Sun

And there was a shelf of volumes bearing this warning:

THESE FILES ARE FOR
PERMANENT RECORD OF

The St. Louis Republic

HANDLE WITH CARE
Positively Must Not be Cut
or Clipped

The warning has not been heeded.

CHAPTER 3

Destroying to Preserve

In April 1999, a few months after my visit to Hy Gordon's warehouses in Rahway, I first came across a brief description of the British Library's disposal project on their website. I was trying to find out whether European libraries keep the originals of their own domestic newspapers after they have microfilm backups made. (They often do; in fact, the British Library, to its great credit, still binds the big English dailies, like the *Telegraph* and the *Guardian.* Many American newspaper librarians would view that activity as eccentric and pointless.) Papers of "special historical importance or illustrative interest are not included in the disposals project," I read—but that couldn't be right, since on the accompanying list was the *World,* the *Chicago Tribune, The New York Times,* the *Herald Tribune,* the New Orleans *Times-Picayune,* Hearst's New York *American* (only two years of it, though), the St. Louis *Globe-Democrat* (during the period that Theodore Dreiser wrote a column for it), the Philadelphia *Public Ledger,* and other major dailies. Each of these runs is of historical importance, needless to say, and some of them are bursting with illustrative interest. And each one has now, thanks to decades of copycat self-plunder in U.S. libraries, reached an almost unimaginable state of artifactual scarcity.

I called up a friendly-sounding person named Bhavna Tailor, who is in charge of Acquisitions and Stock Control at the British Library's Newspaper Library ("stock control," I have since learned, is English librarianship's gentle phrase for "getting rid of the stuff you don't want"), and I did my best to convey to her the preciousness of the things on her disposal list, and the mediocrity of some of the microfilm copies in which the library was placing its trust. The same day, I e-mailed her a letter. "My hope is that this extraordinary trove can be kept intact and available for future scholarship," I said, "not cut up and sold piecemeal by dealers." I would be willing to pay for removal and storage if I had to, I told her, either via a non-profit or as a private citizen, if it came down to a choice between that and seeing the papers irretrievably dispersed. Ten days later, I got a response from Tailor. She would keep my letter on file, she said, "and if there are no takers for the remainder of the US titles, then I will contact you and we can take matters from there." I forwarded the list to Lucy Caswell, because she was the only librarian I knew who was actively taking in large wood-pulp backfiles (as they're called), but she was still trying to digest the tractor-trailer loads of bound volumes and single sheets that her library had bought from Bill Blackbeard.

In August, after sending two further notes of inquiry, I got a letter from the British Library, attached to which was a much longer disposal list, amounting to about a hundred and thirty newspapers and other miscellaneous periodicals—more than three times as many as had been specified in the library's newsletter and on its website. The New York *World* was still there—unbelievably, no library had snapped it up—as were most of the other big papers; and there were pictorial vehicles, such as *Leslie's Illustrated Weekly* and the Chicago *Graphic,* and a bewildering array of ethnic papers and periodicals (the *Gaelic American* from 1916 to 1919, the *American Hebrew* from 1905 to 1920, the Boston *Dielli,* the Jersey City *Svoboda,* the New York *Irish World* from 1880 to 1946, the *British Californian,* the Chicago *Katolik,* the New York *Vienybe Lietuvninku,* the *France Amerique,* and on and on); and political papers (the Yiddish

Forward from 1917 to 1975, for instance, and the *Worker* from 1943 to 1968); and a number of uncommon trade periodicals such as *Combustion* and *Fur Trade Review* (both from the thirties). "It has been decided," Bhavna Tailor stiffly wrote, "that it would not be appropriate for us to donate the remaining material to individuals rather than to institutions." The material, she said, would be "offered to the highest bidder." The list was evidently sent out to newspaper dealers at about the same time I got it; the deadline for bids was September 30, 1999.

As I stared at the titles, I felt a great wave of premonitory misery. The timing of this development was not good. I was two years behind in everything, I owed everybody letters of thanks, apology, correction, or friendly encouragement; and my wife and I had drained our cash reserves, having just bought an eighteenth-century house with no doorknobs in Maine. I didn't want to get caught up in some kind of mind-consuming, hideously expensive wrangle with the British Library.

But, gee, the list was long. The library, while perhaps in technical compliance with disclosure rules, was trying to minimize the scope of their deaccessioning. And then there was the phrase "to the highest bidder." Apparently, it was a matter of indifference to the library whether the newspaper collection held rarities or not; they were willing to act in a way that would all but guarantee its quietus at the hands of the paper knackers. *They wanted the money.* So I made calls, hired lawyers, wrote letters, formed a non-profit corporation, and appealed to the British Library's sense of decency. It didn't work.

The size of newspapers is indispensable to our experience of their content. The newspaper reader proceeds nonlinearly, not as he would holding a typical book, but circling around the opened double-page spread, perhaps clockwise, or counterclockwise, moving his whole head as well his eyes, guided by island landmarks like photos and ads. Even the papers that have no pictures at all have a visual exorbitance, a horizon-usurping presence that microfilm's image (which one observer in the seventies compared to "kissing through a pane of glass") subverts and trivializes.

Still, there is nothing intrinsically wrong with microfilming. Taking tiny black-and-white pictures of things isn't objectionable so long as the picture-taking isn't destructive. In fact, microfilm can be extremely useful: it is portable and reproducible, and for many kinds of simple referential research, it can serve as a stand-in or buffer copy that reduces wear on irreplaceable and fragile originals. Nobody objects to postcards of Dürer woodcuts, or coffee-table books filled with reproductions of vintage ocean-liner posters, because the existence of handy copies of these works of art, in reduced size, does not induce museum curators to slice up or throw away the originals.

But the microfilming of old newspapers (which contain many thousands of woodcuts, by the way, not to mention Easter-egg cutouts, paper dolls, dress patterns, and illustrated sheet music) has, right from the beginning, been intimately linked with their destruction. The disbinding of every volume in order to speed production and avoid gutter shadow (the middle area of an open volume, where the pages turn down toward the binding, a region harder to light and keep in focus) has long been the preferred method of newspaper microphotography in the United States. (European microfilming is more likely to leave the bindings alone.) The technique was systematically applied at the Library of Congress: Luther Evans, who had made a name for himself as head of the WPA's Historical Records Survey, where in the thirties he supervised a large amount of nearly unreadable make-work microfilming around the country, and who eventually became Librarian of Congress, described a pilot project to film a run of the Washington *Evening Star* in 1941: "The entire back of the binding was sheared off under a power cutter and the pages photographed individually." Evans called this "the ideal technique for microfilming bound newspapers." S. Branson Marley, a chief of the library's Serials Division, wrote years later of that disbinding, "This was a major decision, for it meant that in order to film a file for preservation, it was necessary to destroy it; once the volumes were cut for this purpose it was impractical, and usually impossible, to restore them."

That was the practical beginning of the idea of *destroying to preserve,* which has, thanks to the Library of Congress's leadership, become all-powerful in U.S. libraries since the fifties. The notion that printing work of the highest level of technical sophistication, produced in four and five colors in multimillion-dollar plants tended by teams of pressmen working around the clock, would necessarily become the casualty of a crude, error-prone, parallax-warped miniaturizing process, was one that became very attractive to library managers, simply because they didn't want to store the newspapers: newspapers take up lots of space, they are heavy to lug around (a typical ex-library volume weighs twenty pounds), and marginal bits flake off in a messy way, too.

Compared to storing the originals in some big building, microfilming is (like digitization) wildly expensive, even in high-contrast black and white—it costs over a hundred and fifty dollars per volume to film a typical newspaper collection, versus less than five dollars a volume to build outlying storage for it and hire a person to truck to-and-fro whatever people want to see. And newspaper pages are the most difficult of all printed artifacts to photograph (or digitize) well: they are very large, narrow-margined, and filled with tiny type and finely detailed line drawings and photography. You're using the outside area of the lens, where distortion is higher; you're shrinking very small things very small; and you're removing "grayscale" nuances—of course you're going to lose information, and beauty, in the process. Books and journals are easy to work with by comparison.

But these difficulties didn't deter the visionaries of fifty or sixty years ago: the end product might not look that great, but it was thrilling to be able to do the work at all. And once they'd done the heady hobbyistical thing—taken cracker-sized snapshots of the contents of their newspaper shelves, using advanced Recordak film technology—it seemed only sensible to throw the old pages away, rather than to set them aside in an annex in case the microfilm turned out poorly, or had missing issues or pages or months, or in case people had questions (say about the history of American illustration or photography) that only the originals could answer. (In some microfilm, photographs come out as little more than dark rectangles on the page.) Recordak's Charles Z. Case extolled the benefits of "condensing records to microscopic form to save space"; one of the company's promotional pictures from the thirties shows a wall of volumes of *The New York Times* at the New York Public Library, heaped and ranked willy-nilly to heighten the sense of oppressiveness: in front of them stands a prim wooden cabinet full of Kodak-made microfilm. Recordak succeeded early on in winning over Keyes Metcalf, then chief of reference at the New York Public Library, who bought two microfilm readers in the early thirties; later, when he became head librarian at Harvard, he launched, with Rockefeller Foundation money, a large-scale project to film foreign newspapers, in order, as he wrote the foundation's director of humanities, "to help push microphotography." In those early days, microfilm was shot on the same stock as movie film (you can still see the sprocket perforations from the original negative on some prints)—and one has a sense that these library administrators saw themselves in the role of studio moguls, bringing multivolume reference classics to the silver, or at least the gray-green, screen.

Microfilm had an air of enticing sneakiness as well—of important covert operations performed in the national interest. This tradition goes back to the siege of Paris in 1870, when the Prussians cut all telegraph links to the city. In a peasant's disguise, René Patrice Dagron, already a microphotographer of note, snuck his optical apparatus to Tours in wine barrels, and there photographed military communiqués at reduced size on emulsions that he gently rolled up, slid into quills, and affixed to carrier pigeons. The birds, which had been plunging exhausted from the sky when burdened with heavy paper, now flapped to Paris without incident.

In World War II, microfilm again came to prominence.

Eugene Power, the founder of University Microfilms, landed a big contract in 1942 with the Office of Strategic Services, later to become the CIA, to film millions of pages of German scientific papers and other documents gathered by British agents. Around the same time, the OSS needed an efficient way to sort thousands of vacation photographs of Germany that the military had solicited from the public in order to plan bombing runs. A forward-thinker named John F. Langan hired a team of women to mount microfilm snippets of each vacation photo (along with selected stills from Axis newsreels) into a rectangular hole cut in an IBM punch card that was coded to correspond to the subject of the photo. In *The Hole in the Card* (a company history published in 1966 by 3M's Filmsort subsidiary), Neil MacKay writes, "For example, if a request were received for a shot of a bridge in occupied France that the allies wanted blown up, the cards were mechanically sorted at high speed to segregate all 'bridge' cards. The film in the cards was then projected on a screen to select the exact shot wanted."

Langan was helped by another early bird, Vernon D. Tate, who moved to the OSS from the National Archives, where in the thirties he had supervised the filming and destruction of a boatload of primary sources. Tate wrote in 1942 that microfilm "ranks in importance with any secret military weapon thus far disclosed." One of its greatest advantages was the ease with which it could be destroyed, according to Tate:

> Books may not be blown to bits or easily burned by fire; microfilms if capture is inevitable can be rapidly and completely consumed, and as easily replaced through the making of prints from master negatives.

Tate went on to become MIT's head librarian.

After the war, the most influential microfilm booster was a polymathic, bow-tie-wearing career librarian named Verner Clapp. Clapp became the number-two man at the Library of Congress under Luther Evans ("We're going places Verner," Evans wrote him in 1945, "and I'm very glad you're a good sailor"); after narrowly missing the chieftaincy himself, Clapp went on in 1956 to direct the new and very flush Council on Library Resources, which bestowed hundreds of thousands of Ford Foundation dollars on technologies of image shrinkage. In 1958, Clapp chaired a meeting on "Problems of Microform in Libraries" at the Cosmos Club in Washington; the first item on the agenda was "Reduction in bulk—the problems of library storage." One of Verner Clapp's cherished bulk-reducing projects was the "Verac," built by AVCO Corporation (they were at work on the reentry system for the Minuteman missile at the time)—a cubic-foot set of stacked photographic plates layered with super-high-resolution "Lippman emulsion," which could hold a million page-images, each accessed by a servomechanism that, as Clapp put it, "brings the addressed image into the scanning position through a paroxysmic effort of approximately one-tenth of a second's duration." The Verac could make you a hard copy (Clapp uses this Cold War term in 1964), with the help of a Printapix tube, or the image could be made to appear on a "vidicon," or closed-circuit-TV screen. It didn't work, though—the words were blurry. Or perhaps the blur accurately reproduces Clapp's own tears of frustration, for the paroxysmic Verac was an expensive failure. Like missile defense, leading-edge library automation is a money pit.

At the 1959 annual meeting of the National Microfilm Association, Clapp gave the keynote address, entitled "A Good Beginning." He spoke of a hoped-for day in which microfilm machines "can be made a personal accoutrement, as homely and as natural and as essential as the tooth-brush, the ball-point pen, or as eyeglasses." He also told delegates that microfilm "has come to the forefront again and again in time of war, and some of its best-known achievements are associated with espionage." Most of his listeners that day were unaware that Clapp himself was, at the time, a consultant for the CIA, and that since at least 1949, while he was still at the Library of Congress, he had been an official intelligence contact with top-secret clearance. Clapp's CIA file includes "Report of Liaison" forms from 1953 and 1954 which state that his task was to "maintain liaison on mutual library matters as well as monitor certain CIA-financed Library of Congress activity."

What that activity was precisely is hidden behind a censor's busy Magic Marker; some of it probably concerned the contract microfilming of classified documents. In Clapp's handwritten daily minutes, now held at the Library of Congress's manuscripts division, there is a note from November 1951, when he was chief assistant librarian—"Round up on CIA projects," followed by a list of names, including Frederick Wagman (a lifelong microfilm enthusiast, later director of the University of Michigan's library and president of the American Library Association) and John W. Cronin, the Library of Congress's head of processing and member of the American Library Association's committee on cooperative microfilming projects. Around the same time, Clapp notes that he's gotten word from Alexander Toth, the CIA's librarian, that the "CIA contract is in mill."

All Clapp's notes are on paper, easily read today. Clapp's CIA file, on the other hand, is an unfortunate victim of the Cold War mania for micro-preservation: it looks to have been inexpertly filmed at some point, and it has undergone a severe fading, as microfilm does when technicians don't take care to rinse off the hypo fixative. The copy that the CIA sent me is poignantly stamped with the words BEST COPY AVAILABLE on almost every nearly indecipherable page. Some of the pages are, though uncensored, completely unreadable. The same cautionary language—BEST COPY AVAILABLE—accompanies the printouts from microfilmed newspapers that one can order from the Library of Congress and the New York Public Library.

There was a palpable glamour to microfilming in those early days, difficult though it may be to feel it now—a hot chemical whiff of cinematography and of high-stakes intelligence work. And there was, as well, the entrepreneurial appeal of creating a product you could sell to other libraries, and the further compensations that flowed from selling your master negatives and reproduction rights to commercial microfilm companies such as

University Microfilms, as most libraries that possessed early homegrown film eventually did.

But the main reason microfilm (and its rectangular, lower-resolution cousin, microfiche) has always fascinated library administrators is, of course, that it gives them a way to clear the shelves—to "expand without expanding," in the words of a full-page Xerox-UMI advertisement in the July 1976 issue of *Microform Review.* The picture in the ad is of a squeezed, feather-shedding American eagle; the headline is AMERICA'S SPACE PROGRAM IS IN TROUBLE:

> We don't have enough of it. Space. Not in the cities. Not on the land, and, as we don't need to tell you, not in the libraries. University Microfilms can give you more space. More space translates as more ways to expand without expanding, more options open.
>
> Serials Management in Microform is our own slum clearance program.

Newspaper collections were the first slums to be cleared (books came later), and because the Library of Congress had the largest newspaper collection in the country, it was one of the first to go to work. (The Library of Congress had "files of American and foreign newspapers more complete and in greater amount than in any other library," wrote one celebrant a decade before the clearance began.) In 1950, an energetic soul named Clyde S. Edwards was put in charge of the library's Serials Division; an internal report for that year pointed out "the badly congested condition of the bound newspaper collections, and the urgent need for space in which to expand them." But the newspapers were never to have enough space again. Verner Clapp, microfilm futurist, was by this time running day-to-day operations at the library (Luther Evans was out of the country for long periods, on missions for UNESCO), and Clapp was not a believer in "merely more of the same—ever and ever larger bookstacks and ever and ever more complicated catalogs." He subscribed to what is sometimes called the *steady space* model. The ideal research library would (as he described it in his 1964 book *The Future of the Research Library*) reach a certain fixed physical size and stay there forever: techno-shrinkage systems (improved Veracs or, eventually, textual databases) would allow librarians to "retire" their originals (i.e., shear their spines and take their pictures) in favor of ever more densely packed micro-surrogates. The curious twists of meaning that accompany microfilming were not entirely lost on Clapp. "It is an art," he told the conventioneers in 1959, "dedicated to preservation, yet it is often practiced as a preparation for deliberate destruction."

Rather than putting up more shelves for the newsprint collection, or building or leasing a warehouse—traditional reactions to a space shortage—the Library of Congress's response in 1950 was to abandon the binding and storing of many new newspapers: incoming papers were dumped after a few months, as soon as commercial microfilm arrived to put in their place. That practice saved dramatically on binding costs, thus subsidizing the cost of the microfilm, and it "retard[ed] somewhat the normal growth of this congested condition," wrote a still dissatisfied Clyde Edwards, "but will not improve the present state of things." There was only one sure way to relieve the overcrowding, Edwards advised in a later report: "I am convinced that the only solution to this problem lies in an intelligently planned reduction of the original files."

Edwards needed upper-level permission for such a far-reaching disposal program, however. In a "conference decision," the library's managers determined to solve the newspaper problem by, as Branson Marley put it, "permitting the disposal to other libraries of bound newspapers replaced by microfilm." A unobtrusive footnote follows Marley's innocent-sounding sentence: "Volumes for which there are no takers are destroyed." None of this epochal activity, in which the Library of Congress began its slow betrayal of an unknowing nation, was published in contemporary annual reports.

Volumes for which there are no takers are destroyed. Increasingly, there weren't takers, because such is the prestige of our biggest library that whatever its in-house theoreticians come to believe, however nonsensically misinformed, however anathematic to reasoned stewardship, other research libraries will soon believe as well. In 1956, Verner Clapp's last year at the library, the *Annual Report of the Librarian of Congress* was a little more forthright than it had been about what was going on: "The problem of deteriorating newspapers was accentuated by the equally vexing problem of making deck space for newly bound volumes. Following a survey of these problems, orders were placed for a number of microfilm copies of domestic titles available in this form."

But because it takes time to microfilm backfiles amounting to millions of pages, the "planned reduction" went fairly slowly at first. Bill Blackbeard told me that when he first began saving newspapers in the late sixties and early seventies, the Library of Congress still had a huge collection, handsomely bound, stored in a naval warehouse on Duke Street in Alexandria, Virginia. "They had virtually every major American newspaper from a large city," Blackbeard said, "usually from the beginning of the newspaper, or the time that the papers were sent to the Library of Congress—through the nineteen-fifties. Most of these bound files ended about nineteen-fifty." These papers hadn't received the kind of heavy wear that, say, a Kansas City *Star* might have gotten at a public library in Missouri, or *The Detroit News* might have in Detroit.

A few times a year, the library would publish in its *Information Bulletin* a list of the papers it was replacing with film: if no federal agencies wanted them, they could go to other libraries or non-profit organizations; if no non-profits wanted them, they might go into dealers' trucks; if dealers had gotten their fill, they went to the dump. "Their files were just immaculate, white paper, good-looking stuff," Blackbeard said. "They couldn't wait to get rid of them."

Two documents together disclose the enormity of the Library of Congress's print-purgation program over the past several decades. One is a forty-six-page mimeographed list entitled *Holdings of American Nineteenth and Twentieth Century Newspapers Printed on Wood Pulp Paper,* prepared by the Library of Congress's Serials Division in May 1950, just before Clyde S. Edwards strode onto the scene. ("Wood pulp paper" here just seems to mean everything published after 1870, aside from several titles printed especially for libraries in the thirties on ultra-durable rag paper.) The publication served as a hit list of sorts; it includes not only the item counts of post-1870 volumes for more than six hundred different newspapers (everything from the *Alaska Daily Empire* from 1913 to 1949, in 105 volumes, to the Laramie, Wyoming, *Republic and Boomerang* from 1916 to 1949, in 103 volumes) but also the "estimated number of exposures" that it would take to microfilm all of them: sixty-seven million.

The other document is a detailed inventory, prepared in the summer of 1998, entitled "19th and 20th Century U.S. Newspapers in Original Format: Inventory of Volumes Held in Remote Storage."

According to the 1950 count, there were over sixty-seven thousand volumes of post-1870 wood-pulp newspapers in the Library of Congress. From that gigantic land-mass of print, a few thousand volumes now remain. Looking at the numbers a slightly different way, there were, in 1950, around fifty wood-pulp newspaper runs that numbered more than 400 volumes. (661 volumes of *The Cincinnati Enquirer* from 1874, for instance, 498 volumes of the Memphis *Commercial Appeal*, 630 volumes of the Portland *Daily Journal*, 594 volumes of the Brooklyn *Eagle*, 495 volumes of *The Philadelphia Inquirer* from 1874, 413 volumes of Hearst's New York *American*, and so on.) There are no runs of more than four hundred volumes now—and no runs of more than three hundred, or two hundred, or one hundred. Whispers of this secret history are to be found in the small card catalog that librarians keep behind the reference desk in the newspaper reading room: above the typed entry for the New York *Herald Tribune*, for instance, is a handwritten note: ALL ON FILM—(817 VOLS. DISCARDED).

Diane Kresh was until recently in charge of the Library of

Congress's Napoleonically named Preservation Directorate; I brought up the newspapers with her on one of my visits to the library. "Generally we retain the inkprint until we have a microfilm available," she said. I asked her if she thought that was a good policy.

"I do," she said. "I've seen bound newspapers that have become so embrittled that they can't be used. They are still intact—things aren't falling on the floor. But you can't open them, and you can't turn the page."

So the library got rid of the newspapers because of their condition, not because of space requirements? Or was it some combination?

"Oh, no, it wouldn't be the space," said Kresh. "It's the inherent vice of deteriorating paper, and particularly newsprint."

But it was the space, unquestionably. The Library of Congress once owned the *Chicago Tribune, The Detroit News,* the New York *Forward,* and *The New York Times* in rag-paper library editions—printed, in other words, on stock that is significantly stronger than practically all book paper of the twentieth century. The library banished these titles anyway. Charles La Hood, the library's chief of photoduplication in the seventies, wrote: "Microfilming came at a propitious time, as the Library of Congress was experiencing an acute space problem in its newspaper collection."

When I pointed out to Kresh that ex-Library of Congress newspapers find avid buyers every day, and thus could not be nearly as decrepit as she was implying, Kresh admitted that "there is, obviously, ultimately a storage issue."

Why, one wants querulously to ask, is our national library so often in the throes of a space crisis? (In 1997, the library's Working Group on Reference and Research described "a crisis of space, in particular in general collections stacks.") A year of a daily paper would fill fifty-two volumes and occupy less than half the Barbie aisle in a Toys "R" Us. Compared with the sort of human artifacts that the Smithsonian Institution must store (locomotives, dynamos, space capsules), or those that the

National Trust for Historic Preservation is entrusted to protect (office buildings, battlefields, neighborhoods), newspapers and books are marvelously compact. Lack of money isn't the problem. The library has spent huge sums on microfilming, and its preservation budget is more than eleven million dollars a year—enough to buy, build, and outfit a warehouse the size of a Home Depot, which would hold a century of newsprint. Are the library's senior managers really so grotesquely inept that they can't plan for the inevitable growth of the single most important hoard of human knowledge in the country? Why is it so difficult for this great research institution to do what any steadily growing concern—a successful pet-food discounter, say, or a distributor of auto parts, or a museum of sculpture—manages to do year after year, without fuss? Why can't our great libraries have the will to find room to accommodate what we so desperately want them to keep?

I asked James Billington, the current librarian of Congress, what he thought about making room for original papers. Billington, a Russian historian who was, in the fifties, a CIA analyst under Allen Dulles, has raised large quantities of private money to pay for the library's American Memory digitization project. "The embrittlement process is not just a question of degrading—these things disintegrate," Billington said. "There's always a trade-off. The happiness and satisfaction of seeing the whole thing in the original is a short-lived privilege for today's audience. It's likely to be, in the real world, at the expense of the variety and richness of what future generations will be able to see in the microfilm version."

CHAPTER 4

It Can Be Brutal

Inherent vice indeed. Everything goes wrong in time—the germane question is whether the Library of Congress, and the many institutions that followed its example, got rid of things that were, at the time of their jettisoning, both usable and valuable. I bought, on eBay, a 1908 volume of the Panama City *Star and Herald* (published in English during the building of the Panama Canal); it has the Library of Congress's oval stamp on the spine. From a dealer, I bought a volume of the *New York Post* for April 1943, also spine-stamped by the Library of Congress. From another dealer, I bought three issues of the Richmond, Virginia, *Daily Dispatch* from 1879, printed on very strong paper made of straw and rag, each bearing a tiny yellow Library of Congress address label. The issue for Tuesday, June 10, 1879, has this in its editorial columns: "We are pressed for room just now. Do not imagine that your article has been thrown into the waste-basket, (though it may have been.) Some communications keep well. We have several such on hand. We hope to be able to publish them soon." All these objects are in excellent fettle; they can be opened and page-turned with impunity.

I also have a volume of the New York *World-Telegram* from

February 1934. This one has no ownership markings on it, but its marbled boards and triangular cloth corners and spinal typeface resemble those shown in a photo in a 1966 picture book called *The Library of Congress.* In the photo, a man wearing what looks to be a butcher's apron is cutting apart a newspaper volume at a worktable; behind him is an electric guillotine. The caption reads: "Because single sheets are reproduced more quickly and accurately than bound pages, this bindery employee is taking apart newspaper volumes that are to be photographed as part of the Library's program to preserve most of its newspaper files on microfilm."

Timothy Hughes, who sold me the volume of the *World-Telegram* (for $125) couldn't say for sure where he got it. "It possibly came from the Library of Congress—I buy from a variety of sources and even my sources get them from various people—[the items] often get passed down to 3 or 4 dealers before they end up in my hands, so who knows where they originally came from." According to Winifred Gregory's pre-war compendium, *American Newspapers 1821–1936,* there were six libraries that, as of 1936, owned up-to-date bound runs of the *World-Telegram,* which was the leading liberal New York City paper of the time. (The *Herald Tribune* was by reputation conservative; the *Times* was moderate.) These libraries were: the New York Public Library, the Free Library of Philadelphia, the Library of Congress, the Union City (N.J.) Public Library, the Ohio Historical Society, and the State Historical Society of Wisconsin. All have since ditched their *World-Telegrams*. The Library of Congress's catalog card for the *World-Telegram* says NO LONGER IN LC and ALL ON FILM.

Could this volume be described as crumbling? Its pages have yellowed, especially at the outer margins, where light and air have penetrated, but they are whole and sound—no bits and pieces fall out when you carry it around, and it survived the rigors of UPS GroundTrac shipping without mishap. You can open this magnificent public diary without harming it; you can turn its pages without trouble; you can peruse it with a moment's pleasure or a day's fascination. Joseph Mitchell, who was already freelancing at *The New Yorker,* writes about the arrival of Emma Goldman in the United States after her years of exile. "The anarchist wore a snakeskin print dress and a Paisley shawl," he writes—and the photo confirms it. A. J. Liebling, another *World-Telegram* writer, gets a color quote from a cabbie while covering a violent taxi strike: "I come first. The customer comes second, and I don't care if you miss your train, mister." Heywood Broun prints a letter he got from Robert Benchley. Gretta Palmer, on the woman's page, says that the speakeasy ended the male-only bar, but that segregation is returning: "Don't the men like us any more now that their judgement is unclouded by the gasoline in the old-fashioned gin?" In a sports section, a huge cartoon has Robert Moses, the new parks commissioner, hitting a hole in one, because he has promised to spruce up the city's golf courses. And on February 22 there is a nice anonymous lead—maybe by Liebling again?—on page one: "Miss Florence La Bau, an alumna of Goucher College and Columbia University, a young woman of wealth and social position in Ridgewood, N.J., was doing a fourth mate's job on the freighter Wichita when the ship plodded into port today with a cargo of human hair from China, tea from Formosa, silk from Japan, sugar from the Philippines and two strange bears from the mystery land of Tibet." Reading a paper like this is not the only way to understand the lost past life of a city, but no other way will enclose you so completely within one time-stratum's universe of miscellaneous possibility. Nothing makes an amateur historian of you with more dispatch.

Real historians of the late nineteenth and early twentieth centuries aren't reading the old newspapers very much anymore, though—not page by page and month by month, for pleasure—and the texture and content of historical writing has, one suspects, undergone subtle changes (thinnings of specificity, losses of groundedness) as a consequence. Historians don't read the old papers because their libraries don't keep the old papers to read, and microfilm is a brain-poaching, gorge-lifting trial to browse. When you try to survey a series of filmed issues methodically, you miss things that would be obvious to an eye-reader; it's oddly difficult sometimes to do the equivalent of turning the page, especially when you're handling heavily scratched or faded microfilm and must crank up the magnification to make out the words. (This is particularly true at the Library of Congress, where the reader-printers in the newspaper room are in such poor repair that some of them pull forward rhythmically on their own at times, their take-up reels afflicted by a sort of electro-Parkinsonism.) You feel as if you're mowing an endless monochromatic lawn, sliding the film gate this way and that, fiddling with the image-rotation dial and the twitchily restive motor switch. If you have a date and a page number, you look that one citation up and leave; you're rarely tempted to spend several hours splashing in the daily contextual marsh. "Certainly the patron's desire to browse through back issues of newspapers is almost completely gone—people rarely browse through microfilm": so wrote E. E. Duncan in *Microform Review* in 1973. At the Archives of Ontario, one of the microfilm readers had an air-sickness bag taped to it; since the seventies, image-ergonomists have known of a kind of motion sickness that afflicts some microfilm users which seems to be caused by the difficulty of visually tracking the creep and lurch of passing text-scapes. Ben Procter, a recent biographer of William Randolph Hearst, appears stoic, brave, unflinching, because he was actually willing to read what Hearst published: "Oh, yes, microfilm, yes," he told Brian Lamb, on *Booknotes.* "It can be brutal, but you find out a great deal about the man and about his papers."

There are nice things about microfilm, too—the congenial clicks of your neighbor's forward button; the way the chosen image fuzzes and bows modestly offscreen as you press PRINT, as if it must retire to another room to change; the warbly whine of the reel's motor when the glass plate lifts to let the film rewind at straightaway speed; the loud confident slaps of the freed leader that proclaim to everyone in the room that someone has finished his or her research. Because microfilm readers frame text arbitrarily, conferring equal eye-weight on all segments of a page, you occasionally discover tiny items you wouldn't have seen if you read the paper conventionally, favoring the areas that its editors and layout artists expected you to look at first. And of course questing scholars cheerfully endure the ocular and neckular ordeal of microfilm if they have good reason to—if they can't go to a library where the originals are, or if they want to make copies, or if the paper itself is indeed so fragile that it can't be touched or turned without damage. But librarians have lied shamelessly about the extent of paper's fragility, and they continue to lie about it. For over fifty years they have disparaged paper's residual strength, while remaining "blind as lovers" (as Allen Veaner, former editor of *Microform Review,* once wrote) to the failings and infirmities of film.

The infirmities are worrying. After nitrate film stock proved hazardous, a compound called cellulose acetate became, in the nineteen-forties, the medium in which microphotographers placed their faith. At the National Bureau of Standards, experimenters baked samples of it in an oven, tested them for residual strength (the research was subsidized by "several manufacturers of photographic films and equipment"), and declared that "cellulose acetate motion-picture film appears to be very promising for permanent records." Charles Z. Case, of Recordak, seized on this wishful governmental verdict, assuring library administrators (some of whom didn't need much convincing) that his company's product was "in the same category of permanence as the finest book-papers."

But acetate has a way of releasing (or "off-gassing," to use the conservator's term) the acetic acid employed in its manufacture; as the decades pass, afflicted microfilms can begin to shrink, buckle, bubble, or stick together in a solid illegible lump. Responding to what a former chief of microforms at the New York Public Library called "the dreaded vinegar syndrome"—so named for its sinus-clearing smell—the industry switched, by the mid-eighties, from acetate to rip-resistant polyester. (Polyester-base film was developed by Kodak in the early sixties, in part to solve problems encountered by the CIA's

Corona spy satellites: the acetate film tore in orbit.) Millions of rolls of acetate images remain in libraries; indeed, a sizable portion of the preservation budget in some large institutions now must go toward the reduplication, with an attendant loss of detail, of old micro-negatives or positive prints onto fresh polyester.

Better plastic doesn't solve all the problems, either, since microfilm's emulsion—the soft layer of gelatin and silver that holds the image—has vulnerabilities as well. In the early sixties, there were reports of strange spots—some yellow, some red, some with concentric rings—that had developed in the master negatives of collections at the National Archives. In response, inspectors from the National Bureau of Standards examined thousands of rolls of government microfilm; they found "a widespread incidence of defects." The General Services Administration issued Circular No. 326 in 1964 to all heads of federal agencies warning of the spots (I found it filed in Verner Clapp's papers at the Library of Congress) and developed a half-day workshop covering "blemish recognition, inspection techniques, and reporting procedures." No remedy was proffered, because none was known. Still, the GSA quoted the Bureau of Standards report's reassurance that "from the practical point of view, no information has been lost."

This bad news simmered for some years, and manufacturers in the meantime promoted two varieties of non-silver microfilm: vesicular film, whose image results from the heating of polyester until it forms tiny light-absorbing bubbles; and diazo film, which uses a dye made of diazonium salts on exposure to ammonia. Both vesicular and diazo films are cheaper than silver film. But in the early seventies, some librarians were distressed to discover that texts reproduced on "Kalvar"-brand vesicular film had been releasing hydrogen-chloride gas, which (according to Susan Cates Dodson in *Microform Review*) "attacked metal filing cabinets, and reduced the boxes the film came in to dust." The corrosiveness was confined to one formula of film, but all vesiculars proved to be heat sensitive—their tiny gas bubbles begin to collapse above 170 degrees, and above 175 degrees (wrote Carl M. Spaulding, a program officer with the Council on Library Resources, in 1978) "even the most heat-resistant [vesicular films] will suddenly suffer complete image loss." Dodson measured the temperature of the glass film gates of common microfilm readers and found that some reached 180 degrees.

Diazo microfilm, on the other hand, though relatively cheap, is prone to fading on exposure to the light of the reading machine. (It fades in the dark, too, but more slowly.) One piece of research from 1978 found that a frame of diazo film would be likely to suffer serious light-damage after three and a half to twenty hours of use, depending on the brand of film. Major historical dates on diazo—Lincoln's assassination, say, or the moon landing—could rack up enough exposure time to fade away, while frames nearby might still retain good contrast; if somebody left a reader on over a weekend with film in it, that might be the end of the image.

Traditional silver-grained emulsions held up better than that, at least—or did they? Word was getting around that certain species of fungi found nourishment in the film's soft (and easily scratched) gelatin. In his 1978 article, Carl Spaulding wrote that "the extreme susceptibility of silver film to severe damage from water or high humidity is a major concern of micrographics professionals—although relatively unknown to most librarians." Librarians are more aware of the problem now: in 1991, a check of master negatives at the University of Florida's P. K. Yonge Library of Florida History (whose microfilm collection includes "the only extant copy of many Florida newspapers") found that more than half had fungal troubles.

More ill news arrived from the Public Archives of Canada in 1981; a small study there determined that thirty-five percent of a sample of rolls of silver microfilm had "redox blemishes"; five percent of these "revealed a loss of information." In 1988, a group of scientists at the Image Permanence Institute in Rochester, New York, wrote that "there seems to be a much wider scale 'redox blemish' problem in library and archive microfilm collections than is generally believed"; more than twenty percent of the half-million rolls in the Illinois State Archives were affected, for example. And there remained the chronic problems with residual hypo—leftover image-fixing chemicals that weren't rinsed away during the processing of the print or the master. Verner Clapp had himself written about the fading caused by unwashed hypo in a squirmy 1954 *Library Journal* piece called "Are Your Microfilms Deteriorating Acceptably?" The original draft of the article, preserved in Clapp's papers, has the following passage, cut from the published version: "It is horrifying to calculate what the cost of testing, handling, and possible rewashing will be if applied to the entire LC collection of microfilm, now amounting to approximately 100,000 reels. Yet this precaution is indicated."

As a result of Clapp's article, the Library of Congress began a small-scale program of sampling bought microfilm, mostly of newspapers, for "excessive residual hypo, and other defects related to definition or legibility." Between 1972 and 1976 the evaluators rejected, on average, half of the items tested—a "shocking statistic," according to the chief of the Library of Congress's Order Division in that period. Yet so eager were the library's managers to reduce the size of the newspaper collection that "in more than 50 percent of these cases the film rejected by the laboratory is not returned to the vendor but is accepted for addition to the collections"—which is to say that the library knowingly accepted film that wasn't good in order to replace original newsprint that was. And the laboratory's sample during this period was only 0.7 percent of the library's incoming spoolage; the rest passed through unexamined. (Turning disbound pages under a camera day after day is a tedious, trance-inducing job, but checking each frame for mistakes is even worse.)

Microfilm is, Allen Veaner has written, the "invisible product." Librarians file it away unlooked-at, or do a few spot checks, hoping the images it holds are all okay. "Serious defects," writes Veaner, "often do not show up until months or years later (when an angry faculty member or student complains of an illegible or missing page, or when images have faded owing to faulty processing)." For one research project, Shawn Godwin was hired by Old World Wisconsin, a living-history museum, to look at every page of all the newspapers published in Grant County, Wisconsin, between the eighteen-fifties and the nineteen-fifties. Most of the papers were available only on old microfilm; Godwin's task was to find references in them to a certain small African-American community. Some of film was fine, but some of it was not: "Entire years were improperly microfilmed and virtually illegible," he wrote me.

> There is nothing more frustrating than to be trying to reconstruct a specific event, to know it is in the paper, to have references to an article and then to stare and strain at poor quality microfilm and finally acknowledge that what you are looking for is there in name but lost in substance, gone forever into the maw of time.

Nancy Kraft, a librarian at the State Historical Society of Iowa, estimates that about one third of her library's reels of pre-1960 microfilm of Iowa newspapers (seven thousand reels, 8.4 million pages) "represent files that will have to be refilmed"—and many can't be refilmed, she says, because there is no original file left to work from.

When the NEH began paying for mass-microfilming projects in the early eighties, they compelled some improvements in standards; and microfilm labs such as Preservation Resources and the Northeast Document Conservation Center can do fine work. Nevertheless, serious mistakes still occur. Nicholas Noyes, director of the Maine State Historical Society's library, told me that in one recent outsourced job the company failed to film an entire year's worth of newspaper issues. Fortunately his library's policy is to save its originals: the year isn't lost forever. Steve Dalton, who moderates the Northeast Document Conservation Center's popular "School for Scanning" conference, said in 1998 that one of the benefits of microfilming over digital scanning is that microfilmers have had time to learn from their mistakes: "I like to think that after these years and years of experience, we have learned how to do it well." But he added, "I must also admit there is still a ton of really poor quality microfilm that's produced—hopefully not here at NEDCC, but it is produced nonetheless." Dennis Hardin, who runs the microfilming lab at the Indiana Historical Society, told me, "I think there's a lot of film out there that we wouldn't put our names on with a ten-foot pole."

The fading problem is the most serious one, in my own experience. Recently, I tried to read the microfilm of a 1914 issue of *Foster's Weekly Democrat & Dover Enquirer,* published in Dover, New Hampshire. There were whole pages on which little more than the headlines was legible. I was able to read:

NORTHAM COLONISTS

HOLD MEETING

Two Interesting Papers Read
at January Session

And then, below it, there was a column of nothing. No originals of this paper survive, as far as I know: the New Hampshire State Library and the Dover Public Library threw theirs away. The new head librarian in Dover conceded that she's been frustrated at times, looking up a particular article on her library's film and finding that "you just can't read it." On the other hand, as she pointed out, there's more space in the library. "It's so wonderful to have a hundred and fifty years of newspapers in a cabinet," she said.

CHAPTER 5

The Ace Comb Effect

Setting aside the joys and sorrows of the paperless reading experience, and setting aside microfilm's inability to do justice to color printing and halftone photographs, and setting aside the technical troubles with deteriorating emulsions and plastic substrates, one may ask a more basic question: *Are the words the same?* That is, is the microfilm with which the Library of Congress replaced its copy of the *World-Telegram,* say—whether or not it is adequately photographed or physically durable or experientially equivalent—is it, at the very least, a faithful reproduction of what preservation administrators like to call the "intellectual content" of the paper originals? Does microfilm successfully capture the text of the thing it locally replaces? No, often it doesn't, because big-city papers published five or ten or more editions (or "replates") throughout a given day, and most libraries simply bound whichever ones they happened to be sent.

For example, the front page of my bound *World-Telegram* for February 3, 1934 (photographed by Recordak in the thirties and held in microfilm by the New York Public Library and the Library of Congress) has a big right-hand headline, O'LEARY OUSTED BY LA GUARDIA; MOSES TAKES UP TRI-BORO POST, accompanied by prominent pictures of three men recently fired by Mayor Fiorello La Guardia. The microfilm's big right-hand headline, by contrast, is STRIKERS ARM WITH BLACKJACKS; MAYOR APPOINTS TAXI ARBITRATOR, and the only picture is a tiny one of Emmett Toppino, who planned to run the sixty-yard dash at Madison Square Garden that night. Rudy Vallee's divorce problems made the front page in my paper edition—"Supreme Court Justice Richard P. Lydon today reinstated Fay Webb Vallee's suit to restrain her husband, crooning Rudy Vallee, from divorcing her in Mexico"; but in the microfilmed later edition we read instead of the disturbing death of Mrs. Annie Smith, "who rocked too far forward last night and fell into the fire."

The January 1, 1899, *Chicago Tribune* provides another instructive example. In the microfilmed copy of the *Tribune* for that day, a half-inch strip of text is missing from the left margin of the image. The microfilm's headline reads:

> ST HOURS OF
> SPANISH RULE
>
> so's Flag to be Lowered
> the Forts and Public
> Buildings of Havana
> at Noon Today.

The article itself, cabled in by Richard Henry Somebody—his surname is gone—clearly had to do with the end of the Spanish-American War (a war created by newspapers, incidentally, just as *Citizen Kane* suggests), but the text is too corrupt to follow. There is a nine-frame political cartoon running across the middle of the page entitled "Pen Pictures of the Leading Events of the Week," but the first box of the cartoon isn't comprehensible:

> ENTLE ART
> OISONING
> URAGED
> AL.

Turning now to the massive *Chicago Tribune* volume owned by the Cartoon Research Library at Ohio State, formerly of Harvard (this one bearing a bookplate that said it was paid for out of the bequest of "Mrs. Anne A. P. Sever, Widow of Col. James Warren Sever, Class of 1817"): everything for January 1, 1899, is legible; Alfonso's flag, as it happens, was to be lowered at noon. Moreover, the page Harvard kept safe for a hundred years differs substantially in content from the text of the microfilmed copy. One of Harvard's above-the-fold headliners was a long account of the heroic efforts of Henry Nehf, a druggist and volunteer fireman from Terre Haute, Indiana, whose body had been found in the remains of a burned and collapsed building, his right arm over his head, as if to fend off the ceiling, and his left around the nozzle of a fire hose. When Nehf had disappeared twelve days earlier, he had at first been suspected of starting the fire or otherwise being on a "debauch"; now, he was a hero. Nehf's watch was stopped at 6:08. "It is not an unreasonable conjecture that the falling débris which stopped the watch caused his death, as the watch was in a vest pocket over his chest, which was crushed in," wrote the unflinching reporter. Later that day, however, in the edition that was later microfilmed, the article was drastically shortened to make room for coverage of a gas explosion in Hartford City, Indiana. A world that keeps only microfilm for January 1, 1899, will be a world that does not know that Henry Nehf, martyr druggist, owned a watch that stopped suddenly at 6:08.

Very often, when I have been able to check the microfilm of a big-city daily against an original that was discarded from some library, I have found editional differences. The existence and uses of these variations were once well-known: Alfred McClung Lee's classic book *The Daily Newspaper in America* (1937) quotes an early textbook of journalism:

> News is selected for each edition with a nicety of judgment as to values, each newspaper keeping in mind the territory that is

> covered by the edition. Mail editions, intended for out-of-town readers, will emphasize the national and state news. . . . City editions . . . will lay emphasis on the local news as far as its value justifies that action. Late afternoon editions concentrate on the sports scores and decisions. Street editions, designed for the café and theater crowds of the night, herald the latest sensations with their headlines.

Joseph Herzberg, city editor at the *Herald Tribune,* described how it worked in 1947 at his paper:

> Papers are torn apart each edition on the night desk as late stories develop. The city desk may have a late fire or homicide, a terrible quake may have killed thousands abroad, or an important man may die at any hour. So highly skilled is the organization and so dovetailed the work of the separate desks that these late stories get in, although they may require many changes in the make-up of the paper. Stories are shifted from page to page, new pictures constantly arrive, space must be made for late theater or music reviews. The presses roll through the night and when they stop another twenty-four hours of world history has been set down.

The miracle is that libraries, collectively—not by design but just because it happened that way—once held on their shelves a surprising stash of this multi-editional diversity. Now (with a few exceptions) they don't know, or don't care, that it exists—and in fact most of it no longer does exist, because as each variant run leaves a library, copies of the unvarying microfilm take its place.

Even for the recent past, administrative indifference to variation can make for odd informational losses. *The New York Times* currently publishes, aside from its city edition, two national editions. Libraries hold these papers for a month or two or six and then throw them away after the microfilm arrives. But the Bell and Howell/UMI microfilm that all libraries subscribe to is a copy of the late city edition, not a copy of either of the national editions. This leads to sticky moments for reference librarians: somebody in California or Boston shows up wanting to look up a particular article or photo or ad that he or she clearly recalls from *The New York Times*—an article that is even listed in one of the available indexes of the *Times* (Gale Research dutifully indexes one national edition even though no library keeps it)—only to discover that the item is not part of the public record. Three years before, it was printed and read by thousands; now you can't see it anywhere. James F. Green, a librarian at Michigan State, posted a newsgroup message in 1994 about this predicament; he said "there will be many times that I will have to try to convince a disbelieving patron that an article from the New York Times which is cited in our locally mounted Expanded Academic Index database is not available from any library."

Early editions of the September 17, 1970, Chicago *Sun-Times* published a story that quoted off-the-record remarks by President Nixon (apparently aimed at the Soviet Union) about a crisis in the Middle East. Nixon's staff called the paper to complain, and the remarks were cut from later editions. The early edition was probably the one that was delivered to local libraries: if one or two of them had collected the *Sun-Times* in paper from that era, it is very likely that Nixon's words would have survived in their complete and original form. But libraries didn't keep the paper; and Jeffrey Kimball, author of *Nixon's Vietnam War,* has for several years sought in vain for a copy of the afternoon edition of that date. "For my new research project, a larger study of 'smoking-gun' documents, Nixon's quoted remarks have a critical bearing," Kimball wrote me, "but all I can get hold of now is the microfilm copy of the evening edition of the *Sun-Times,* which does not quote Nixon's comments; that is, all microfilm copies of this newspaper for this date seem to be of the evening edition. I have been to the Library of Congress, phoned libraries around the country, contacted the *Sun-Times,* written old-newspaper dealers, searched the Nixon archives, talked to the Chicago Historical Society staff, and so on." *Time* magazine once had the *Sun-Times* article in its clip files, where Walter Isaacson saw it and cited it in his book *Kissinger,* but since then (so Isaacson told Kimball), these files "don't really exist anymore."

Few microfilm copies of old newspapers are complete,

either—not necessarily because the microfilmers skipped pages by mistake (although they have certainly been known to do that) but because the original run lacked issues or had items razored out of it by maniacal collectors. But in a marvelous bit of redefinitional insanity, a microfilmed newspaper is "considered complete" by the Library of Congress (according to its *Newspapers in Microform* reference volumes) if "only a few issues per month are missing." Taking "a few" to mean "two" (conservatively), a microfilm is all there, for the Library of Congress's purposes, even when more than six percent of it *isn't* there. If collection managers in major research libraries replace their own imperfect, even badly broken original runs of a given daily paper with copies of a single filmed set that, though known to be incomplete, is "considered complete" by indexers, and believed to be complete by trusting buyers, the replacement process necessarily leaves permanent, unfixable impairments in the documentary record. Before we had four different Ace combs in our pocket, each with a different missing tooth; now we have four miniature photographs of the same Ace comb with the same missing tooth. If that tooth happens to contain an article about the building of the new gymnasium in the high school where your parents met, or about the trolley-car line that once went down your street, forget it, you're out of luck.

How does the Ace-comb syndrome affect historical research? Some years ago, David Bosse, who is now the librarian at the Historic Deerfield Library in Massachusetts, was compiling an annotated list of maps published in northern newspapers during the Civil War, when he found that the microfilm for some of the Chicago papers had "significant gaps"—gaps that couldn't be filled, because there was no surviving original paper for that period. Worse, he discovered a six-month void in the filmed record of the New York *Sun* for 1862. (The *Sun* is one of the great New York dailies; in a later era it published Don Marquis's "Archy and Mehitabel" columns.) "What I discovered was that everyone that I contacted had purchased the film from the New York Public Library," Bosse said. "Some of them, I think, probably had runs of originals, decided to get rid of them, and replaced them with the New York Public Library film—and there was a six-month gap in the film." Bosse was unable to locate any extant originals of the *Sun* that could supplement what the film lacked. "My own experience is that information does perish through this process," he said.

Lucy Caswell, of the Cartoon Research Library at Ohio State, was working on a study of one of the first women political cartoonists, Edwina Dumm, who drew for the Columbus *Monitor* in the teens. Caswell had a scrapbook of original cartoons cut out of the paper, which Dumm had given her before she died, but they lacked dates and surrounding news. Using the microfilm of the Columbus *Monitor,* she was able to locate some of the cartoons, but some of them weren't to be found, as a result of either missing issues or editional variation. Caswell tried to locate an original set of the paper, but there isn't one: the copy in Columbus was destroyed after microfilming, and the Ohio Historical Society's copy was given or sold to a man in Detroit who cut it up for the circus ads and threw the rest away.

I asked Caswell what she thought, given this sort of difficulty, about the prudence of keeping originals. "You're talking to somebody who values the object, so I would always keep the paper master," she said. "I know my cohorts in the past have not." Caswell is diplomatic, as I'm not, about the losses: "I think that people did it in good conscience under circumstances that in some cases were beyond their control. Boards of trustees and administrators were saying, 'You have to do this, we can't afford to do otherwise.' " She senses a change of outlook, though. "It seems to me that maybe, for lots of reasons, our collective consciousness about history is getting a little better, and maybe we won't repeat the errors we've made in the past."

CHAPTER 6

Virgin Mummies

Ah, but we will almost certainly repeat some of the errors we made in the past. They keep coming back around, the counterfeit justifications, the false economies. The truth is that certain purificationally destructive transformations of old things into new things seem to excite people—otherwise polite, educated, law-abiding people—and it's up to other normally polite people to try to stop them. I arrived at this conclusion late one night at the kitchen table, as I read through a Ph.D. dissertation from 1995 by a man named William Richard Lemberg, who directs the library at Saint Mary's University in Minnesota. Lemberg's webpage picture shows him with a push-broom mustache and a cheerfully bald forehead; he is a robe-wearing member of a Catholic order, the Brothers of the Christian Schools. To judge from our phone conversation, he is a gentle, genial man.

Brother Lemberg's idea, supported by pages of statistical analysis and marvelously detailed cost assumptions, is that American libraries would collectively save a whole lot of money—about forty-four billion dollars over the next one hundred years, in fact—if they digitally scanned about twenty million books and got rid of more than four hundred million duplicates. Our libraries would be better off, in other words, if they destroyed about ninety-five percent of their accumulated collections. Brother Lemberg writes that "information professionals have begun to doubt the usefulness of paper-based technology as a long-term foundation for providing cost-effective information services." The miniaturization of the newspapers was only a beginning.

The estimates and calculations in Lemberg's work reminded me, as I looked over them, of a proposal by an enterprising nineteenth-century geologist named Dr. Isaiah Deck. Like Brother Lemberg, Dr. Deck was interested in the future of paper-based technology. He was English by birth; sometime before 1854, he came to the United States and set up an office at 113 Nassau Street in Manhattan, in the building where *Vanity Fair* had its offices, and where *The New York Times* was founded in 1851. Just down the street were other big-circulation newspapers: James Gordon Bennett's New York *Herald,* Moses Beach's *Sun,* and Horace Greeley's New York *Tribune.* Their high-volume cylinder presses, built by Richard Hoe and Company, demanded an enormous volume of paper every day; according to an estimate made in 1856, it would have taken a caravan of six thousand wagons, each bearing two tons of paper, to carry the newsprint consumed in one year by the newspapers of New York City. In 1855, as the price of paper rose, Dr. Deck proposed to dig up two and a half million tons of Egyptian mummies, ship them to New York, unroll them, and use their linen wrappings to make paper.

It was all rag paper then, remember. Mill women sorted towering mounds and bales of linen and cotton castoffs, cutting the cloth by hand into four-inch squares or sending it through a cutting machine invented by Moses Beach of the *Sun.* (Moses's son Alfred Beach, incidentally, edited *Scientific American* and invented the subway tunnel-boring machine.) The rags went into a tumbling drum, to rid them of dirt and buttons (rubber was almost impossible to remove completely, and left black specks in the paper), and they were boiled in chemicals to soften the cloth, and then they went into a rotary engine called—because it was invented by the Dutch—a Hollander. The Hollander, an oval trough with a metal-edged paddle wheel in it, tore and mashed the broth of half-digested rags until their cellulose fibers won independence, and this pulp, poured out onto a wire-mesh (or "web") conveyor belt and squeezed through rollers, dried into paper—book paper and newsprint.

By the eighteen-fifties, the United States published more newspapers than any other country; U.S. paper consumption was equal to England's and France's combined. Rag imports flowed in from twenty countries, but most came from Italy—twelve million pounds of Italian rags in 1852 and, by 1854, twenty-four million pounds. But there were ominous developments: part of the crop of Tuscan rags, which had formerly gone in its entirety to the United States, went to England instead. "Complaints of the price and scarcity of paper were universal," according to Joel Munsell's nineteenth-century *Chronology of the Origin and Progress of Paper and Paper-Making.* Both the *Tribune* and the *Sun* reduced their size that year to save on paper costs, and the Philadelphia *Daily Evening Register* discontinued publication "on account of the high price of paper."

Writing in 1854, Dr. Deck envisioned a "famine of paper material looming up in the distance." And where there is famine, there is money to be made. On a trip to Jamaica, prospecting for copper, Deck had taken time to evaluate several possible rag substitutes—aloe, plantain, banana, and dagger-grass—but none was satisfactory. Several generations of papermakers before him had experimented with alternative "furnishes" for their product. Bamboo waste, old rope, corncobs, grass, and straw were important American pulp additives; European research had roamed farther afield. Jacob Christian Schäffer, an authority on the fungi of Bavaria, had attempted, in a series of works in the seventeen-seventies, to make paper from potatoes (both the skins and the insides), dandelion roots, cabbage stumps, thistles, grapevines, lilies of the valley, and Bavarian peat—but none of his *papierstoffen* found favor in commercial mills. An Englishman named Hill produced, in 1854, a paper made from horseradish; also one from manure, "bleached and reduced to pulp by the usual modes."

Pulpwood chips or sawdust had held promise ever since 1719, when René de Réaumur, a scholar of insects, observed to the Academie Royale that certain American wasps make excellent paper from trees—they "seem to invite us to try." But only in Asia did arboreal paper have a long tradition: the Japanese used the beaten inner bark of the mulberry to produce a medium of enviable durability. A few wood-pulp practitioners claimed success in America: the October 28, 1830, issue of the *Crawford Messenger,* published in Meadville, Pennsylvania, was reportedly printed on paper made from lime and aspen wood. When Dard Hunter, the eminent twentieth-century paper historian, wrote his *Papermaking,* there was a set of bound volumes of the *Crawford Messenger* at the library of Allegheny College in Meadville. A librarian there wrote Hunter that the issue of the *Messenger* for that day looked and felt smoother than the others in the volume: "All the other edges are frayed, stained, or creased while this one is clear cut as if it had been shaped with shears." Hunter proposed taking a sample of the paper to test whether it had wood pulp, but his request was refused: "The librarians," Hunter wrote, "are reluctant to spare even a fragment of the paper for this purpose."

When I called the Allegheny College library to ask after the October 28, 1830, issue of the *Crawford Messenger,* I was told that it was gone. There is a run of the *Messenger* on microfilm, but a shrunken picture of a page can't reveal much about the composition of its paper. And the particular set of the newspaper that the microfilmers laid out under the camera had lacked certain issues, including the one for October 28, 1830—the Ace comb problem again. Are there any originals left? The Library of Congress owns one original volume of the *Messenger,* for 1828—they kept a lot of newspapers printed before 1870. (Several years ago, however, they did give away, to the American Antiquarian Society, a number of runs from states with letters that come early in the alphabet; they planned to give away more, but there were protests, and the project was dropped.) And the American Antiquarian Society itself holds a few scattered issues, but not the one supposedly made of lime and aspen. There is, however, at least one remaining set, at the Crawford County Historical Society. Rose Deka, a librarian there, told me that the October 28, 1830, issue is still in "excellent condition." Thanks to libraries like hers, which keep what they own, the physical history and durability of early wood-pulp paper is still a subject that can be studied, just barely.

But circa 1847, when Dr. Deck made a trip to Egypt in search of Cleopatra's lost emerald mines, wood-pulp paper was by no means a sure thing. Deck enjoyed digging things up—he fancied himself something of an archaeologist as well as a prospector. (He had written about some Anglo-Saxon relics for the *Archeological Review.*) His father had known Giovanni Belzoni, the famous Egyptian-tomb plunderer, and thus Deck had inherited a few interesting items, including a piece of mummy linen of a "remarkably delicate texture." Though the expedition to Egypt was a failure—no emerald mines turned up—the explorers did encounter some major "mummy pits," as Deck called them. Where the winds had scoured the plains of sand, Deck reported that he had seen "fragments and limbs exposed in such plenty and variety that the wanderer would be impressed with the idea that he was in the studio of a Frankenstein, in an extensive line of business."

He made some calculations. Assume two thousand years of widespread embalming, an average life span of thirty-three years, and a stable Nilotic population of eight million people. That left you with five hundred million mummies, just "rotting in the ground." The numbers were "incredible." What to do with that many mummies? How might an enlightened Western visitor best put them to use?

We could set them on fire, of course. In H. Rider Haggard's novel *She,* mummies are used as torches—the bituminous preservatives burn so fiercely that "flames would literally spout out of the ears and mouth in tongues of fire a foot or more in length." Combustion this intense could generate steam. The railroad from Cairo to Alexandria, imposed on the Abbas Pasha by the English in the early 1850s, runs through several bustling necropolises; Egypt had no indigenous coal and very little wood. A small item in the September 27, 1859, edition of the Syracuse *Daily Standard* reads: "Egypt has 300 miles of railroad. On the first locomotive run, mummies were used for fuel, making a hot fire. The supply of mummies is said to be almost inexhaustible, and are used by the cord." Dard Hunter's *Papermaking* cites an informant's report that "during a ten-year period the locomotives of Egypt made use of no other fuel than that furnished by the well-wrapped, compact mummies."

But Deck's geological training convinced him that there was a better way for entrepreneurs to profit from Egypt's buried resources. He estimated that each mummy would yield on average eight pounds of linen, of a quality ideal for modern papermaking; and the "superior class of mummies" would yield much more than that. A mummy from the collection of one Mr. Davidson, Deck reports, was bandaged in nearly three hundred yards of fabric, "which weighed, when bleached, 32 lbs." You could get dozens of four-page newspapers out of thirty-two pounds of linen. And there would be secondary compensations, as well, since within the layers of linen would reside winged orbs and other bijouterie with resale value; and the distillation of the "animal remains" would produce aromatic gums, such as olibanum, "issoponax," and ambergris. Even the bituminous compounds employed in the embalming of the "inferior mummies" could be made into varnishes and machinery oils, according to Deck. Mummy soap was another of his suggestions. He possesses, he says, paper samples available for inspection, including banknote and writing stock "of the finest but toughest texture" made from cloth from the tombs of the kings at Thebes.

A preliminary sketch of Deck's proposal appeared in 1847, in the *Spettatore Egiziano,* a newspaper overseen by the Abbas Pasha in Cairo. I haven't been able to track this paper down, but *Punch* saw the item and produced an anonymous poem about it in the May 29, 1847, issue. "Cheops and Ramses, shake in your cere-cloths!" the poet writes:

> They're going to take the bier-cloths
> That wrap the sons and daughters of old Nile,
> From gilded kings to rough-dressed rank and file,
> And turn them into paper!

Scientific American also got wind of the article, and published a brief note entitled "New Speculation" on June 19, 1847:

> Mehemet Ali has found a new source of revenue, in the fine linen in which the immense deposits of mummies are wrapped, by applying it to the manufacture of paper. Calculations, founded upon mummy statistics, make the linen swathings of the ancient Egyptians worth $21,000,000. This is better than stealing pennies from the eyes of dead men.

In England, the paper industry possibly took the hint: Munsell's record for 1850 includes for the first time a mention of Egyptian rags—twenty-three tons of them—imported by Great Britain. Then Deck sailed for America, and in 1854 his expanded proposal appeared in a publication received by some of New York City's leading printers, newspaper editors, and papermakers: the yearly *Transactions* of the American Institute, a New York society devoted to the advancement of industrial and agricultural arts. Deck was aware that some readers, the "over sensitive," may be repulsed by the notion of large-scale mummy mining, and he says that he himself would hesitate to despoil the fascinating science of archaeology of its choicest gems, "unless the requirements of the age demand it." He poses this question for the squeamish:

> I would ask them whether it is not preferable to employ clean and sound linen wrappings from a virgin mummy to the dubious rags collected from the loathsome persons of the Lazaroni who swarm the quays of the chief seaports of Italy and Spain, and are equally the pest and annoyance of travellers to the interior, and

> from which source more than four-fifths of the present raw material for paper is obtained.

A modern-day Abelard and Heloise, he suggests, might soon correspond on stationery that was once the "chemisette enveloping the bosom of Joseph's fair temptress"—i.e., enveloping the corpse of Potiphar's wife. And was it not conceivable that "a sheet of the 'New-York Times' be issued on the indestructible shroud of Moses's fairer (Pharaoh) stepmother"? And the supply, oh, the supply! It was beyond calculation. There weren't only humans in those mummy pits, after all. There were all the wrappings of crocodiles and cats, and those of the sacred bulls at Dashour, the burned bones of which, as Deck points out, were already being used to clarify syrup in the sugar refineries of lower Egypt. The tenderness that other cultures reserve for infants—the swaddling and cradling and bathing—Egyptian culture redirected at their dead. Dr. Deck invites inquiries from "companies or private speculators."

Did the rag dealers and papermakers ever act on these suggestions? We know that Egyptian rags appeared for the first time in America in 1855, exactly contemporary with the publication of Deck's proposal: one J. Priestly bought 1,215 bales of Egyptian rags at a little over four cents a pound. The next year, a reporter for the New York *Tribune* wrote: "It is within a very short time that rags have come from the Nile, and now it is quite a business. About two and a quarter millions of pounds came to New York from Alexandria last year." That's an awful lot of Nile rags. Some of these imports might have come from living people, but many, it seems fairly certain, came from the long dead. A number of the Alexandrian bales found their way up the Hudson and west as far as Syracuse, where the Syracuse *Daily Standard*—the same paper that would soon publish the tidbit about the Egyptian railroad's fuel—printed a veiled confession in its July 31, 1856, issue:

> Rags from Egypt.—Our Daily is now printed on paper made from rags imported directly from the land of the Pharaohs, on

> the banks of the Nile. They were imported by Mr. G. W. Ryan, the veteran paper manufacturer at Marcellus Falls, in this county, and he thinks them quite as good as the general run of English and French rags.

News of papermaker Ryan's novel material reached an editorial writer for *The Albany Journal,* who described a paper "made from the wrappages of mummies." The editorialist asked, "Could anything better illustrate . . . the intense materialism of America?" In 1858, the Syracuse *Daily Standard* included another corroborating tidbit: a Boston importer had bought forty thousand pounds of linen rags "said to be taken from Egyptain [*sic*] mummies"; when he threshed them, he produced thirteen thousand pounds of sand. And in 1866 a clergyman gave a sermon in which he claimed that during the Civil War, a New York merchant sold a shipload of mummies to a papermaker in Connecticut, who threw them all "into the hopper." Said the clergyman to his parishioners: "And the words I am now reading to you, are written on some of this paper."

Dard Hunter was oddly hesitant about the mummies. He didn't mention the clergyman's tale (given in Munsell's *Chronology*), he doubted the existence of the Syracuse "Rags from Egypt" item, and, although he included further reports of mummy linen in paper mills in Broadalbin, New York, and Gardiner, Maine (the Maine rag-sorters attributed a typhoid epidemic to the Egyptian linen), he wanted us to imagine that the "grewsome" material was used to make wrapping paper, not printing paper.

But upstate paper companies often supplied New York printers—the New York *Tribune,* for instance, got its paper from a mill near Niagara Falls—and Deck hadn't established himself near Printing House Square in order to argue the cause of *wrapping* paper. Nor would the gentlemen of the American Institute (whose members included Horace Greeley, the *Tribune*'s editor; Richard Hoe, the leading manufacturer of printing presses; and Nathaniel Currier, of Currier and Ives) have bothered to publish Deck's "On a Supply of Paper Material from the Mummy Pits of Egypt," following an article about street-paving, if the idea had appalled them. On the contrary, the idea interested them. Why not make mummies into newsboys, speaking in ink-begotten Bodoni?

Was *The New York Times* (or the *Tribune,* or the *Sun*) ever printed on stock made, at least in part, from Egyptian mummies? Only a microscopic analysis of the constituent pulps would tell for sure, and even then the microscope might fail us, since papermakers mixed their furnish the way whiskey blenders mix their mashes, adding several pulps to one vat. One hesitates, in any case, to chop hundreds of little test samples out of old pages in the service of science—first do no harm. But there is a fair chance, I think, that some of the remaining bound volumes of the biggest New York dailies from 1855 through, say, 1870 entomb more than the history of the United States.

I called the Syracuse University Library and the Syracuse Public Library to see whether they still owned their old volumes of the Syracuse *Daily Standard,* since it is the one newspaper that we know was printed on Nile rags. They don't. A firm called Hall and McChesney, long gone, microfilmed the *Standard* on acetate stock sometime before 1972, and both libraries deemed it an acceptable substitute. On microfilm, the "Rags from Egypt" page is blurred but legible, except at the outermost corners. The Syracuse Public Library gave its volumes of the *Standard* to the Onondaga Historical Association, which accepted them even though they had no space and already had their own copy. Richard Wright, the director of the Historical Association in the seventies, went through the duplicate set of papers clipping items of interest: he and his wife discovered several of the choicest mummy quotations I have cited here.

Both of the Wrights are gone now, but their files of local history are not. Judy Haven, the Historical Association's librarian until 2000, is not sure how much longer they can hold on to their mass of papers—they have no money, there have been water problems in the basement, and people don't understand that a historical society needs public support to function. "Everybody wants us to hang on to the newspapers," she said, "but nobody wants to help us with the cost of storing them in any way." The pages of the *Daily Standard*'s mummy issue rattle when you turn them.

CHAPTER 7

Already Worthless

And that's why, when I was reading Brother Lemberg's quietly titled work, "A Life-Cycle Cost Analysis for the Creation, Storage, and Dissemination of a Digitized Document Collection," which proposes to pay for the digitization of American libraries by annihilating thousands of established book collections, I thought of Dr. Deck. Four hundred million library discards? Of course not that many will end up going, just as Dr. Deck's entrepreneurial idea didn't in the end consume five hundred million mummies; instead American papermakers learned how to handle wood pulp, while in under-forested England, esparto grass became (Munsell writes) "the most valuable fibre yet discovered as a substitute for that of linen." (Esparto, not wood pulp, was the dominant English papermaking furnish even after the Second World War, until Swedish wood-pulp suppliers dumped their product on the British market and forced esparto out.)

But people *were* willing to give Egyptian linen a try—mummies were incontestably imported and unwrapped, their coverings tossed into papermaking macerators and, possibly, inked into issues of the New York *Tribune,* and then volumes of the New York *Tribune* were microfilmed by Kodak's Recordak Corporation in the thirties, and all over the country old volumes of the *Tribune* and the *Sun* and the *Times* were thrown away or auctioned off, and now much of the transfigured shroudage is reburied once again, though in less pharaonic company, in the company of a million old, undecaying phone books. (The Library of Congress is now microfilming and tossing its early phone-book collection, too, by the way.)

"Duplication in libraries is a real problem," Brother Lemberg explained to me when I called him. "We all have the same thing! What if just one library owned a paper copy, and we had an electronic library for the rest of them? They could all get rid of theirs. It's an exciting kind of idea for retrospective work." Of the books that would be purged in accordance with Lemberg's cost analysis, about thirty million of them, according to one of his statistical tables, would date from 1896 or before.

I learned about Lemberg's dissertation from a recent textbook by Michael Lesk, *Practical Digital Libraries: Books, Bytes and Bucks.* Lesk works at the National Science Foundation, where, as division director of Information and Intelligent Systems, he helps administer the government's omni-tentacled Digital Library Initiative, which has dispensed many millions of federal dollars for library projects. The National Science Foundation began its sponsorship of the digital initiative in 1992, with the help of NASA and DARPA, the Defense Advanced Research Projects Agency; now the Library of Congress and the National Endowment for the Humanities are also participating. In an early round of funding, six universities—including Harvard, Berkeley, Stanford, and the University of Michigan—received about four million dollars apiece to help them find their way to the all-electric word kitchen. Lesk agrees with Brother Lemberg: in order for libraries to provide the best service to the most people for the least money, they ought to begin large-scale scanning projects right now, and simultaneously divest themselves of their originals.

When I interviewed Lesk (in December 1998), he offered

me an example of what a library might do to help finance a digitization project. Stanford was spending, he said, about fifty-five million dollars to repair its on-campus library building, damaged in the 1989 earthquake. "You could scan the entire contents of that building for less. Now the problem is that letting that building fall down is not acceptable to the Stanford community." Later he said: "I routinely suggest to libraries, 'You know, gee, maybe you should think about repairing your building. Maybe you don't want to do it, because maybe you want to do something else.' " Lesk would not get rid of all scanned duplicate books, however. "There are various caveats," he said.

> You might feel that you wanted more than one copy, just in case there was a fire in Washington. Suppose the book had been bound by a famous bookbinder, you might not want to tear that copy apart. But basically, yes, for the vast majority of nineteenth-century material, where you don't particularly care about the binding or the paper, the book is falling apart, there are no illustrations, I would say, yes, you would be better off with one digital copy and one carefully watched paper copy, than you are with relying on eight different or ten different decaying paper copies and no digital access.

Why not both? Why can't we have the benefits of the new and extravagantly expensive digital copy *and* keep the convenience and beauty and historical testimony of the original books resting on the shelves, where they've always been, thanks to the sweat equity of our prescient predecessors? We can't have both, in Michael Lesk's view, because the destruction of the old library will help pay for the creation of the new library. The fewer books that remain on the shelves, the lower the storage cost—that's the first-order "benefit" to Lesk's government-financed plan. And the fewer physical books that are on the shelves—the more they must fly by wire—the more the public will be obliged to consent to the spending of ongoingly immense sums necessary for global conversion, storage, networked delivery, and "platform migration." Lesk used to work at

Bellcore, the research group owned until recently by NYNEX and other Baby Bell phone companies; it isn't entirely surprising that millions of dollars of the National Science Foundation's grant money are going to telecommunications networks, notably to the creation of a joint MCI WorldCom/NSF "very high performance Backbone Network Service," or vBNS, and hookups thereto, that will connect phone companies, university science labs, and university libraries, for the benefit of all concerned.

None of this would disturb me—who can quarrel with high-performance backbones?—if an attack on low-tech book spines weren't also part of the plan. The attack is part of the plan, though, just as it was when the Library of Congress began destroying the newspapers. The single "carefully watched paper copy" that Lesk thinks we should keep will generally not be the one that is actually scanned, because the scanned book is thrown away afterward: big projects like JSTOR (Journal STORage, the Andrew W. Mellon Foundation's digitally copied database of scholarly periodicals, many going back to the nineteenth century) and the Making of America (Cornell's and the University of Michigan's growing collection of digital books) routinely prepare for digitization by cutting up the book or journal volume they have in hand, so that the pages can lie flat on the scanner's glass. Michigan's librarians choose digital conversion, according Carla Montori, the head of preservation, "knowing that the original will be disbound, and that there will be little chance it can be rebound." The disbound Making of America books are, some of them, uncommon mid-nineteenth-century titles; e.g., Henry Cheever's *The Island World of the Pacific* (1856), *The American Mission in the Sandwich Islands* (1866), Josiah Parsons Cooke's *Religion and Chemistry; or, Proofs of God's Plan in the Atmosphere and its Elements* (1865), John C. Duval's *The Adventures of Big-Foot Wallace, the Texas Ranger and Hunter* (1870), and Mary Grey Lundie Duncan's *America As I Found It* (1852). Michigan's preservation department maintains that the thousands of books they have scanned were all terminally brittle—but the term "brittle" has shown itself to be remarkably pliant in recent decades, and nobody now can evaluate Michigan's diagnoses, since most of the scanned remnants went in the trash.

"At the moment it looks as if [disbinding] is the cheapest way to do things," Lesk told me. He is even bolder in a paper entitled "Substituting Images for Books: The Economics for Libraries," where he argues for the outright hashing of a better copy of a book over one that is worn out or very brittle, simply because it's less expensive to destroy the book in better condition. "It is substantially cheaper to scan a book if the paper is strong and can be fed through a stack feeder, rather than requiring manual handling of each page," he writes; thus "it may turn out that a small library located in a rural and cold mountain location with few readers and clean air has a copy in much better shape, and one that can be scanned more economically."

Of course, that small mountain library, having done such a fine job of safekeeping all those years, may have "less motivation to scan a book which is not yet deteriorating"—hence the need, in Lesk's central-plannerly view, for a nationwide cooperative authority that will order that library to guillotine its copy and feed it to the scanner for the greater good.

Lesk's candor is impressive: he acknowledges that the resolution of today's scanned offerings may be crude by tomorrow's standards, or even by comparison with today's microfilm. "I would like to see, as soon as possible, a lot of scanning, so that momentum builds for doing this job," he told me. "It is likely that to build support for a conversion of this sort, what matters much more is that a lot of stuff gets done, than that the stuff that gets done is of the ultimate highest quality." Better to have to scan some things twice, in Lesk's view, than not to scan at all—assuming, of course, that there is still a physical copy left to destroy when it comes time for the retake. Lesk also recognizes that in a cooperative project involving millions of volumes, there will be errors and omissions. "The odds are that there will be things lost," he said. Some projects, such as JSTOR, have the money to do a careful preliminary check to be sure that no pages or issues are missing, but most places, he says, "won't be able to afford the JSTOR quality standards."

I was interested to hear Lesk offer JSTOR as a paragon of quality. JSTOR is the most successful of the large-scale digitization projects; it has big money and big names behind it (including lifelong library automator Richard De Gennaro, former chief librarian at Harvard and, before that, at the New York Public Library); it can be marvelously helpful in finding things that you didn't know existed, or that you do know exist but don't have handy. Its intent, however, is not supplemental but *substitutional:* back issues of scholarly journals are, in the words of its creator, William G. Bowen, ex-president of the Andrew W. Mellon Foundation and of Princeton, "avaricious in [their] consumption of stack space"; JSTOR will allow libraries "to save valuable shelf space on the campus by moving the back issues off campus or, in some instances, by discarding the paper issues altogether." Taking this cue, Barbara Sagraves, head of preservation at the Dartmouth library, wrote in an online discussion group in 1997 that questions about weeding the collection had "bubbled up" at her library. "The development of JSTOR and the promise of electronic archiving creates the possibility of withdrawing paper copies and relying solely on the electronic version," she writes. Although she wants to make clear that Dartmouth is "in no way considering that option," she says that construction planning has made librarians there "step back and question retention decisions in light of new means of information delivery." In a survey conducted by JSTOR in 1999, thirteen percent of the respondents had already "discarded outright" bound volumes of which electronic copies exist on JSTOR, and another twenty-five percent had plans to do so; twenty-four percent have stopped binding incoming issues.

Lesk likes JSTOR for that very reason. He wants to divert capital funds from book-stack square footage into database maintenance, to create a habit of dependence on the electronic copy over the paper original, to increase the market share of digital archives. And he is right that JSTOR's staff takes pains in the preparation of what they reproduce: they make sure that a given run of back issues is as complete as possible before they scan and dump it.

What about quality, though? The printable, black-and-white page-pictures that JSTOR stores are good—their resolution is six hundred dots per inch, about the same as what you would get using a photocopier. (What you see on-screen is less good than that, because the images are compressed for faster loading, and the computer screen imposes its own limitations.) But the searchable text that JSTOR derives from these page-pictures is, by normal nineteenth- and twentieth-century publishing standards, intolerably corrupt. OCR (optical character recognition) software, which has the job of transmuting a digital picture of a page into a searchable series of letters, has made astonishing improvements, but it can't yet equal even a middling typesetter, especially on old fonts. Thus JSTOR's OCR accuracy rate is held (with editorial intervention) to 99.95 percent. This may sound exacting, but the percentage measures errors per hundred letters, not per hundred words or pages. A full-text electronic version of a typical JSTOR article will introduce into the clickstream a newly minted typo every two thousand characters—that is, one every page or two. For instance, I searched JSTOR for "modem life" and got hits going back to the April 1895 issue of *Mind:* the character-recognition software has difficulty distinguishing between "rn" and "m" and hasn't yet been told that there were no modems in 1895.

It's easy to fix individual flukes like this, once they are pointed out, but the unpredictable OCR misreads of characters in proper names, in dates, in page numbers, in statistics, and in foreign quotations are much costlier to control. That's why JSTOR allows you to see only the image of the page, and prevents you from scrolling through its searchable text: if scholars were free to read the naked OCR output, they might, after a few days, be disturbed by the frequency and strangeness of its mistakes, especially in the smaller type of footnotes and bibliographies, and they might no longer be willing to put their trust in the scholarly integrity of the database.

Half joking, I pointed out to Michael Lesk that if a great

many libraries follow his advice by scanning everything in sight and clearing their shelves once they do, the used-book market will collapse. Lesk replied evenly, "If you've ever tried taking a pile of used books to a local bookseller, you know that for practical purposes, most used books are already worthless. Certainly old scientific journals are worse than worthless. You will have to pay somebody to cart them away, in general." (Online used-book sites, such as abebooks.com, Bibliofind, and Alibris, where millions of dollars worth of ex-library books and journals change hands, might contest that statement.) I asked Lesk whether he owned many books. He said he had several thousand of them—most of them printed on "crummy paper."

CHAPTER 8

A Chance to Begin Again

Before Michael Lesk, though, came the grand old men of microfilm—people like M. Llewellyn Raney (director of libraries at the University of Chicago, who in 1936 wrote that the "application of the camera to the production of literature ranks next to that of the printing press"); and Fremont Rider, the slightly askew head librarian at Wesleyan; and Rider's authoritative follower, Verner Clapp. We must learn more about these men.

In an article in a 1940 issue of the *Journal of Documentary Reproduction,* Llewellyn Raney provided an early hint of developments to come: he coyly described a dinner at the Cosmos Club in Washington, where "a couple of curious librarians and a Foundation scout" discussed with some microphotography experts the economics of book storage versus "miniature reproduction." The question was whether "discarding might introduce a new economy":

> If the volumes in question could be abandoned afterward, then the bindings might be removed and the books reduced to loose sheets in case anything were gained by this course. Gain there

> would be, because sheets could be fed down the chute to a rotary camera glimpsing both sides at once far more rapidly than the open volume on a cradle by successive turning of the leaves.

Not only would the microfilm's images look better—the activity would be cheaper. "So ended an intriguing night out," wrote Raney. "The participants are of a mind to repeat it—often."

A few years later, Fremont Rider had a revelation. He conceived of a kind of bibliographical perpetual-motion machine: a book-conversion plan that would operate at a profit. In 1953, he described it as follows:

> Every research library would actually save money if it absolutely threw away almost all of the volumes now lying on its shelves—volumes which it has already bought, bound and cataloged, and would save money even if it had to pay out cold cash to acquire microtextual copies of them to replace them! This is the startling fact which most librarians are not yet really aware of.

Assume, Rider goes on to say, that each discarded volume would have a salvage value of two dollars. Out of that income, the library would pay for the book's microtext replacement, house the microtext in perpetuity, and derive, besides, "an actual cash profit on the substitution." He writes: "If there was ever a case in library technology of having one's cake and eating it too this substitution of microtext books for salvageable bookform books would seem to be it!"

A cash profit—*sounds mighty good.* Miles O. Price, then the director of Columbia's library, said in the discussion that followed this presentation that he has "long been a microtext enthusiast." But (and this is where I got my comment to Michael Lesk about the collapse of the used-book market) he quibbled with the cost analysis: "Discarded material will have low salvage value because of the number of libraries which will be discarding." James T. Babb of Yale "felt the need for the physical book to exist somewhere in the Northeast," but he thought that the need would decrease. According to the synopsis of the discussion, only one library manager that day reacted with anything like revulsion or outrage at Rider's plan. Charles David, head of the University of Pennsylvania's library, found the economic analysis "exasperating" and questioned its soundness. He said that it was an "invitation to librarians to destroy books by the millions."

And that is what it was. Fremont Rider was a giant of twentieth-century librarianship; his erratic career repays study. He had a persuasive and colorful prose style, and his poems (a number of which he published in his autobiography) have a certain sorrowful throb:

Roses, jasmine,
  Frankincense, myrrh—
Grey death dust
  In the soul's sepulchre.

(Read it slowly, Rider recommends.) At Syracuse University, he edited the *Onondagan*—this was back in 1905, when they still had their run of the Syracuse *Daily Standard*—then he went to library school in Albany, where Melvil Dewey (whose biography Rider later wrote) hired him as a secretary. But Dewey's adjustments to the decimal system couldn't hold Rider's attention, and by 1907 he was in New York turning out pulp mystery stories and, very briefly, headlines for Hearst's yellow-pennanted flagship, the New York *American*. For *The Delineator* (a magazine edited by Theodore Dreiser) he produced a series of pieces on spirit rappings, levitation, astral bodies, multiple personalities, and other phenomena that have "converted to psychism the greatest scientists of Europe, and are now creating widespread comment in every intelligent center of the globe." These were collected in his first book, *Are the Dead Alive?* It isn't an entirely dispassionate work: "the *fact* that tables and other articles of furniture do under certain conditions move, apparently of their own accord, *must be admitted as established*." (Rider was a fervent italicizer.)

Soon he was writing guidebooks to Bermuda, California, and New York; he was managing editor of *Library Journal* and *Publishers Weekly* for a while; he founded a company that did the printing work for R. R. Bowker; he started a monthly magazine called *Information* and one called *The International Military Digest.* He began to make money in Florida real estate.

Then came an apparent manic episode, followed by crisis and collapse. Rider bought a Vanderbilt estate, Idlehour, on the south shore of Long Island, and spent several hundred thousand dollars fixing it up as a self-help college and "vacation hotel-club." Promoters sold life memberships in the club, but because (as Rider tells it) he refused to operate it as a speakeasy, nobody came, and he declared bankruptcy in 1929. But in 1932 he rose from the dead with a powerful (although pseudonymous) pamphlet called "Are Our Banks Betraying Us?" In it, possibly conscious of his own reduced financial position, he called for a moratorium on the payment of mortgages, and he said that people are "deeply and dangerously embittered."

> They are thoroughly disgusted and disappointed with the present "system," not merely because their fingers have been burned, but because they realize perfectly well that, in many cases, the burning was neither just nor justified. They want a "new deal."

The pamphlet produced, according to Rider, an "astonishing flood of enthusiastic approval." He mailed a copy to Franklin Roosevelt; Roosevelt shot off a thank-you letter that ended, handwritten, "You are right! Keep it up!" This was two months before Roosevelt's first use of the phrase "new deal" in his nomination speech.

In 1933, needing steady money, Rider accepted the librarianship of Wesleyan, in Middletown, Connecticut, his native city. He began a system of buying books in bulk and selling off the discards. Though a bankrupt himself, he did wonderful things for the library's finances, and he wrote a "Study of Library Cost Accounting" that, in his words, "enkindled" the profession. But his great work, his extraordinary New Deal for librarians, came in 1944: *The Scholar and the Future of the Research Library,* handsomely self-published, as most of his books were. Rider had discovered a "mathematical fact," almost a "natural law" of library growth, which is that over the past three centuries library collections have doubled every sixteen years. Rider devotes a page to an elongated graph plotting collection size against years—the "parabolic" trend lines zoom up to near verticality. The chart of this "veritable tidal wave of printed materials" would make anyone in charge of a library bolt for high ground. We confront, Rider says, far more than a library problem: "It is a problem—and a problem to the *n*th degree complex and baffling—of civilization itself." How can we respond, when "mere palliatives are going to be utterly ineffective"?

> We absolutely *must* analyze our whole problem from entirely fresh viewpoints, and must endeavor to find, in one direction or another, sweepingly new solutions for it.

As it turns out, Rider was wrong—later students of library progress have demonstrated that collections don't double every sixteen years and have not done so in the past. No matter—Rider believed his figures to be true, or at he least hoped they were more or less true (he liked and wrote science fiction), and books do undeniably pile up fast. What is a library to do to contain this doubling and redoubling growth? It could build an annex or a new building and shelve the hideous growth in it—that's what once would have happened. Ah, but the "storage warehouse" is, Rider holds, a "tacit confession of past failure"—all it does is change where the growth takes place, and "it, of itself, creates new expenses and fresh problems." The library could adopt a severe policy of "weeding out" its stacks, but, says Rider, with justification, a library that weeds is a library that is *"no longer providing its users with the material it has weeded out!"*

Microphotography should have saved us long ago, but it hadn't, and Fremont Rider knew why: librarians had been treating micro-materials *"as though they were books."* They were not books—they were "a brand-new form, an utterly and completely and basically different form," and therein lay our historic opportunity:

> No one seems to have realized that, abruptly, for the first time in over two thousand years, libraries *were being offered a chance to begin all over again.*

Rider's version of the new beginning was the Microcard library: a set of catalog cards bearing the usual author-title information on the front, and the highly reduced images of every page printed in emulsion on the back. Since card catalogs already had cabinet space assigned to them, a complete Microcard replacement of the existing card catalog, accompanied by a disposal of the physical books it stood for, would result in a savings in storage cost "that comes gratifyingly close to 100%." Rider had grand visions for his Microcards—he even envisioned "micro-reading machines built into organs, pianos, and the like, [and] special reading machines on easels for orchestra use."

He set up the non-profit Microcard Foundation, controlled by a board of trustees that included several prominent librarians (Keyes Metcalf, by then running Harvard's libraries, and Archibald MacLeish, Librarian of Congress, among them), and with the help of Kodak and other companies he began to sell Microcard reproductions of volumes of genealogy and local history, publications of the Early English Text Society, and the Rolls Series of medieval chronicles. In the fifties, librarians at the Atomic Energy Commission became interested; they reproduced older reports on Microcards, so that weapons laboratories could throw out their originals; soon the AEC was distributing current reports on Microcards, too.

There were difficulties with the reading machines, though—for one thing, Microcards, being opaque, demanded lots of reflected light, and this light (in the cautious words of an early enthusiast) "produces heat which, when concentrated on the small section of the card being read, would be apt to have serious effects." The installation of a cooling fan reduced the hazard of fire, but the viewed image never achieved enough contrast or crispness—it wasn't as good as the screen-shadows of conventional microfilm, scratched and faded though they may be. Nonetheless, libraries made heavy investments in these book-substitutes: in 1954 there were twenty-five Microcard publishers (Barnes and Noble produced some titles) and 1,600 Microcard-viewing machines in the United States. All for naught. "To any one who has New England blood in his veins," Rider wrote late in life, "waste—absolute, and completely unnecessary waste—is more than an economic loss: it is a venal sin." Rider died a sinner in 1962.

But there is no lasting shame in taking a wrong turn. The shame comes in the fact that physical books were spent, wasted, too, as part of Rider's brainsick spendthrift-frugality. For a topological question arises: how can one get all the pages of a given book onto the back of a card (or several cards, if the book is long), when book pages are double-sided? Rider's answer was simple—destroy twice as many books:

> All that we have to do is to take *two* copies of the book that we are proposing to micro-copy, return these two copies to their original unbound form, and then *spread them out*. How do we do this? We take the two copies; trim off all the waste paper margins on all the four sides of the pages; and then "reimpose" the resulting pages *in an order and layout especially adapted for the easy reading of them on the back of a catalog card.*

The notion that in these acts of petty vandalism we would be somehow "returning the books to their original unbound form" is a characteristic Rideresque flourish—as if the book's binding were a bit of Victorian gingerbread, an excrescence, a superficial late addition to the primordial, Promethean page-heap. (Fortunately a number of Microcard publishers found ways to reproduce pages without disbinding—by re-photographing microphotographs—or concentrated their work on manuscript papers that weren't bound in the first place. They also gradually abandoned the idea of opacity, and began using clear plastic rectangles through which light passed—microfiches—instead.)

Library leaders were hypnotized by Rider's book. It was the talk of conferences; it gave a heroic forward tilt to the administrator's cause. The journal *College and Research Libraries* published a symposium called "The Promise of Microprint," in which Keyes Metcalf wrote that *The Scholar and the Future of the Research Library* "should be made required reading for library school students" and said that it "may well prove to be one of the most important books dealing with libraries in this generation." A senior librarian from Brown University wrote excitedly that "it is difficult, to put it mildly, in the absence of some still more efficient space-saving device, not to embrace micro-cards as the panacea for libraries 'growing pains' "; this informationalist dreamed of a time when libraries would have a fixed size: "When will the rate at which material is published on micro-cards permit a library to withdraw . . . enough books from its shelves to balance the amount of material which is newly published in conventional book form and must be added?" Ever the self-promoter, Rider includes in his 1955 autobiography, *And Master of None,* a page full of praise for *The Scholar* from eminent librarians. Archibald MacLeish: "a superb job, superbly done"; James T. Babb of Yale: "by far the most interesting and stimulating piece of library literature I have tackled in a long time"; Harold Leupp of the University of California: "the most constructive approach to the problem I have heard from any source"; William Warner Bishop, of the University of Michigan: "The book fairly takes my breath away. You have given librarians much to think about and to think about furiously."

Never mind that Rider's "constructive approach" advocated the dissection (in matched pairs) and deacquisition of millions of volumes over time (excepting, to be sure, "prestige material," gift collections, and some special cases—books with color illustrations, for instance); never mind that Rider was proposing that the central research trove of a large academic library would shrivel, "by inexorable mathematical law," into "endless aisles of [Microcard] file cases," aisles in which the scholar would, Rider wrote, "find most of his materials, and do most of his work." One might have expected library generals to have kept their distance from this amiable entrepreneurial crank. Instead, these furious thinkers served on his Microcard Foundation and Microcard Committee; they helped him plan and standardize and refine his conception; they bought his product; they were clearly intrigued by the potential despoliation that his proposal held out to them.

Rider had successfully found and cultivated their fear, fear of the demon Growth that was alive in the stacks, doubling relentlessly, a monstrous exploding pustule of cellulose. The only reason there wasn't more actual damage done to research collections as a result of *The Scholar and the Future of the Research Library* is that Microcards were so obviously inadequate to the demands of the scholarly eye and mind that the hundred-percent-space-saving swap-out couldn't proceed as its promoter envisioned.

CHAPTER 9

Dingy, Dreary, Dog-eared, and Dead

Fremont Rider's enduring achievement was to convince the heads of research libraries that it was somehow embarrassing to add more low-cost storage space. Any outlay, no matter how lavish (and the act of microfilming a little-used book is, and has always been, at least twenty times more costly than the act of putting it in storage), seemed preferable to the face-loss of having to rent an old building and set up ranks of shelves in it. Book-storage warehouses were, Rider told his quaking readers, "not 'solutions' of the growth problem, but simply 'confessions of avoidance' "—which is like saying that it is a confession of avoidance to buy new shoes for your child because he or she is sure to outgrow them. They were determined foot-binders, this crew—Metcalf at Harvard, Tate at the National Archives and MIT, Wagman from Michigan, Babb from Yale, Raney and Fussler from the University of Chicago—men who were pledged, in spite of every setback, to bring the costs of mass-microfilming down to the parity point of new construction, so that their Mr. Fixit hungers, their joy in lenses and basement darkrooms and hand cranks and developing fluids, would seem to be the result of the soberest, the most parsimoniously conservative calculations.

Foremost among these determined cost-reducers was Rider's friend and ally Verner Clapp at the Library of Congress. Rider was harmless, in a way: his ideas were deranged, but he seems to have been slow in applying them to Wesleyan's collections. (He did, however, perform what he called a "full cropping" on some wide-margined Wesleyan books, slicing off their tops, bottoms, and fore-edges—cover-boards and all—"so as not to store forever a lot of accompanying waste paper.") Verner Clapp, on the other hand, spent more than thirty years at the Library of Congress, serving under four different chief librarians, and the impetuously technophilic decisions he and other managers made there have done irreversible damage to what was once our library of last resort. Rider barked, Clapp bit.

Clapp's book *The Future of the Research Library* (1964) begins with a respectful tribute:

> As World War II drew to a close, Fremont Rider, at that time the librarian of Wesleyan University, threw a bombshell into the library world by his demonstration of the exponential growth of research library collections. . . . But Rider, ever a constructive critic, provided along with his prophecy of doom a gospel of salvation: the research library of the future, he foresaw, would consist of microtext.

Clapp believed in this gospel; after he left the Library of Congress to launch the Council on Library Resources, he contracted with the Microcard Corporation to create an improved, portable micro-viewer, and he funded the first scientific journal to be published exclusively in a micro-format—*Wildlife Disease.* The viewer-development program was a failure, but the prototypes, notably a tripod-mounted model with a segmented, insectoid abdomen and a staring monocle of an eye, are fine examples of late-fifties futurism. In the Council's annual report for 1959, Clapp includes a section on "The Problem of Size" that contained up-leaping growth graphs based largely on Rider's errant statistics of fifteen years earlier. Like Rider, Clapp was a man of wide reading and humanistic polish—he studied Herodotus in the original and wanted people to know it, and he thought that C. P. Snow's division between the two cultures was "baloney, baloney, thorough baloney"—but his attitude toward old books (except the obviously valuable items in rare-book rooms) was marked at times by a puzzling vehemence, as in this description of a visit to a small-town library:

> After numerous inquiries we find someone who knows where the public library is, and we visit it. Dingy, dreary, dogeared and dead! Stupid people and stupid books that no one reads, that no one should read!

The persistence of this dingy paper patrimony troubled Clapp: "The world's population is laid to rest each generation; the world's books have a way of lingering on," he writes. How can we "extract profit and usefulness from this inheritance of the past," he goes on to inquire, and yet at the same time "prevent it from clogging the channels of the present"? How can libraries, in other words, maintain the self-sufficiency that is essential for scholarly exactitude, without actually putting up more shelves?

"Massive dissemination in microfacsimile"—that's how. Microfilm is compact and clean, as fresh as only plastic can be (at least initially). Clapp's fantasy of institutional transformation was a variation on Rider's idea of making money by throwing books away—if you reduced the cost of creating and distributing microcopies and at the same time made them easier to use, then "the storage library would no longer hold much meaning." Groups of cooperating libraries would, once a decade, agree upon a corpus of "lesser-used books to be retired to microtext." The mass retirements would be sufficient to hold each collection fixed at "whatever millions of original volumes the future shows to be optimum for a research library." Growth—exponential, geometrical, even linear—would stop altogether. The size problem would be solved. Clapp worries in passing about the researcher's inability to stand and browse a comprehensively microfilmed collection, but he thinks, happy man, that better cataloging would somehow compensate for this difficulty.

Warren Haas, who assumed the presidency of the Council

on Library Resources in the seventies, described Clapp to me as "bubbling" and "full of beans." Deanna Marcum, the current president of the (renamed and substantially repurposed) Council on Library and Information Resources, has written that Clapp "loved gadgets, and was forever thinking about what could be invented to make library jobs more efficient or streamlined." Clapp was looking for "solutions to the problems of libraries"; and in his search he had help from his board of directors—a group that included some extremely bright war scientists and CIA consultants.

Warren Weaver was one of the Council's founding board members. He had been chief of the Applied Mathematics Panel during World War II, performing the ballistics computations necessary to create machines that shot down planes with the help of radar (work known as "fire control"); this war effort led Weaver to the nascent field of Operations Research (OR), which endeavored to calculate, with the help of glittering curlicues of equations superimposed on a gaunt gray skeleton of simplifying assumptions, the least costly way to transport troops, position anti-aircraft guns, or bomb cities. Weaver was also interested in the statistical mathematics of human communication and the possibility of machine translation—and from there it was only a hop and a skip to the Council on Library Resources. (It didn't hurt, either, that Weaver was a vice president at the Rockefeller Foundation, which had paid for much of the early work of newspaper microfilming at Harvard and the Library of Congress.)

Philip Morse, an MIT acoustician and founder of Rand Corporation, the Air Force's non-profit think tank, had spent much of his career evaluating the destructive efficacy of missiles, depth charges, and nuclear weapons, first during the war, as director of the highly successful Anti-submarine Warfare Group, and then later at the Defense Department's Weapons Systems Evaluation Group (where Morse argued in favor of the hydrogen bomb) and its successor, the Institute for Defense Analysis; in 1947 he became the first director of the Brookhaven nuclear laboratory and (in his account) the first person to suggest to the Navy that it should start building nuclear submarines; in 1963 he became a board member of the Council on Library Resources. Around that time, as director of MIT's Operations Research Center, he had the idea of applying OR's mathematical methods to the workings of MIT's library; out of that grew Morse's thickly mathematical treatise, *Library Effectiveness* (1968), which uses a technique called Markov analysis to determine whether a book of a particular age and number of previous circulations is likely to remain useful; in order to gather detailed circulation statistics, Morse wanted to computerize the library. The modern library, he felt, "cannot now be operated as though it were a passive repository for printed material."

One of Warren Weaver's disciples from the Applied Mathematics Panel was Merrill Flood, a game theorist at Rand who had, during the war, produced a secret OR analysis of the ways that B-29s might bomb Japan. (Bombing with or without propaganda leaflets, incendiaries, or "poison gas" were some of the options listed by Flood.) Flood had risen to become president of the Operations Research Society of America (a group Philip Morse had founded) in the early sixties; Flood believed that OR's heuristic techniques could help the nation take "very major steps to 'modernize' its vast transportation system," and that sophisticated war games and business games, in which "many of the decisions normally made by humans in real life are made by the computer," would teach us how to design a better world. Flood's nuclear-powered wonderland was just around the corner, in fact: "an abundance of nearly free energy, and economical computers for controlling it, are scientific accomplishments already in sight," he wrote in 1962. About that time, Verner Clapp hired Flood, along with a team of military-intelligence experts, to produce an OR-influenced cost-benefit study, *Automation and the Library of Congress.* The team was headed up by Gilbert W. King, chief of research at Itek Corporation; Itek was (in those days) a stealthy company run by ex-CIA paramilitarist Frank Lindsay, charged with producing the high-resolution spy-satellite cameras used to microfilm the Russian hinterlands from many miles up. Gilbert King, Merrill Flood, and the others proposed that the Library of Congress's cataloging and processing functions undergo a comprehensive computerization, using a "trillion bit memory"; the stacks would be closed to researchers, so that monitoring software could track book usage, and so that books themselves might be shelved, unbrowsably, not by call number but by "demand frequency." (There would be "a complete independence of the physical location of items from their descriptive mapping in the catalogs and files"—in other words, a total reliance on the location records held in the computer.) Microfilm was getting so good, according to the King Report, that soon "the circulation of most documents in their printed form may become unnecessary"; the report suggested that several of the library's divisions (including the Defense Research Division, funded by the Department of Defense but administered by the Library of Congress, and the Legislative Reference Service, which answered legislators' questions) might convert their holdings to a computer-coded microfilm-storage system called Filesearch. (Fortunately they didn't: the U.S. military used the Filesearch system to index thousands of microfilmed North Vietnamese documents as part of its intelligence work; when the hardware was superseded, all the indexing information was lost.) None of this would be cheap: the King Report's writers unanimously proposed that the Library of Congress devote between fifty and eighty million dollars—three times the library's total annual budget—to the automation of its basic functions.

Quincy Mumford, the Librarian of Congress, wasn't quite so adventurous as Clapp, and he couldn't put together that kind of money. But the wiry, energetic Clapp wasn't too discouraged; in 1964 he hired Lawrence F. Buckland to study the practical questions of computerizing the Library of Congress's catalog-card printing operation. Buckland had been an officer at the Air Force's Rome Air Development Center in the fifties, where he had helped underwrite Gilbert King's large-capacity "photoscopic" computer memory (as part of an attempt to create an automatic Russian-to-English translation machine); later Buckland moved to Itek and then, in 1962, he founded Inforonics, a database consulting and publishing company whose early clients were the Air Force, the CIA, and the National Science Foundation. (Buckland's company produced the first major reference book to be typeset directly from a digital database, the 1969 edition of the *American Heritage Dictionary*.) A team of systems specialists at United Aircraft also got involved with the Library of Congress's computer-cataloging project (with the help of steady grants from the Council on Library Resources), and a person named Henriette Avram was engaged to tune and manage the increasingly costly effort—Avram's résumé included assignments at the National Security Agency, the secretive federal monolith devoted to electronic surveillance and cryptanalysis, and the American Research Bureau, the company that produced the Arbitron television ratings. By the late sixties, after some stops and starts, Clapp and the library he was trying to manage from afar finally had a machine-readable cataloging (MARC) record—ungainly, cabalistically coded, but twenty years ahead of its time. Some of Verner Clapp's ideas and enthusiasms "have seemed a bit quixotic," said William S. Dix, then librarian at Princeton, "but in his hands the impossible dream had a way of approaching reality. For he never gave up." Clapp was a classic bleeding-edge man. Just about every machine dream that administrators now have, Clapp had, and funded, forty years ago.

Helping large research libraries to disencumber themselves of old books was a top priority: Clapp gave a grant to his erstwhile Library of Congress colleague John H. Ottemiller (a former OSS documents-gatherer who ended up at Yale's library), which Ottemiller used to pay faculty members to go through the Yale stacks, deciding what to get rid of or move offsite, as part of a "selective book retirement" study; Ottemiller wrote that he saw "a possible need for putting greater emphasis on the *discarding* of materials rather than their storage." (Paying the faculty weeders was necessary, Ottemiller said, to overcome "a loss of enthusiasm for the project.") But discarding was maybe a little ho-hum—how about holographic storage? Clapp hired Arthur Carson, of Carson Laboratories (who had spent much of his career at United Aircraft working on the Air Force's flightless nuclear-powered airplane), to investigate the recording of texts in rectangular crystals of doped potassium chloride; unfortunately, the stored images faded a little every time the lasers read them. Fiber optics? Clapp asked the Institute for Scientific Information to use "minute but flexible threads of light-conducting material" in a handheld copying device. Clapp was especially drawn to closed-circuit TV; it was attractive, he wrote, because it promised to contribute to the efficiency of library work by "reducing the required number of collections of specialized or little-used material." If you could combine closed-circuit TV with an automatic, pneumatic page-turning machine, say, you might really have something. Thus in 1958, Clapp's council contracted with the de Florez Company to develop a pneumatic page-turner, which would allow books to be microfilmed on autopilot, or read remotely by closed-circuit television. (The machine was very handsome: with its air tubes and angled lights, it looked like an expensive piece of dental-office equipment.) The de Florez company was founded by Admiral Luis de Florez, the first chairman of the CIA's Research Board—an ingenious inventor of oil-drilling equipment and flight-control instrumentation who also advised the CIA about the potential for radiological weapons (whether to use "light dosage contamination" for example) and the promise of drug-facilitated interrogation. For a time, Clapp and his board of directors thought that there might be commercial possibilities for the de Florez page-turner, but it didn't live up to expectations. After many tinkerings and infusions of capital, and a trial period in the microphotography lab of the New York Public Library, the machine was set aside; eventually it was pronounced "not particularly suited to the handling of library materials."

On the public relations front, the Council gave the go-ahead to Joseph Becker, a senior information specialist at the CIA, to develop a demonstration of (as Clapp wrote in the annual report) "some of the realities behind the talk of 'push-button libraries' " for the 1962 Seattle World's Fair. This exhibition, "with an emphasis on the 'library of the future,' " was sponsored by the Council on Library Resources (via a pass-through grant from the American Library Association); other sponsors were the Air Force, Radio Corporation of America, and National Cash Register. In the council's annual report, a photograph shows Secretary of State Dean Rusk (who incidentally was that same year trying to figure out whether the CIA should use Mafia hit men or poisons to assassinate Castro) looking mildly amused as someone hands him a printout from a Sperry Rand Univac computer. Two years later, a modified version of the library-of-the-future exhibition, this time using IBM computers but again supervised by Joseph Becker, was on display at the New York World's Fair. As part of a demonstration of networked information, fair-goers were able to pick up a handset from a bank of telephones and listen in on taped reviews of young-adult books.

Faxing was another of Clapp's preoccupations—if libraries could fax things easily here and there, then they wouldn't need to keep as many physical books near to hand. But the hefty Xerox Magnavox Telecopier was too slow: "Transceiving time for an average 10-page request is about one hour." There were all sorts of other possibilities, though. Clapp thought highly of the now legendary defense-worker J. C. R. (Lick) Licklider—who had spent his twenties studying what happens to white rats if you force them to stay awake for several days by putting them on slowly turning treadmills surrounded by water (they die), and who had developed time-sharing computer systems for the Air Force's SAGE air-defense system. Clapp hired Lick to look into the elements of man-machine symbiosis as they might shape libraries in the twenty-first century; Licklider got to work in 1961, just before he went on to triumph as the creator of the ARPANET, the Pentagon's precursor to the Internet—the

Internet being itself a leading cause of sleep deprivation. The result, published in 1964, was a coolly abstruse book called *Libraries of the Future,* written by Licklider and a team of missile-minded members of the artificial intelligentsia, without the aid of a single librarian, historian, or humanist; Verner Clapp proudly wrote the foreword.

Clapp well knew that some of the projects in which the Council was taking an interest were aimed at "special manifestations of library work such as the handling of in-house industrial research reports or of military intelligence." But he had no doubt that "libraries generally will eventually benefit." He was plainly impressed by the work in indexing and retrieval going forward at the Air Force, the Atomic Energy Commission, and the CIA (in 1953 he had even applied for the job of Air Force Librarian): as a lifelong Republican and a patriot who had, while at the Library of Congress, fired or allowed to resign a number of employees when FBI checks found clear evidence of political disloyalty or homosexuality, Clapp wanted to do his part to win the Cold War (which was a war of secret science, demanding speedy but eyes-only informational flow) and to help civilian research libraries at the same time.

Not all the CIA contacts at the Council came through Clapp, however. Other members of the Council's board of directors—Barnaby Keeney, Caryl Haskins, and Frederick Wagman, for example—had their own affiliations. Wagman, as we know from Clapp's papers, worked on unspecified CIA-financed projects with Clapp at the Library of Congress; his career in intelligence began during the war, at the Office of Censorship, an agency responsible for intercepting, reading, and (if they proved interesting) microfilming private letters on their way to and from the United States. Barnaby Keeney, a medievalist and Rhodes scholar, worked for the CIA in the fifties and continued to consult for the agency while he was president of Brown University; he is now perhaps best remembered for his role as board chairman (beginning in 1962, while he was still on Clapp's Council) of the Human Ecology Fund, a CIA front organization that paid for some of the experiments in which LSD and other drugs were given to unwitting Canadian subjects. (Intrigued by Russian psychiatric research and the possibility of "brainwashing"—a Korean War word—the CIA wanted to improve its interrogational techniques and perfect new methods of what its department heads called "mind-control.")

After Barnaby Keeney left the Council's board—he went on to become the chief of the newly chartered National Endowment for the Humanities—Caryl Haskins (wealthy entomologist, president of the Carnegie Institution of Washington) joined Clapp's team in 1965. Haskins was the founder of Haskins Laboratories and a student of radiation's effects on living organisms; in 1949 he chaired the Secretary of Defense's Ad Hoc Committee on Biological Warfare, producing a report that contained some startling talk about the possibility of "radiological weapons" and "weapons causing epidemics, glandular or hereditary changes, or other biological 'chain reactions.' " In the fifties Haskins was a consultant for the CIA's mind-control research: his name appears in a 1952 CIA memo on Project Artichoke, which is described as "a special agency program established for the development and application of special techniques in CIA interrogations and in other CIA covert activities where control of an individual is desired." (The memo comments on the possible utility of sodium pentathol, barbiturates, hypnosis, neurosurgery, electric shock, heroin, alcohol, Benzedrine, and "lycergic acid" as interrogational aids, and reports that a scientific panel has been established, with Haskins at its head, "to evaluate possibilities and give direction in the field of research and experimentation.") As a Project Artichoke emissary, Haskins traveled to Canada to discuss the brainwashing experiments with a psychologist at McGill University; and he agreed to remain available to the CIA as a consultant when his attempts to recruit other researchers met with little success.

Clapp's library council had traditionalists on its board, too—the gruff and likeable Louis B. Wright was one, director of the Folger Shakespeare Library. Wright had first felt a need for such a council in the mid-fifties (he just wanted a better way to reproduce pages from rare books and manuscripts); and he had raised Ford Foundation money to fund it and chosen Clapp to run it. A few years into the enterprise, however, he became alarmed by Clapp's unrelenting gizmology. Wright was overruled; by then Clapp had a physicist on staff and was in full futuristic swing; in 1960, the Ford Foundation board strongly endorsed Clapp, saying that "the most informed point of contact between the computer man, the optics man and the scientific linguist, on the one hand, and the world of bibliographic storage and access, on the other, is the president of the Council on Library Resources." A number of Clapp's old Library of Congress co-workers got contracts: CIA consultant Mortimer Taube (an ex-Library of Congress weapons-research abstractor and an Atomic Energy Commission information specialist, described by one of his contemporaries as being possibly "the first library millionaire") was given the job of developing another hand-reader for microfilm and microfiche, after the Microcard Corporation's attempts failed. This prototype didn't work either.

Clapp's last and most ambitious mechanization scheme—an attempt to create a working electronic library at MIT—was called Project Intrex. In the early sixties, Intrex (administered by Carl Overhage and other veterans of air-defense engineering at MIT's Lincoln Laboratory) had been sponsored by the Independence Foundation, a conduit for CIA money in that era; in 1967, the Council on Library Resources assumed lead financial responsibility. Clapp took a personal interest in Intrex, serving on its steering committee even after his retirement from the presidency of the Council; the project envisioned, among other things, "better and more economical systems for weeding," as well as "digital storage of encoded full-text in massive random-acccess storage." ("Massive" and "mass" were thermonuclear words that seemed to get the hearts of information scientists beating faster.) But Intrex's historian, Colin Burke, sums up the project thus:

> Project INTREX fell very short of the expectations of all its sponsors. After some eight years INTREX ended with little

> more than a few pieces of soon outdated hardware, some homeless software, and twenty thousand indexed articles in a limited field called "material science."

Intrex's only visible achievement, Burke adds, was a set of paper finding aids called "Pathfinders," which helped students get around the reference collection.

Why couldn't Clapp have shown a little patience, and funded more quiet inquiries into techniques of cataloging Persian works (as some traditionalist members of his board would have much preferred him to do), reconciling himself to the fact that whatever glorious man-machine couplings were in the offing, they weren't going to happen in his lifetime? Why couldn't he have left library administrators alone, rather than forever distracting them from their primary task as paper-keepers by dangling the lure of convulsive change before them, long before the change was practical, and long before it had revealed its many risks? Clapp especially goaded his alma mater, the Library of Congress, to invest in seductive prematurities, early systems that broke down, cost a fortune, spread confusion, didn't focus, made life more difficult, and failed in general to do what they were built or bought to do. Forty years and many generations of scrapped prototypes later, libraries are still trying to get Clapp's remote-access full-text wish-list to fly.

But brute shrinkage was the idea closest to Clapp's heart, and there (despite the disappointments of machines like the Verac) the basic technology was already mature. Microtext, he wrote, has "rescued many millions of pages of newspapers from oblivion at comparatively low cost and with a concomitant saving of space"—the next step, then, was to perform a similar sort of "rescue" on journals and then books. The question was how to pay for it. In *College and Research Libraries,* Alan Pritsker and William Sadler had, in 1957, dealt an inadvertent blow to the burgeoning micro-movement in a cost study that found microfilming to be of financial appeal as an alternative form of storage only if libraries (and their patrons) were willing to tolerate (1) somewhat fuzzy print, (2) minimal quality control, and (3) "the destruction of the text." (The researchers assumed textual destruction because the microfilming system that they were using in their estimates of work-flow, the RemRand Model 12, required that pages be "fed automatically into the machine." That in itself was not a problem, the authors wrote: "Since the purpose of microfilming is to reduce the space requirements, the cutting of the bindings is considered inconsequential. Any possible gain from the resale value of these books would be more than offset by the increased efficiency in filming.") And yet, despite their diligent efforts, Pritsker and Sadler found microfilm conversion to be a costlier means of storage for research libraries than bookshelves. (Alan Pritsker, incidentally, went on to become a pioneer of digital simulation, creating the computer languages JASP for the Air Force and GERT for NASA.)

Clapp responded to these unwelcome results by having the Council commission a similar study, completed in 1961. The Crerar Library in Chicago, a privately endowed reference library whose social sciences collection had been sold off by Clapp's former Library of Congress colleague Herman Henkle, was supporting itself by marketing its services to places like the Atomic Energy Commission, whose *Nuclear Science Abstracts* Crerar's librarians produced. The library was moving from an old building to a squat glass box on the campus of the Illinois Institute of Technology; there were many pre-1920s journals in the collection which took up space. Clapp and Henkle felt, or hoped, that microfilming these volumes might be cheaper than continuing to store them, but they couldn't be sure, especially with Pritsker's discouraging results; so Clapp asked a small consulting firm to perform an operations-research analysis on the problem, "Costs and Material Handling Problems in Miniaturizing 100,000 Volumes of Bound Periodicals." Clapp, too, allowed his engineers to assume "shearing of spines" in their estimates, since spine-shearing allows for "considerable labor saving in the photographic operation by avoiding the necessity for raising and lowering the pressure plate each time a page is turned."

This time around, the cost comparisons came out a little

better. It now appeared, according to Clapp's summary of the research, that with enough buyers of prints of the microfilm, a large microfilming project could successfully reduce a library's storage costs without any of the sacrifices that Pritsker and Sadler enumerated—no sacrifices, that is, "except that of destruction of the text."

CHAPTER 10

The Preservation Microfilming Office

The newspapers went first, but as the filmable remainder of their own bound backfiles dwindled, library planners began to look around for other ways to occupy their now fully staffed and equipped information-renewal programs. "It's like having a sausage factory, in a way," one former Library of Congress department head told me. "You've got to feed the beast." (The library owned twenty-four microfilm cameras in 1973; they were shooting seven thousand feet of negative film per day.) Books with brittle paper were one good possibility—shabby, unattractively aging, toned by time. In the mid-sixties, the library, again in the vanguard, began segregating thousands of books that were (as the 1968 annual report of the Council on Library Resources phrased it) "otherwise beyond redemption." Coincidentally, the library needed more space: "Space was a key word in the thinking and activities of this division [the Office of Collections Maintenance and Preservation] during fiscal 1966," reported the *Library of Congress Information Bulletin*. In 1967, Verner Clapp's last year as president, the Council gave the Library of Congress (via the Association of Research Libraries) a grant for a Pilot Preservation Project, to explore "arrangements for assuring the preservation of these [brittle] books for the continuing uses of the research community."

One interesting idea, which had been propounded by Gordon Williams in a 1962 study (also prepared with the help of a grant from the Council), was to save a physical copy of every significant book in a central, low-temperature storage warehouse, where it would be available for microfilming on demand. A benefit of the plan, according to Williams, was that libraries would then know what they could "safely discard" if they wanted to, since there was one backup in deep freeze. This well-intentioned conceit proved in the end administratively unwieldy, but the research done in connection with it, which compared some of the Library of Congress's books with the same titles held in other libraries, showed that the condition of a given book "varied greatly" from library to library: an important observation, since it implied that book longevity depends on local variables (humidity and temperature, rough treatment, styles of rebinding) as much as it does on the innate chemical properties—the "inherent vice"—of the paper.

Then it came time to relocate all those brittle books to high-density, low-cost housing. (In a later era, some stack areas in the Library of Congress's Jefferson building were reportedly known as "the slums.") The library hired Frazer G. Poole as preservation officer; Poole had a degree in aerological engineering from the U.S. Naval Academy (aerology, in Navy parlance, is the study of flying weather; the usage dates back to dirigibles) and eight years of experience directing the Library Technology Project of the American Library Association, where, at Clapp's suggestion and with Clapp's money, Poole developed performance standards for commercial bookbinding—which may be the reason that the Library of Congress did so much indiscriminate rebinding in those days. In 1968, Poole created a Preservation Office, whence blossomed the Preservation Microfilming Office (PMO), which filmed ninety-three million pages (three hundred thousand non-newspaper volumes) betweeen 1968 and 1984. In the eighties, the PMO had a staff of nineteen; they were transfiguring two hundred thousand guillotined pages per week. All of this material was pronounced "embrittled to the extent that it was no longer serviceable." We'll never know what "no longer serviceable" means, because the vast majority of those books are gone. One of the PMO's managers explained the eventual disposition of these three hundred thousand items:

> The volumes are cut, filmed by the Photoduplication Services, and the negative and positive copies are edited. All volumes, except those unique titles to be retained after filming, are sent to the Exchange and Gift Division. If the material is not claimed by interested institutions, it is pulped.

We are, wrote Deputy Librarian of Congress William Welsh in 1985, "running our cameras against the clock in the race to save as much as possible."

How many institutions, as a practical matter, are going to claim books that have been cut out of their bindings? Individual citizens might want mutilated books, but they weren't allowed to have them, according to Joanna Biggar, who wrote a 1984 article for *The Washington Post Magazine,* "Must the Library of Congress Destroy Books to Save Them?" The article, by identifying a few of those three hundred thousand volumes referred to by the head of the PMO, makes clear what did and what didn't qualify as a "unique title" in the Library's thinking in that era.

Biggar describes an illustrated 1909 book, *Peaks and Glaciers of Nun Kun: A Record of Pioneer Exploration and Mountaineering in the Punjab Himalaya,* by an explorer named Fanny Workman. The Library of Congress guillotined and filmed it in 1975; when a researcher who had recently used the book requested the disbound remains, she was told that the library wasn't allowed to transfer books to individuals. The Preservation Microfilming Office wouldn't let her take even the map. Fanny Workman's book, with its ninety-some illustrations, went to a Baltimore pulpery. Last time I checked on Bibliofind, on April 20, 2000, there were two copies of Fanny Workman's *Peaks and Glaciers of Nun Kun* for sale. One, "slightly rubbed and worn" and recased with new endpapers, was going for $2,200; the other, "slightly spotted" but crisp, for $2,400.

Assuming, conservatively, that the books the Library of Congress got rid of have a replacement value of forty dollars apiece (some would be worth less, some a great deal more), and assuming (generously) that the library kept ten percent of the originals after filming them, the Preservation Microfilming Office threw out more than ten million dollars' worth of public property between 1968 and 1984.

Spring-balanced book cradles, which hold bound books open evenly under a camera without cracking their spines, have been around since the thirties. Gutter shadow isn't as dark and deep in books as it is in newspaper volumes, because books aren't as thick, and their margins are usually wider. Very few of those three hundred thousand volumes would have had to be terminated in order to be "preserved," except that the PMO's mandate was to condense efficiently, per Verner Clapp's cost-estimating subcontractors. A 1987 Library of Congress Discussion Document titled "Preservation Selection Decisions," written by Ricky Erway, then of the Planning Office, includes a list of pros and cons to "keeping the material in its original format." One of the cons is "no space savings." If you keep the original but microfilm it in order to reduce the risk of damage to it, Erway points out, you actually provide "negative space savings." (Meaning that you must store the boxes of microfilm, too.) Erway also writes: "To save space, it is beneficial to transfer to a new format those materials which can then be discarded or can at least be stored offsite." The "primary solution" for brittle books, according to Erway's paper, was "Discard original."

In turning over this document—and it took me more than four months to extract it from the library, after I saw it mentioned in a UNESCO report on methods of library preservation—the head of the library's Office Systems Services and Records Office wanted me to know (1) that the Library of Congress is not bound by the Freedom of Information Act, (2) that the report "was never shared broadly within the Library," and (3) that its recommendations "never became Library policy." Oh, and another thing: "The report you are requesting is not of record at the Library of Congress." Ricky Erway herself now works at the Research Libraries Group; when I called her, she was kind enough to fax a copy of "Preservation Selection Decisions" to her former employer so that they could send it to me, since they seemed to be unable to locate it on their own. The document is, Erway says, "an artifact of its time"; when she looked it over recently, though, she thought, "Well, this seems pretty rational to me."

A year after Erway submitted her report, the new librarian of Congress, James Billington, dropped in on the library's Cataloging-in-Publication division, where he said a friendly hello to a publishers' liaison named Victoria Boucher. Boucher and Billington chatted for a moment, and then she brought up what was on her mind: the library was destroying books and calling it preservation. Knowing Billington's interests, she mentioned the loss of pre-Revolutionary Russian works in good condition. Billington seemed, as Boucher recalled afterward, "annoyed and embarrassed." She asked him if he'd yet been into the stacks (where books had slips in them marking them for microfilming), and he said he hadn't. When Billington left, the head of the department snapped at Boucher, "I'm glad he has you to tell him how to run a library!"

Boucher also went to the library's European Division and protested the sacrificial microfilming; she was told that she was "preaching to the choir." Eventually she had a talk with the head of the Preservation Microfilming Office at the time, Bohdan Yasinsky. Yasinsky reassured her, saying that people from Rare Books see the books before they are destroyed and have a chance to save them. "Quite a few people feel the way you do," Yasinsky told Boucher. "I am known as 'the butcher of books.' " The Library of Congress wasn't really a lending library, he said, so it didn't matter whether books remained in portable form. Boucher asked him if there had been any complaints from members of Congress (who can take books out); he said that there hadn't been. He fixed her with a basilisk gaze, according to Boucher, and said, "They know it won't do them any good anyway." When I telephoned Yasinsky (who is now a Ukranian specialist at the library), he promptly confirmed the butcher-of-books epithet. There were those, he said, who were "very skeptical" when he told them that he had to cut a book in order to film it. Yasinsky attributed their unhappiness to "nostalgia."

There have been reforms at the Library of Congress since the late 1980s. Decision trees and definitions of "serviceable" in reference to book stock have evolved considerably, I'm told—now the library supposedly keeps almost everything. Or rather, everything that has been allowed to become part of its collections; everything processed for retention, cataloged, and shelved. For, in fact, librarians reject and discard a huge mass of books that the library is given, free, by publishers every year (as the national library, the one library to have this privilege, they should be shelving everything they are sent); the only items that the library is required by law to store in perpetuity, oddly enough, are unpublished but formally copyrighted manuscripts. Anything published they can discard at any time. ("I am happy to announce that the Copyright Discard project is going very well, and all of your efforts are most appreciated," one recent internal memo began; the question was whether a certain class of material should go in the "regular Discard tub" or the copyright-discard tub.) And the library doesn't necessarily keep its second copies, either; one notable duplicate they deaccessioned some years ago was one of five known copies of an interim edition of *Finnegans Wake* from the twenties; the library bartered it for ten thousand dollars' worth of fine press books.

A great research library must keep its duplicates, even its triplicates, for a number of reasons, the most basic ones being that books become worn with use, lost, stolen, or misshelved. (A recent survey of nineteenth-century American books at the Library of Congress found that "the number of Not on Shelf, misshelved, and missing books is alarming.") Curious, I searched, on May 18, 2000, for phrases like "Surplus Library of Congress" and "Library of Congress Duplicate" on Bibliofind and turned up these: a rare printing of Henry Adams's *A Radical Indictment!* (1872) for sale for $2,000; a very fragile Hebrew grammar by John Smith published in 1803, with early ownership signatures on front and rear pastedowns (and a Library of Congress duplicate release stamp on the verso of the title page), for sale for $295; Mary Ellen Mark's *Ward 81* (1979), with an introduction by Milos Forman, rubber-stamped as a Library of Congress duplicate and for sale for $500; two volumes called *Chosen Kobunka Sokan* by Sueji Umehara, with approximately one hundred plates and an LC surplus stamp, for sale for $650; an anonymous 1881 book titled *Ploughed Under; the Story of an Indian Chief,* written with the assistance of "Bright Eyes," a.k.a. Susette La Flesche Tibbles, a full-blooded Omaha Indian, stamped "Library of Congress Surplus Duplicate" and spine-labeled "Reserve Storage Collection," for sale for $450; a children's book from 1861 by Jane Andrews called *The Seven Little Sisters Who Live on the Round Ball That Floats in the Air,* with eight illustrations (described as "a Library of Congress duplicate surplus"), for sale for $150; an 1831 edition of *The Federalist, on the New Constitution,* by Alexander Hamilton, John Jay, and James Madison, with a duplicate stamp on the first flyleaf, for sale for $400; E. H. Barton's *Cause and Prevention of Yellow Fever,* inscribed by the author to the Smithsonian Library in October 1858, with a Library of Congress release stamp on the first flyleaf, for sale for $450; and a book called *The Army of the Potomac* by Major General George McClellan, published in 1863, inscribed by McClellan to "His Excellency, General Count von Moltke, Chief of Staff etc etc with the sincere respect of George McClellan, Jun/69," with a Library of Congress duplicate stamp on the copyright page, for sale for $12,500.

The National Historic Preservation Act of 1966, as amended, requires federal agencies to disclose to the public, and to the Advisory Council on Historic Preservation, any plans that would affect districts, sites, buildings, or "objects" that are on the National Register of Historic Sites or that meet the register's criteria for inclusion. One of the criteria is that the building or object has "yielded, or may be likely to yield, information important in prehistory or history." No better description of a library collection could be had, and yet nobody as far as I know has tried to apply this law to the Library of Congress's collection (although the library's Jefferson building is on the National Register); no other law sets limits on what the library can or can't do to, say, its surviving newspapers, or to its decks of books and periodicals. If the library's management wanted to reduce their original holdings by one third over the next several years, they could do so without holding a single public hearing; and the library has not in the past felt any obligation to alert the public to what they are planning to micro-mutilate or to sell off. It is a strangely secretive place, underscrutinized by comparison with other federal bureaucracies, its maladministration undetected by virtue of its reputation as an ark of culture. The library has gone astray partly because we trusted the librarians so completely.

I asked Diane Kresh, head of the Preservation Directorate, whether there were any decisions that, with benefit of hindsight, she wished had gone differently. Any pieces of the collection that she would have liked to have seen retained that weren't?

"As far as I'm aware, everything we've acquired we've retained, at least in my tenure here," Kresh answered. What about serials, I asked—bound newspapers and journals and magazines? She said that the library *had* maintained the newspapers—they were just maintained on film. I don't doubt Kresh's sincere belief in the equivalence of microcopies and originals, but if a cop was told that some missing diamonds *were* still on display in the museum, they were just "maintained" as cubic zirconiums, the cop might arrive at a slightly different interpretation of the event. "I feel even with the newspaper example I'm comfortable with the decision," Kresh told me. "And as for other collections, I'm not aware of any that we've gotten rid of."

Kresh could so easily have said, "Yes, there were hundreds of thousands of books that we had that we should not have pulped after we filmed them. Their destruction was totally unnecessary and motivated in large part by a need for space." And she could have added, "As a matter of fact, there is currently a dire space crunch in both the Jefferson and Madison buildings—we've got stuff piled on the floors, it's a mess—and we're getting rid of things right now that we would probably keep if we were willing to rent another warehouse to tide us over until our remote-storage facility in Fort Meade is finished." Of course, Kresh is loyal to her employer and wouldn't say anything like that; I shouldn't have expected her to. But it would be true.

CHAPTER 11

Thugs and Pansies

The chief of the Preservation Reformatting Division of the Library of Congress, Irene Schubert, contributed to an electronic discussion group a few years ago. In a case where some of a periodical's run is brittle and some is not, Schubert wrote, the library would consider tossing it all out anyway: "Space is always a problem it seems, so we may get some encouragement to microfilm the entire run and discard the paper copies."

I asked, ahead of time, to interview Irene Schubert as part of an appointed visit to the Library of Congress's Madison building one afternoon. Diane Kresh told me that Schubert was unavailable. "If you have any issues," she said, "you can give them to me."

Kresh did, however, take me on a complete circuit of the library's renowned conservation lab, which I hadn't asked to see but was of course very glad to admire nonetheless. ("I wanted to start the tour by saying that we have the premier lab in the world," said Kresh flatly.) The full-bearded senior rare-book conservator, Thomas Albro, was working on an elegant box for a fifteenth-century edition of Ptolemy's *Geography* that he had just finished restoring. He had disbound the book, which was "inoperable" as a result of a bad rebinding in the nineteenth century—"shoddy work," he said—and he had washed the paper to remove yellowed sizing (sizing is the layer of gelatin that papermakers used to keep inks from soaking in and spreading, or "feathering"), and he had beautifully rebound this treasure in pale leather. Elsewhere, I saw very old Japanese softcover books for which a staff member was making lovely cases with bone fasteners. One conservator was worrying about what to do about some yellowed Wite-Out on one of Bill Mauldin's original drawings. Mauldin, a political cartoonist, published some of his work in the Army newspaper, *Stars and Stripes.* The Library of Congress once had a run of *Stars and Stripes;* it has microfilm now. Nonetheless, Mauldin's art is getting the most exquisite restoration treatment imaginable.

At another worktable lay parts of an enormous Hebrew scroll of the Book of Esther: a conservator had gone over its surface with a tiny vacuum cleaner and painted over each of its letters with gelatin parchment size. In the Collection Care Section, the purpose of which is to deal non-violently with books from the library's general collections, I admired the recently acquired pneumatic box-making machine, which stamps out custom-fitted boxes to hold books that in an earlier era would have gone under the lens, or to a commercial bindery to be reclothed in radiant pyroxylin (plastic-coated cloth). (The Library of Congress had a zealous rebinding policy for many decades—they sent books to the bindery rather than make minor repairs in-house, and thousands of ornate bindings were lost in consequence.)

All of this was genuinely impressive, and it helped to remind me of the befuddling divergence, in library language, between *conservation* and *preservation.* The two are no longer synonyms—in fact, they are more often antonymic, although library spokespersons have been known to rely on the lay confusion that surrounds their undisclosed redefinition. *Conservation* refers to the repair or restoration of the original object, the book or manuscript, the empirical, thumbable thing; *preservation,* on the other hand, though it may embrace the act of conservation, has more generally come to mean, in response to powerful euphemistic requirements, any act that carries on or propagates, in any chosen medium (e.g., the original pages, photocopies, fiche, film, tape cartridge, Microcard, diskette, CD-ROM, Norsam metal disk, and so on), the words or images of the original object. Thus *preservation* can mean dumping or other more remunerative forms of dispersal, whereas *conservation* never does, although of course conservational practices have at times caused unintentional harm. (The Scotch-taping of the Dead Sea Scrolls comes to mind.) Reversibility—the potential to undo what you or your predecessors have done—is a watchword of modern book conservation; book preservation, by contrast, is often irreversible, because the book is gone. "This cannot be emphasized too strongly—the filming process is often damaging and irreversible," according to the primary textbook of the eighties, *Preservation Microfilming: A Guide for Librarians and Archivists.* Often *intentionally* damaging and irreversible, one wants to add—for on the next page the textbook says: "It must be stressed that if you do remove bindings from bound volumes before filming, the quality of the film is usually improved, and the cost of producing the film is significantly reduced."

So all conservation is preservation, but not all preservation is conservation. And here's a troubling organizational fact: book conservators generally report to directors of preservation departments. This is true even though a book conservator's training is a slow apprenticeship, over many years, while the preservation administrator needs but an extra year of library-science courses to earn the right to decide, or help decide, what to do with a stackful of artifacts about which he or she might know almost nothing.

Complicating matters further, the manager of the library's reformatting lab (the microfilm and/or digital lab) also usually reports to the director of preservation. Thus the top person, the preservation administrator, or P.A.—who more often than not (although there are exceptions) has had no bench training and has only a slender acquaintance with the manual repair of books—has jurisdiction over two labs whose aims are in opposition to each other. The conservation lab wants to save the book; the preservation lab wants to "save" the book. The conservation lab costs money and progresses deliberately, item by item, sewing, gluing, restoring (although small fixes take only a matter of minutes)—and all of its work must go back on the shelf. The microfilming and digitization labs seem fast, because the planetary camera's white über-flash and the scanner's green underglide occur hundreds of times an hour, as on a production line, and though these departments have high overheads, they also *make* money, sometimes packets of it, through federal grants, state grants, foundation grants, and the selling of copies—and not everything that gets imaged has to go back on the shelf. (The New York Public Library had agreements with "various commercial publishers and micropublishers," according to former director David H. Stam: "With few exceptions, the income and royalties from these publications have been put back into the library's preservation programs.")

So the P.A. presides over one department that pays at least part of its way with outside money and one that doesn't; one that helps the library with its storage problem and one that doesn't. If you were a P.A.—a real cost-sphinctering conehead (not all are, of course)—with the managers of those two departments beneath you, of whom would you feel fonder? When you moved up to a senior post, whom would you promote to your old job: the chief of the microfilm lab, who steadily pulled in money, or the chief conservator, who seemed only to be able to spend it? More than a few former spine-whacking micro-managers are now preservation administrators.

In the early eighties, Wesley Boomgaarden briefly ran the preservation-microfilming operation at the New York Public Library, where his crew filmed more than two million pages, or ten thousand book and journal volumes, per year ("a lot of material from the Jewish division," Boomgaarden recalls, "a lot of material from Slavonic"); now he is the preservation officer at

Ohio State. In 1988, writing in the pages of an anthology called *Preservation Microfilming: Planning and Production,* Boomgaarden nicely captured the tension that existed between preservers and conservators:

> When my hard-working preservation microfilming staff wheeled truck after truck of brittle volumes into the conservation laboratory each week—to use their "low tech" power cutter in the process of cutting off spines to make filming easier, faster, cheaper, and better—they were villified [*sic*] by the conservation shop staff and called "thugs" who were destroying books in order to save them. And, because of the accusers' pitiful statistics in conserving those minute numbers of dainty things—we "thugs" in turn labeled our conservation studio colleagues as "pansies."

"That was a long time ago," Boomgaarden now says. "We've learned so much since then." In a recent big preservation project that Boomgaarden led, "most of the filmed volumes [were] retained in the collections." About five to ten percent of what is currently microfilmed at Ohio State is, by Boomgaarden's estimate, thrown out—an improvement, at least. One crucial difference between then and now is that Ohio State has an enormous new remote book-storage facility; its space crisis has abated.

CHAPTER 12

Really Wicked Stuff

I was very glad to meet the talented people in the Library of Congress's conservation lab, to be sure, but since I was trying to learn more about past and present microfilming practices, I was disappointed that Preservation Reformatting was not on the tour, too, as previously requested. I did get a chance, however, to have a talk with the library's chief scientist, Chandru Shahani, a friendly man in a gray suit. On one side of the table, Dr. Shahani and I sat discussing things like the fold test for paper strength and the predictive value of accelerated-aging experiments; on the other side sat Diane Kresh and Helen Dalrymple. Kresh was Shahani's boss; Dalrymple was a formidable woman from the library's Public Affairs Office whose job, as far as I can tell, was to obstruct inquiry. The two women monitored the interview, saying nothing, taking a note from time to time.

But this didn't seem to cramp Shahani's style, and presently we came to the subject of mass deacidification—another consuming interest at the Library of Congress over the past three decades. Before 1850 or so, papermakers passed their freshly made webs of paper through tubs of animal gelatin, which added the necessary ink-resisting layer to the page. But the gelatin smelled bad, and, more important, its application was a separate, costly step. Then they learned that they could pour some new liquids and powders into the pulp vat, *before* the material was squeeze-dried into paper, that would leave it with ink-fixing properties similar to those of gelatin sizing. They mixed in rosin, distilled (as is turpentine) from pine sap, and aluminum sulphate (alum), which helped the rosin migrate to the outside surface of the newly formed paper and stay there. This technique was called "vat sizing" or "engine sizing," because it happened right up front in the rag engine. The alum-rosin additive worked very well, but rosin contains abeitic acid, and alum creates sulphuric acid; and those various acidities, through branching sequences of chemical reactions (with air, with water, with lignin, with bleaches, with starches, clays, and other additives)—reactions that nobody, not even Dr. Shahani, understands very well—weaken the fibrous mat of civilization-sustaining cellulose.

So, the thinking went, if you could find a way to tame the acids in books en masse, using some magical process of dipping or gassing, you would help library collections stay healthy longer—and you would get to use a great deal of very expensive machinery, besides. Beginning in the late fifties at Verner Clapp's Council on Library Resources, and then later at the Library of Congress, there evolved a two-roads-diverged book-treatment plan: inoculate, through some sort of chemical treatment, the books that were still relatively healthy, and microfilm and destroy those beyond redemption.

The father of modern mass-deacidification was a former clothes-factory foreman named William James Barrow, whom we will meet a few chapters on. For now, we need to know only two words: *diethyl zinc.* Diethyl zinc (or DEZ, as it's jauntily acronymed) was the active ingredient in a patented technique developed at the Library of Congress in the early seventies. You arrange your acid-beset books in milk crates, spine down, up to five thousand of them at a time, and stack the crates in a ten-foot-high retrofitted space-simulation chamber that bears some resemblance to a railroad tank car; then you shut the round door at the end, suck out the air, and let the miracle DEZ fog creep in. "The beauty of this process," Chandru Shahani told me, "was that diethyl zinc, being so reactive with water, would go seek out water, wherever it is. It would just go, *shoosh,* just like that. It would penetrate a closed book." If all went well, the diethyl zinc would bind with oxygen in the water and turn into zinc oxide. Zinc oxide is a mundane, mildly alkaline substance; it is used in cosmetics and as a vitamin supplement; it would remain fixed in the paper's fibers as an "alkaline buffer," ready to obliterate any acidity that might ripen in time.

Early on, the library hoped their ingenious invention would lead to "licensing arrangements to the private sector"—that deacidification would perhaps subsidize itself—but things didn't quite work out; and as Dr. Shahani began recounting what happened at the Goddard Space Flight Center, where there were "mishaps" in 1985 and 1986, I thought I sensed Diane Kresh and Helen Dalrymple beginning to fidget. Diethyl zinc is a colorless liquid, but it is not exactly odorless—for one thing, your nose would promptly burst into flame if you opened a test tube of it and took a sniff. It is not at home in our world: it ignites instantaneously and fiercely on contact with air, and it explodes on contact with more than trace amounts of water.

During the conflagration, it releases a terrible smell. "Oh, the odor when it burns!" said Scott Eidt, a retired chemist who worked with diethyl zinc at Texas Alkyls in the eighties. Ahti Koski, who did his graduate work on the pyrolysis of diethyl zinc, reports a smell "best described as similar to burning chicken feathers in a rubber boot," but he cautions that this might be a by-product of other reactions occuring along with the burning of DEZ. Heavily diluted (so that it will fume but not inflame), diethyl zinc functions as a polymerization catalyst—meaning that very small amounts, mixed with other chemicals, will cause some species of rubber or plastic to form out of their molecular constituents. That has been its primary civilian use.

The technical term for things that burst into flame on contact with air is "pyrophoric," and pyrophoric substances are, naturally, of interest to the military. Richard Smith, inventor of a rival (and unpyrophoric) deacidification method called the Wei T'o process—named in honor of an ancient Chinese god who protects books from harmful forces such as bookworms, thieves, and fire—suspects that diethyl zinc was employed in the early days of the space program. "In the late fifties and early sixties," Smith told me, "most of America's rockets didn't get off the launching pad, or they got just a few feet up in the air and they fell over. Do you remember seeing pictures of those? One after the other. I've always thought that the reason that they had so much trouble is that they were using diethyl zinc as their ignition material. I think that this stuff was definitely involved in our early failures in space."

I haven't been able to verify Smith's launch-failure theory, but there is no question that both German and American propulsionists have experimented on and off with diethyl zinc since the thirties, putting a slug of it near the outgoing nozzle to kindle a blastoff, or squirting a little into a ramjet engine to give their payload a high-altitude boost and increase its range. Ballistic-missile engineers at places like Rocketdyne, Aerojet, and the University of Texas tested diethyl zinc and other hypergolic fuels—that is, fuels that light themselves. According to Robert McComb, one of the scientists who worked on the deacidification process at the Library of Congress, "Diethyl zinc had been used back in the sixties in some rockets for air augmentation and things like that, but it—um, I'm getting into confidential information—but anyway it was not publicized per se." Before moving to the library, McComb was employed by the Allegheny Ballistics Laboratory, a Navy-owned missile- and ordnance-testing center operated by Hercules, Inc. (manufacturer of TNT, missiles, bombs, tanks, black powder, and what-have-you); Hercules and Stauffer Chemical were co-owners of Texas Alkyls, the chemical factory that made the library's diethyl zinc.

Hawley's Condensed Chemical Dictionary says that diethyl zinc is a "high-energy aircraft and missile fuel"—but missiles were just the beginning. U.S. troops have used DEZ to create firewalls, according to an Army scientist at Fort Belvoir, Maryland, by the name of Divyakant Patel. "During the war," Patel told me (he didn't make clear which war) "when they want to separate out one section from another section, they can throw this vapor in the air, just like creating a screen, a big screen of fire." Patel has himself recently experimented with diethyl zinc: using a hypodermic syringe, he filled bullets with the chemical and shot them at land mines. A few drops of DEZ, diluted in toluene, is more than enough to set TNT on fire, and the bullet hole releases the combustion pressure so that the mine doesn't explode—or at least not quite so violently.

Dr. Allen Tulis, current chairman of the International Pyrotechnics Seminar (where investigators in the fields of combustion, explosion, and flame propagation gather every year to share their research), has worked with diethyl zinc on and off for decades and knows its behavior as well as anyone. In the sixties, as a researcher at the Illinois Institute of Technology Research Institute, a not-for-profit contractor that does weapons testing and development for the Department of Defense, Tulis found diethyl zinc's properties useful in his "encapsulated flamethrower," which was later weaponized, to use the military's verb, for the U.S. Army. Previous to Tulis's work, soldiers operating flamethrowers didn't survive very long in battle, because the plumes of fire revealed their whereabouts and they were quickly shot. An encapsulated flamethrower, so I gather, launched frangible capsules containing diethyl zinc. When they hit their target and broke, the capsules created the sort of deflagrational mayhem that was produced by a standard flamethrower, but without betraying the thrower's location.

Diethyl zinc is one of a class of tricky organometallic compounds called metal alkyls; it grabs any available oxygen atoms, including those in cellulose and in human tissue, and uses them to create fire. Tulis recalls one time when some droplets of diethyl zinc blew out of a prototype flamethrower capsule and splattered onto his lab notebook, scorching the pages. "It's very dangerous," Dr. Tulis says, "because if you spill a few drops on your body somewhere, it will eat right into the flesh, and you can't really stop it. It continues to react with moisture and your flesh as it eats into your body." Chemists have on occasion been badly burned—as have enemy troops, presumably.

In the seventies, bomb designers also saw possibilities in DEZ, as they searched for a suitable "initiator" to employ in a fancy new kind of fuel-air weapon. The old fashioned fuel-air bombs, used in Vietnam and much later in Iraq, blew out a cloud of fuel into the air above a target and then, using a second, delayed charge (or a cluster of charges), lit the cloud. The result was a doughnut-shaped firestorm accompanied by a high-pressure shockwave that could be substantially more destructive than that created by a conventional bomb—an "overpressure" closer, in fact, to that produced by a small nuclear detonation. Fuel-air bombs were used to clear landing zones for helicopters (they could blow a stand of trees flat), to clear minefields by triggering all the mines, and simply to kill or stun people in quantity. Even for those who escaped the worst effects of the blast, the shock wave's implosive undertow could rupture eardums, collapse lungs, and cause a bubbling in the blood similar to a deep-sea diver's case of the bends.

The military wasn't completely satisfied with these fuel-air bombs, however. In 1979, the Air Force's Office of Scientific Research funded a workshop at McGill University in Montreal in which scientists from Atlantic Research Corporation and elsewhere discussed possible ingredients for a "FAE III" (that is, a third-generation Fuel-Air Explosive bomb)—a weapon whose fuel cloud would be lit as it expanded not by small secondary explosives, but by its own voraciously combustive chemistry. Dr. John Lee, a scientist at McGill, experimented with a number of compounds, including triethyl aluminum and diethyl zinc, as potential initiators and shock-wave amplifiers for this new bomb. Lee recalls an unsettling incident in his laboratory. A holding tank was supposedly empty, but in fact it still contained a tiny amount of diethyl zinc. "We thought it was completely, completely gone," Lee told me; but when air was allowed to enter the test chamber where the tank sat, there was a "small explosion." Diethyl zinc is, Lee said, "really wicked stuff." If he heard that someone was playing around with hundreds of pounds of it, "it would scare the hell out of me."

CHAPTER 13

Getting the Champagne out of the Bottle

The Library of Congress was playing around with hundreds of pounds of it. Their aim was to build a processing facility that would deacidify a million books per year: to do that, they would need about forty-five thousand pounds of their fractious agent—three percent of the weight of the books, assuming that an average book weighs a pound and a half. Every five-thousand-book run would require between two and three hundred pounds of vaporized diethyl zinc: the word "sobering" comes to mind. (Compare this to the manufacture of plastic or rubber, where to make, say, twenty tons of your final product you might need a single pound of diethyl zinc intermingled with other catalysts and a non-pyrophoric solvent such as hexane.) The scientists' task was made more complicated by the fact that DEZ, as it reacts with water, produces quantities of ethane, which is flammable. I described the deacidification process to Allen Tulis. "Ethane is a very good fuel," Tulis said. "Now the problem I see there is: How do you discharge this material [the diethyl zinc and ethane] and properly neutralize it? Because you've got the makings of a fuel-air in there. If the vacuum would be breached and air would blow into the system, you'd have a humongous explosion." The library had in effect designed a large fuel-air bomb that happened to contain books.

The strangeness of the idea seems not to have troubled the scientists' sleep, however. There were two principal developers of the DEZ process: Dr. John Williams, the library's head of the Research and Testing Department, who had designed water filters and had made an improved inflatable rubber bag during the war (a bag used for gluing helmet liners into Army helmets); and a quiet, deliberate man named George Kelly, Jr., whom Williams hired in 1971, with the help of a grant from the Council on Library Resources.

Kelly had a B.A. in chemistry from the University of Maryland; during World War II, he taught recruits at the Army's Chemical Corps School how to fire 4.2-inch chemical mortars. He did some research on floor tiles and had an unhappy time at a pesticide company, and then moved to Westvaco, where he tested the methods of refining trona to make bicarbonate of soda (trona is a kind of rock mined deep below Wyoming) and was part of a team that made a couple of hundred thousand pounds of a rocket fuel called hydrazine. In the sixties, Kelly moved to Union Carbide, where he experimented with water-soluble polymers as paper coatings. "I'm pretty much a problem solver," Kelly said. After Union Carbide canceled his project, Kelly wrote John Williams and asked if there was a job for him at the Library of Congress.

Williams liked Kelly's work on paper coatings, and assigned him the job of testing potential agents for deacidification. Kelly was willing—in fact, he did so much work with a pungent group of compounds called amines that his sense of smell was destroyed. After a few years, he and Williams together narrowed their search down to diethyl zinc, which they ordered in quart bottles from Texas Alkyls. With a hypodermic syringe, Kelly sucked some DEZ from the bottle and quickly plunged the needle of the syringe into a cork; to start a test run, he stabbed the needle through a rubber gasket in the crypto-pressure-cooker that held five or six test books and gave them a shot. The library's safety officer was not happy with these experiments, according to Kelly. "You're going to burn our library down!" the officer would say. "No, I'm not," Kelly would answer. Recalling an early visit from Kelly, Scott Eidt, the chemist from Texas Alkyls, told me: "We made a joke of it, because of what he was going to do. We'd call it 'book burning.' "

Williams and Kelly, both intelligent applied scientists with no practical knowledge of traditional book conservation, got their first diethyl-zinc patent in 1976. Kelly convinced a somewhat doubtful manager at General Electric's aerospace unit to let them use a vacuum chamber in Valley Forge, Pennsylvania, for some early tests. Each test, performed on lots of four hundred books, consumed between thirty and seventy pounds of liquid DEZ. The testing proceeded without any scares, except once when Texas Alkyls shipped the wrong colorless liquid: scientists unknowingly filled the vacuum chamber with it, leaving the books "thoroughly acidified."

There were problems with the process, though—book covers decorated with rainbow-colored auras of zinc-oxide residues, binding adhesives weakened, papers darkened, scorched, or bad smelling—and the penetration of the acid-neutralizing vapor was incomplete in many cases. Treated books also proved to be more sensitive to light damage than untreated papers. General Electric was lukewarm about the project, and it and the library parted ways in the late seventies—which was just as well, since the GE chamber had "small air leaks" anyway. But by 1980, an optimistic Kelly announced that the process was "now ready for commercial use." He warned, however, that diethyl zinc was "extremely hazardous" and must be used only in an industrial setting by trained personnel. But, he said, "we have demonstrated it can be used successfully and safely to treat books." Neither Kelly nor anyone else at the library alluded to the missile-propulsive and incendiary incarnations of their chosen chemical: it was described as a polymer catalyst, *tout court.* "We deliberately stayed away from so-called military uses," one former Library of Congress scientist told me.

Kelly and Williams retired from the library—Kelly went back to consult for his old company, FMC (which had bought Westvaco), and Williams took a job working on artillery propellants for Armtec, a defense contractor in California. Ideally, that would have been the end of diethyl-zinc deacidification forever. But the process found a new and ardent friend in Peter Sparks, the aptly named head of the library's Preservation Directorate, who arrived in 1981.

Sparks took up the organometallic cause, began feeding quoteworthy quarter-truths to the press, and succeeded in extracting millions more in deacidificational funding from Congress. He and the librarian of Congress, Daniel Boorstin, liked big, round numbers; Sparks told a writer for the Associated Press that a diethyl-zinc treatment would add "400 to 600 years" to the life of a book. He showed off a guillotined copy of Thomas Carlyle's *Sartor Resartus* to reporters and claimed that seventy-seven thousand books a year go brittle at the Library of Congress. (The Library of Congress had fun with Carlyle, microfilming eight separate old editions of *Sartor Resartus,* three editions of his *Life of Schiller,* Lecky's edition of his *French Revolution,* and a shelfload more.) *The New York Times* believed Sparks in 1984 (why shouldn't they?): "The pages of at least five million volumes now crumble at the touch of a finger, simply because daily exposure to the elements has turned them brittle. Every year 77,000 more volumes are affected." Sparks was "a very good marketing person," Chandru Shahani told me. "He was, I think, too good a salesperson, so he sold this with a lot of promises when the process wasn't ready. He hadn't really anticipated the problems." Daniel Boorstin authoritatively backed up Sparks's salesmanship, too: the same *New York Times* article quoted Boorstin as saying that the diethyl-zinc process was "one of the most important steps toward the preservation of knowledge around the world. . . . It would be hard to overstate its significance."

As for safety, not to worry, the "handling of diethyl zinc by trained operators has been reduced to a routine matter," according to the library's *Information Bulletin*. Daniel Boorstin wrote a letter to Congress assuring them that there were "no known safety risks to personnel or books with the Library of Congress' process."

Once funding was secured, an idle vacuum chamber at NASA's Goddard Space Flight Center, conveniently located in suburban Washington, D.C., became the center of testing operations. In 1982, the library (through NASA) hired Northrup Services to draw up plans and operating procedures. Several Northrup engineers went down to Texas Alkyls for an eyebrow-raising diethyl-zinc briefing. One of the engineers began to feel that the Library of Congress had not been forthcoming in its description of the hazards of the process. "Basically what you had was a huge combustion chamber," the engineer told me. "It became patently clear to me that we were heading for trouble, because we were modifying a system that was not designed for chemical processes." NASA's vacuum chambers were built to simulate conditions in outer space, after all, and the engineers at Northrup Services were thermal-vacuum scientists, with no experience in the design of prototype chemical plants.

Northrup needed the work, according to the engineer; they therefore played down some of the difficulties and hazards in their pro forma presentations to NASA. "What we were told to say to [NASA's] safety committee versus what was really going on were a little divergent," the engineer says. And there were too many managers. The project was paid for by the Library of Congress, constructed in NASA's buildings, employing Northrup: nobody was really in charge, and nobody really knew what they were doing. The detailed chemistry of diethyl zinc's reactions with most of the hundreds of filler substances in old paper were undocumented. The library had never published detailed descriptions, in peer-reviewed journals, of the evolving permutations of their invasive treatment and its often discouraging experimental results. The Library of Congress planned to do something radical and irreversible to millions of its books, and yet, rather than inviting outside comment and help, they were behaving like weapons procurers at the Department of Defense.

The first NASA run, in November 1982, was the most ambitious one—after months of preparation, the testers loaded five thousand ex-library books into the chamber, the number they planned to treat each time when they were at full production volume. The process wasn't particularly kind to the books, as it took almost two weeks and involved extremes of heat and cold. First, they heated the books to 113 degrees Fahrenheit for a few days in order to drive off most of their moisture; next, they pulled a vacuum, slowly, which caused the temperature to drop. When they were sure the air was gone, they began fogging the chamber with the necessary two to three hundred pounds of their chemical. As the reactions progressed, the chamber grew first warm, then quite hot, although it was supposedly kept "well below" 212 degrees. (It wouldn't be at all good if the temperature rose above 250 degrees because diethyl zinc begins to decompose above that point; at pot-roast temperatures, the decomposition becomes "self-sustaining and uncontrollable," and, depending on conditions and quantities, you could have a thermal explosion.)

Four thousand of the books were discards, a thousand were from the library's shelves. For six days, in this iron lung, they underwent their hot chemotherapy. Then the technicians created another vacuum, and the temperature dropped again—but slowly: it would be bad if the books froze, because the DEZ vapor might condense on them and remain to cause trouble upon repressurization. In an effort to prolong these books' lives, the scientists were subjecting them to conditions that mimicked a rigorous accelerated-aging experiment, minus the air—no wonder the paper sometimes tested weaker immediately after treatment.

The five-thousand-book run was not a success. (The results were "mixed," according to Congress's Office of Technology Assessment.) Analysis determined that a cloud of ethane gas had taken up position at the top of the chamber, while a cloud of heavier diethyl zinc pooled at the bottom; because the vapor was in a vacuum, there was little convectional mixing. Thus many of the stacked books got no deacidificational benefit, while some got too much. There were "tide marks," darkened paper, and distasteful odors. ("Cause of odor a mystery since known chemistry cannot explain it," noted the still-baffled scientists years later.) Also the library couldn't possibly meet its stated goal of deacidifying a million books a year if each five-thousand-book run had a cycle time of two weeks—things had to move along much quicker than that. Hoping to work out the problems, the scientists made a number of much smaller tests in another NASA vacuum chamber, and then, in the spring of 1985, with funds running low and many uncertainties dangling, the library decided to abandon the prototype plant altogether and build still another, smaller pilot facility, in a different NASA building, with a rectilinear chamber this time instead of a round one, so that the DEZ gas wouldn't idle in the waste space, and with faster pumps, so that the gas cloud would swirl turbulently around the books, reacting with all of them. There was an air of desperate haste at this stage—a NASA electrician later reported that in November 1985, "a Library of Congress representative tried to talk [name whited out] into running DEZ into the chamber when there were system leaks and no procedures." The electrician stopped them by "explaining the consequences of those size leaks, but did not feel he should have been the one to do this."

The hurry had to do with money: the library had spent several million on the NASA project so far (and the NASA project followed the GE project, which hadn't been cheap), and Peter Sparks and William Welsh (the deputy librarian of Congress) needed to get beyond feasibility studies and tap into the $11.5 million that Congress had budgeted for a bona fide high-volume treatment plant, to be built at Fort Detrick, which would possibly handle books for other libraries as well. Later, Welsh admitted that the library had diverted $1.7 million from the library's personnel accounts into the diethyl-zinc fund without congressional permission. ("The time drivers on this project [were] the limited funding, and the Library of Congress pushing to get the job done," said one anonymous respondent in an official NASA report. "There were overruns, and budget problems in October 1985 that caused the Library of Congress to pressure Northrup on this project.")

On December 5, 1985, Dr. Anand Apte, one of Northrup's senior project engineers, was nearing the end of the first test cycle of the new plant in NASA's Building 306. There were no books in the chamber. Apte couldn't tell how much diethyl zinc was left inside—the temperature gauges were reading cold, indicating the presence of a liquid, but they weren't reliable. At 6:45 A.M., hoping to neutralize whatever was left, he opened a valve and allowed some water in. The door of the vacuum chamber blew open. "Shortly after the water injection," according to the mishap report, "Dr. Apte observed flames shooting out of the chamber door and immediately vacated the building." The walls and ceiling were charred; the chamber door and O-rings had fire damage; the sprinkler system went off.

Yes, it was bad, but not horrible, and the library was determined to get the system purged and proceed—a congressional appropriations-subcommittee meeting was on the calendar for the end of February 1986. ("[Name whited out] has been applying pressure to get the job done even after the December 5, 1985 incident," reads the NASA report.) Before NASA had completed its investigation into the accident—the agency was in turmoil anyway after the explosion of the *Challenger* space shuttle on January 28, which also involved hypergolic fuels—a "disenchanted" electrician was called in to make some repairs to the DEZ delivery system, and workers cleaned the inside of the reaction chamber. Not all the diethyl zinc had been consumed in the fire, as it turned out; a substantial volume still lurked in the complex of delivery pipes and brine-seal tanks. (Afterward, in a weighing of a supply tank, seven hundred and thirty pounds of the chemical were unaccounted for.) A jet of "black goop" spurted from one valve on February 11, 1986; the next day, a copper elbow pipe was discovered to have mysteriously straightened. Other plumbing was too hot to touch. Northrup did not inform NASA of these anomalies. On February 14, at a signal from one of his colleagues, the hapless Dr. Apte pressed a switch to open valve V-303. The pressure gauge spiked, there was a boom and a flash, and (said the NASA report) "the walls were blown apart, and the two doors leading into the room were blown off." The NASA report theorizes that something pyrophoric happened in one of the vapor condensers: "The violence of the explosion suggests a mixture of DEZ and water (brine) or air resulting in a rapid overpressurization of the condenser and subsequent rupture of adjacent piping and blower housing." Nobody was hurt, though.

February 20 was looming—the day of the crucial appropriations-subcommittee meeting. Daniel Boorstin was planning to make a cri de coeur for more money. Meanwhile, engineers from Texas Alkyls were flown up to take a look at the situation in Building 306; they noticed, among other things, that there were no relief valves to vent trapped fluids in the piping. And the piping itself wasn't going to hold forever—the DEZ was attacking the seals, and there was a thought that it could even react with the metal oxides in stainless steel. NASA, unable to figure out how to drain all the abscesses safely, called Welsh and said, "We're going to blow it." Welsh was upset. He offered to go in himself, wielding an infrared camera, escorted by armored vehicles if need be, to locate pressure spots. But NASA said no.

On Thursday the twentieth, the congressional subcommittee was called to order. Daniel Boorstin, a chronic bow-tie-wearer who could really crank it out when he needed to, told the members that the "vast and unprecedented cuts in the Library's budget" were "dangerous, and could become tragic for our nation, the Congress, and the whole world of learning." (The library was being asked to cut about seven percent.) Boorstin was not an alarmist, he told them—far from it. His library had, he hoped, acquired "a reputation for honesty and conservatism" in its budgetary requests. The current crisis "has not been created by inexpertise, neglect, waste, indolence, or dishonesty in the

Library of Congress." No—the crisis was created by Congress. "We will fail in our duty to our posterity," Boorstin said, "if we do not hand on to them the fully stocked, properly organized treasure of wisdom of the past which it has taken us two centuries to accumulate."

The next day, an Army demolition unit drove over from Fort Meade. Welsh wanted to be there, but he wasn't allowed to watch. Half a million dollars worth of pilot-plant piping was, to quote the NASA report, "disassembled by means of shaped explosives." There was a *whoomp* and a surprisingly large fireball. The DEZ bomb had finally gone off.

The marvel is, though, that even this disaster wasn't the end of the program. Leading off a rather grim discussion of diethyl zinc before the subcommittee in 1987, Boorstin said that "there has never been an important technological advance that was not controverted by people who had rival schemes or who didn't think any scheme should be pursued." There were still large sums to be spent—including over a million devoted to forcing rats to inhale megadoses of zinc-oxide dust in order to demonstrate that deacidified books weren't toxic. (The library had already paid to have rats gassed with a mixture of diethyl zinc and hexane vapor—the tests were "inconclusive" because it wasn't clear which of the two poisons killed the animals.) What were a few rodents, though, when all of written history was on the brink of disaster? Peter Sparks was a very determined man, and William Welsh's pride was also on the line. The two of them had been talking up DEZ for years as one of the library's two top-priority projects (the other was the optical-disk program)—it just had to work.

The first step was to muffle the NASA disaster with some confusing specificity. "On Friday, February 21," said the Library of Congress's *Information Bulletin* several weeks after the fireball, "the line cutting charges were set off opening the pipes. Liquid diethyl zinc in the lines spilled out and burned for about 30 seconds and the wood structure burned for about one hour, causing considerable damage to the temporary building frame, walls, and roof that was over the chemical delivery section of the test facility." The second step was to shift blame from the library to Northrup and NASA—which wasn't difficult to do, since the space shuttle had just blown up, and Northrup had been incontrovertibly sloppy. "The Library's own review of the test facility has revealed serious design and procedural deficiencies in the prototype chemical delivery system that will be addressed and corrected in a redesign of the facility," reported an article in the *Information Bulletin* in July. Welsh told the congressional subcommittee that he hadn't known that NASA and Northrup "didn't have the chemical processing experience."

Welsh himself may not have known, but surely the library's scientific staff had reviewed the plans and signed off on them many months before the black goop began to squirt? They were the process's inventors; they'd designed the tests; they'd seen and used the hardware; they'd been driving to the Goddard vacuum-chamber sites and fine-tuning their dream for years, longer than anyone, and they claimed that they had reduced the handling of DEZ to a matter of mere routine. If Peter Sparks and his crew didn't have the competence to evaluate the chemical-delivery system as detailed by Northrup Services ahead of time, shouldn't they have shown the schematics to engineers who knew how to handle large volumes of extremely dangerous gases and liquids? Offering an aerospace vendor like Northrup the job of designing the diethyl-zinc plant was like asking three heart surgeons and a urologist to design an offshore drilling platform: the probability was high that they would make mistakes.

Peter Sparks was unsinkable. He transferred the project to Deer Park, Texas; the library began paying Texas Alkyls to engineer yet another plant. *Library Journal* protested—"It's Time to Dump DEZ" was one of their editorial headlines in the fall of 1986. The editorial's author, Karl Nyren, suggested that, like a gambling addict, the library was unable to "abandon behavior that is manifestly unfruitful." Nyren wrote:

> Sometimes it seems that there is an epidemic of "entrapment" in government: the Sergeant York gun that, after millions spent

> upon it, just doesn't work; the predilection for backing the finally discredited losers in international affairs; the loss of the *Challenger.* The DEZ process belongs right alongside these failures.

Neither Congress nor the library community had been told, said Nyren, "of the preponderance of evidence for the danger and unmanageability of DEZ."

William Welsh published a rebuttal in a later issue of *Library Journal;* he said that diethyl zinc "has for many years been used as a catalyst in the production of common plastics, including polyethylene, polystyrene, polypropylene, and polyester." Welsh does not mention that the plastics industry, when it does use DEZ as a so-called Ziegler-Natta catalyst in the manufacture of polyethylene and related compounds (and it has never been commonly used), uses it in tiny amounts, in diluted form, whereas the library's preservation factory would at full capacity consume DEZ neat and by the ton. Not surprisingly, there is in Welsh's reply no breath of missiles or incendiaries. Then, to further allay fears, Welsh engages in a little semantic subterfuge: "DEZ is produced as a liquid, and in that form is pyrophoric, i.e., it burns spontaneously when it comes in contact with the air. When used as a deacidification agent, DEZ is vaporized into a gas in a contained vacuum environment where, as a gas, it is not pyrophoric." Whether diethyl zinc is a liquid or a gas has nothing to do with its pyrophoricity—it burns either way. And since "pyrophoric" just means "inflames on contact with air" it is highly misleading to tell librarians that it isn't pyrophoric in a vacuum. DEZ gas *is* pyrophoric in a vacuum; there just doesn't happen to be any air around to demonstrate that fact, and the danger is that there is a world of air outside the vacuum that wants to get in. "DEZ is and always will be pyrophoric," Ahti Koski wrote me.

In 1988, the newly appointed librarian of Congress, James Billington, and his senior staff—William Welsh and Peter Sparks included—greeted eminent library visitors at the brand-new $2.8 million Texas Alkyls deacidification plant, which could handle three hundred and fifty books at a go. Curious preservation administrators peered into the yawning vacuum chamber, and saw custom-made book carts with wire spacers, and lots of purposeful plumbing, and it all looked very scientific. "I think the safety questions are completely resolved," Sparks told *The Washington Post* in 1988. "We now know how to use this technology and this material safely. It works very well. And we're getting ready to scale up to a major facility that will meet our needs and also be able to treat books for other libraries."

Trusting the Sparksian sell-job, a number of universities, including Harvard and Johns Hopkins, began sending batches of books to Texas for treatment at a cost of about ten dollars a book. But although the engineering was much better this time, the process itself failed. In 1991, Robert J. Milevski, who was then the preservation librarian at Johns Hopkins, found, on examining books that he had sent to Texas, that the effects of treatment "were so startling that I had to wonder why these results had not been known earlier, considering especially all the DEZ research conducted by and for the Library of Congress." Milevski wrote:

> In some cases, the physical damage to some items was so great that it required commercial rebinding, or replacement. Covering material components—binding adhesives, cloth, paper, and illustration colors and inks—were all affected to one degree or another, depending upon the items selected for treatment. Book paper cockled. All paper discolored somewhat and emanated an odor.

Out of 667 books treated by Akzo Chemical (the Dutch company which had by then absorbed Texas Alkyls), forty-four percent had some sort of damage (not counting cockling, smell, and yellowing, which was pretty much universal), and twenty-four percent might need "remedial treatment." And some books were not deacidified, either. One of the pictures that Milevski includes illustrates what he calls the "edge-burn effect": evidently not enough of the residual moisture had been baked out of some books; when the diethyl zinc found it, the reaction was hot enough to leave scorch marks. Peter Waters was invited to Texas once when he was head of conservation at the Library of Congress (head of *conservation,* not preservation—Peter Sparks was head of preservation). "While Peter Sparks and the rest were having a meeting," Waters says, "I got taken into the site and saw one of the chambers being opened. I was totally horrified with what I saw." He saw distorted books and books burned around the edges. There was a kind of "metallic-musty" smell.

Sparks, though, was still talking about full-scale plants in Fort Detrick, and about one-hundred-million-dollar twenty-year contracts, and about sending tank trucks full of neat diethyl zinc across the country. And he'd boosted his figure: he told Congress that the library hoped to treat thirty thousand books a week, or a million and a half books a year. That way, presumably, the plant could catch up on the Library of Congress's own arrearage of acidity and also serve the nation. Eventually, reality took hold: doubts were pointedly expressed to James Billington; Sparks left the library in 1990. "When Billington heard about some of the problems that he hadn't been told about, after Sparks had left, he totally blew his top," one former employee told me. "And if you know Billington, when he blows his top, the foundations of the library vibrate." Sparks is now a consultant; on a webpage for Neilsen Bainbridge, a framing-supplies company, beneath a picture of Sparks standing before some statuary, he is quoted as endorsing the Alphamat Artcare line of framing supplies, which feature patented life-extending "MicroChamber" technology: "Laboratory observations made on these test photographs clearly show that Alphamat Artcare inhibits yellowing and fading of these color images. With Alphamat Artcare, you achieve worry-free framing every time." The fine print says that the matboards were exposed to nitrogen dioxide (a pollutant) "in an accelerated laboratory test that simulates 77 years of aging."

It wasn't that James Billington was against spending lots of money on machinery—he likes doing that. It's just that he was more interested in mass digitization than mass deacidification. The Library of Congress's collections were, as he told the Senate in 1994, part of the nation's " 'strategic information reserve' that will provide the intellectual cargo on the information superhighways." The library, he said, "hopes to contribute to the electronic future by being an exemplary catalyst for the library community more broadly in building the National Information Infrastructure." He told the Information Industry Association that the Library of Congress was "substituting technology for paper" in its digitization of "key American collections." He wanted to "get the champagne out of the bottle." Putting old books in gas chambers was not his thing.

Even so, diethyl zinc clung to life. Something about it appealed to the scientists—its unnaturalness, perhaps, its counterintuitiveness, its racy propulsiveness, its danger. Between 1992 and 1994, Chandru Shahani (who worked at India's Bhabha Atomic Research Center before he emigrated) commissioned twelve more test runs in Deer Park, Texas. By the last run, he and his coworkers felt they had beaten the stench problem: a panel of conservator-sniffers determined that "95.2 percent of the books have acceptable odors"—meaning that if you diethyl-zincked a million books a year, forty-eight thousand of them would smell bad. Better, but not great. "The tragedy is," Shahani told me, with genuine regret, "we perfected the process just as the rug was being pulled from under the process."

Shahani remains scornful of Northrup and NASA. In a 1994 write-up of the last twelve test runs, he and Kenneth Harris refer to the "pathetically poor engineering practice and design" at the NASA pilot plant. When I talked to Shahani in 1998 (seated across from Diane Kresh and Helen Dalrymple of the Public Affairs Office), he said: "I had been here long enough to see how bumbling those people were, the contractors who were contracting those tests. I don't know if that's how DoD contractors are or what, I don't know. I mean, I'm saying this on tape. But I hope they aren't like this one." Shahani briefly detailed their lack of qualifications and explained the chemist's responsibility to maintain mass balance in reactive processes, a responsibility not met at the NASA installation. Then he went on: "And these people were so bad. In the first place, every run that they did—I was there for five or six runs before this thing happened—every run they would do, some gauge or another would not be working. Nothing was ever a hundred percent functional. They would still go on with it."

And then something went wrong. "Instead of pumping out from the chamber, they were pumping in," Shahani said. "And then they sent water in there. I mean, how could you do that? I just cannot imagine that. And then NASA made it worse. They took them off. I mean, those guys at least would have been able to pump the thing out. When there was the fire, NASA said, 'Go, you're out of here.' They wouldn't let them pump it out, even. So then the diethyl zinc sat there for months—weeks, maybe, or days, I don't remember now. But enough so that the diethyl began to react with the plumbing. It will find any moisture anywhere, the slightest amount of moisture—and all materials contain some moisture. So they had all kinds of problems, and then we lost track at that point, because we were not in the picture."

Here Helen Dalrymple finally bestirred herself. "If we're going to get on to anything else," she said, with forced gaiety, "we do need to move on, because Mr. Baker needs to leave at two-thirty."

Okay, we'll move on—enough about diethyl zinc. Now, in a modest ongoing program, the Library of Congress pays a small company in Cranberry Township, Pennsylvania, to strap minor works of American poetry onto steel-finned agitators, seal them in drums that fill up with a costly inert liquid called perfluoroalkane, which is made milky by the presence of quadrillions (approximately) of very tiny magnesium-oxide particles, in which liquid the books rise and fall, turning first one way, then the other, their pages waving like pale seaweeds, until some of the magnesium-oxide particles, small as they are, tumble into declivities in the surface of the paper, where they are allegedly held in place by static electricity. After twenty minutes, a vacuum pump sucks out the carrier liquid, and the books, unstrapped and stacked on metal tables, look and feel almost as they did beforehand, except, in some cases, for a slight powdery texture to the paper.

Dr. Shahani contributed some refinements to this procedure, but it was developed by several alumni of Koppers Chemicals, principally a smiley, self-effacing man named Richard Spatz, who knew a lot about pressure-treating wood and applied that knowledge to wood-pulp paper. Spatz was dipping books in his garage for years, and air-drying them in the game room, before the world began to pay attention. The Bookkeeper system, as it is known, is inherently safer for organic life-forms than diethyl zinc, and it is apparently benign for books, too, but of course nobody can be certain of its benignancy for a hundred years or more. If you test the paper after its Bookkeeper bath, it shows a higher (less acidic) pH, which is good, but whether magnesium oxide's neutralizing powers will endure in the book as it is repeatedly breathed on, paged through, and photocopied, and even whether the substance, assuming it does stick where it was put, is ultimately of any significant value to the health of the paper, is unknowable now as well. Perhaps those few minutes spent splayed in a vacuum will shorten a book's life more than the alkaline deposits will prolong it. Acidity discourages paper-eating bugs; over hundreds of years, that may be very helpful. Some conservators believe that all mass deacidification is a mistake: given the near infinitude of recipes for paper, new and old, and the impossibly complex reactions that ensue over time, the alkaline buffer may do bad things to fibers, and to inks and dyes and bindings, that we cannot foresee.

If Bookkeeper is harmless, and it may possibly be, the good thing about it is that it allows preservation administrators (who seem to have a hard time simply leaving things alone) to feel that they're taking the initiative and doing something powerful and talismanic, that requires pipes and gauges and special vocabularies, for their chosen volumes. For once you dunk or spritz or gas a group of books, they immediately become charmed objects, *items on which your preservation dollars have been spent,* and as such are less likely to find themselves carted off to the discard area (called "Gifts and Exchanges" at the Library of Congress) the next year. Deacidification buys time for them in that managerial sense, at least.

But then the books that you haven't dunked or spritzed or gassed may begin to seem suspect. At the Library of Congress, deacidified books are now identified with a white dot on the spine, like Dr. Seuss's Star-Bellies. Two subclasses of material thus arise: the chemically purified, and the mortally diseased. Those that haven't earned their white dots may in time become easier to sacrifice to a reformatting project—they've been passed over once, after all, and their untreated acidity makes them (if you accept the prevailing view) an imminent danger to themselves on the shelf. If in fifty years the chemical purification turns out to be itself harmful in some unexpected way, the polarity will simply reverse: those books that underwent the therapy will become the newly diseased, the white dot will signal distress, the distress will pull in fresh grant money, and new treatments will come into play to undo the damage of well-meaning earlier maltreatments. Waste may be the only constant.

Leave the books alone, I say, leave them alone, leave them alone.

CHAPTER 14

Bursting at the Seams

We will never know how much capital the Library of Congress spent on organometallic R and D over those decades—the costs were bundled in and hidden. Millions more were tossed into the other gaping preservational cash pit, the Optical Disk Pilot Project, an early digitization experiment also pushed by William Welsh and Peter Sparks. By Department of Defense standards, the amounts were minuscule, but they were lost at a time of great hardship for the library—when operating hours and staff were being cut—and their redirection has left our historical record compromised and disfigured. With all the money the library spent noodling with fire in a vacuum, and testing the longevity of the acrylic layer on soon-to-be-outmoded optical disks, they could have put up several large, unflashy, dimly lit, air-conditioned print-shelters out in Virginia or Maryland that would have kept millions of low-use books, newspapers, and bound periodicals out of the summer heat, shelved in call-number order, awaiting their infrequent summons. (The library did rent some space, in Landover, Maryland, beginning in 1976, but it wasn't nearly enough.) The library's scientists could have spent those decades learning more about the chemistry and aging characteristics of old paper, rather than studying the behavior of an exotic metal alkyl *on* old paper. Coolness is pertinent because, as with cut flowers, film, diskettes, or hamburger, lower temperatures slow down intermolecular couplings and scissions and thus attenuate time's asymptotic slide. One study in 1966 compared a long-frozen Everyman's Library edition of Poe's *Tales of Mystery and Imagination*—it had traveled to Antarctica with Scott's expedition and wasn't retrieved until 1959—with the identical edition from used-book stores in Manchester and Glasgow: the paper in the polar Poe was stronger.

There were knowledgeable staff members during this period—most notably Peter Waters, Head of Conservation—who argued that for the vast majority of books, simply placing them on a shelf somewhere was the best and cheapest first step to preserving them, but Deputy Librarian Welsh's heart was not in adding raw shelf storage. Welsh is, he told me, a people person—when he was at the library he knew hundreds of employees by name, and even now he immediately remembers lesser figures from fifty years ago, such as Clyde Edwards, the man who began systematically replacing newspapers with microfilm. Welsh is not a book person. He is the last of the Cold War librarians—he arrived in 1947 after six years in the Air Force, where he was promoted to major and served as librarian of the Alaskan Division Headquarters of the Air Transport Command; he rose under Clapp and Luther Evans, worked on the CIA-sponsored *East European Accessions List* in the fifties, wrote the foreword to *Newspapers in Microfilm* in 1972 (the one, that is, which said that a microfilmed newspaper was considered complete if only a few issues per month were missing), and was made deputy librarian in 1976. Welsh believed that libraries shouldn't be regarded as "warehouses of little-used material." (Actually, that's exactly what they are.) Though he boasted that the Library of Congress produces "vastly more than the microfilming programs of any other library" and that "we probably produce more [microfilm] than all other libraries put together," he felt that film didn't squeeze things down enough. So he turned to optical disks: "Disk storage is attractive because it is very much more compact than film—ten to twenty thousand pages on one side of a twelve-inch disk, compared to about a one-thousand-page capacity on a single reel of film," he wrote. And the thousands of tiny copies on the twelve-inch disks are actually easier to read than the originals, Welsh held: "the extremely high resolution of the electronic scanning process improves the accuracy of the captured image, even making it possible to improve the readability of a faded or discolored original." The scan is *better* than the original—and if it's better, why keep the original? The digital process will, according to the *Library of Congress Information Bulletin* for September 12, 1983, "reproduce items with sufficient quality to permit the library to consider discarding the original." In 1984, Welsh told *The Washington Post* that his optical disk jukeboxes could reduce the three Library of Congress buildings to one. As it turned out, the resolution of the images on the disks was a migraineiferous three hundred dots per inch—six hundred dpi is considered middling now—and the twelve-inch format never caught on. Copyright holders made strenuous objections, too, as they will when someone is trying to re-publish their work without paying them.

Ainsworth Spofford, the late-nineteenth-century director of the Library of Congress, collected books and built new wings and fireproof buildings to hold them. John Russell Young and the great and glorious Herbert Putnam collected more books, and Putnam built a huge annex that opened in 1939. Then came Archibald MacLeish, a poet of some anthologization, who became distracted by the idea of using the library for military intelligence and war propaganda. (In 1941, MacLeish signed a letter of agreement with OSS founder William "Wild Bill" Donovan, undisclosed to Congress, which, for an initial fee of seventy-five thousand dollars plus expenses, committed the Library of Congress to intelligence-gathering for Donovan's new Office of Coordinator of Information; the library would, for example, "build up biographical data on key men in public and military affairs in foreign nations.") With MacLeish came the hiring of Luther Evans and the promotion of MacLeish's personal assistant and vision-man, Verner Clapp. No storage edifice went up during Clapp's long years of influence. That is why, after Clapp left the library to invent the new tomorrow by hiring defense contractors, Quincy Mumford inherited a collection that was, as he told Congress in 1958, "bursting at the seams." But Congress was slow to respond to Mumford's plea. In the end they combined a project to build a memorial to James Madison with the library's request for a new building, and the architects, straining mightily, came up with the colossal, marble-finned kitsch box now permanently stuck to Independence Avenue. There are bronze sculptures of flying books welded above the doorway, covered with chicken wire to keep birds from perching on them.

Never mind the architecture, though: *the building wasn't ready to store anything until 1980.* From the forties through the eighties, while other government agencies built like pharaohs, the country's pre-eminent records-storage-and-retrieval system didn't have, largely as a result of Clapp's philosophical disdain for mere shelves, enough room to hold what it needed to hold. Welsh inherited the ill-starred Madison building, and he oversaw it after his fashion, but he stood in Verner Clapp's long shadow, and he was by temperament and training a steady-spacer. Libraries should not grow, they should "grow." In 1989, he was still extolling the virtues of "interdependence" and "miniaturiz[ing] existing collections." (As soon as library managers start talking about resource sharing, or cooperative projects, or interdependence, you know they have local shelf-clearing in mind: they want somebody else to keep what they once had.) "Networking can and should enable us to avoid costs," Welsh wrote. "If we can depend upon the network to help meet some of our needs, we can reduce our acquisitions, cataloging, and preservation costs and, perhaps most important, defer construction costs for new library space."

It wasn't incompetence that led to the library's five-decade space crisis, as it turns out, it was ideology—it was a steadfast unwillingness to build or rent enough buildings. That's why, during this period, so many fine old things were undeservedly destroyed. The bones of the collection were deformed in a deliberate squeeze.

CHAPTER 15

The Road to Avernus

In 1957, aided by a large grant from Verner Clapp's Council on Library Resources, a document laminator named William James Barrow began a ten-year program of research into paper's deterioration. As a first step, he assembled, from the collection of the Virginia State Library, five hundred nonfiction books printed between 1900 and 1949. Most were duplicates, all were undamaged. ("Bindings showed no wear, and leaves of some were unopened.") Here are some of Barrow's experimental victims, all published in the early decades of the twentieth century: John W. Foster's *Diplomatic Memoirs,* Andrew Carnegie's *The Empire of Business,* Seneca Egbert's *Manual of Hygiene and Sanitation, A Text-Book of True Temperance,* published by the United States Brewers' Association, Thomas Mosby's *Causes and Cures of Crime,* Arthur Pound's *The Telephone Idea, The National Formulary of Unofficial Preparations,* John Hearley's *Pope or Mussolini,* and Mary S. Cutting's *Little Stories of Married Life.*

Out of each of these five hundred books, Barrow and his assistants cut eighteen test strips, from the middles of random pages. These he tested in various ways, tearing them in half using the Elmendorf Tear Tester, folding them under tension, analyzing their fiber content. The fold test, which he performed using a custom-made machine that worked the strip of paper back and forth through ninety degrees while subjecting it to a tugging force of one kilogram, was the most helpful, he found. Paper from older books survived many fewer oscillations between the clamps of his fold tester than paper from newer books. Correlating the fold-test data with some groundless guesswork (Barrow believed that three days in an artificial-aging oven at 212 degrees Fahrenheit was equivalent to twenty-five years of real life), he came up with a set of estimates of the life expectancy of the books whose pages he had minced.

Here are Barrow's results, summarized in the celebrated book called *Deterioration of Book Stock, Causes and Remedies:* thirty-nine percent fell in the *Very Weak* category, meaning they would "hardly last 25 years" and if unused "might be intact after 50 years." Forty-nine percent were *Low Strength,* which would "deteriorate to the *Very Weak* category in 25 years. Their endurance would be less than newsprint." Nine percent were *Medium Strength A,* likely to survive from twenty-five to fifty years with moderate usage; two percent were *Medium Strength B* and might be expected to last fifty years or more; one percent were *High Strength.* "If material which should be preserved indefinitely is going to pieces as rapidly as these figures indicate," Barrow and his editors wrote, "it seems probable that most library books printed in the first half of the 20th century will be in an unusable condition in the next century." Library administrators liked these numbers—some simply added together everything except *High Strength* and *Medium Strength B* and got a really frightening percentage: "The research carried out by William J. Barrow at the Virginia State Library indicated that 97% of the non-fiction books printed between 1900 and 1939 will have deteriorated to the point of being useless by the end of the century," wrote a Preservation Committee at Pennsylvania State. Or you could flip it around, as Yale's librarian Rutherford Rogers did in 1985: "Barrow startled the library world with his research results, which suggested that only 3 percent of the papers in books published between 1900 and 1949 could be expected to last for more than fifty years." In any case, the numbers were disturbing. "Librarians will recognize that the problem is not a new one," Barrow concludes, "but few will fail to be astonished at its magnitude."

But Barrow was wrong. There are today millions of usable library books dating from the first half of the twentieth century. As far as I can tell, all of the editions listed in his experiment exist now in libraries, available to readers. (Readers can't use the specific copies that the Barrow Laboratory cut up, however.) There has been no apocalypse of paper. Perhaps Barrow sincerely believed in the estimates, perhaps not. Perhaps all those who, like Peter Sparks, cited Barrow believed in the estimates, perhaps not. In 1998, I read the numbers to William Wilson, the paper scientist who was measuring the natural aging of paper until someone tossed out his experiment. "A lot of these predictions were made to get people's attention," Wilson said. "I knew Mr. Barrow, by the way. I don't know whether he really believed that or what. But it's almost the end of the century, and somehow most of those books haven't known that they were supposed to disappear."

Verner Clapp was the first to seize on Barrow's numbers (he had paid for them, after all); in his *Future of the Research Library,* he used them as justification for his preferred path. "From the investigations of W. J. Barrow, it is now known that few of the books printed in the first half of this century can be expected to be of much use by its end," Clapp wrote. In the early sixties, he paid the Association of Research Libraries to hire some statisticians to apply Barrow's overeager deterioration model to a random sample of books in the National Union Catalog. They did some arithmetic and came up with 1.75 billion imperiled book-pages. Now the question became, as Clapp put it, "what to do about these 1.75 billion pages, many—perhaps most—of which are doomed within a relatively brief foreseeable future."

Deacidification was one possible course of action, wrote Clapp; and in the sixties the Council on Library Resources duly paid Barrow's lab to test various early mass-deacidification treatments in Virginia. Barrow gassed books overnight with ammonia fumes, and he sprayed them with solutions of "magnesium acetate, urea, magnesium carbonate, calcium oxide (with the addition of sugar), and magnesium bicarbonate." He tried "pickling" a book: spraying it with chemicals and wrapping it in aluminum foil. None of these methods took. In 1966, Clapp encouraged Barrow to experiment with a treatment that a British liquor chemist had developed, using cyclohexylamine carbonate, CHC. The Barrow technicians interleaved books with CHC-impregnated sheets, and put sachets full of CHC granules in manuscript boxes; but the paper changed color, and the CHC reacted with humid air to form cyclohexylamine, which had "carcinogenic potential." So that was out.

After Barrow died in 1967, Clapp's Council continued to fund the Barrow Lab, which forged on under the direction of Dr. Robert N. DuPuis, who in the fifties was director of research at Philip Morris. DuPuis wrote memos at Philip Morris that plaintiffs have since used as evidence of the tobacco industry's extensive foreknowledge of the medical dangers of smoking; in 1955, he assured viewers of *See It Now,* Edward R. Murrow's TV show, "If we do find any [components in tobacco smoke] that we consider harmful, and so far we have not, we'll remove these from smoke and still retain the pleasure of your favorite cigarette." In 1970, DuPuis became interested in the promise of morpholine, used in floor polish, to lift acid paper's pH. Eventually, the Barrow Lab and George Kelly at the Library of Congress began some morpholine "vapor phase deacidification" tests, precursors to the diethyl-zinc trials. The Barrow Lab used treatment chambers made by Vacudyne, a company whose processing units, coincidentally, were helpful to cigarette manufacturers in their "vapor phase ammoniation" of tobacco leaves. (Ammonia raises the pH of smoke, allowing for a more powerful buzz per gram-unit of nicotine; morpholine raises the pH of paper—transiently, as it turned out.) Morpholine probably wasn't a carcinogen—so Litton Bionetics determined through assays paid for by the Council on Library Resources in 1977—but it had a dead-fish smell, caused headaches and nausea, yellowed some paper, and sometimes changed the color of leather and pyroxylin-coated book jackets. Henry Grunder, a librarian at the Library of Virginia (formerly the Virginia State Library), wrote me that the Barrow Lab experimented with morpholine on his library's books: "We frequently run into the tell-tale rubber stamp, with the lot number written in; and the darkening discoloration that it is said the process induced in some papers is also present. (It left that behind, although no residual alkalization.)"

But in 1964, Clapp's feelings about mass deacidification and other prolongations of incarnate bookness were only mildly enthusiastic anyway. Even if deacidification could be made to work, he wrote, he expected it to be "comparatively expensive"; and he mentions "storage at reduced temperatures" only in passing. Those were fine techniques to fiddle around with, but microfilm was for pragmatists: "The sensible solution to look to is, again, a solution based upon replacement of originals by high-reduction microfacsimile."

Notice the rhetorical fine-tuning. In 1961, Clapp was attempting to demonstrate that microfilm was good for libraries purely on economic grounds, because it was cheaper than the safekeeping of originals. Now, several years later, perhaps chastened by some of the less-than-fruitful hardware-development outlays the Council had made, he was saying that even if microfilming always remains more expensive than safekeeping, it is the best answer to a different problem—the problem of catastrophic deterioration—an answer that, he points out, has the *side benefit* of reducing "storage, binding, and other maintenance costs" as well. Microphotography is, he notes, "already the standard method for preserving newspapers"—why not books as well? Microfilm and attendant book-riddance is always the solution, but the primary problem it solves is beginning to shift. The idea of destroying to preserve is gaining ground.

Late in life, Clapp wrote a long, multi-part essay for *Scholarly Publishing* about W. J. Barrow and the quest for permanent paper. It is required reading in some library schools, and for good reason: it is engagingly written and full of interesting sidelights about the development of papermaking. Clapp portrays his friend Barrow (whom he had known and advised since 1948) as a hero—"an essentially solitary worker lacking formal training" who single-handedly identifies the true causes of paper's demise (*not* wood pulp, *not* polluted air, *not* gaslights, but alum-rosin sizing), and who invents an alternative acid-free recipe (or possibly adapts it without attribution from a formula developed by the S. D. Warren Company) that changes publishing forever.

Clapp's essay has helped move along reforms in the paper industry, and for that we should be grateful. But Barrow was not the pioneering self-taught visionary that Clapp made him out to be; one book conservator, Thomas Conroy, writes that Barrow

> treated his sources crudely, refusing to correct theory in the light of observation, and (a greater personal defect, but a smaller scientific one) giving inadequate credit to his predecessors. Much of Barrow's appeal to librarians was that he proposed simple solutions to extremely complex and unfashionable problems. When serious attention was again given to preservation, starting in the late 1960s, Barrow's writings were taken as given, and used directly as foundations for further work; his articulations were not challenged or confirmed.

Sally Roggia, in a recent dissertation, writes that Barrow was an "aggressive promoter" who in the fifties and sixties began to be "widely, if incorrectly, credited with original scientific research and findings that were essentially confirmations of work that had been known for decades, and not new discoveries." Roggia says that librarians and archivists must "stop holding onto myths especially when, as in Barrow's case, the myth contradicts reason and common sense."

Clapp's authority, his steady money, and his careful shaping of the truth created the Barrow myth. "I have spent many hundreds of hours—yes many hundreds" editing Barrow's writing, Clapp informed Barrow's son after his death; "I do not mean to denigrate your Father's achievement in any way when I say that in the programs of research which he conducted with assistance from this Council we were a full, if a junior partner." So when Clapp talks about Barrow's amazing discovery of the "catastrophic decline" in fold endurance and the "disastrous condition of paper in the second half of the nineteenth century"; when he titles a historical section "The Road to Avernus" (i.e., hell) and describes papermaker's alum as "the librarian/archivist's worst enemy," we should pause for a moment, and recall that Clapp was a man besotted with microtext, who had spent lots of Ford Foundation money in attempts to perfect micro-machines and image-storers that would allow research libraries to unload their shelved and cataloged book inventory, and that in his role as chief assistant librarian of the Library of Congress he presided over the undoing of its peerless newspaper stock, a willed act that has undermined American historiography far more seriously than anything that alum-tormented newsprint could possibly have done to itself. Clapp, with Barrow's laboratorial help, demonized old paper; he did so partly in order to compel improvements in new paper, and partly to make a convincingly urgent case for filmed replacements.

CHAPTER 16

It's Not Working Out

Clapp says that W. J. Barrow "knew more about old papers than anyone else alive." If so, it was a taxidermist's knowledge. Barrow spent his life coating old papers with melted plastic—not an activity that one normally associates with paper connoisseurship. He quit college in the twenties to work in his cousin's company, the Barrow Corporation, which made work clothes. He managed clothes factories until 1931, when the company collapsed; a year later he set up shop as a conservator at the Virginia State Library. There, experimenting on the library's collections, he gradually refined the now infamous Barrow method of document lamination.

You take a fragile manuscript, or the disbound leaf of a book or newspaper, you layer it between two sheets of plastic, with some tissue included for strength and some chemicals to counteract acidity, and heat this sandwich up. Then you run it through a pair of rollers at great pressure until the plastic fuses permanently to the paper. It's similar to what happens to new drivers' licenses at the Department of Motor Vehicles, but instead of wallet IDs, Barrow was operating on eighteenth-century historical documents. The method became very popular; unlike traditional techniques of paper conservation, the procedure was quick and cheap and could be performed by anyone. "The Barrow laminating process," wrote Clapp, "thus perfected by 1942, has withstood the test of time and has become the standard method."

But time's test run had not ended. No conservation lab uses lamination now; and one website for newspaper collectors advises: "Don't laminate any item in your collection. Lamination irrevocably destroys any value!" The plastic that Barrow used was cellulose acetate, the same substance that microfilm of that era was made of. In 1933, around the time Recordak's Charles Z. Case began selling microfilm to libraries, a salesman from the Celluloid Corporation pitched a new product, Protectoid, to the National Archives. People at the archives began laminating documents between flat plates, in a 750-ton hydraulic press. Barrow couldn't afford the flat-plate machine and used rollers instead. (Perhaps he'd had some experience with the making of celluloid collars from his factory work.) But acetate laminations, like acetate microfilms, aren't stable at ambient temperatures and humidities. They go brittle. The reason that Barrow knew so much about deacidification, in fact, is that he'd had to figure out how to counteract the paper-attacking acetic acid that was awakened in the hot plastic as it squeezed through the rollers. (His method was hotter and squeezed harder than the National Archives's flat-plate method.) Some laminated papers turned yellow or brown; some vintages of acetate contained particular plasticizers that weakened the paper they protected; and as the Barrow Lab sold its patented lamination machines to enthusiasts around the country, and the fame of the method spread from Virginia to other state archives—and to the New York Public Library and the Library of Congress—bad things began happening. "We have found that some materials are permanently damaged by lamination," wrote David Stam, head of the NYPL, in 1984. Someone at a state land agency in Pennsylvania treated a great many early American manuscripts, including papers by William Penn and papers with wax seals, to a rustic version of the

Barrow hot-rolled process. When the Pennsylvania State Archives inherited these documents, and saw the shape they were in, they got a grant from the Pew Charitable Trust to "disemBarrow" or delaminate them.

It was slow work. Jane Smith, a conservator, spent three years with a face mask on, using acetone and other solvents to remove the coating. "They were deteriorating rapidly, much more rapidly than anybody ever imagined," she told me. "You could pick one up and twenty were stuck to it." Plasticizers were "exuding from the lamination plastic," and the result was "actually damaging the document physically, because as lamination breaks down, it lets off many nasty things—acetic acid, formic acid." Most laminated documents aren't this bad: "I've seen plenty of collections of documents that have been 'Barrowed,' and they're in okay condition," Smith said. "They're inherently changed, because you've just melted plastic into the interstices of the paper, so you do not have a piece of paper anymore. You've introduced thermal oxidation and heavy pressure, and you've just filled all of the pores of the paper with melted plastic, which causes some forms of paper to become translucent. You can see through them—not completely through them like a sheet of glass, you're not able to read them as clearly, because you're getting conflicting information from both sides all at once." Rumor has it that one state archive which owns a great many documents laminated by a Barrow disciple "smells like a pickle works"—the vinegar syndrome at work.

I asked Smith what the satisfactions were to her delamination work. "Anybody at all, if they were interested, could see the tremendous difference between a piece of plastic that looks like a place mat at your dinner table, for your children, and a beautiful piece of seventeenth-century British-import or early Pennsylvania paper. You went from a piece of plastic to a piece of paper, and it was phenomenal. The texture reappeared. It was really a glorious thing." When old microfilm contorts, and the emulsioned image separates from the base, you have nothing at all left to read; when lamination buckles, on the other hand, you still have the surviving document underneath.

Swayed by the doctrine of reversibility, some paper conservators now use, in place of lamination, a much gentler technique called polyester film encapsulation, whenever they must enclose paper in plastic in order to protect it. William Minter, of Woodbury, Pennsylvania, developed this method: the document lives between two sheets of polyester that are sealed around the edges by a tiny, ultrasonically actuated titanium jackhammer that vibrates forty thousand times a second. The paper doesn't get heated or squashed in rollers, and if for some reason you need to get your hands on the original, you can slice the margins of the encapsulation to free the paper. Less reversibly, a German company called ZFB (Zentrum für Bucherhaltung, or Center for Conservation) has built a room-sized machine that is able to pull apart, or "split," a fragile newspaper or book page into two extremely thin surfaces and then glue these layers together, with a new, stronger paper sandwiched within. Barrow was "working with the best technology and the best materials available at the time," Minter told me. "Unfortunately, it's not working the way it was intended."

CHAPTER 17

Double Fold

Barrow's breathtakingly confident predictions—as to the impermanency of twentieth-century paper and as to the permanency of twentieth-century plastic—haven't come true, but it was his misuse of the fold test that really overstimulated librarianship. In the paper-science lab, the test is almost always performed with the help of a small desktop machine called the MIT Fold Tester, which turns a strip of paper back and forth through 270 degrees at the rate of 175 double folds per minute. It is the most sensitive of all the physical tests for paper—sensitive in the scientific sense, meaning that test strips which are strong in every other way may seem weak when fold-tested. "Changes in folding endurance of paper," write D. F. Caulfield and D. E. Gunderson of the Forest Products Research Laboratory, "show up long before there is a change in the tensile strength, bursting strength, or tearing resistance." If you are interested in proving that a page of a book has undergone a dramatic degradation, the fold test is the test for you.

But it is an inconsistent test, according to B. L. Browning, a paper scientist who was a contemporary of Barrow: "The folding endurance test is less reproducible than most other physical tests, and a considerable scatter of values is commonly obtained even on relatively uniform machine-made papers." Especially when you're testing differences between old book papers, which can break after one, two, or five folds, the results are so variable that they must be discounted. "Values of one or only a few folds are not usually considered significant," Browning writes. Of all tests, folding endurance is most influenced by humidity. The muggier the day, the more times your sample will be willing to fold, all other things being equal. In order to get meaningful results, you have to precondition your paper in an environment of known humidity. Barrow, self-taught, with no scientific background, only gradually became aware of these difficulties.

None of that would matter much, except to paper scientists, if the fold test, allowing for all of its invalidating irreproducibilities, were a useful rough indicator of paper's ability to do what readers ask of it. Is it? We ask of a book that its pages remain attached to their binding and turn. Maps must fold and unfold as a condition of use, dollar bills must survive pocket-crumpling and repeated wallet-bound contortions—book paper must turn without breaking. The late Klaus Hendriks, a scientist at the Canadian Conservation Institute, wrote:

> While folding endurance is more sensitive to changes in paper than any other strength test, papermakers essentially use it only in the manufacture of paper for applications such as bank notes and maps.

The fold test, in other words, is the wrong test to be using on books. Indeed, Hendriks rejects other currently available mechanical measurements as well: "None of the commonly used paper tests bear any resemblance to the way a paper document or book is handled in practice," he writes.

Nonetheless, Barrow favored the fold test above all others because, he contended, it "simulates the bending of a leaf to and fro in a book in use," and because it "seems to lend itself most readily to analysis"—meaning it made the best graphs. (In one of the Barrow Laboratory's books, Verner Clapp and Barrow are photographed together as they admire a large wall-mounted graph of the precipitous decline in paper's fold endurance; the inverse, in a way, of Fremont Rider's exponential growth chart.) In 1967, as part of one of the last big experiments he designed before his death, Barrow put his team of technicians to work on five hundred more books—this time imprints published between 1800 and 1899. Some of these books would be nice to have now—an 1817 edition of Marmontel's *Les Incas, ou la destruction de l'empire du Pérou* (with plates); Bayard Taylor's *A Visit to China, India, and Japan in the Year 1853* (1855); Jones's *Medical Electricity* (1895); the 1857 edition of William Cowper Prime's *Boat Life in Egypt and Nubia; Secret Journals of the Acts and Proceedings of Congress* (1821 ed.); and Margaret Oliphant's *Makers of Venice.* But Barrow, ever the dissector, had them snipped and clamped into the fold testers, which must have been waggling away into the wee hours, since the experimental regime demanded thirty strips per book—ten strips cut across the lines of print, ten cut from inkless paper, and ten cut parallel to the lines of print—not to mention another eight strips per book to be clamped and torn in the Elmendorf Tester. Barrow, who sometimes seems really to despise paper, found the "debasement of quality" to be "pervasive" in the books published between 1850 and 1869, but it "reached an all time low" at century's end. (The descriptive writing here is probably Verner Clapp's, not Barrow's; Clapp's literary assistance at times amounted to ghostwriting.) Over two thirds of the 1870–1899 group endured one fold or less, which meant they were, he said, "not suitable for regular library use."

All these test books, along with the five hundred from 1900 to 1949, and assorted other lots (including seven books printed between 1534 and 1722, "all of which were in excellent condition after several centuries of use"), have now disappeared from view—temporarily, one hopes. The Barrow lab closed in the seventies; the books reportedly went to the Library of Congress. Bill Minter, the encapsulator, observed to me that even in their mutilated state these books would be interesting to study now: using Barrow's baseline fold data, we might measure whether the paper had become appreciably weaker after thirty further years of natural aging, and how well deacidified paper held its deacidification, and we could get a better sense of what Barrow meant by "not suitable for regular library use." Minter proposed to Chandru Shahani that the Library of Congress do some experiments on the Barrow test specimens ("For the past ten years I've been talking about this!" Minter says), but to judge by his research, Shahani is not terribly interested in the actual aging of paper—he remains fascinated by laboratory ovens, and by the possibility of developing an improved and simplified artificial-aging test.

Many of the books may be gone, but their quotably quantified test results live on in the hearts and bibliographies of preservation managers, who by the late seventies began to have fantasies of sampling the paper in their own collections, in order to see how catastrophically degraded and grant-gettably reformattable it was. Most libraries don't have MIT Fold Testers, though—and anyway you wouldn't want to be cutting strips out of your library's books with Barrow's abandon; you need something quicker and less extreme, albeit variable and imprecise. You also want something that undergraduates and other low-wagers can do with minimal training. And that's how the library world settled on the *double-fold test.*

Anyone can do it. Open a book to a random page and fold its lower right corner in toward you, forming a triangle against the paper, until you feel it crease under your thumb. Then fold it back in the opposite direction until it folds against the far side of the page. That is one double fold. Do that until the paper breaks, or until you reach some stopping point, as specified by your library's preservation department—one double fold, two, four, five. Double folding may seem oddly familiar to some, for it is how kindergarteners are taught to divide a piece of paper without scissors. Now, however, it is used to survey research collections in order to determine their "usability" and hence their fate.

"Usable," as it happens, is another piece of specialized

preservo-vocabulary. A unusable book is not a book that you can't use. "An 'unusable' record," wrote Gordon Williams in 1964, "is one already so deteriorated the paper breaks when folded once. A 'usable' record is one with obvious signs of past use but that might be expected to last at least another twenty-five years if untreated and stored under average library conditions." But that is just one of dozens of definitions and regional variations. Indiana University defines a brittle book as one that doesn't survive three double folds followed by a gentle tug, while an extremely brittle book is one whose page "breaks off in your hand when folded once"—in such cases, "it is often best to withdraw, replace or reformat the item." At Northwestern, staff members are urged to do the "four corner test" for brittleness, "because we might end up reformatting the item," but they are advised *not* to pull the corner. At Cornell and Berkeley, a brittle book is one that doesn't withstand one double fold. At Johns Hopkins, when I called, it was one-and-a-half double folds; i.e., "three half folds." The Library of Congress also uses three half folds. Ohio State defines brittleness as a paper's breakage "when a lower corner is folded back and forth four (4) times (the 'two-double-fold test')." It's two double folds at the University of Maryland, too, "at a width of no more than 1/2 inch," followed by "a very gentle tug"; books that fail this test are "in jeopardy when anyone simply turns the leaves." David Lowe, who manages an NEH-funded microfilming project at Columbia University, explained his library's procedure to me: "Three-eighths of an inch from the corner you fold once, then back under for a single double fold, and then try to tug gently. Then single folds after that up to a total of four single folds—so only twice, after the double fold. Four is the max. If it withstands four, we don't torture it any more."

The University of Florida has an even tougher standard: "A book is considered brittle for University of Florida's Preservation purposes, when the paper is weak enough to fail the 'double-fold test' at five [double] folds or less." (Perhaps it's five because of Florida's humidity; you need to do more folding to get the results you would get up north.) A library staff member who encounters what is by this extreme definition a brittle book routes it to the Brittle Books Department, with a flag in it bearing the "dft result" ("dft" means double-fold test)—from there the marked book enters the twilight realm of "planned deterioration." If and when the book produces a double-fold test number of less than one, it is withdrawn.

This is of course utter horseshit and craziness. A leaf of a book is a semi-pliant mechanism. It was made for non-acute curves, not for origami. If you wanted to test the effective springiness of a watch spring or a Slinky, would you bend a short segment of it back and forth until it broke? If you had a tree in your yard that survived storms by bending and dipping in the wind, would you consider cutting it into firewood because one of its twigs snapped when you bent it in two? Would you check the resilience, and hence the utility, of a diving board by counting how many times you could fold it back on itself before it failed? No, you would not. In fact, a diving board that you could double-fold ten times might be an unacceptably floppy diving board.

The point is that if you bend an intentionally stiff-but-flexible item past the point of its return-memory, you will begin to break it, and that incremental breakage brings a separate set of physical processes into play, with their own plottable curves and points of final rupture. Klaus Hendriks, the paper scientist from Canada, wrote that "one cannot qualify a book page that can be turned over and read as being at the end of its lifespan, even if a corner breaks off after one fold. As long as no mechanical force acts upon it, it will survive a while longer. One will be able to read it and turn it over for years to come."

CHAPTER 18

A New Test

Late one night, after the children were in bed, I began some random experimentation at the household bookshelves. My wife asked me what I was up to.

"I'm—I'm performing the fold test," I said.

"Please stop breaking the corners off our books," my wife said. "It can't be doing them any good."

Before the survey was suspended, I had found that Saintsbury's *Essays in English Literature,* Thomas De Quincey's study of Richard Bentley, Lessing's *Laocoon,* and Christopher Morley's *The Haunted Bookshop* flunked their fold tests. A few months later, I bought a book of essays by Edmund Gosse called *Questions at Issue,* published by Appleton in 1893. The more I read it, the more I liked it, and the more I liked it, the more I wanted to find out how it would rate in the eyes of a preservation administrator. I put my thumb to work on a lower corner of page 153, the last page of an essay called "The Limits of Realism in Fiction." There was almost instant breakage—the corner fell away before it had completed the first leg of the double-fold cycle. If I were doing a survey of my collection, I would be forced to assign this book a dft result of 0.4 or so—a death sentence in some libraries. If I cut a strip out of page 153—which I am unlikely to do—I probably wouldn't even be able to get it clamped and under proper tension in the MIT machine before it would break. This was the sort of book over which preservation people shake their heads and say, "It's got one read left in it." Or, in a sad but firm voice, "We've got just one chance to turn these pages, and it better be when they're under the camera." Untold numbers of books with fold-test results better than that of my copy of *Questions at Issue* have met their unmaker in windowless offices of preservation reformatting.

And yet this was clearly a usable book: I was using it, and not gently, either. I don't cover books with plastic sleeves; I pile them on the floor around my chair, and sometimes the piles topple. Any manual procedure that would conclude that my book was "unusable" or "unserviceable" was a flawed procedure. Klaus Hendriks was right, I thought—the existing tests are inadequate. To test a toaster you toast with it, to test a circuit board you run it for a burn-in period, to test tires you drive them on a test track, to test a heart muscle you put its owner on a treadmill. Suddenly something came to me: a new test for paper.

You don't have to be a scientist or a conservator to perform my "Turn Endurance Test," and it's nondestructive. The protocol is as follows. Open a book to a middle page. Lift the top of the page a little with your right forefinger. Now, when you're ready, *turn the page,* as if you had just read it. Then, with your left hand, restore the page you just turned to its initial position. Turn the page, turn it back; turn the page, turn it back. Each turn cycle may be called one *double turn,* or DT.

I performed a full-scale Turn Endurance Test on page 153 of Gosse's *Questions at Issue,* the very page that had acquitted itself so poorly in a regulation fold test. I turned the page once . . . and nothing happened. The paper did not crack, disintegrate, or compromise itself in any way. Again I turned—and the paper was sound. I turned the page ten times—then twenty, then fifty. Each time, I let it return all the way to a point of rest on the right-hand page-block, so that in lifting it for the next cycle I would duplicate all the top-edge stresses of normal use. Each round trip took me about two seconds.

After two hundred turns, I began to enjoy myself. It wasn't tedious; I got good at it. At the beginning of each cycle, the title of Gosse's next essay disclosed itself on the page beneath: "Is Verse in Danger?" (Gosse believes that it is.) I looked down at the lower corner I'd broken off and regretted that I'd done it, and yet if that lost corner indirectly saves a few books it will not have been creased in vain.

After four hundred double turns I stopped. Barrow claimed that the test for fold endurance simulated the to-and-fro bending of a leaf in actual use—but that can't be right, since my fold-failing page 153 had just flexed eight hundred times (at two bends per cycle) with no hint of damage. Its top edge, where my fingerprint ridges caught and curled it back slightly each time to initiate the turn, was unmarked. *Questions at Issue* was (by definition) a very brittle book, if you compared it with brand-new paper, or old rag paper, but my ten minutes of research indicated that I would be able to read it four hundred times, which was plenty. There is, then, a broad infrared spectrum of serviceable frailty below "breaks at one-half fold" that the act of folding simply cannot sense. In the early sixties, Barrow once took a reporter for the Richmond *News Leader* down to his lab:

> "See," he said, taking a yellowed book off a shelf of yellowed books. It was an old cookbook. "Printed in 1905," he said, as page 282 came out in his fingers. We folded the paper over, then back. Two folds were all the paper could take. The page fell into two pieces, and the recipe for Chicken a la Terrapin was cut in half.

The reporter was shocked, but we needn't be. If Barrow hadn't chosen to destroy yet another page in order to perform his parlor trick, the recipe for Chicken à la Terrapin would very likely be with us today. (And it would be an interesting recipe, too: a terrapin is a large freshwater turtle.)

One root of the word "duplicity" is *duplicitas,* "doublefoldedness." The fold test, as it has been institutionalized in research libraries, is often an instrument of deception, almost always of self-deception. It creates a uniform class of condemnable objects—"brittle material," or better yet, *embrittled* material (for somehow the em-prefix adds a further wiggle of worry)—whose population can be adjusted up or down to suit rhetorical needs simply by altering the number of repetitions demanded in the procedure. It takes no intelligence or experience to fold a corner, and yet the action radiates an air of judicious connoisseurship. Because it is so undiscriminatingly inclusive, and cheap, and quantifiable—because it can be tuned to tell administrators precisely what they want to hear—the fold test has become an easy way for libraries to free up shelves with a clear conscience. *It isn't that we'd like more space,* one can almost hear them whispering to themselves, as they work the corners back and forth, *it's that the books are, sadly, doomed.*

CHAPTER 19

Great Magnitude

The eighties became the decade of the Barrow-inspired statistical-deterioration survey. Stanford University set the pattern in 1979 by subjecting the corners of four hundred books to three double folds (*three,* followed by a gentle pull, just to be sure), with additional demerits for bad bindings, crumbly margins, and poor paper color—they found that twenty-six percent of the books had "deteriorated." In 1984, the Library of Congress cut strips from the fore-edges of twelve hundred of its books and mounted them on MIT Fold Testers; a statistical consultant found that twenty-five percent had fold values of less than one, meaning that "in the judgement of experienced Library of Congress personnel in the preservation field" (i.e., Peter Sparks and his crew), these books "should be preserved by microfilming rather than deacidification."

And then in 1985, in the pages of *College and Research Libraries,* came a monster from New Haven. It was called "The Yale Survey: A Large-Scale Study of Book Deterioration in the Yale University Library." A team of interns (salaried by the National Endowment for the Humanities and the Mellon Foundation) performed double-fold tests on an incredible 36,500 books. The corners were to be "folded four times, and the crease pinched on each fold," an appendix confides—*pinched,* just to be sure. "Of the books surveyed in the main Sterling [Memorial Library] stacks, 44.7 percent did not survive the four-fold paper test—a percentage that represents between 1,351,600 and 1,420,420 books." What were we to conclude from these huge numbers? "These findings signal the need for expanded replacement and reproduction programs"—more microfilming. The current preservation librarian at Harvard, Jan Merrill-Oldham, was one of the team of dedicated folders.

The Yale survey was executed with care and thoroughness, and it's worth studying. If we look at its results in a slightly different way, they argue for the astonishing fortitude of acidic paper, not for its endangeredness. A few years before the publication of the survey, Gay Walker, Yale's head of preservation, delivered a paper to preservation administrators that described the environmental conditions in the Sterling stacks. There were, she said, "major problems with the ventilation system." There was no air-conditioning, and humidity levels in the summer were extremely high. Worse than that, heating problems raised wintertime stack temperatures into the nineties and dropped the humidity to ten or fifteen percent. "Water leaks occurred from time to time and a pigeon's nest with eggs could be found now and then on the upper floors," Walker informed her colleagues. "It seemed that the Sterling stack tower was purposefully built to serve as a giant aging oven—planned deterioration indeed!"

And yet, according to the survey report (which doesn't spell out these environmental rigors), even after decades of being dry-baked, summer-steamed, leaked on, bird-nested, and even occasionally read, the Yale collection wasn't doing too badly: "Surprisingly, the percentage of books needing immediate treatment was much lower than we had believed," the surveyors candidly admit. Their advance guess was that thirty or forty percent of Yale's books would need attention, but that proved, they wrote, to be an overestimate—an overestimate, that is, unless the surveyors redefined the needing-attention category "to include all books with brittle paper" (those, in other words, that failed their mystical manipulation), whether the books actually needed attention or not. Without the fold test, Yale had no marketable preservation crisis.

And marketing was the key, it seemed, because marketing pulled in money. At the same preservation conference at which Gay Walker recounted the sorry state of Yale's Sterling stacks, Peter Sparks gave a brief pep talk called "Marketing for Preservation." Charities, he told his fellow folders, raise an "amazing" amount of money every year—over forty billion dollars in 1979. But the competition was keen:

> To get a piece of the action, an organized, systematic approach must be devised to convince donor agencies that one's cause is worthwhile. Library preservation is a salable item; one must simply formulate an approach that will convince donor publics to invest substantially in this cause.

What was the systematic approach going to be? How could library leaders repackage the idea of mass microfilming in such a way that it would leap to a top spot on the worthy-cause roster?

Warren Haas, Verner Clapp's successor (after a brief interregnum) as president of the Council on Library Resources, had been meditating on these questions for a long time. He was a deep believer in Barrow's *Deterioration of Book Stock, Causes and Remedies,* and an equally deep believer in microforms. (Microforms haven't returned the favor: Haas's undergraduate thesis on British book censorship is available on microfiche, but the copy I got through interlibrary loan was faded to the point of unreadability, although I was able to print legible pages by changing the print setting to "negative," so that the type stood out white on black.) In 1972, the year of Verner Clapp's death, Haas chaired a committee on preservation for the Association of Research Libraries, and wrote its final report: *Preparation of Detailed Specifications for a National System for the Preservation of Library Materials.* (The work was supported by a grant from the

Department of Health, Education, and Welfare.) Haas proposed that a consortium of big libraries embark on a "planned program of microfilming" that would include "collective ownership of any master negatives produced as part of any text preservation project." The ownership of the masters was a matter of some concern to a library director like Haas, because, as he explained, "much master negative microfilm made from volumes in research library collections, at times even at the sacrifice of the original volume, is now in commercial film vaults." The microfilm business had boomed—companies were selling enormous motley collections on "ultrafiche" (very high reduction microfiche) to libraries who needed to build up their title counts fast. (In a later CD-ROM era, such a product would be called "shovelware.") Haas's consortium would in effect become a micropublishing and reprinting concern to rival commercial micropublishers; the marketability of collections they microfilmed, Haas believed, "should weigh heavily in initial preservation program designations, both for the potential income and the high level of program visibility." But before they could get their consortial shutters clicking, they would need money. A program of the scope that Haas envisioned would require, he wrote, "federal financial support of great magnitude."

To raise money, Haas felt that they would have to "expand awareness among the general public"—and among librarians—and to do that they would need a set of traveling exhibits about paper and its decline, and a "carefully written and well designed booklet describing the dangers of collection deterioration," even perhaps a film.

Haas couldn't get all this rolling in 1972, but he was a patient man. Jack Sawyer, president of the Mellon Foundation (and former OSS outpost chief in Paris), liked Haas's "savvy, shrewdness, battle-weariness, and enthusiasm," and had him installed as head of the Council on Library Resources; by the mid-eighties, Haas, with the horrifying fold-test statistics from Yale and the Library of Congress in his back pocket, was ready for a second big push. In 1986, he wrote and published a yellow booklet, carefully written and moderately well designed, called *Brittle Books.* (No author appears on the title page, but when I asked Haas who had written it, he said, "I wrote it.") The booklet summarized several meetings of a certain Committee on Preservation and Access (meetings paid for by the Exxon Education Foundation), whose attendees included the Library of Congress's own Peter Sparks and William Welsh, Sidney Verba from Harvard, Gay Walker from Yale, Harold Cannon from the NEH, and other interested parties. "Careful analytical work undertaken in several leading libraries confirms that books printed on acidic paper begin to deteriorate rapidly fifty years or so after publication," Haas wrote in the little yellow book. (No analytical work undertaken anywhere confirms that; if anything, acidic paper deteriorates more slowly after fifty years, as available reactants are used up.) A fourth of the volumes in old, large research libraries are "so embrittled that they will soon become useless," Haas asserts, citing Yale's survey and the others—brittleness being defined as a paper's liability to break "after one or two double folds of a page corner." We must preserve these books and, just as important, provide "wider and more equitable access" to them. The goal of the microfilming effort is to create "a new national library of preserved materials." Books with intrinsic value (those with "important marginal notes," for example) ought to be "safeguarded as artifacts"—but for most brittle books "reproduction of content is the only realistic course of action; otherwise, an important segment of the human record will be lost forever."

There, that's how to market it. Tell the people that if libraries aren't given the money to microfilm these books (and to chuck them out when they're done, but probably best not to stress the chucking-out part too much), people will lose the human record forever. That will get them to listen. "Extraordinary means for capturing the attention of a wide and diverse audience must be found," Haas wrote. "The Committee is agreed that those who are concerned with preserving our intellectual heritage must speak with one voice if funding and participation are to reach required levels."

Haas was himself a dogged fund-raiser, and he soon convinced the Exxon Education Foundation to give the Council another grant of $1.2 million; part of the money would found a regional microfilming service-bureau called MAPS (Mid-Atlantic Preservation Services, later Preservation Resources) and part would help pay for a movie. Haas began interviewing filmmakers.

CHAPTER 20

Special Offer

By this time, the microfilm industry—University Microfilms and the other commercial micropublishers and service bureaus, along with the big library labs at the New York Public Library, Yale, Harvard, Michigan, Columbia, Chicago, Berkeley, Stanford, and the Library of Congress—needed a major crisis of paper deterioration in order to divert attention from the many misfortunes besetting their own medium. Library users did not like microfilm, that was clear, and they didn't like microfiche any better—whether spooled or cut into rectangular sheets, the microphotographic medium was a bust. Even some formerly enthusiastic librarians were becoming more cautious about buying lots of microtext for their collection—the entire micropublishing industry had acquired a faint cheesiness of tone. Allen Veaner, of *Microform Review,* mentions the sixties influx of federal money for "collection building" in college libraries: some libraries bought lots of film or fiche in order to boost their title counts quickly to a level that would allow them to receive one kind of accreditation or another. Overheated demand increased the number of micropublishers, and some of them were, writes Veaner,

> shady entrepreneurs anxious to cash in on quick profits from micropublication schemes. Unfortunately, with the exception of the largest professional producers, malpractice is often the rule rather than the exception.

One interestingly shady practice was the offer to take old bound journals and newspapers in trade for new microfilm. A library would allow a film salesman to pick up several hundred bound volumes, expecting to get a microfilmed set in return. But the microfilm wouldn't arrive, and the salesman would begin spinning stories, and the volumes were never seen again—sold to dealers. A man named Charles Venick, who reportedly "perspires a lot," worked the substitution scam on librarians in California, Iowa, Florida, Pennsylvania, and Oklahoma in the late sixties and early seventies, until he was finally arrested. One library lost bound volumes "valuing in excess of $10,000." Murray Martin, who first exposed the practice, wrote that librarians were seeking the benefit of "disposing easily and profitably of shelf-eating stock."

But these deals didn't always end unhappily. Pamela Darling, head of the preservation office at the New York Public Library in the seventies, wrote in *Library Journal* that one way to pay for microfilming is "to cooperate with micropublishers who plan to market microform copies. In most such cases, the library will receive free film in return for the loan of the original material; reprint fees or royalty payments on sales are sometimes involved." Since as a rule, according to Darling, once the microfilm is obtained, "the original material may then be disposed of" (except for rare books), this sort of arrangement "can be of great benefit to the library," if entered into cautiously and carefully.

Financial inducements to get rid of originals by offering free filming continue today. In 1998, Heritage Microfilm, out of Cedar Rapids, Iowa (which did a lot of microfilming for Iowa's NEH- and state-funded newspaper project), had this come-on on its website:

> SPECIAL OFFER
>
> FREE filming for newspapers with a subscription to your own film. Call 888-870-0484 or email us for a quote on your next filming project.

(They've removed it now; now their website says "We will return your documents after filming if desired. Or, material will be destructed after a 90 day holding period to ensure you are completely satisfied. All destroyed materials are recycled.") The digital world has picked up on the swap offer, too—the Mellon Foundation's JSTOR project recently offered libraries a thirty-dollar credit against annual database fees for the first five bound volumes of a set that a library donated for scanning, five dollars per volume after that. If you weren't a JSTOR subscriber, they would send you a check. If you wanted to "loan" the volumes, JSTOR would pay or credit you twenty dollars per volume, five dollars per volume after the first five—that is, if you allowed disbinding and didn't require that the loose remains be boxed individually. (Suppose you let someone borrow your car and they returned it to you as a pile of scrap metal, along with a photograph of it. Would you define the transaction as a loan?) In this way, JSTOR gets fresh journal sets to chop and scan, and at the same time, by including a financial incentive for libraries to reduce their nonvirtual stores, they sharpen the need for centrally sourced digital surrogates. The more physical texts that leave the shelves, the more electronic copies must go through wires, which makes the people who control the tariffs on the wires happy: one form of marketing for preservation.

Yes, the seventies were, writes one historian, the "gilded age of microforms in libraries," but there were signs of rebellion even then. In the pages of *Microform Review,* Stephen Salmon published a critique of microfilm's quality and usability: "Let's suppose that the user has found the microform he wants, found a reader, and somehow managed to get one mounted on the other. Then what does he see? The answer seems to be: all kinds of things but not necessarily what he might expect—fingers;

smudges and stains; scratches; dirt and dust; text cut off in the margin; missing pages; images reversed, upside down, or out of order; and assorted blurs, caused by improper lighting, improper contrast, poor resolution, and lack of proper focus." Salmon also quotes a survey respondent who said that microfilm was "an information burial system."

And then there was the question of longevity. Reviewing microfilm's silver-emulsional troubles in 1978, Carl Spaulding, at the Council on Library Resources, pointed out that since libraries don't usually store their film at the extremely low humidity levels specified by industry standards, "the plain fact is that almost no libraries can claim to have archivally permanent film." He ended with a series of bluntly bulleted recommendations, of which the first was: "Most libraries abandon the delusion that their microform collections are permanent." Well, then, why bother? Unless the desire to save space overrides all other motives, why struggle to reproduce books and newspapers in salts or vesicles or silver gelatins that may well not last as long as the originals would have?

The reason Spaulding gives is interesting. He, like many others who were once stimulated by microphotography, was already, by the late seventies, tiring of it, and responding instead to the high-pitched digitarian dog whistle. It is difficult to believe, Spaulding predicted, that in fifty or even twenty-five years libraries would own lots of microfilm; it seemed to him much more likely that "information now commonly recorded on microform will be stored in electronic form in a few central locations to be accessed from any one of the countless online terminals." We needn't worry about microfilm's deterioriation, Spaulding implies—we'll be throwing it all out anyway.

You might expect, with all of microfilm's woes—the illegible early projects, the user-resistance studies that showed a widespread dissatisfaction with the reading experience, the periodic lapses of quality combined with the practical impossibility of checking for lapses, the frauds and malpractices, the abandoned formats, and the various physical afflictions that the film itself was heir to—that preservation visionaries would have become cautious, by the mid-1980s, in their plans to "salvage" major collections by this means. Instead, the preservationists' scare numbers grew, and their imagery became more extreme, as they gradually learned how to sell the problem of aging books as a crisis for the civilized world. They spoke with one voice, as Warren Haas hoped they would, but what they said was increasingly estranged from reality.

Margaret Child, a consultant for the Council on Library Resources and a former NEH strategizer who had attended Haas's brittle-books summits, wrote in 1985 that in order to build a preservational infrastructure, "we need massive infusions of 'foreign aid'—subsidies from government and private foundations, direct funding by local and national governments, and the diversion of institutional funding to preservation programs of all kinds." University administrators must be "persuaded that there is indeed a crisis serious enough to demand diversion of substantial amounts of funding," and scholars "need to be targeted," for although they are the "primary users of the materials endangered, [they] remain remarkably unsupportive of any kind of reformatting." (Unsupportive, possibly, because they know the tribulations of microfilm, and the boon of having the original book in hand; with a very few exceptions—such as Randy Silverman, the director of preservation at the University of Utah, who is an expert in nineteenth-century bookbinding—preservation librarians don't do the kind of historical research that would require them to give their library a regular workout.) Moreover, says Margaret Child,

> the general public needs to be alerted that the threatened loss of our collective memories has at least as commanding a claim to its attention and its tax dollars as the deterioration of historic buildings or the natural environment.

Child is at pains, however, to emphasize that reformatting is not a "universal panacea":

> Microfilming is only *one* of the treatments at our command for dealing with the plague of paper deterioration, just as radiation therapy is but one of the options to be considered by an oncologist confronted by a malignancy.

Like radiation therapy, microfilming isn't "an ideal or very pleasant method of treatment," Child writes, but "in the last analysis, its value as a treatment is indisputable in those cases in which the patient would die." The weakness of this analogy is that your typical doctor believes that when he prescribes radiation therapy he has a reasonable chance of keeping a patient alive, while your typical late-eighties preservation-reformatter disposed of the patient after a last afternoon on the X-ray table. In fact, it was better if you dismembered the patient first, because you could get higher quality X rays that way for less.

As the metaphorized stridency intensified, Haas, Child, Sparks, Welsh, and the other brittle-bookers began to see results. In 1985, Haas met with William (*Book of Virtues*) Bennett at the National Endowment for the Humanities, and he "talked passionately," as he describes it, on behalf of preservation. Bennett acted; a week before he was to leave for his new job in Ronald Reagan's cabinet as secretary of education, he founded an Office of Preservation at the NEH. That gave the lobbyists something to fix on: entreat Congress to give the Office of Preservation more money. "That was the beginning of real effort," Haas recalls, "as opposed to Library of Congress effort."

Now—how much money would the effort require?

CHAPTER 21

3.3 Million Books, 358 Million Dollars

To answer the extremely important money question, Haas hired (circa November 1984) Robert M. Hayes, distinguished dean of UCLA's School of Library and Information Science, to write, against a six-week deadline, a report entitled "Analysis of the Magnitude, Costs, and Benefits of the Preservation of Research Library Books." Hayes was a network consultant for libraries and an early computer-connectivity expert; his digital career went back to the vacuum-tube days, when he used the National Bureau of Standards' very fast fifties machine, the SWAC, now esteemed by historians of computer evolution. At Hughes Aircraft, at Magnavox, and then as head of a venture called Advanced Information Systems, Hayes helped design data-management systems for the National Security Agency, the Air Force's Ballistic Missiles Division, the National Science Foundation, and Douglas Aircraft. But in the early sixties, Hayes decided to make library automation his life; he and the CIA's Joseph Becker, who became his business partner, developed the library-of-the-future exhibition in Seattle, and Verner Clapp gave the two of them a grant to write *Information Storage and Retrieval* (1963), a rich compendium of hardware and methods.

Like Clapp and Fremont Rider, Hayes was troubled by the problem of growth. He, too, had an answer, and it wasn't more shelves. "The most far-reaching solution to the problems posed by library growth," he and Becker wrote in the *Handbook of Data Processing for Libraries* (1970), "is the creation of cooperative library networks." Hayes might seem to be an unlikely person to write a manifesto for a gigantic microfilming program, since he had spent a good three decades as a database frontiersman, and yet once Hayes got going, and the macroeconomic numbers started rolling like flatcars through his brain, he demonstrated why he was the ideal choice for the job.

What Hayes did was sift through all the statistical deterioration surveys—Yale's, Stanford's, the Library of Congress's, and others—pulling percentages from dozens of places, cleaving to the ideal of consistency wherever possible and, where it wasn't, saying so and plunging ahead anyway. And he did some arithmetic.

Assume, he began, that the nation's libraries hold 305 million books—or volumes, rather, since the figure includes periodicals. If you apply the Library of Congress's MIT Fold Test results to that figure, and call twenty-five percent of them brittle, you have 76 million volumes currently "at risk." Assume that in another twenty years, 38 million more will attain "at-risk" status. Assume that of those 114 million volumes, nine out of ten are duplicates. That leaves you with 11.4 million at-risk volumes that would be available over the next twenty years for microfilming. In most cases (as Hayes points out in a supplemental report), the work would require guillotining, "effectively destroying the original as a book."

Not all 11.4 million would have to be filmed, though. To estimate how many would, Hayes relied on a 1984 "Preservation Plan for Textual (Paper) Records for the National Archives of the United States," which recommends that the archives repair or otherwise conserve seventeen percent of its holdings, mass-deacidify twenty-eight percent, "dispose" of six percent, leave twenty-four percent alone for now (as part of their planned deterioration), and microfilm the remaining thirty-three percent. (Why these numbers add up to more than a hundred Hayes does not explain.)

Now we're almost there. If we apply the National Archives' number, and assume that one third of the national at-risk population is microfilm-worthy, that brings us to 3.8 million volumes. But some of those have already been microfilmed—the Library of Congress and the New York Public Library, to name but two, have not been idle. Hayes invoked a percentage from an American Theological Libraries study, where 13.3 percent of the sample had existing microfilm.

Now, 13.3 percent of 3.8 million is about five hundred thousand, subtract that—okay, that brings us down to our final number: *3.3 million brittle volumes to microfilm in the next twenty years.*

And now to figure out how much it's going to cost. Assume a rate of twenty cents a page, sixty dollars a book, to film the chosen ones, and assume another twenty-two dollars in library overhead to do the choosing and cataloging and processing necessary before and after the work is done. Slap on another $88 million for things like training, research, program management, and communications, and you end up with a Brittle Books Program cost of $358 million.

That's a lot of money, true, but Dean Hayes is ready in chapter 6 of his report to point out the advantages, as well. At the top of his list is "Saving of Storage Costs." If each of the 3.3 million books that get microfilmed induces five out of ten of the libraries which hold duplicates to get rid of their own copies of those books, replacing them with "some other means of access to [their] content" (at an undisclosed cost), then all libraries, considered together, will be the net beneficiaries of liberated stack space. One must assign a dollar value to that space. It costs, Hayes estimates, only $1.25 per year to store a book, but if you do some quick things with present values and interest rates, you come up with a present value of the future cost of storage of $12.50 per book. Since five books are being dumped for every one microfilmed, you can multiply that number by five: $62.50 per volume—that is, slightly more than the estimated basic cost of microfilming. To put it another way: Yes, we'll be spending $358 million on the program, but since as a result of the program, libraries will be relieving themselves of 16.5 million books, we're going to be saving $206 million in storage costs—3.3 million books times the present value of the storage cost for five books at $62.50 per book. The savings that result from this spectacular book blowout is a "societal benefit" rather than a local benefit, Hayes points out: "The bulk of the savings will be experienced by other libraries that replace their duplicates with the converted form."

Then Hayes (whose Ph.D. thesis for the UCLA math department was entitled "Iterative Methods of Solving Linear Problems on Hilbert Space") performs a last operations-research calculation that I'm not sure I can follow. Five of the ten duplicates for every unique microfilmed title are, under Hayes's model, going out the back door, but even so, Hayes thinks that once the shutter has stopped clicking over a given book, a library will save money on interlibrary-loan costs connected with it—$149 in present value per microfilmed original, he estimates. He gives no costs for the duplication of the microfilm that would make interlibrary loans unnecessary; he talks about various forms of alternative delivery ("online, download"), but he assigns no financial outlays to them—the high-speed digital backbones will apparently be free. Never mind—for Hayes's purposes, the enormous "savings" on forgone interlibrary-loan costs gets us past the break-even point. The project is not a wash, it's a profit. As a nation, we would end up richer if we spent $358 million to microfilm 3.3 million tragically doomed books and threw out sixteen million tragically doomed duplicates: we would save space, save money, and save civilization, too.

Fremont Rider would have been proud.

CHAPTER 22

Six Thousand Bodies a Day

It was a national emergency. So Congressman Pat Williams of Montana believed. He and his staff had gotten the story from Warren Haas, who was using the numbers he'd gotten from Robert Hayes. On March 3, 1987, Congressman Williams's Subcommittee on Postsecondary Education assembled a group of experts at an "Oversight Hearing on the Problem of 'Brittle Books' in our Nation's Libraries." "Today," Williams announced, "many documents that represent this Nation's cultural and intellectual heritage are literally eroding away." Acid paper was the culprit; "librarians tell us that millions of books in America's libraries are now in great danger." The principal solution, in Congressman Williams's considered opinion, was microfilm—lots of it, and soon. "It is our Nation's very memory that is at risk."

The testimony that followed was vigorous and persuasive. Daniel Boorstin, accompanied by Deputy Librarian Welsh and Peter Sparks of the Preservation Directorate, tendered as fact the notion that each year at his library seventy thousand volumes were moving into a "dangerously brittle state"—a numerical whimsy that Sparks had been passing around to reporters for years. "Across the country," Boorstin said, "in libraries and learned institutions, in every State of the Union, books are becoming so brittle that their contents can only be salvaged by microfilming and then only if funds are available soon." Vartan Gregorian, who was at the time head of the New York Public Library (and a member of Warren Haas's Commission on Preservation and Access), told the hearing room that seventy-seven million volumes in the United States were "facing extinction" (Robert Hayes's estimate, plus a million, and with an injection of endangered-species rhetoric), and he compared his staff to "French generals in charge of triage" who must take care of the "immediate death problem" for some books while "putting others in nursing homes, and some others in ambulatory care, while waiting for their turn." Gregorian held up what he called "almost a dead book"—the history of a French town during the Battle of the Marne. "We have resurrected it through microfilming," he said. He closed by quoting the slogan of the United Negro College Fund—"A mind is a terrible thing to waste"—and said that "we stand to waste the fruit of many minds, indeed, many cultures, if we hesitate in our response to this national crisis."

Lynne Cheney, the new chairperson of the National Endowment for the Humanities, said: "Our thrust at the Endowment has been on intellectual content rather than on the book itself"—hence the Endowment's predilection for microfilming over low-cost book repairing. The problem of brittle books "has only been in the forefront of my mind for eight or nine months now," Cheney confessed, but still, the carnage had to stop: "As we speak, the war continues, and every day Dan Boorstin gets 6,000 more bodies brought into the Library of Congress."

One of the congressmen asked Cheney for some cost estimates, and she used Robert Hayes's: "We are dependent upon people to whom we give grants to come up with figures for the amount of money needed to save these [volumes]. The Council on Library Resources estimates that in order to film 3 million volumes over the next 20 years, $358 million is needed, or about $15 million annually."

Carole Huxley, an official at the New York State Education Department (who had also participated in Haas's brittle-books committee), offered no corpses or French generals, but she did assert that what was going on in the New York State Library was a "calamity." Brandishing an old book, she said: "Our research houses are on fire."

Eventually, it was Warren Haas's turn. The time had come, said Haas, for the federal government to "join in the task as a constructive partner and to do its share." Lots had been accomplished already, "but a kind of giant step is needed. . . . I have just no question that the time is right." In recent years, the general public has begun protecting historical buildings, Haas observed; now, as a mature society, we must do the same for our documentary past:

> The purpose of the work we have set for ourselves is to protect the human record as it is and has been. In this cause, we have the advantage of starting with collections that have been assembled by librarians and scholars over more than a century; we already have what has been judged important at many points in time.

Let's think for a second about what Warren Haas has just said. He is quite right. It is a marvel, for which we should all be thankful, that libraries have such breadth and multifariousness. It is no easy thing to make a great library. It doesn't just happen—it is something that nineteenth- and twentieth-century librarians (and legislators, university presidents, boards of directors, faculty members, and rich people, too) decided was worth doing, for themselves and for us. It took three hundred million discrete acts of inclusive judgment to build the empires of locally available paper that we inherit and use, and we would like to be able to pass on this congregated boon to those who follow, trusting them to do the same. Trust makes it work. Now, imagine if the National Trust for Historic Preservation asked Congress to devote fifteen million dollars a year to the making of measured architectural drawings and floor-by-floor blueprints of thousands of old buildings in need of repair, and then, once they had "intellectually preserved" the ogives and molding profiles and pediments and interior vistas of these buildings, tore half of them down. "The books themselves, as items, cannot be saved," Haas declared, "but their contents can."

The crisis offered a major opportunity, as well. Once a library has saved the "contents" of a book, Haas told the assembly, "new technology suggests that there may be additional ways to use the item":

> It is not unlikely, I think, that the wealth of film that we are building up as a national archive can be used to convert to digital form for reading on a computer terminal, for using it as a base for printing a new edition in small numbers.

Haas doesn't stress the point: it wouldn't do to give the impression that the government was being asked to provide venture capital for a prodigious electronic-publishing venture. But in fact that was the plan: get money now to have a whole lot of "endangered" (and incidentally out of copyright) material shot on film, then digitize from the film later, for ease of access.

At no point during that morning in Washington did anyone mention the documented vulnerabilities of "archival" silver-halide microfilm, although the Council on Library Resources's own program officer had pointed them out in print a decade earlier. Nobody explained that the word "brittle" as used in their statistics had a narrow, technical definition. Nobody felt the need to suggest to those present that just because you take pictures of something doesn't mean you must throw it away, and that in fact the low-cost storage of the source originals ought to be a part of any prudent effort to "protect the human record."

And, most interestingly, none of the expert witnesses uttered a syllable about space.

Had these seasoned library leaders—Welsh, Haas, Gregorian,

and others—all suddenly forgotten the shelving squabbles that they'd had to adjudicate in their own institutions? Were they entirely unconscious of the fact that if you cut up and "save" three million books on film you have three million fewer books to store, and that the creation of a databased union list of what has been filmed may well have a fivefold effect on discarding, just as Robert Hayes had suggested in the very report on which they were basing their twenty-year action plan? ("The great argument in favor of microfilm is space saving," Hayes wrote in the expanded 1987 version of his report.) Had they blanked on fifty years of pro-condensational oratory? Of course they hadn't. Space assuagement was what they longed for, and yet, as if by prior agreement, they mentioned it not.

Since the perfection of the Xerox machine, microfilming has been unnecessary to any book-preservational act. If I were a preservation administrator, and I were absolutely sure, because I had an infallible accelerated-aging test for paper, that all surviving copies of Edmund Gosse's *Questions at Issue* at my library and everywhere else were going to disintegrate into illegibility tomorrow at 3:30 P.M., and if I were determined to preserve the contents of that book for the human record, and if I had no secret craving to make use of the shelf space that Gosse's book occupied, would I have the book microfilmed? Certainly not. I would instead make two full-sized eye-readable photocopies, one bound and one unbound. The bound copy would go on the shelf tomorrow, and the unbound one would become the master, and go into storage in order to make copies for other libraries as they wanted them. Preservation photocopying, as it is called, is faster and cheaper than microfilming, and much easier to check for errors and to correct when errors are found than film is (the film technician must splice retakes into the frame sequence, and there is a stipulated limit of three splices per roll), and the image is cleaner on a paper copy, and you don't need to read it on a screen in a windowless hellhole—*and* you will get a better digital scan and searchable OCR text from it as well, when or if that time comes.

Savage, ungovernable space yearnings, in concert with an ill-conceived long-term plan to stock the sparkling digital pond with film-hatchery trout—these, and not groundwood pulp or alum-rosin sizing, were the real root causes of the brittle-books crisis.

CHAPTER 23

Burning Up

At several points during their congressional testimony, Vartan Gregorian, Lynne Cheney, and others referred admiringly to a brand-new movie called *Slow Fires.* This documentary, conceived and commissioned by Warren Haas, paid for by money given to the Council on Library Resources from the Exxon and Mellon Foundations, with further infusions from the National Endowment for the Humanities and the Library of Congress, is the most successful piece of library propaganda ever created. Haas chose Terry Sanders, an Oscar-winning documentary filmmaker, to produce and direct; Haas had heard good things about Sanders on a visit to UCLA, and during their interview Sanders struck Haas as a person who was willing to listen. At the outset, Sanders was a blank slate—"Basically, it's not a subject that I know the slightest bit about," Sanders told me—but he was, Haas recalls, a "quick study." Sanders got Haas, Welsh, Sparks, and a few others to come up with a wish list of what they wanted the film to do and say, and he read the packets of material he was sent. He felt that he could use some help with the writing: "I'm not particularly a wordsmith—this needed some poetry to it." So he asked Ben Maddow, whose *Asphalt Jungle* had been nominated for an Oscar in 1951, to come up with the screenplay.

Still, Sanders was worried. "When I would tell people about the film that I was doing, about the paper and books turning to dust and the acid eating away—as I told them, their eyes would literally glaze over. It was not an exciting topic to anyone. So that was a good early warning signal that [we'd] better do everything possible to make it an interesting film. We were running scared the whole way." They spent months trying to think of a title; finally, Ben Maddow came up with a real grabber: *Slow Fires.*

Haas himself (blue shirt, wise-looking eyebrows) begins the movie quietly, saying something innocuous about how we can't get carried away by electronic fads; but soon we are in a lushly photographed, somberly sound-tracked world, visiting the Austrian National Library in Vienna, where expressionless international preservationists have convened to discuss (at a meeting funded by the Council on Library Resources) the world's paper crisis; and then we're at Harvard's Widener Library, in a gorgeous slow dolly shot of bookshelves accompanied by narrator Robert MacNeil's voice of literate probity: "Here Nobel Prize winners roam the open stacks—historians reevaluating the past, scientists looking to see what other scientists have already done." Then MacNeil's voice drops slightly: "Yet month by month, year by year, these precious volumes are burning away with insidious *slow fires.*"

Lap-dissolve to a pair of stone lions: at the New York Public Library, we learn, "millions of books are victims of a chemical disease." The NYPL's chief of conservation, John Baker, says that the books may not look so bad (he's right, they don't): "But when you open them, many, many of them are so brittle and deteriorated that they simply fall apart in your hands." (We never see such an outcome in the film, however.) Then we're off to the Library of Congress, containing, MacNeil narrates, "the cumulative daily life of the nation, invaluable and irreplaceable."

> Yet even here, inside this shell of splendid masonry, millions of volumes are falling apart, inside their covers, and within the very fortress meant to preserve them.

At this, there is a stare-shot of a worn and tattered book and a sudden (but soft) violin-tremolo of fear on the sound track. Vartan Gregorian comes on, a jolly charmer, but serious now, announcing that there are "seven million disintegrating books" in the Library of Congress.

The film's kidney-punch is delivered in William Welsh's office. Welsh, who from some angles looks a bit like Kirk Douglas, or maybe I'm thinking of Frank Gorshin as the Riddler in the TV version of *Batman,* holds a small old book while he describes the library's 1984 deterioration survey. "So we had a survey made of our collections," he says, "and we discovered, much to my horror, that twenty-five percent of our book collections of thirteen million books—*twenty-five percent*—were embrittled. That means they would crumble." Welsh does not describe the MIT Fold Test that was the basis of this embrittlement percentage, but he does vividly demonstrate what he means by the temporally indeterminate phrase "would crumble." He opens the book he is holding. It has a loose binding, but its pages are not falling apart; indeed, they appear abundantly readable. Nothing breaks off or crumbles away as Welsh flips through it.

"This is a book taken from our collections that shows the condition that I've described, embrittlement," he says, and he pulls a page out and crumples it in his fist. Working his fingers, he allows the illegible confetti that he has just created to flutter onto his lap. He looks meaningfully at the camera, as if what he has done is devastating in its irrefutability. "You see what happens when you do that to it," he says.

Slow Fires has a sequel, *Into the Future* (1997), about the novel burdens of keeping digital media alive. *Into the Future* is very good, but *Slow Fires* has moments of trying tendentiousness. It would be a better film if what it was saying happened to be truth and not head-slapping exaggeration—then its use of crisis language borrowed from struggles over DDT, AIDS, and acid rain, and its footage of murmuring papyrologists attempting to reassemble fragments of ruined Egyptian texts ("within a generation or two our own books in our own libraries will look like this unless we take heed"), and its pity-inducing pans over shots of charred library interiors and of the Florence flood, would have some justification. But one mustn't chide the director of a made-to-order film for doing his best to tell the story that the people who hired him asked him to tell. "I'm not the expert at all," Terry Sanders told me. No prominent paper scientists—not William Wilson, or Chandru Shahani, or Klaus Hendriks—were interviewed in the film or asked to review the script for accuracy. Nonetheless, the film won Grand Prize in the science category of the 1989 Salerno Film Festival.

One interesting difficulty Sanders had was in getting some actual shots of the devastation of the "chemical disease." "Librarians were very sensitive about showing me their really, really badly damaged books, because it didn't seem right," Sanders says. "I said, 'You know, you can't do a whole film on this without showing the seriously damaged books.' So finally I got to film some, and they're in there." And yet there is in the film no shot of a book—one of millions of allegedly afflicted books that were said to be available to the film crew "in every nation, in every culture"—whose pages have slowly burned away or otherwise self-destructed to the point of unreadability as a result of acid hydrolysis. That is because no such population of books exists. There are some pictures of books with brown or yellow paper that is obviously acidic, paper that is fragile and edge-crumbled, that would fail the fold test; there are books in obvious need of care (or at least more attentive shelving), with loose, damaged pages that could do with a protective box or a librarian's pink shoestring to keep them together. There is a shot of a row of intact old quartos onto which some paper looks to have been crumbled and sprinkled for dramatic effect. But there is no book or newspaper volume shown that wouldn't stay right where it was, disclosing its intellectual contents to the careful-fingered inquirer, for centuries.

The movie's melancholiest moment comes in a scene at the Northeast Document Conservation Center, in Andover,

Massachusetts. A prep person in the film lab talks as she cuts open a very well preserved volume of the Portland *Evening News.* (An unusually valuable volume, by the way: one of the headlines is AMELIA EARHART'S PLANE CRASHES.) The prep woman explains: "As you can tell from the color of the newspaper, they're turning brown, and they're highly acidic. They're burning up." Suddenly the piteous atrocity of her task asserts itself for an instant: "It kind of bothers me to guillotine newspaper collections, because I know the actual papers are not going to go back on the shelves," she says. Then she is able to reassure herself with the received ideology: "But to contain the information on microfilm is the ideal way to preserve the newspapers."

Slow Fires was an enormous hit for its sponsors. It was a highly persuasive, credible (thanks to Robert MacNeil), tastefully photographed piece of intentional fear-mongering that targeted the various "donor publics" that Peter Sparks, Haas, and Welsh had in mind—not only legislators, who were invited to special screenings of the movie on the Hill, but right-minded, library-card-carrying TV-viewers who cared about books and history and, in the movie's own solemn words, "the preservation of civilization itself." (Peter Sparks appears in the movie, by the way, pointing out features of a brightly colored scale model of the diethyl-zinc plant, complete with little plastic people in lab coats.) It first appeared on PBS stations in December 1987, and it was re-broadcast twice in the United States thereafter; after seeing it on WNET, one anxious banker called and volunteered to "do anything to help save brittle books." *Slow Fires* has been translated into Russian, Chinese, French, Portuguese, and Spanish; it has appeared on TV in at least seventeen countries and at two of the directorates of the Commission of the European Community; it has made the rounds along with a "giant Brittle Books exhibit" created by Kent State's audio-visual lab, and over the years it has enlivened hundreds of regional library conferences and library-school classes and scholarly get-togethers like those of the American Philosophical Association and the Medieval Academy. The title has been absorbed into the working language of librarianship: an exhibit entitled "Slow Fires at Harvard's Libraries" carried the torch in Cambridge in 1991; while the all-important Association of Research Libraries prepared a briefing paper that read thus: " 'slow fires,' triggered by the acids in paper, are spreading through research libraries, transforming book and journal collections into piles of paper fragments."

In some libraries, according to Terry Sanders, the movie is shown to new employees as part of orientation and training programs. "I can virtually go into the library anywhere in the world and mention *Slow Fires* and suddenly I'm a celebrity," Sanders told me. "I've written the *Gone with the Wind* of the library world." Because the movie has been part of the basic training of a generation of librarians, many have come to accept what it says unquestioningly; and library-loving lay viewers, who have no independent way of verifying the film's dismaying claims, can only defer to the professionals.

CHAPTER 24

Going, Going, Gone

Representative Pat Williams was one of *Slow Fires*'s first converts. Having heard Daniel Boorstin make a last plea for more federal money, Williams ended the subcommittee meeting by saying that he and his fellow committee members wanted to "help sound the alarm and see what we can do to fight these slow fires." Soon afterward, Williams got in touch with Sidney Yates, the powerful Democratic congressman from Illinois who oversaw the budgets of the National Endowment for the Arts and the National Endowment for the Humanities. Warren Haas set up a screening of *Slow Fires* for Yates and his staff. "I've never been so impressed by a congressman making himself an expert in a very short time," Haas says. "He's a remarkable guy."

With such a magnificent launch to the idea that microfilm was the key to the survival of civilization, it seemed a fair bet that Congress would increase its funding to the NEH's Office of Preservation. But how much would the increase be? To make sure the campaign continued to gain ground, Haas decided that he needed somebody doing full-time advocacy work at the Commission on Preservation and Access, which he formally spun off as a separate non-profit charity, with the help of a million or two from the Mellon Foundation, while he continued to run the Council on Library Resources. Late in 1987, he brought in a woman who would prove to be a more determined brittle-book reverberator than any who had come before. She was Columbia University's librarian and vice president for information services, Patricia Battin. "She will emerge," said one of her colleagues at an awards ceremony in 1996, "as one of the most important figures of the second half of the twentieth century."

Warren Haas knew Patricia Battin's aptitudes well—in 1974, at Columbia, he had hired her away from SUNY Binghamton's small library; several years later, he left her in charge of Columbia's huge library system when he went to Washington to take up foundation work. "She's sharp as hell," Haas told me. "She's a good manager—an extremely good manager—very articulate, and has for a long time been one of these people who look twenty years in the future, understanding that print and digital information are all part of the same game." In the early seventies, when at Columbia, Haas had gotten the Council on Library Resources to hire some efficiency experts at Booz, Allen and Hamilton (a consulting firm that had done mechanization studies for various libraries in the Air Force, the Navy, and the Army) to come up with a plan for reorganizing the Columbia library's administration and readjusting its position within the university. The result of this consultational scrutiny was that Haas became the first library director who was also vice president for information. "I had the computer center under my wing," Haas says.

But in Haas's era, computing and library management, while joined at the top, remained more or less functionally independent of each other. As personal computers began to appear in the early eighties, Patricia Battin (who had already bought a million-dollar mainframe system in her role as an executive at the Research Libraries Group), decided that it was time to bring her subordinate divisions closer together. In her 1984 article "The Electronic Library—a Vision for the Future," she is at pains to say that "the personal computer does not mean an end to books," but she goes on to describe the requirements of the "wired scholar," and she calls for "merging the Libraries and the Computer Center to provide an information infra-structure to stimulate the continuing autonomous use of information sources." In practice, that meant buying more databases and new hardware, fusing library and computer budgets, and spreading around IBM seed money as part of something called Project Aurora—"which is the dawn," she explained to me. About the partnership with IBM, she now says, with some justice, "This is what the vendors had done from time immemorial. They get their feet in the door by giving you all this free stuff and then you become indebted to them for ever—'indentured' I guess is the word."

Even with IBM's self-interested help, however, Battin's vision of the scholarly future would have major start-up costs. And Columbia was not rich at the time; in fact, one of the tough-love things Battin did as university librarian was cut almost a tenth of her workforce. "It was hard because . . . the whole online automation started, and so forth, and so we were really trying to transform operations as well as reduce expenses," she told me. Naturally, there was tension—"opposition everywhere" is how she summed it up to me. Some of her staff didn't understand the new Scholarly Information Center that she and IBM had brought into being: they asked where it was. Battin told them, "There isn't any center, it's in your mind." And some faculty "failed to understand the kinds of unattractive decisions that have to be made." Libraries are, Battin observed to me, "the lifeblood of scholarship and instruction, and when you start tinkering with somebody's lifeblood, they're not going to like it." In particular, she says, "the scientists were on me all the time because we weren't moving fast enough, the humanists were on us all the time because we were destroying the book—which we weren't."

Columbia had space problems, too. ("Everybody has space problems," Battin says.) She finally convinced the board to buy a five-million-dollar building on 131st Street in Manhattan to use for book storage (the fact that it was off-limits to patrons caused some fussing from the faculty), but she also tried to get the president and the provost to understand that they must amortize the book budget just as they amortize computers, "because every time you buy a book, you buy a space cost." (Fremont Rider's old point.) Battin never quite says that her notion of the library of the future was premised on the elimination of a good part of Columbia's old book collection—instead she says, in her essay on the electronic library, oblique things such as: "We expect the preservation medium of the future to be optical disk"; and, "The basic shape of our collections will change as we develop programs for shared collection management and shared preservation."

Battin—very tall, square-shoulderedly elegant, with (in the eighties, at least) large rectilinear glasses similar to those Joyce Carol Oates used to wear in pictures—was an enthusiastic early digitarian, but, like Haas before her, she did not spurn traditional microfilm, either. In 1983, she told her preservationist peers that Columbia's library had four microfilm cameras going full-time; the library depended on "outside funding and cooperative projects for an active assault on our large collection of brittle materials." On her arrival at Columbia, she had been horrified by what she called "yellow snow" in the stacks—the wisps and shards that crack off the margins and flutter down from inside the bindings of wood-pulp book-paper and old newsprint. (An ill-fated technique of commercial rebinding called oversewing, which arrived in the twenties and by the mid-1930s had been incorporated into the specifications for library binding—a technique that knits together the back of the milled-off text-block by means of dozens of angled needle-punctures, effectively perforating the inner margins—is a major cause of yellow snow.) Such fragments have been a fact of library life for many decades ("scraps of faded, rusted, brittle paper litter the floor and present insistent questions," said the *Bulletin* of the New York Public Library in 1929), but Battin, freshly arrived from SUNY Binghamton's young and relatively small collection, was not prepared for what she found. "It was so shocking," she told me; in yellow snow she found evidence of a silent post-industrial cataclysm. It led her to propose that "we will not add to our collections any material in poor condition, regardless of its intellectual content," since "it makes no sense to spend an enormous amount of money on materials that are simply going to deteriorate."

An active assault—that was the sort of aggressive zest Battin brought to her work at the Commission on Preservation and Access. She gave the Commission "full-time energy," Warren Haas told me, "and a point of view that was exactly right. You just have to talk to Pat to understand Pat. She's a great animal." Her organization's tax-exempt status prohibited her from lobbying on behalf of legislation, in the strict legal sense, but she could and did get the heads of twenty of the largest research libraries in the country to write letters expressing their deep concern over brittle books, and she could and did (as she told me) "work with Mr. Yates's office giving him the kind of information that he needed as to how severe this problem was." And she could, of course, write speeches, which she gave across the country and around the world, showing the incendiary *Slow Fires* as she went.

Some years later, in an awards-acceptance ceremony sponsored by an IT firm, Battin claimed that she owed her success to "affirmative action and the old boy network." But in this she did herself an injustice. Battin owed her success to the missionary intensity of her desire for informational reform, and to her capacity for exaggerative repetition. Her knowledge of paper's deterioration and of the techno-preservational alternatives to paper came for the most part from people like Warren Haas, William Welsh, and Peter Sparks, but she had the convert's desire to convince and conquer. With the help of a little word, *dust,* she scaled the heights of funding.

Until Battin came to Washington, librarians (with the exception perhaps of Peter Sparks) had not prominently claimed that books were turning to dust. It wasn't true, for one thing. *Slow Fires* alluded to the idea, but only in passing, and there had been a March 1987 piece by Eric Stange in *The New York Times Book Review,* based on interviews with Welsh, Sparks, and others, entitled "Millions of Books Are Turning to Dust—Can They Be Saved?" But Stange was a print journalist, not a librarian, and he tells me that the title wasn't his idea anyway—editors came up with it. Battin, however, with an authority derived from nearly ten years as director of one of the country's great book collections, used *dust* boldly, repeatedly. In one of her early communiqués from the Commission on Preservation and Access, in June 1988, she outlined the specifics of the cooperative microfilming plan that she and the NEH had just presented to Congress. Twenty libraries would each microfilm 7,500 of their volumes every year for twenty years, for a total of three million volumes—the three million being "the estimated number of volumes it would be important to save in order to preserve a representative portion of the 10 million or more volumes that will turn to dust by that time." Robert M. Hayes had estimated that 11.4 million books were going to enter the "at-risk" category in the next twenty years—now suddenly ten million of them were going to turn to dust.

In a publication called *Change,* Battin wrote that "approximately 25 percent of the world's great collections are already brittle and turning to dust because of the alum sizing introduced into paper-making around 1850"; in a 1989 piece for *Educational Record* called "Institutions Have Moral Responsibility to Preserve Great Book Collections," she mentioned those "university librarians who have long witnessed and attempted to stay the crumbling pages of books as they slowly turn to dust." The 1990 annual report for the Commission added the red-flag adverb *literally:* "Books, along with other paper-based materials, are literally turning to dust because of the chemically unstable acid-based paper that became popular in the mid-1800s."

Battin's articles went out to libraries around the country, accompanied by a leaflet written by one of the Commission's interns: "Ideas for Preservation Fund Raising: A Support Package for Libraries & Archives." Here is its first paragraph:

> Have you seen a first edition copy of Emily Bronte's *Wuthering Heights,* or perhaps a 1847 edition of her sister's *Jane Eyre*? They

> are most likely in the same condition as Milne's 1926 *Winnie the Pooh* and Huxley's 1932 *Brave New World:* Dust. . . . Each copy slowly destroyed as it sits quietly unnoticed in the literature section of your library. (Ellipses in original)

Have no fear—the first editions of the Brontës, Huxley, and Milne are doing fine. The statements in this passage are so untrue that they induce a kind of blinking awe. Once the dust delusion took hold, it seems to have neutralized any scruple of restraint among its proponents. They just started making things up.

The Commission was also a clearinghouse for inspirational fund-raising publicity. They copied and distributed, for instance, an article from the University of Tennessee's alumni magazine that begins: "A slow fire is burning in Hodges Library. It's destroying books that can't be replaced. There isn't any smoke, nor are there flames. But thousands of books are crumbling into dust, fatally burned by the acid in their own pages." The article, "Goodness Gracious, Great Books Afire," ends with a request for checks made payable to the Library Preservation Fund.

The more the word *dust* was repeated by library folk, the more real the idea became. Sidney Verba, Director of the Harvard University Library (and a member of the founding board of the Commission on Preservation and Access), pounded the broadloom before Congress in 1989:

> If what differentiates humans from other species is the ability to use language, and if what differentiates civilization from pre-civilized forms of life is the ability to record that language by written words, then it follows that our essence as humans is contained in the written words we pass from generation to generation. These written words, entrusted to library collections, are turning to dust—and with that part of our lives is going as well.

In 1990, the Canadian Broadcasting Corporation series *The Nature of Things* aired an episode about brittle books called simply "Turning to Dust"; staff of the Commission on Preservation and Access "collaborated" (so its 1989 annual report stated) with the CBC during the development of the show.

Perhaps the most arresting document from those consciousness-raising days is a flyer produced by the American Library Association in 1990. On the front are three sequential photographs of *A Handful of Dust,* by Evelyn Waugh. (It appears to be a dummy book, not a real edition of the novel.) In the first picture, a few raggedy-edged pages poke out of the text-block; in the second picture, the front cover has developed three black lesions that look to have been made with a blowtorch, while cornflake-sized paper bits hemorrhage from the fore-edge; in the third picture, there is a cremational pile of fine dark powder and tiny fragments—only the vestigial word *Dust* is still legible. Below the three pictures are the words *Going, Going, Gone.* The sequence is a fictional simulation, needless to say; no book ever, anywhere, has spontaneously disintegrated in this manner—not in a research library, and not during a photo shoot for a publicity brochure. Inside the front flap, the American Library Association's text informs us that "literally" millions of books are turning to dust, that more than a quarter of the books in libraries "may not survive the century," that the one "tried-and-true" technology is microfilming; and we are urged to "let Congress know that money spent on book preservation is money well spent." On the back of the flyer it says: "Funded in part by the Commission on Preservation and Access."

CHAPTER 25

Absolute Nonsense

Not only are people liable to spend more money on a problem when they are good and scared, but they are also more likely to accede to things that they would otherwise find abhorrent, such as mass-disbinding, if they believe that a state of emergency warrants them. Was it a state of emergency? Were millions of books turning to dust? I called up Peter Waters to get an idea of what he thought of *Slow Fires* and the embrittlement crisis.

From 1971 until he retired from the Library of Congress in 1995, Waters oversaw the training of a generation of conservators; he has been sewing, gluing, rehinging, resizing, washing, de-verminizing, and generally giving careful thought to paper and print and their future prospects for most of his life; and, like all great book conservators, he has eavesdropped on the history of papermaking through his fingertips. But Waters is also one of the world's experts on book emergencies. His experience began in Florence in 1966, when the Arno's sludge, admixed with "undesirable wastes," filled the treasuries of the Biblioteca Nazionale. There were two major disasters in Florence, according to Waters—the first was the flood itself, and the second was the "extreme post-recovery damage" to the books resulting from the manner in which they were handled (piled wet to head height) and dried in their mud-beplastered state. (Interestingly, volumes of twentieth-century newspapers fared better than some two-hundred-year-old gelatin-sized rag-paper books in the tobacco dryers that officials used for some of the collection.) Waters was consulted about recovery efforts after the 1986 fire at the Los Angeles Public Library, and after the 1988 inferno at the Russian Academy of Sciences Library in Saint Petersburg. He was called in to advise after a fire in 1978 at the Klein Law Library in Philadelphia—Klein was building a new library building; the entire collection was insured; Klein's librarian, who "seemed to be in a total state of shock," said he had "no plans" to enter the rare-book room for several days; when Waters and his colleagues finally convinced him to allow them into the room, they found that water from the fire hoses had risen to a height of three feet before it had drained away, causing the swollen books to burst from the shelves; many were "covered with mold to a thickness of at least a centimeter."

I read Waters a passage from one of Patricia Battin's articles, "The Silent Books of the Future: Initiatives to Save Yesterday's Literature for Tomorrow," published in 1991. "If swift and drastic action is not taken," Battin writes, "the great voices of 19th century scholarship will be stilled far more effectively and finally than by war, flood, censorship or fire." Then comes the parade of scary numbers: "80% of the materials in our libraries are published on acid paper and will inevitably crumble. The Library of Congress alone reports that 77,000 volumes in its collections move each year from the 'endangered' state to brittleness and thence to crumbs."

Thence to crumbs? What did Waters think of that kind of talk? "Well, unfortunately I think I have to say that it's absolute nonsense," Waters said. "The truth of the matter is, you have to go and look very, very hard indeed to find really crumbled books." Waters does not question that books become brittle with age; he does question the notion that a diagnosis of brittleness means the end of a book. "Only if the collections are physically abused will they start breaking up," he told me; the phenomenon of "yellow snow," associated with oversewn bindings, should simply move us to handle books with more care, even enclose them in protective boxes. (Peter Waters's son Michael Waters designed a computer-controlled box-making device to enclose thousands of fire-damaged books in Saint Petersburg at a cost of roughly a dollar per boxed volume; the Library of Congress's custom-box maker is also one of the younger Waters's machines.) "If books are protected in boxes, and left in good order, even in the normal environmental conditions of a library, there is no mechanism—not chemical or physical—for them to crumble. It simply can't happen."

Waters has reviewed the statistical deterioration survey of the Library of Congress's collections and found that its data fail to support the endlessly repeated estimate of seventy thousand (or seventy-seven thousand) books going brittle yearly—never mind Battin's "and thence to crumbs" fillip at the end. "You're still going to meet a great number of people who believe that time is running out, or has run out, and that all this material is going to crumble," he told me. "And there really is not one single piece of hard evidence to support it."

Waters calls *Slow Fires* "that ridiculous movie"; of the phrase "slow fires" itself, Waters says that it "misrepresents the real-time state and conditions of the Library of Congress's collections" and that it has "given birth to ignorance as to the survivability of so-called brittle book material." He has been saying these things publicly for years. In a 1992 speech entitled "The Deterioration of Library Materials: A Doomsday Inevitability or a Manageable Preservation Challenge?" delivered while he was still at the Library of Congress, he said:

> Let us first dispense with the most commonly held belief, which in my opinion has led to panic and uncontrolled and ineffective reformatting policies throughout the United States. It is, *that once paper reaches the brittle condition, it will not survive.* There is no basis in truth or scientific evidence to support this belief. Brittle book material can and will survive for an indefinite period of time, if

> they are physically protected and not abused by stack attendants, readers, poor housing conditions *and administrative policies that ignore or write off their existence.* (Emphases in original)

As an example of the longevity of extremely weak paper, Waters instances the Library of Congress's dime-novel collection. These books were printed on groundwood pulp; for years they were stored in poor conditions (high heat and humidity). The collection now contains, Waters says, "some of the most brittle material that you could ever wish to see. Now the whole collection has been boxed, and if I could live for five hundred years, I would still expect them to be in the condition they are now, providing they're not physically abused." (The boxes also serve to caution dime-novel researchers to handle the paperbacks carefully.) Waters writes: "Here is a crucial question—does *any* library have a substantial inventory of losses caused by brittle books crumbling to dust? I think not. Total loss is much more likely from theft and vandalism."

But in 1980, Peter Waters unwittingly supplied one of the reformattisti's most potent images, printed in the *Smithsonian Magazine* and subsequently in *The New York Times Book Review,* the *Christian Science Monitor,* and on the cover of *American Scientist.* When *Smithsonian* was doing a piece on the opening of the Madison building ("called by some a monstrosity"), they sent a talented photographer named Yoichi R. Okamoto to take pictures. One of Okamoto's tasks was to document the problems of preservation; he showed up in Peter Waters's office in the Adams building. "He was talking about what he'd been told about brittle books," Waters recalls, "and he said, 'Is there some way you can demonstrate this?' " So Waters manually "scrumpled up" a page into a handful of fragments—as his old boss Frazer Poole had done in many a brittleness demonstration before him, and as William Welsh was to do some years later in *Slow Fires.*

Okamoto said, "Well, supposing you blew it?" They went out to the corridor with several books and began blowing around fragments. Okamoto wasn't satisfied with these shots and returned to take more. "Although I shall go down in history as destroying books at the library," Waters says, "it was a great photograph." When it appeared in *Smithsonian* (full page and in color), the caption somewhat misleadingly read, " 'Brittle book' flies apart as conservator Peter Waters blows on it. Slowing decay is major Library job."

The brittle book in the photograph would not have flown apart if Waters hadn't first reduced it to cornflakes by hand. "I scrumpled it and blew the remains," he says.

CHAPTER 26

Drumbeat

Peter Waters is not alone in his opinion that the brittle-books petitioners, most notably the Commission on Preservation and Access, used Rachel Carsonesque language that was, in Waters's words, "designed to dramatize a situation, which can lead to funding support, rather than depicting an accurate reflection of the state and rate of collections deterioration." Paul Conway, Yale's head of preservation, calls it "the Henny Penny school," where you say the sky is falling, "and then it turns out to be something else." Conway explains: "There were principled people who felt that the way to build national money is to focus, focus, focus and raise the issue to the national agenda. So it became a political process, which is focusing and narrowing, where voices are raised and attention is gained. If you take that logic to its extreme, you have to build a crisis state. You read the literature from the late eighties, you get this constant drumbeat." *Fire . . . calamity . . . crumbs . . . endangered . . . chemical disease . . . dying patients . . . facing extinction . . . dust.* Patricia Battin at one point even wrote of "millions of rotting books," a counterfactualism of brazen repulsiveness. She probably plucked it from *Slow Fires,* which talks of books "rotting on the shelves."

But it was the earnest avowal that books were "turning to dust" that really enlisted sympathy outside the library world, because "dust" as a terminal state is so siftably granular, so irreclaimably fragmented, so impossible to copy. *What was words is now dust.* The phrase certainly worked on me. Even though I had spent a fair amount of time in library stacks around the country and had never encountered a book that could be described as having attained a near-dustlike (as opposed to dust*y*) condition, I believed that millions of these books, or at least thousands of them, must be hidden away in places that visitors never saw. I trusted that library authorities were saying something that was close to the truth.

But it seems they weren't. I had lunch with two learned booksellers, Ian Jackson and Peter Howard, who between them have examined hundreds of thousands of library discards from all over the world, as well as private caches in attics and sheds and all kinds of hot, inclement places. I read them some sample *dust*-passages, along with a statement from the Commission on Preservation and Access's 1992 annual report that offered "the fact that over twenty-five percent of the world's great collections was embrittled and lost to future scholarship." Lost to future scholarship? Peter Howard blinked and said, "Seems like nonsense to me." Ian Jackson observed that late-nineteenth-century South American book-paper was some of the worst he had come across; its manufacture was influenced by the German chemical industry, which created, Jackson said, "the horrible paper that browns." He gave as an example the hundred-odd volumes produced by a Chilean scholar, José Toribio Medina, between 1880 and 1930, books that "remain the bedrock of South American bibliography." They were all reprinted in the sixties, because the original paper couldn't hold up to heavy reference-room use: it was brown and fragile. "The paper is just—it's worse than German," Jackson said. And yet even copies of Medina in the original exist and are collected. Jackson owns thirty thousand books, most from the acid-paper era; in his life he has run into "a few dozen"—not thousands or hundreds—that have reached what he called the Wheat Chex stage.

Since German paper seemed to present unusual problems, I also talked to Helmut Bansa, editor of *Restaurator,* an English-language conservation journal published in Munich. Bansa said that books can become so brittle that they can be handled only with the "utmost care." "But they will not embrittle to dust," he said. "This is not true." Nor has he ever seen (and this is a very important point) a book that could not be copied. "The worst state is if you have a sheet of paper and you turn it around an angle, let's say, of ninety degrees, then it will break. This is the worst state I've ever seen."

I also talked to Peter Jarmann, a bookbinder and conservator at St. Bonaventure University, south of Buffalo, who has perfected a technique called "quarter-joint binding" that allows books to open flatter (while facedown on photocopiers, say) with less damage. Jarmann has encountered books, especially those with oversewn bindings, that are so brittle that their pages cannot be turned without breaking them out of the binding. Has he come across any books that are turning to dust? "I think they've slowly discovered that this idea that they'll all turn to dust is a myth," he said. "The books get weak to a point, and they kind of stop at that point. And whether they break out of the binding kind of depends on the binding. They're more likely to fall apart in a stiff binding than in a binding that gives."

John Dean, head of preservation at Cornell, told me that his library has the usual problems with flakes of paper at the photocopiers and that their Southeast Asian collections are extremely delicate. "But as far as actually, literally turning to dust," Dean said, "I must confess I have never really seen that phenomenon myself, and I don't think any of the research has actually demonstrated that this is the case. I think that that particular rhetoric is a metaphor, and it may be an attention grabber, I'm not really sure."

I brought up the dust question with Robert McComb, the former paper scientist from the Library of Congress. McComb said: "What they were afraid of is if they even took the book off the shelf and put it on a book cart, it might start falling apart. There have been a few examples of that. I didn't say a lot, but there's been a few." He's seen exactly two books that "when you opened the covers a little bit they just broke into hundreds of little pieces." McComb says he once came across a book in which a piece of bacon had been used as a bookmark. "How long it had been in there, Lord knows, but wherever that bacon grease had gone, that paper was exceedingly fragile."

I asked Ellen McCrady, who edits the *Abbey Newsletter,* the periodical of record for U.S. book preservationists and conservators, about the Commission's notion that we must convene a vast communal filming bee right now because millions of books will crumble over the next twenty years. "I think they leapt at that solution and oversold it," McCrady said. "Pat Battin was gung ho on microfilming, and to her this was the solution. I used to resent that. She used to call it 'preservation.' Microfilming is not preservation. Microfilming is microfilming—it's copying. She was overstating her case, and associating herself with higher things, and so on." McCrady believes that microfilm ought to be used to save things that would not otherwise survive, but Battin took it too far. "If you want to be a leader, you have to have credibility, and you shouldn't distort reality in order to gain the favor of the masses. It'll backfire."

CHAPTER 27

Unparalleled Crisis

Lots of microfilming—that was the important thing. Get as much under the camera as possible, as soon as possible, using "a comprehensive mass-production strategy." And yet Battin's "major attack" on the brittle-books problem was not just about microfilm. There was also the deacidificational thrust and the alkaline-paper thrust. To further the cause of deacidification, the Commission on Preservation and Access hired Peter Sparks, who was by then looking for work as a freelance consultant, to write a slim study called "Technical Considerations in Choosing Mass Deacidification Processes." And that was about it.

The alkaline-paper thrust, on the other hand, was a commendable attempt to convince publishers to use (in a slight misnomer) acid-free paper: paper that had not merely a neutral pH when it came off the roll, but an extra dose of Rolaidsian additive mixed in, a buffer or "alkaline reserve" which would counteract any hydrolytic toxins that the fibers might secrete or otherwise encounter in their golden years. In adopting this goal, the Commission nudged its way into a campaign already in progress, headed by Ellen McCrady, who had for years argued for the use of acid-neutral paper; her Abbey pH pens are used by librarians as a quick check of acidity. (The pen line comes out a pale purple if the book is alkaline, yellow if it is acid.) Allied alkaline forces were able to celebrate a victory sooner than anyone could have foretold, mainly because stricter EPA regulations were compelling papermakers to redesign their plants in order to reduce the acidity of manufacturing effluents. March 7, 1989, was the big day for acid-free paper: urged on by Vartan Gregorian and a writer named Barbara Goldsmith (who later joined the board of directors of the Commission on Preservation and Access), a group of authors (including Robert Caro, Joan Didion, and Kurt Vonnegut) and publishers (including Harper, Random House, and Simon and Schuster) pledged that they would publish first printings on acid-free paper. (Actually, some of the publishers had gone acid-free for hardcovers several years before.)

In time, most of the bigger papermakers switched to alkaline-buffered output, following the lead of the S. D. Warren Company; some of the smaller ones couldn't afford to and closed. Today, most hardcover books state on the copyright page that they are printed on acid-free paper. (The competing hope that the industry also employ recycled postconsumer fibers, the chemistry of which is difficult to control, has possibly lopped some years off the life expectancy of some "permanent" papers, however.) Vartan Gregorian's New York Public Library placed a full-page ad in *The New York Times* to celebrate acid-free "pledge day," and its public-relations office took the opportunity to issue a press release filled with some further alarming (and false) numbers—such as "35 out of the 88 miles of shelves in the Central Research Library contain 2½ million dying books"; "Seventy percent of all books printed in this century will be unusable in the year 2000"—followed by a deferential nod to the NYPL preservation program, which runs "one of the largest and most sophisticated microfilming laboratories in the world."

It always went back to dying books and microphotography. And yet Patricia Battin was well aware that, as she told me, "everybody hates microfilm." There were two ways of alkalizing this hatred: the long-term way and the short-term way. The long-term way was to perfect digital successors to microfilm (since, as Robert Hayes wrote, "There appears to be high user acceptance of quality CRT display; why else would so many people watch 'the tube' so avidly?") and begin converting the subsidized film scrolls as soon as electro-storage technologies had developed standards, or even sooner. The short-term way, though, was to scare "the masses" (to use Ellen McCrady's word) into thinking that big-money microfilm was, for now at least, a necessary evil. In the world of research libraries, the masses are the faculty and students who use the collections. Over several decades, these groups had successfully been eased into the conviction that the replacement of original newspapers with rolls of transparent plastic was a historical inevitability; now they had to be persuaded, as well, that a planet's worth of old books was at death's door. That's where the Scholarly Advisory Committees, or SACs, came in.

With the help of money from the Mellon Foundation and the William and Flora Hewlett Foundation, the Commission on Preservation and Access invited dozens of academics to spend some time in restful settings outside Washington (at the Belmont Conference Center in Elkridge, Maryland, or in Bellagio, Italy), where they would sit through presentations by Battin and others, read handouts, hear more presentations, talk earnestly about the task they faced, read more handouts, and return to their home campuses in a state of double-folded enlightenment. There was the Scholarly Advisory Committee on Art History, the Medieval Studies SAC, the Text and Image SAC, and the Modern Language and Literature SAC. "Making clear to scholars that their own perhaps narrow specialty is far from the only area affected is an early task in the development of a scholarly advisory committee," the Commission's annual report stated in 1992. "This awareness usually leads to the desire to spread the word—to inform colleagues of the impending disaster and to rouse them to action." Eventually, the Commission's various committees were expected to produce reports and (since two thirds of the brittle books would be allowed to die spontaneously) "help plan strategies for making the hard choices as to what and how to preserve."

There were scholars who were somewhat puzzled by the proceedings. My father-in-law, Robert Brentano, a medievalist at Berkeley who was invited to participate in the Text and Image SAC, found himself explaining the usefulness to historians (and their students) of seeing the actual books and documents from a certain period, rather than many separate pictures of them. Others were completely taken in, used by the Commission to spread panic. Larry Silver, a member of the Art History SAC, delivered an addled talk at the annual conference of the College Art Association. He said that being asked to select what to preserve was "like playing God, or at least Solomon." One had to play Solomon, said Silver, because wood-pulp paper was "filled with acid that literally causes it to self-destruct, like the tapes on the old television show, *Mission Impossible.*" J. Hillis Miller, famed deconstructionist from the University of California at Irvine, wrote the final report for the Modern Language and Literature SAC. The Commission passed out copies of Miller's report at its brand-new "modular brittle books display" at the Modern Language Association meeting in 1992: "Large resources need to be deployed to preserve as many books as possible," Miller announced (that must have pleased the Commission!), and he said that "every possible action should be taken to educate our colleague[s] and our libraries in the magnitude of the problem." Members of the committee were of course mindful of the value of "actual physical books," Miller wrote,

> But if these original books in all their copies and editions, along with all the papers in archives, printed or written on paper from the 1850's to the recent past, are slowly burning up, then microfilmed or digitalized preservation is obviously demanded.

By then, Patricia Battin's planful indefatigability—the articles, the newsletters, the roving exhibits, the scholarly committee meetings, the grueling international tours—had paid off substantially. The word "dust" had been singularly helpful, and the word "crisis" had been given a walk on the wild side, as well. Warren Haas, recall, had staidly said there was a "brittle books problem"; then Margaret Child said that there was "indeed a crisis"; then Vartan Gregorian told the congressional subcommittee that it was a "national crisis"; then *Slow Fires* called it a "universal crisis." But in 1988, before Congress, Patricia Battin, never to be outdone, held up the shining orb of the National Endowment of the Humanities, which she says constitutes an "unparalleled resource to solve an unparalleled crisis." Congress, marshaled by Sidney Yates and abuzz with the novelty of the disaster they were being called upon to relieve, nearly tripled the budget for the NEH's Office of Preservation—soon to be renamed the Division of Preservation and Access, mirroring Battin's Commission. A year later, Battin told Congress that embrittlement was "an unprecedented crisis"—no, wait, it was a "crisis of alarming proportions." Congress scaled up the budget even more. Suddenly George F. Farr, Jr., a polite, plummy man who was then and is still the director of the NEH's preservation program, had many millions to give away for filming projects. "The Endowment could not have advanced its current plan for brittle books without the groundwork laid by the Commission and, at an earlier date, by the Council on Library Resources," Farr wrote. Hefty applications and testimonial letters came in from libraries, each describing a particular collection (a thematic subcomponent of American history, say) that especially deserved to have its pictures taken, page by page, before it succumbed. The review panels met; the winners were announced; the disbinding began. The Library of Congress's Preservation Microfilming Office got a congressional budget-boost as well, so that its squad of camera operators could keep pace with the national effort. The civilization-saving plan to microfilm over three million books was under way.

In the first few years, the wave of soft money went mostly to libraries with existing photoduplication programs—Columbia, NYPL, Harvard, Yale, Chicago—but that changed as more universities created preservation departments of their own, hiring full-time preservation administrators to run them. The preservation administrator could perform a local deterioration survey that would produce some shocking percentages, choose an enticing subset of the collection to present to the NEH in a grant proposal, negotiate contracts with nonprofit or commercial microfilming shops, and convince the subject specialists in charge of that piece of the collection to come up with five or ten thousand brittle books. The institutionalization of the preservationist's profession was one of Patricia Battin's cherished dreams—indeed, just before she left Columbia, she had secured for its library school nearly half a million dollars from the NEH to train more fresh, green P.A.s. "We didn't have a manufacturing infrastructure," Battin explained to me. "I mean, how are we going to film all this stuff?"

There is a direct correlation between the spread of preservation administration as a career and the widening toll on old books. Battin wrote in 1988 that the "number of preservation operations in American research libraries has increased from about 5 in 1978 to more than 50 in 1988, as universities have acted to institutionalize the activities necessary for the preservation of scholarly collections printed on acid paper." She adds: "And we haven't yet begun to fight!"

There are about eighty preservation administrators at work now. The only major research library in the country that still has no full-time or part-time preservation administrator is the Boston Public Library. It is also the only large library in the country that has kept all of its post-1870 bound newspaper collection.

Some pages from the New York *World*

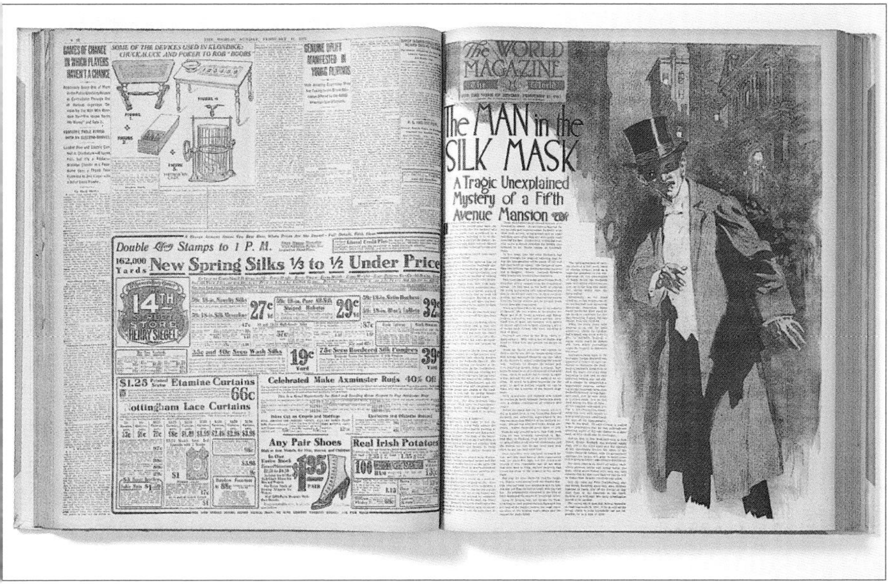

"The Man in the Silk Mask," New York *World*, February 11, 1912, from a set formerly owned by the British Library.

"The Man in the Silk Mask" as reproduced on black-and-white microfilm. The New York Public Library microfilmed its run of the *World* in 1951, and duplicates of this microfilm have since replaced nearly all print copies of this paper.

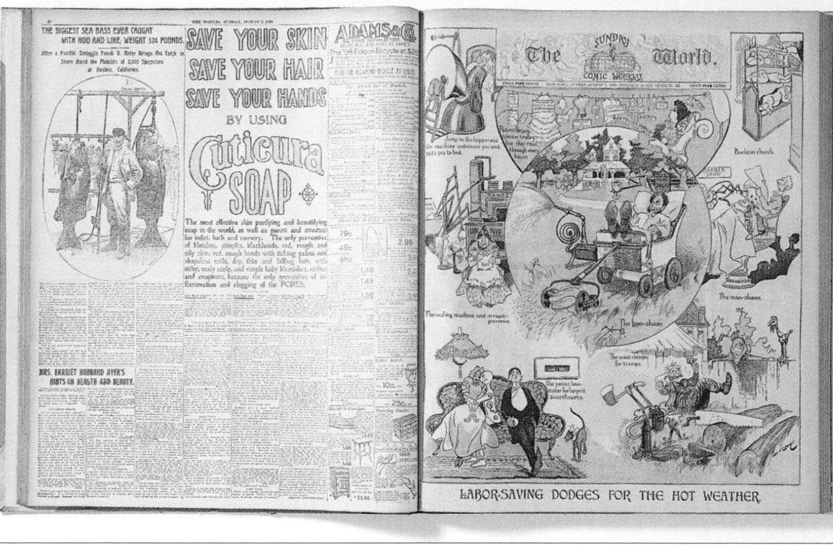

"Labor-Saving Dodges for the Hot Weather," New York *World*, August 7, 1898. D. McCarthy's cartoon includes a robotic lover, a "lawn-shaver," and an undressing machine.

"Too Much for Any One Man to Believe," New York *World*, May 19, 1901. Possibly the last copy extant.

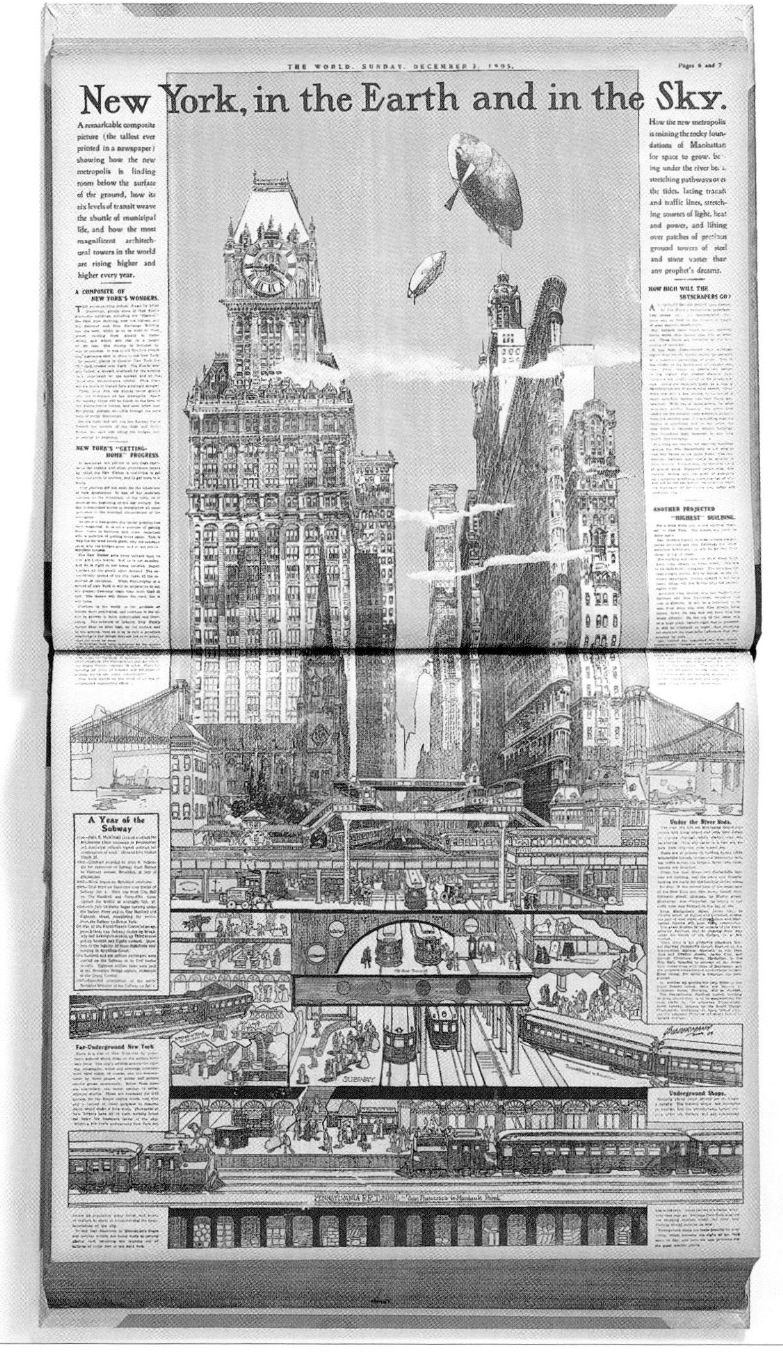

THE WORLD. SUNDAY. DECEMBER 3, 1905. Pages 6 and 7

New York, in the Earth and in the Sky.

A remarkable composite picture (the tallest ever printed in a newspaper) showing how the new metropolis is finding room below the surface of the ground, how its six levels of transit weave the shuttle of municipal life, and how the most magnificent architectural towers in the world are rising higher and higher every year.

How the new metropolis is mining the rocky foundations of Manhattan for space to grow, be- ing under the river be[illegible] stretching pathways o[illegible] the tides, lacing transit and traffic lines, stretching courses of light, heat and power, and lifting over patches of precious ground towers of steel and stone vaster than any prophet's dreams.

A COMPOSITE OF NEW YORK'S WONDERS.

NEW YORK'S "GETTING-HOME" PROGRESS.

HOW HIGH WILL THE SKYSCRAPERS GO?

ANOTHER PROJECTED "HIGHEST" BUILDING.

A Year of the Subway

Under the River Beds.

Far-Underground New York

Underground Shops.

SUBWAY

PENNSYLVANIA R.R. TUNNEL — San Francisco to Montauk Point.

"New York, in the Earth and in the Sky," New York *World*, December 3, 1905. A composite illustration by Louis Biedermann of New York's marvels—"the tallest ever printed in a newspaper." Possibly the last copy extant.

SPAIN'S MOST DARING EXPLOIT OF THE WAR

The World.

CERVERA'S SQUADRON DISCOVERED BY WORLD.

THE MORRO THREATENED BY GUNS OF VESUVIUS.

WHAT THE VESUVIUS MAY HAVE DONE TO THE MORRO AT SANTIAGO.

GEN. SHAFTER'S ARMY IS NEARING SANTIAGO.

SPANIARDS ROUTED AT OLD CAVITE.

HUNTING A LANDING FOR GEN. SHAFTER.

"Spain's Most Daring Exploit of the War," New York *World*, June 19, 1898. During the Spanish-American War, Pulitzer's *World* and William Randolph Hearst's *Journal* strove to outdo each other's battle illustrations.

"New York's Costliest Spring Hat," New York *World*, April 7, 1907. On the facing page is an art supplement by Charles Dana Gibson, printed on thick card-stock; few of these supplements were microfilmed. Sheet music, comics, and occasionally whole news sections are missing from the microfilm as well.

CHAPTER 28

Microfix

Not all preservation administrators approved of what the Commission on Preservation and Access was up to, though. "I just saw Pat as leading the whole profession down a tube," says Randy Silverman, the director of preservation at the University of Utah's library. Utah has a dry climate, and Silverman, a practicing bookbinder and conservator, knew that there wasn't a brittle-paper crisis in his library. In fact, he wasn't running into many brittle books at all, and in the ones he did see "gutter-snap," as he called it, was often the problem: the pages broke at the perforations of an oversewn binding. He and Matthew Nickerson, a graduate student, replicated the standard double-fold survey procedures on a random sample of books from the university's collections and found, as they expected, brittleness rates at about two percent—their point being that storing books at lower humidity was possibly a better (and far cheaper) way of extending their lives than cutting them up to take pictures of them.

Silverman's main objection to Battin's NEH-funded program, however, was that in the first several years there was no money for book repair. "The profession was steered by this great fear," he told me, and the fear led to mass microfilming, which "took the focus away from other activities. My hobbyhorse is trying to repair books—you know, fix them—and there was no money left for conservation. All the money was going to film. And every time you got done filming, you were able, in some people's minds, to simply throw the books away." There were plenty of things, Silverman knew, that an experienced book-repair person could do for a population of damaged or fragile books to keep them on the shelf and available for use—and the repairs wouldn't cost nearly as much as would microfilming them or giving them high-end conservation treatment. Detached pages, flapping spines, a broken text-block—many troubles were fixable if you knew what you were doing. But most preservation administrators were trained as reformatters and managers and not as practitioners of a traditional craft; having no personal experience doing repair, they sent things to the microfilmers that would have required only a little thread, some paste and Japanese paper, and some close attention.

Early on, Silverman began writing a polemic against the Commission and its selling of "microfix" (his word) as the sole solution, but he buried it. "It was really loaded ten years ago. I would shoot off my mouth in private. It was too dangerous to say stuff, because in fact you couldn't change it." Some of his colleagues had private misgivings, as well; but, as Silverman wrote me after we talked, "the reality was nobody could stand up to Ms. Battin because they all had their hand in the NEH till that she was stockpiling."

Once, however, Silverman challenged Battin publicly. It happened at an American Library Association convention, circa 1991; Battin was giving an update on the national microfilming campaign. "She made it clear that people really needed to participate in the brittle book program by writing grant proposals," Silverman says. There was a lot of money that year for microfilming, and it was in danger of not being spent: "If it wasn't used she feared that Congress would determine that the brittle-book crisis (as she had promoted it to them) would appear not to require funding and once the critical momentum was gone she feared it would never be reestablished." Silverman spoke up during the question-and-answer period. "I tried to make a point that the exclusive focus on microfilming equaling 'preservation' was leaving the repair of the physical collections unaddressed. She told me that book repair was a local maintenance issue and did not qualify for national funding because it was each library's responsibility to maintain its own collection."

Battin wrote authoritatively in 1990: "The issue of repair as an alternative to microfilm was not considered as a federal responsibility in the initial legislation." Later, apparently in response to protests from some grantees, the NEH changed the rules somewhat; George Farr was at pains to point out several times to me that the NEH has "provided support" for the repair and reboxing of more than fifty thousand books (out of more than eight hundred thousand that were filmed), but when I repeated Farr's claim to one preservation manager, this manager (who asked for anonymity) said, "Whoa, whoa, first, the assertion is wrong. He hasn't paid for fifty thousand books. He has allowed *us* to pay for the repair of books as part of our cost share. Do you know how these grants work? We write a grant to NEH, NEH gives us two dollars, and we have to add in a dollar of our own. It's two to one. The NEH guidelines allow us to repair books that have gone through the process, as part of our contribution. In the ultimate bottom line, which is the total of what we've contributed, [along] with what NEH provides, he's technically correct. But there is no money in the federal budget to support the repair of collections."

CHAPTER 29

Slash and Burn

Patricia Battin gave me a brittle book when we met one afternoon in Washington, at the offices of the Council on Library and Information Resources on Massachusetts Avenue. The book is a play by Robert de Flers and Francis de Croisset, in French, accompanied by a memoir and a frontispiece photograph of de Flers in profile (he's reading a sheet of manuscript) and a facsimile of his handwriting. It is a charming little book, published in Paris in 1929 and library-bound in pink, black, and red marbled boards soon thereafter (since it originally came out in paperback), and now tied with a soft, salmon-colored shoestring. The bookplate says "Columbia University in the City of New York" in Gothic letters, and bears the seal of the university, in which Wisdom, or some nobly enthroned woman, says something in Hebrew while holding up a book to three naked children. There is a scriptural reference at the feet of the children, citing a passage in Peter: "Laying aside all malice and guile and as newborn babes, desire the sincere milk of the Word, that ye may grow thereby."

In 1986, as part of a "Cooperative Preservation Microfilming Project" organized by the Research Libraries Group (which

Patricia Battin had run for a time), Columbia stamped the book WITHDRAWN and sent it to Micrographic Systems of Connecticut, where it was neatly guillotined and then filmed, with financial support from the NEH and the Mellon Foundation—whereupon Patricia Battin took it with her to Washington as a sample. The paper is brown around the edges and has the Necco-wafer smell of acidic paper, but it is otherwise intact; somebody has apparently performed a fold test on the lower corner of page 115. Fifteen years ago, Columbia's preservation administrators decided that this book was at risk for immediate disintegration and deserved emergency filming with our tax money; today, though a photographer reduced it to a stack of loose leaves, nothing remotely decompositional has occurred. On a hot day recently, I untied its string and held up some of its pages; they did not tear or shatter or do anything except move air and make interesting soft flapping noises. Columbia University has a reel of master microfilm now and no book.

Guillotining was de rigueur in the 1988 Brittle Books plan. Not every book was cut, but most were. "I'll try to explain this in a way that I don't get misunderstood," Battin said to me, when I asked her why the books couldn't simply have gone back on the shelf after they were microfilmed. "Here we have a disaster of major proportions, and I do believe that. We have limited amounts of money. If you do it in a cottage-industry way, in which you try not to disbind the book, it's going to cost you a lot more than if you say, okay, we have to make this economic decision, and we can save the knowledge in more books if we do it on this kind of mass—" Battin hesitated for an instant and then continued, "which means disbinding."

Battin went on to tell me that a German company, Herrmann & Kraemer, has developed advanced book cradles "which allow you to do a good job of filming without disbinding the book. We didn't have those at that time." Battin is correct that such cradles exist. But the best U.S. microfilming establishments—Preservation Resources and NEDCC—do not use them. It is possible to film all but the most tightly bound books well with a traditional cradle, it just takes longer: almost all programs do less disbinding now than they did at the height of the craze in the early nineties, even though they have traditional cradles to work with. The desire to disbind, then, was independent of what was technologically possible. "I think by and large if we were going to do as much as we thought the majority of the scholarly world wanted, we had to disbind," Battin told me, "and then the book wouldn't go back on the shelf."

We could save more books for less right now if we destroyed more books right now, and we had to act right now because it was a "disaster of major proportions," and we knew it was a disaster of major proportions because corners were breaking when space-craving preservation administrators running microfilm labs folded and pinched them. George Farr, the NEH's preservation person, was on board with this cross-eyed logic; and in the early years of NEH funding, with the *Slow Fires* panic and Battin's cost-saving mass-production strategy uppermost in participants' minds, filming activity often took a "vacuum-cleaner approach," as it came to be called. Operators bundled off whole stack-ranges that were determined to be at risk, rather than going through the shelves book by book to figure out what physically ought to happen to individual items: it takes time and therefore money to sort a shelf-full of books into "basket cases" (a widely used and wonderfully elastic term for books in bad shape), books that may need minor repair, and books that were merely published in the acid-paper era and are otherwise okay. "Yes, I'm sure there are books that were microfilmed that probably were not that brittle," Battin says now. "We had great debates among the populace as to whether you took the collection approach or the individual-copy approach, and decided for the initial filming grants that the collection approach made the most sense." To me she quoted the French adage, "The best is the enemy of the good." Of course, the bad can be the enemy of the good, too.

Yale was one of the big libraries that took the collection approach. In a paper about a microfilm-to-digital experiment at Yale called Project Open Book, Paul Conway described one of the challenges the conversion team faced. *"Slash and burn preservation,"* he named it: "For some key collections in a single library, most of the brittle books are now gone." Determining the dimensions of an original page or the fidelity of its microfilmed reproduction is "severely hampered," wrote Conway, "if the original volume is in a landfill."

"We had to slash our way through these collections in order to save them"—that was the thinking in the eighties and early nineties, Conway said when I reached him. The sense was that "these books were on their last legs, if not already dead: 'Put them out of their misery and move on to a better technology.' The first seven or eight years of large-scale microfilming had that mentality." (Conway was not director of preservation at Yale during that period.)

I asked him if the sudden surge of NEH money had perhaps seduced libraries into destroying the very things we meant them to preserve. "Yes, we were seduced," Conway said. Yale's American history collection, for example, took a hit early on. "Half of what was there is now filmed and not on the shelf anymore. And everyone was seduced. But at some point we started waking up and saying 'Wait a minute, this is crazy.' " In a recent NEH-funded project, Yale filmed twenty-one thousand books, and they threw "maybe two hundred" away, he said. Like Ohio State, Yale now has a new remote-storage warehouse, where books are sorted by size rather than by subject, and shelved in arbitrary order in computer-indexed cardboard boxes on thirty-foot-high shelves that you reach on a cherry picker. "There's a lot of criticism about them because they're not browsable," said Conway, "but what those buildings have effectively done is make space a non-issue."

Libraries everywhere, one is told and wants to believe, are now dispatching many fewer books than they were ten years ago, in the heyday of Battin's hatchet fever. Jan Merrill-Oldham,

Preservation Librarian at Harvard, wrote me that Harvard is currently filming nine to ten thousand "brittle volumes" per year, of which only one or two a month are completely disbound and guillotined. (In a partial disbind, the prep person cuts some of the threads, loosening the book so that it can open flatter under the glass pressure plate.) One of Harvard's recent NEH grant proposals states that "approximately 7% of all volumes filmed as part of this project will require disbinding or removal of folded pages prior to microfilming. Disbinding is a strategy of last resort." But Merrill-Oldham insisted that even the seven-percent figure was "an artifact" (numbers, like lucky books, can sometimes attain artifactual status), produced by cutting and pasting the language from older grant proposals. "There are very few libraries these days that do the kind of discarding that went on right at the beginning," she says. "We just hadn't pulled it all together, I don't think, right at the beginning. And I'm not sure that libraries should be faulted for feeling their way to some kind of solution. It's not like there was tons of help all over the place."

At Columbia, when I called (December 1998), David Lowe's NEH-funded technicians were working methodically through the business and economics stacks, classifying books as Brittle or Not-Brittle by using their variant of the double-fold test. If the book was brittle, they checked the binding. If the binding was damaged, they designated the book as a "BD"—Brittle and Damaged. If it was a BD, and it was published after 1850, they segregated it for "selector review," the selector being a librarian with expertise in the book's subject area. He or she was to decide whether the book merited microfilming (if no film existed somewhere already) and whether or not to reshelve it. "If it's a 'Reshelve No,' it's basically a withdraw," Lowe explained. The selector took circulation into account. "I think I said, 'If it's circulated in the last ten years I think you should consider reshelving it,' and the selector said, 'Maybe *twice* in the last ten years.' So that's the sort of thing we get involved in."

I said to Lowe that I wished that the classification of an item as brittle wouldn't act to seal its doom. "Well," Lowe replied, "when you're pressed for space and you're only given so much money to build new places for books, you start thinking, 'Hmm, microfilming, and then get rid of them, that makes a lot of sense.' It's administrator-think, and it's convenience, and most of the stuff isn't circulating that much." (Circulation is, however, a meritless measure of a book's interest or usefulness in a research library; interests change from one generation to the next.) Lowe couldn't offer any estimates of the percentage of books disbound; he did say, though, that they had just finished filming several thousand "pams" (pamphlets), and most of those were cut apart in the process and thrown away. "I mean, they don't have much of a binding to begin with," he said.

CHAPTER 30

A Swifter Conflagration

That some librarians realized that what they were doing was crazy, as Paul Conway says they did, and that the guillotinage got no worse than it got, is due in large part to the abolitional insistence of one scholar, G. Thomas Tanselle. Tanselle, an editor of Melville, is vice president of the John Simon Guggenheim Memorial Foundation and a former president of the Grolier Club; he teaches classes on bibliographical analysis and scholarly editing at Columbia, and he owns a large collection of books produced by several dozen American publishers between 1890 and 1930. (Nothing in his collection has crumbled, by the way.) In December 1990, at Columbia's library school (now disbanded), and a month later at the New York Public Library, Tanselle delivered a pointed but civil speech, "Libraries, Museums, and Reading":

> Scarcely a day now passes that the microfilming epidemic does not thrust itself on my attention in some way, either through my discovering that certain materials are no longer available in original form in a particular library or my being asked to join an appeal aimed at rescuing a category of material scheduled for destruction.

Tanselle mentions seeing, at the New York Public Library's annex, "a whole range of shelves of nineteenth-century newspapers marked with signs that read 'Microfilmed. To be discarded.' " He says: "One makes do, of course, with whatever survives, for there is no alternative. But when we are confronted with such recent loss of evidence, loss produced intentionally in the name of preservation, we have yet another reason to remark on the pervasiveness of human folly."

As the human folly continued, Tanselle in 1992 gave an address at Harvard's Houghton Library (published in the *Harvard Library Bulletin*) in which he said that all library books should be "placed in the charge of those who are experienced in the care of artifacts," and he quoted a nineteenth-century bibliographer: "The most worthless book of a bygone day is a record worthy of preservation." (A wish to keep what is physically on the shelf does not, however, have to "stand in the way," Tanselle observed, "of an enthusiastic acceptance of the developing technology for the electronic dissemination of texts.") In 1993, with mass-microfix still at large, he produced a strongly worded but still remarkably gentlemanly screed for *Common Knowledge*, which began, "The present time will be regarded in the future as an age of book destruction." Its title, "The Latest Forms of Book-Burning," proves to be a direct reference to *Slow Fires* and its sponsor:

> The term "preservation" in the title of the Commission on Preservation and Access was never intended to refer to preservation of physical objects containing texts, but only to texts abstracted from objects; and in practice this "preservation" has been an agent of destruction for the objects. *Slow Fires* is the title of the Commission's widely publicized film about the self-destruction of books containing acidic paper; the copies used in the Commission's program of microfilming, however, are doomed to a much swifter conflagration.

That piece turned some heads, and then in 1995 Tanselle wrote, for a Modern Language Association committee, a "Statement on the Significance of Primary Records" that was adopted by the MLA's executive council. Tanselle again praises organized efforts to film and to scan, but he says that regardless of how texts may travel among minds in the future, we have decisions to make about the tangible objects that are in libraries now. Unless the public grasps the value of these primary records, he writes, "sizable portions of certain classes of textual artifacts face destruction."

Tanselle's tenets, though they were ridiculed by some as being impractical or self-marginalizingly extreme, are really quite simple and helpful. One is that we shouldn't spend lots of time trying to determine which books have artifactual value (or "intrinsic value") and which don't. According to standard library theory, your rank-and-file book is assumed to have no intrinsic value; it is a dented and tarnished word canteen whose contents may be poured off at will into other, often smaller receptacles. A relatively few books—ones that bear a famous person's signature or marginalia, for example—may qualify as objects of artifactual value, and these objects often live in rare-book departments. In practice, writes Tanselle, this categorization is influenced mainly by book dealers' price lists: "Books of high market value will receive expensive conservation treatment, and other books will be microfilmed or photocopied and then thrown out. Such a policy is not worthy of a research library." The distinction between rare books and utilitarian word-ware is not only impossible to make—because the degree of future rare-bookishness is unforeseeable now, as is the degree of informational interest—but harmful, as well: "I think it is undeniable that the common attitude of disregard for the physical evidence in books has produced an insensitivity to the destruction of books that would not be condoned by professionals dealing with any other category of artifact," Tanselle writes.

The truth is that all books are physical artifacts, without exception, just as all books are bowls of ideas. They are things and utterances both. And libraries, Tanselle believes, since they own, whether they like it or not, collections of physical artifacts, must aspire to the condition of museums. All their books are treasures, in a sense; the general stacks become a sort of comprehensive rare-book room—not staffed and serviced as rare-book rooms are, obviously, but understood as occupying the same kind of unreformattable sensorium. Only by "approaching books as museum objects do we most fully and productively read them," Tanselle provocatively writes. Once a large research library makes the decision to add a particular book to its collection, it has a responsibility to try to keep that physical book in its collection forever. That duty continues in force even if publishing undergoes revolutionary changes and libraries buy only electronic texts from some moment forth. The keeping needn't involve expensive measures, however: "Most books are not frequently used, and neglect can sometimes be an artifact's best friend."

There are plenty of vicissitudes of the flesh, to be sure, and libraries, like museums, will inevitably get rid of things, but if they can at least try to begin to understand, as museums generally do, that everything they own is a piece of human handiwork as well as a bitmappable or re-keyable or filmable sequence of words, then we have a better chance of avoiding some of the damage that will otherwise accompany the ongoing shrinkathon.

Once the Modern Language Association came out in favor of primary records, feelings began to shift a little. The indiscriminate spine-shearers and the upper-tier administrators who approved their work began to get the sense that they'd gone a little overboard. Patricia Battin retired from the Commission on Preservation and Access in 1994—succeeded for a brief period by an equally radical futurist from Cornell named Stuart Lynn, and then eventually, mercifully, as the Commission was folded back into the renamed Council on Library and Information Resources, by a moderate, historically minded humanist, Deanna Marcum. And there is now a new book category in some libraries: "semi-rare," as at the New York Public Library, or "medium rare." The medium-rare book is defined as possessing more intrinsic value than the common book, but not so much as a rare book. Tanselle would rightly question the taxonomic confusion in these distinctions, but at least they indicate improvement. Possibly you won't be allowed to copy a medium-rare book facedown on a library's copying machine (which can be rough on spines and pages); on the other hand, you won't necessarily need to read it in a special room with white gloves on.

Nobody has yet tried to do what Tanselle repeatedly recommended, though: he suggested that we store somewhere all the casualties—books, journals, or newspapers; bound, disbound, or never bound in the first place—of mass-microfilming or preservation photocopying. "A central repository could be established for receiving the books, if the libraries that possessed them before microfilming did not wish to keep them," he wrote in 1989; and four years later, "Although it is a pity that the Commission did not make such a repository a part of its plan, it is not too late to establish one now." As the amount of digital scanning increases, the repository would hold those paper remains as well. The cost of this *salon des refusés* would be a tithe of the total cost of copying.

The NEH requires many expensive things of its grantees—among them the storage of microfilm master negatives at low humidity and temperature (often in commercial storage vaults at a cost of a dollar per year per roll) and the creation of a second-generation negative from which to make positive "service copies" of film as needed—but the NEH never required, should so manifestly have required, should this *instant* begin requiring, that any microfilming or digital scanning that it pays for will without exception result in the physical storage somewhere (either in the host library or, if the host library was enticed into applying for the NEH grant partly to be rid of the incremental bulk of the book, in a low-cost book-refugee ziggurat) of every original "master-positive" book or bound newspaper.

CHAPTER 31

Crunch

Despite Tanselle's influence, the basic outlook of the reformatters has not changed that much. Steve Dalton began his 1998 seminar at the Northeast Document Conservation Center, "To Film or to Scan," with a paper-demonization demo. "Chemical deterioration takes place because paper has what we can call *inherent vice.* Inherent vice, I like to say, is the original sin of paper. It's born to a goodness, with high ideals, to live a long and prosperous life. But it has this tendency to go wrong." Dalton crumpled up a piece of blank, eighteenth-century rag stock and demonstrated that it could be flattened out again without damage. "It almost feels like a fabric, rather than a paper," he said. While we students handed around the artifact, Dalton crisply summarized the decline in nineteenth-century papermaking—the bleaches, the sizings, the lignins, the tannins.

Then, from a shelf in his podium, he took out a small blue book in an old library binding, its serifed title stamped in gold. "This is a book from 1903," he said, "and that paper that we passed around is from roughly 1785 or '90." He pulled out a page from the book, crumpled it in both hands, and let the manufactured confetti fall onto the wood-grain vinyl veneer of a conference table. "I think librarians secretly have the urge to do this once in a while," Dalton volunteered; there was some light laughter. "So if you feel the urge, I'll leave this book up here. But one page per person, please." He repeated the old estimates from Robert Hayes: "So we're talking probably over three hundred million volumes in research collections in the United States that have this terrible inherent vice to self-destruct."

Soon we were hearing some blunt talk about a primary advantage to preservation microfilming. "A lot of times institutions that we deal with, when we do preservation planning surveys, are wrestling with significant storage problems," Dalton said. "Does anyone here have a storage problem in your institution?" Hands went up around the room. "Space is really—it's a big factor." If you merely photocopy a brittle book in order to preserve it, you've done nothing to, as Dalton put it, "crunch space," whereas with microfilm, "if you're discarding materials after filming, then you can take a large volume of material, and crunch it into a one-hundred-foot roll of film."

At break time, I asked Dalton if I could take a look at the brittle book. It was called *The Life Radiant* by Lilian Whiting (Little, Brown, and Co., 1903). On the copyright page were blue and pale-purple stamps identifying it as the property of the New York Public Library, Astor, Lenox, and Tilden Foundations. On the inside cover, in red letters, was stamped:

MICROFILMED
Date Feb 07 1990
TOO POOR TO BIND

Every page I turned was legible; turning did no damage. On page 80, I read: "The demands of modern life absolutely require the development of some means of communication that shall obviate the necessity of the present laborious means of handwriting." On page 82 was a quote from H. G. Wells on the discovery of the future. Pages 83 and 84 were gone, though—crumpled in workshops to demonstrate the urgent necessity of microfilm.

I asked Dalton where he had gotten the book; he gave me an odd look. Perhaps it occurred to him that I wasn't a librarian. "Uh, this is just something that when people go around here from the center to yard sales and things, if they see something like this they scoop it up," he said. He smiled: "Always on the lookout!" The New York Public Library owns only microfilm now for *The Life Radiant;* its catalog record lists the 1990 reformatting as sponsored by a grant from the National Endowment for the Humanities. I suppose it is possible that the New York Public Library's book happened to find its way to a yard sale in the environs of Andover, Massachusetts. It's more likely that Dalton's own staff at the Northeast Document Conservation Center microfilmed the book, and that the NYPL didn't want it back afterward.

At Dalton's "School for Scanning" seminars (also brought to you by the Mellon Foundation and the NEH), librarians go to hear current thinking on embedded metadata, SGML tagging, lossless compression, TIFF formats, emulation, refreshment, and disbinding. Why disbinding? "To get a digital image that's really well captured, it's still best to disbind," Dalton advised us.

CHAPTER 32

A Figure We Did Not Collect

How high, one wonders, was the national toll? How much destruction did we as a nation pay for? The National Endowment for the Humanities doesn't know and doesn't want to know. I asked George Farr whether the NEH ever kept track of the number of volumes that physically went back on the shelves after their contents entered the Paradiso of spools (though I didn't put it that way), and whether the NEH required its grant recipients to provide any counts or percentages of physical books discarded or disbound as part of their project reports. "We have not done so" was Farr's written reply. "NEH has never taken a position on the eventual disposition of brittle volumes that have been microfilmed to preserve their intellectual content. We believe that this is a decision that is more appropriate for the grantee libraries to make."

The most confidently flourished post-microfilm discard percentage that I have come across was offered by Carla Montori, head of preservation at the University of Michigan, in a posting to the Preservation Administrators Discussion Group. Montori writes:

> Analysis of 15 years of disposition decisions [at Michigan] indicates that something less than 40% of brittle originals are

> withdrawn after reformatting into or replacement by a stable format copy.

Michigan has a long-established microfilming program, begun by Verner Clapp's close friend Frederick Wagman. Perhaps, I thought, this forty-percent figure would make a good conservative estimate?

I ran it by Ellen McCrady, editor of the *Abbey Newsletter.* She said she had no way of knowing, since libraries weren't eager to make that sort of information public, but that it seemed on the low side. "I would guess that forty percent were saved whole," she said. She told me to check the Association of Research Libraries' annual preservation statistics, which might offer some clues. So I ordered a copy of the latest year then available, 1996–1997.

You can learn all kinds of things from this staple-bound purple booklet. Harvard got $1.3 million in outside preservation money (a good chunk of it from the NEH); Boston Public Library got $3,522. Michigan digitized 1,350 "bound volumes" (they were no longer bound by the time they were digitized), and microfilmed 5,547. You can check how many volumes were deacidified, filmed, scanned, commercially bound, boxed, and treated to three different intensities of physical repair at each of over a hundred really big U.S. and Canadian libraries. Since 1988, according to these figures, which for technical reasons under-report actual levels, libraries microfilmed about one million volumes, most of the work paid for by the federal government. But you will not find in this purple book of preservation statistics—perhaps because the Association of Research Libraries is too tactful to demand it of its members—how many volumes were in fact preserved, in the old-fashioned sense.

I asked Julia Blixrud, one of the people who compiled the numbers, whether there had ever been an attempt to track how many books survived reformatting. She said she didn't think so. Was that possibly, I said, because it would be embarrassing to poll members for such a statistic? "That I don't know, I've not been a preservation librarian," Blixrud said. "I would guess that it was not as much of interest to us." And she added, "The political nature of this survey has been to assist in some ways in getting funds to continue to do the preservation microfilming." She told me to talk to Jutta Reed-Scott, who with Harvard's Jan Merrill-Oldham designed the survey in the late eighties.

"That unfortunately is a figure we did not collect," said Reed-Scott. "I am not aware that anyone collected that. It would be a really difficult figure to keep track of. There are so many variables that go into returning items to the shelf." (Oh, piffle. It would be no more difficult to track this figure than to track any other.) I asked Reed-Scott if the need for such a number had ever come up during the planning stage. "I do not recall that that ever arose as a question," she said. I told her that my sense from talking to people was that there had been a sudden drop-off in preservational disbinds and discards around 1993. (The year, incidentally, of Thomas Tanselle's book-burning piece.) "I think that's exactly what happened," Reed-Scott said. Now the problem was scanning. "That is the arena where the issue will become much more difficult than the preservation-microfilming arena," she said. "You can film from a bound volume, with some difficulty, but it is certainly possible. It becomes far more difficult to scan from a bound volume, because obviously you get the distortion, if the margin is narrow." In the evolution of scanning theory and praxis, we're about where we were in 1953 in microfilm.

There is a further fact to note about Jutta Reed-Scott. In the seventies, she was not a preservationist at all; she was a hard-core space freer-upper. In 1976, as Jutta Reed, then collections development librarian at MIT, she published a wonderfully cut-and-dried paper for *Microform Review* arguing that if you subscribed to the microfilm of the journal *Daedalus,* for example, and dumped all but current paper issues, you would save $1.35 per year in binding costs. Add to that the "dramatic reduction of storage costs of micropublications over hard copy periodicals," as determined by the formulas

$$\text{storage cost} = \tfrac{1}{2}av(t(t+1))$$

and

$$\text{storage cost} = \tfrac{1}{2}bv(t(t+1))$$

(where a is the yearly cost of storing one bound volume, and b is the yearly cost of storing one volume copied onto microfilm; where t is the storage time in years, and v is the number of volumes per year), and you really begin to save, save, save. Assuming an annual storage cost of $0.38 per journal volume and $0.034 for microfilm, our soi-disant preservationist calculates that if you replaced bound volumes of *Scientific American* with microcopies, you would over a twenty-year period save over *$145* in storage costs. (Of course, you will no longer be able to interpret *Scientific American*'s color-keyed illustrations properly, and over that same period you'll have paid University Microfilms a fortune for the microfilm subscription.) "In the long run microforms will increase the storage capacity of present library buildings and can postpone the construction of additional storage space," Jutta Reed unwaveringly writes.

Perhaps it isn't so surprising, then, that Reed-Scott exhibited an indifference, a listless lack of curiosity, as to how many original volumes were saved after they were microfilmed, since in an earlier life she believed in the "decisive economic advantage" of the dump-and-replace method without any consideration of embrittlement whatsoever.

CHAPTER 33

Leaf Masters

The NEH didn't know and didn't care; the national preservation statistics were mute on the subject; but still I kept an eye out for estimates and demi-disclosures, because I believe we need to know how much was lost. In 1984, David Stam, then director of the New York Public Library, wrote that "a heavy proportion of our embrittled material has been discarded after microfilming" (by "our" he meant in the United States), and he said that "the practice of disposal has often included materials that could have been adequately preserved in the original." There is, however, no way to quantify the words "heavy proportion"—does it mean over half? I called Yale's Paul Conway back and asked him whether a fifty-percent discard figure was a reasonable guess through 1993 or so. He said that "fifty percent rings true" for the years between 1983 to 1993. "But since then libraries are trying a lot harder."

Gary Frost, who was for years in the business of making sumptuous preservation photocopies (sometimes with color-copied title pages) at a place in Texas called Booklab, wrote in 1998:

> If the current compulsion toward digital scanning of library materials is really the dawning of a New Age era of microfilming

> what is the preservation implication? The implication may be the same; that the new technology will be considered a preservation method that results in the discard of library materials. The microfilming process, by one estimate, has resulted in the discard of over 60% of the originals recorded.

Over sixty percent? Was that a reasonable estimate? Gary Frost is an interestingly ambivalent—one almost wants to say "tortured"—soul. He strongly believes that librarians should continue to function as custodians of the "source original." Conservators should "support developments in storage facilities and delivery systems that enable the survival of originals." He told me that Michael Lesk's and Brother Lemberg's idea of discarding millions of books in favor of networked digital page-scans is "a right-wing paramilitary objective—or no, a left-wing paramilitary objective." He regrets the "very strong undercurrent in the USA toward disposability, toward favoring clean copy over soiled original."

But in producing Booklab's fabled preservation photocopies, Frost's team of operators severed spines just as microfilmers would, to get pages to lie flat. Frost gave his *mutilés de guerre* a nice name, though: he called them *leaf masters.* Libraries were supposed to put their pristine, acid-free Booklab photocopies on the shelf and store the soiled leaf masters in cool sanctums, using them like the frozen sperm from great racehorses whenever the circulating photocopy had done too many laps. Originals were not for "eye reading," but for "machine reading"—for the infinite propagation of copies. ("I've never seen a book I couldn't copy," Frost said, when I asked about the extent of crumblement or dusthood.) Not so many libraries were interested in storing boxed or shrink-wrapped bundles of loose pages, though; the leaf masters often went in the compost pile.

"We've cut two or three hundred thousand books here in flat platen work," he told me. "It is what it is. I know that the types of materials that we were working from were such combat-battered brittle materials anyway that there wasn't any circulation left in them. I also realize the dilemma of in any way projecting a preservation agenda based on destruction, even though that's been possible in a couple of weird ways."

I wondered what percentage of the disbound Booklab books were kept by libraries afterward. If I was to go to a university and ask to see their disbound, shrink-wrapped Booklab originals, I said, what would my chances be of seeing something?

"I would say that your chances are probably very minimal," Frost answered. "Certainly in the ten- to twenty-percent category of stuff that we did. I could be wrong." The libraries at the Metropolitan Museum of Art don't throw away their leaf masters, according to Frost. "They don't believe in brittle books. That's almost seven or eight or nine libraries right there, in that one museum. But that's kind of the exception that proves the rule that most of these would be thrown away."

I asked him who had been the verbal source original for the estimate that microfilming had resulted in the discard of "over sixty percent" of the books recorded. John Dean, of Cornell, had come up with that a long time ago, Frost said.

"I don't think so," said John Dean, when I reached him. "I have no basis for that kind of number at all." Dean did confirm a discussion in 1993 (at an annual meeting of the NEH's Office of Preservation) of how much to keep after microfilming. "Faculty and bibliographers and curators were saying, 'Hey, if you're going to throw this stuff away, I don't want it filming.' " The idea that libraries should now digitize their goods so that other libraries can throw out their copies is one he attributes to "the brutalist school."

The oddity here is that Cornell has been a hotbed, or testbed, of crypto-brutalists—but that's a matter for a later chapter. Perhaps the sixty-percent estimate Gary Frost had in mind came not from Cornell's John Dean, who disowned it, but from Yale's Gay Walker. Walker wrote in 1989: "Based on a non-scientific survey of the field, the majority of filmed volumes are subsequently withdrawn from collections." The survey to which Walker refers was eventually distributed as part of an informational compilation called *Brittle Books Programs,* produced by the Association of Research Libraries. "Of all responding libraries," write the surveyors, Jan Merrill-Oldham and Gay Walker, "nearly half discard 90 percent or more of the original copies of volumes after they have been reproduced." Almost a quarter of the thirty-five libraries surveyed kept none of the volumes after reformatting, they found; two libraries declined to answer. Walker does not volunteer Yale's own percentage; but included in this compilation is another 1986 document in which she writes that items at Yale designated for withdrawal should "have all ownership marks removed or marked out and a 'discard' stamp applied to the inside front flyleaf and the inside back cover as well as the title page . . . items are sent to the Gifts and Exchanges Unit when a truckload has accumulated." In a 1987 article for *Restaurator,* Walker offers another hint: "In the great majority of cases, the very deteriorated, brittle, disbound original is withdrawn from the collection and often placed in a library booksale for a minimal amount." Walker was "Arts of the Book Librarian" at Yale when she wrote that.

Walker and Merrill-Oldham's survey is, in any event, the best estimate I've found of discarding practices at the height of the brittle-books agitation. To be cautious, though, let's say that only half of the books, not (as Walker says) "the majority," were thrown out. Between 1988 and 1993, the NEH paid for the microfilming of about 500,000 books, and the Library of Congress's Preservation Microfilming Office filmed another 150,000 volumes or so. At a fifty-percent retention rate (which is, for the Library of Congress of that era, extremely conservative), 325,000 books were removed from U.S. libraries as a direct result of federal money. Add the newspapers to that.

But the losses exceed that number. In the same paper, Walker wrote that the "filmed copy must be a perfect one—other copies of the book will be discarded upon the strength of the listing." Does this still seem strange—that libraries would cast aside their own copies of books simply because they have been judged by others worthy of filmed preservation? It was never a strange idea within the preservation movement. Recall that Robert Hayes had built it into his cost-benefit analysis: the creation of a film would have a multiplier effect around the country, triggering local bibliectomies. (Sometimes a library would buy the microfilm from the filming library to replace its original; but sometimes the library would simply feel better about deselecting its original in the knowledge that preservation-quality microfilm was potentially there to be bought, even if it wasn't actually bought.) Hayes figured that five physical copies would disappear from libraries for every book filmed, but let's say, more conservatively, that from 1988 through 1993 fifty percent of the filmed books spawned three physical disappearances—one at the filming library and two of duplicates somewhere else. And let's say that none of the remaining fifty percent (i.e., those books that were physically reshelved post-microfilming) prompted any parallel discards elsewhere—highly unlikely, but also conservative. That triples the loss-estimate and brings it to 975,000 books. Almost all these books were old and out of print, so the replacement cost, assuming that these original editions could be found on the used-book market, and ignoring costs of recataloging and reprocessing, is high—say (again conservatively) forty dollars a book. As a very rough, lowball guess, thirty-nine million dollars' worth of originals left our nation's libraries, thanks to federal largesse. It's as if the National Park Service felled vast wild tracts of pointed firs and replaced them with plastic Christmas trees.

It isn't just accessible physical copies of books that we lost during that awful period; we also lost content. "A major concern about filming is that many filmed titles have missing pages, even though the film was inspected," Gay Walker wrote—the Ace comb effect applies to books, too. (That is, when libraries replace several differently damaged copies of a book with microfilm of the same copy of a book, and the microfilm turns out to lack something, we're less well off, informationally as well as artifactually, than we were before the program began.) In the late eighties, the University of California at Berkeley sent test shipments of thirty to fifty books each to five top-notch microfilm labs, telling them that they wanted "the highest quality film of the books sent to them, totally reproducing the text of the volumes." Even in the test batch, one of the five filmers was discovered to have missed pages. Other problems continue to crop up: a 1993 audit of microfilm from Ohio State, Yale, and Harvard found that one third of the film collections "did not resolve to the established ANSI [American National Standards Institute] resolution standards"; the auditors hypothesized that "some camera or processing settings were incorrect."

Helmut Bansa, editor of *Restaurator,* told me that he has heard that some U.S. libraries "want to have the originals back." He wouldn't give details, though. "I can only report that some American libraries that have done this microfilming and throwing away now regret to have done that." Which ones in particular? "Even if I would know I wouldn't tell you," Bansa said.

CHAPTER 34

Turn the Pages Once

"This is all about Pat Battin's vision of a digital library," Randy Silverman, Utah's conservator, said to me: "One digital library fits all." Microfilm is really only a passing spasm, a "cost-effective buffer technology" (as one of the newsletters of the Commission on Preservation and Access has it) that will carry us closer to the far digital shore. Silverman sums up the Commission's thinking as follows: "How to fund technology in a time of barely increasing acquisition funds? And even if all the scholars have monitors, it's like having a color TV in 1964. What are you going to watch? Somehow we've got to get some goods online. Preservation was a natural cause to help justify the conversion to an international electronic library. Battin played it for all it was worth." If you unwrapped three million word-mummies—if you mined them from the stacks, shredded them, and cooked their brittle bookstock with the help of steady disaster-relief money—you could pump the borderless bitstream full of rich new content.

In 1994, shortly before Battin retired from the Commission, her newsletter published a special "Working Paper on the Future." Its authorship is credited to the Commission's board and staff, but it reads like one of her own heartfelt manifestos. "The next step for our nation's libraries and archives is an affordable and orderly transition into the digital library of the future," the working paper contends. All "information repositories," large and small, private and public, "must" make this transition. (Why must they all?) We're going to need continuing propaganda for it to be successful, too: "Changing a well-entrenched paradigm requires frequent and public articulation of the new mind set required in many arenas." And, yes, there will be "high initial costs" involved in making the transition; these may threaten to "paralyze initiative," unless we make a "thoughtful" comparison to what is described as "the rapidly escalating costs of traditional library storage and services."

Doesn't that sound a lot like Michael Lesk—once of Bellcore, now at the National Science Foundation handing out bags of seed money for digital library projects, who believes that libraries would save money if they got rid of the vast majority of their nineteenth-century duplicates in favor of middling-resolution networked facsimiles, and who says he routinely tells libraries that they might not want to repair their buildings, since they could digidump most of what their stacks held instead?

One reason Battin sounds like Lesk is that she worked closely with him for several years; she invited him to serve, along with a number of other resolute anti-artifactualists, on what has proved to be her most consequential committee: the Technology Assessment Advisory Committee. Lesk wrote the TAAC committee's first report, "Image Formats for Preservation and Access": "Because microfilm to digital image conversion is going to be relatively straightforward," Lesk mispredicted, "and the primary cost of either microfilming or digital scanning is in selecting the book, handling it, and turning the pages, librarians should use either method as they can manage, expecting to convert to digital form over the next decade." He and another non-librarian, Stuart Lynn—at the time Cornell's vice president for information technologies (who retired in 1999 from the chief information officership of the University of California, where he kept an eye on digital-library projects partially funded by

Michael Lesk's National Science Foundation)—took the position in the advisory committee's discussions that the costs of digital conversion and storage had dropped to the point (Verner Clapp's long-dreamed-of point) that it was almost as cheap to scan-and-discard as to build.

Michael Lesk is uncharismatic and plodding; Stuart Lynn, however, is an Oxford-educated mathematician with a measure of brusque charm. He and his onetime colleague Anne Kenney (currently Cornell's assistant director of preservation) became, with the financial support of Battin's Commission, the Mellon Foundation (always ready to help), and Xerox Corporation, the progenitors of some of the most successful digital-library projects of the nineties. Stuart Lynn believed in an economic model in which digital preservation would be, as he told me, "self-funding." If you were able to "funge immortality dollars into operating dollars"—that is, if you assumed a certain (fairly high) per-item cost for physical book storage, and if you ejected the original books once you digitized them and relied on virtual storage, and if you sold facsimiles-on-demand produced on a Xerox DocuTech high-speed printer (Lynn was serving on an advisory panel at Xerox at the time), you would, so his hopeful model suggested, come out more or less even—and you'd have all the emoluments of networked access.

But digital storage, with its eternally morphing and data-orphaning formats, was not then and is not now an accepted archival-storage medium. A true archive must be able to tolerate years of relative inattention; scanned copies of little-used books, however, demand constant refreshment, software-revision-upgrading, and new machinery, the long-term costs of which are unknowable but high. The relatively simple substitution of electronic databases for paper card catalogs, and the yearly maintenance of these databases, has very nearly blown the head gaskets of many libraries. They have smiled bravely through their pain, while hewing madly away at staffing and book-buying budgets behind the scenes; and there is still greater pain to come. Since an average book, whose description in an online catalog takes up less than a page's worth of text, is about two hundred pages long, a fully digitized library collection requires a live data-swamp roughly two hundred times the size of its online catalog. And that's just for an old-fashioned full-text ASCII digital library—not one that captures the appearance of the original typeset pages. If you want to see those old pages as scanned images, the storage and transmission requirements are going to be, say, twenty-five times higher than that of plain ASCII text—Lesk says it's a hundred times higher, but let's assume advances in compression and the economies of shared effort—which means that the overhead cost of a digital library that delivers the look (if not the feel) of former pages at medium resolution is going to run about five thousand times the overhead of the digital catalog. If your library spends three hundred thousand dollars per year to maintain its online catalog, it will have to come up with $1.5 billion a year to maintain copies of those books on its servers in the form of remotely accessible scanned files. If you want color scans, as people increasingly do, because they feel more attuned to the surrogate when they can see the particular creamy hue of the paper or the brown tint of the ink, it'll cost you a few billion more than that. These figures are very loose and undoubtedly wrong—but the truth is that nobody has ever underestimated the cost of any computer project, and the costs will be yodelingly high in any case. "Our biggest misjudgment was underestimating the cost of automation," William Welsh told an interviewer in 1984. "Way back when a consultant predicted the cost of an automated systems approach, we thought it was beyond our means. Later, we went ahead, not realizing that even the first cost predictions were greatly underestimated. The costs of software and maintenance just explode the totals."

Things that cost a lot, year after year, are subject, during lean decades, to deferred maintenance or outright abandonment. If you put some books and papers in a locked storage closet and come back fifteen years later, the documents will be readable without the typesetting systems and printing presses and binding machines that produced them; if you lock up computer media for the same interval (some once-standard eight-inch floppy disks from the mid-eighties, say), the documents they hold will be extremely difficult to reconstitute. We will certainly get more adept at long-term data storage, but even so, a collection of live book-facsimiles on a computer network is like a family of elephants at a zoo: if the zoo runs out of money for hay and bananas, for vets and dung-trucks, the elephants will sicken and die.

This is an alternative route to a point that Walt Crawford and Michael Gorman make very well in their snappy 1995 book *Future Libraries: Dreams, Madness, and Reality.* It would take, Crawford and Gorman estimate, about 168 gigabytes of memory, after compression, to store one year's worth of page-images of *The New Yorker,* scanned at moderate resolution, in color; thus, if you wanted to make two decades of old *New Yorker*s accessible in an electronic archive, you would consume more memory than OCLC uses to hold its entire ASCII bibliographic database. "No amount of handwaving, mumbo-jumbo, or blithe assumptions that the future will answer all problems can disguise the plain fact that society cannot afford anything even approaching universal conversion," Crawford and Gorman write. "We have not the money or time to do the conversion and cannot provide the storage."

E-futurists of a certain sort—those who talk dismissively of books as tree-corpses—sometimes respond to observations about digital expense and impermanency by shrugging and saying that if people want to keep reading some electronic copy whose paper source was trashed, they'll find the money to keep it alive on whatever software and hardware wins out in the market. This is the use-it-or-lose-it argument, and it is a deadly way to run a culture. Over a few centuries, library books (and newspapers and journals) that were ignored can become suddenly interesting, and heavily read books, newspapers, and journals can drop way down in the charts; one of the important functions, and pleasures, of writing history is that of cultural tillage, or soil renewal: you trowel around in unfashionable holding places for things that have lain untouched for decades to see what particularities they may yield to a new eye. We mustn't model the digital library on the day-to-day operation of a single human brain, which quite properly uses-or-loses, keeps uppermost in mind what it needs most often, and does not refresh, and eventually forgets, what it very infrequently considers—after all, the principal reason groups of rememberers invented writing and printing was to record accurately what they sensed was otherwise likely to be forgotten.

Mindful of the unprovenness of long-term digital storage, yet eager to spend large amounts of money right away, Lesk, Lynn, Battin, and the Technology Assessment Advisory Committee adopted Warren Haas's position: microfilm strenuously in the short term, digitize from the microfilm (rather than from originals) in the fullness of time. *Turn the pages once* was the TAAC's motto. Microfilm has, Stuart Lynn noted in 1992, higher resolution and superior archival quality, and we can convert later to digital images at "only a small increment of the original cost" of the microfilming. He sums up: "The key point is, either way, we can have our cake and eat it, too."

As ill luck would have it, the cake went stale quickly: people just don't want to scan from microfilm if they can avoid it. It isn't cheap, for one thing: Stuart Lynn's "small incremental cost" is somewhere around $40 per roll—that is, to digitize one white box of preexisting microfilm, without any secondary OCR processing, you are going to spend half as much again to convert from the film to the digital file as it cost you to produce the film in the first place. If you must manually adjust for variations in the contrast of the microfilm or in the size of the images, the cost climbs dramatically from there. And resolution is, as always, an obstacle: if you want to convert a newspaper page that was shrunk on film to a sixteenth of its original size, your scanner, lasering gamely away on each film-frame, is going to have to resolve to 9,600 dots per inch in order to achieve an "output resolution" of six hundred dots per inch. This is at or beyond the outer limits of microfilm scanners now.

And six hundred dots per inch doesn't do justice to the tiny printing used on the editorial pages of nineteenth-century newspapers anyway. In an experiment called Project Open Book, Paul Conway demonstrated that it was possible to scan and reanimate digitally two thousand shrunken microfilm copies of monographs from Yale's diminished history collection (1,000 volumes of Civil War history, 200 volumes of Native American history, 400 volumes on the history of Spain before the Civil War, and 400 volumes having to do with the histories of communism, socialism, and fascism)—but Conway was working from post-1983, preservation-quality microfilm made at the relatively low reduction-ratios employed for books. "We've pretty much figured out how to do books and serials and things up to about the size of, oh, eleven by seventeen, in various formats, whether it's microfilm or paper," Conway says. "We've kind of got that one nailed down, and the affordable technology is there to support digitization from either the original document or from its microfilm copy. But once you get larger than that, the technology isn't there yet, [and] the testing of the existing technology to find out where it falls off is not there." Conway hasn't been able to put these scanned-from-microfilm books on the Web yet. "The files are not available now," he wrote me,

> because we chose (unwisely it now turns out) to build the system around a set of proprietary software and hardware products marketed by the Xerox Corporation. Our relationship with Xerox soured when the corporation would not give us the tools we needed to export the image and index data out of the Xerox system into an open, non-proprietary system. About two years ago, we decided not to upgrade the image management system that Xerox built for us. Almost immediately we started having a series of system troubles that resulted in us abandoning (temporarily) our goal of getting the books online. . . . In the meantime, the images are safe on a quite stable medium (for now anyway).

The medium is magneto-optical disk; the project was paid for in part by the National Endowment for the Humanities.

Newspapers have pages that are about twenty-three by seventeen inches—twice as big as the upper limits Conway gives. The combination of severe reduction ratios, small type, dreadful photography, and image fading in the microfilmed inventory make scanning from much of it next to impossible; one of the great sorrows of newspaper history is that the most important U.S. papers (the New York *Herald Tribune,* the New York *World,* the *Chicago Tribune,* etc.) were microfilmed earliest and least well, because they would sell best to other libraries. We may in time be able to apply Hubble-telescopic software corrections to mitigate some of microfilm's focal foibles, but a state-of-the-art full-color multimegabyte digital copy of a big-city daily derived, not from the original but from black-and-white Recordak microfilm, is obviously never going to be a thing of beauty. And no image-enhancement software can know what lies behind a pox of redox, or what was on the page that a harried technician missed.

In the late eighties, the Commission on Preservation and Access wanted an all-in-one machine that would reformat in every direction. It commissioned Xerox to develop specifications for "a special composing reducing camera capable of digitizing 35mm film, producing film in difference reductions (roll and fiche), paper, and creating CD-ROM products." As with Verner Clapp's early hardware-development projects at the Council on Library Resources, this one didn't get very far. The master digitizers—Stuart Lynn, Anne Kenney, and others at Cornell, and the Mellon Foundation's JSTOR team, for example—realized almost immediately that they shouldn't waste time with microfilm if they didn't have to. "The closer you are to the original, the better the quality," Anne Kenney told me. "So all things being equal, if you have microfilm and the original, you scan from the original." JSTOR came to the same conclusion:

> One interesting discovery that we made in the process of obtaining bids is that working from paper copies of back issues of journals, rather than from microfilm, produces higher quality results and is—to our surprise—considerably cheaper. This conclusion has important implications beyond JSTOR.

It sure does have important implications: it means that most of the things that libraries chopped and chucked in the cause of filming died for nothing, since the new generation of facsimilians may, unless we can make them see reason, demand to do it all over again.

CHAPTER 35

Suibtermanean Convumision

The second major wave of book wastage and mutilation, comparable to the microfilm wave but potentially much more extensive, is just beginning. At the upper echelons of the University of California's library system, a certain "Task Force on Collection Management Strategies in the Digital Environment" met early in 1999 to begin thinking about scanning and discarding components of its multi-library collections. Two of the librarians "anticipated resistance to the loss of printed resources, especially by faculty in the Humanities, but agreed that the conversation had to begin." Others prudently pointed out that the "dollar and space savings would likely be minimal for the foreseeable future and should not be used to justify budget reductions or delays in needed building improvements." Still others wanted to be sure that the organizers of the program arranged things so that the "campuses which discarded their copies would not be disadvantaged."

For some years, Cornell's Anne Kenney has been a leader of the scan clan. She knows (as she told the attendees at a Mellon Foundation-sponsored conference in 1997) that "the costs of selecting, converting, and making digital information available can be staggering." Since it is so horribly expensive, she believes that the only way libraries will be able to pay for it is if "digital collections can alleviate the need to support full traditional libraries at the local level." Therefore, over the past decade, in its various grant-funded scanning projects, Cornell University has snarfed its way through a banquet of old material, employing the language of earnest preservationism whenever it was expedient. (The books are "deteriorating," "rapidly self-destructing," etc.) They have disbound a collection of what are in some cases extremely rare math books of a century ago (and printed up germ-free facsimiles of them on a Xerox DocuTech printer), and books on Peruvian guano and butterflies and forestry. The paper facsimiles are a way of easing the transition to the digital library: "Conceivably, this may at some point allow librarians to propose other service alternatives as a substitute for traditional shelf storage," says a footnote to the report—meaning that to use a book, you would have it printed out on demand or you would read it on-screen. Of course, if the book had to be printed out, there was an opportunity to generate a little revenue, too: "There may also be opportunities to underwrite some of the costs of preservation through the sale of facsimile editions."

A few years later, Cornell got Mellon money to scan original runs of nineteenth-century American magazines like *Scribner's, Scientific American, Harper's,* and *Atlantic Monthly.* A wonderful nineteenth-century monthly magazine, replete with many hundreds of engravings, called *The Manufacturer and Builder* (already microfilmed in 1989 by the Northeast Document Conservation Center), was unmade by Cornell as one of its contributions to the digital Making of America project. (The Making of America was conceived by Stuart Lynn and others at Cornell in part to alleviate the problem of the "escalating cost of storage and the lack of adjacent building space.") Ah, but it's searchable, you may say, and neither the microfilm nor the original issues are: it's worth destroying an illustrated run of *The Manufacturer and Builder* to get a fully searchable copy of it up on the Web. Yes, it is searchable, but because the type of the original is small and the resolution of the scanning is only six hundred dots per inch, the image-processing software doesn't have enough information to chew on. As a result, while the images Cornell offers are legible, the OCR text available for your searches sometimes speaks in a language entirely its own. Here, for example, is Cornell's searchable text of the beginning of an 1883 article about a subterranean convulsion in Java:

> As intimated in our editomial remnarks last month, the gm-eat suibtermanean convumision imi, Java gmoxvs mom-c appalling as time facts relating to it become better kumouvum, antI time meal magnitude of time tlisturbance can be mucasumably compiehended.

"It xviii be unnecessamy," the writer continues, "for us to enter into further details of time catastrophic, save to remark that all we mepouted of time changes in time configumation of time hind lmadi time suiruounding ocemun bottom, has beemi comifimmed, amid much mom-c extensive changes noticed." An explanatory note about viewing the plain text derived from Making of America page-images says that "OCR accuracy is high but varies from page-to-page depending on a number of variables"; the note blames the errors on the "brittle, faded, and foxed" originals, saying that proofreading "would be very expensive and time consuming." A production note preceding the OCR text says that Cornell did the work in order "to preserve the informational content of the deteriorated original." The "best available copy" of the original was used, of course. The originals were disbound, we learn elsewhere, "due to the brittle nature of many of the items." I asked Anne Kenney how the library determined brittleness; she said they used the double-fold test. "I'm not as wedded to retaining, at each site, the original sources as some may be," she said.

It's extremely kind of Cornell's librarians to put these images on the Web, and one can't blame them for the untutoredness of their OCR software (which despite its sometimes garbled output unquestionably helps researchers in their truffle hunting), but it's truly a shame, after the decades of havoc wrought by microfilming, that pages bearing such a wealth of engravings are once again needlessly dying to feed the sausage factory. The faculty and students of Cornell were not asked whether they wanted valuable runs of nineteenth-century magazines sacrificed for this experiment. "These things were never aired out in a public forum," says Joel Silbey, a Cornell historian who served on an advisory board to the library. "I was stunned when I first heard that they would have to disembowel the things." He began to "express consternation." The response of Anne Kenney and her colleagues was, according to Silbey, that "this was the only way it could be done and that it had to be done or we would lose things." Which is a curious rationale, since the intellectual content of *The Manufacturer and Builder,* along with many other Making of America titles, was already backed up on microfilm when Cornell began their work—the emergency last-ditch "rescue" of this supposedly at-risk title had already happened. After some discussion, several of the disbound runs were sent to Rare Books, where they are or will be boxed. It was too late for *The Manufacturer and Builder,* though.

So the machine-induced loss begins all over again. But it can be stopped: there is no reason why one medium must mandatorily stab another one in the back. John Warnock, head of Adobe Software and a book collector of catholic tastes and deep pockets, discovered that he could create extremely fine-grained, full-color electronic copies of his own antiquarian books, using an overhead camera with a four-by-five-inch digital camera-back, without doing anything to them more injurious than turning their pages. He founded Octavo Corporation, which has published searchable facsimiles of early editions of Robert Hooke, William Harvey, Franklin, Galileo, Newton, and Copernicus; Octavo recently finished photographing one of the Folger Library's First Folio editions of Shakespeare. It takes several minutes for the array of sensors in the camera to process the detail in one double-page spread, each of which consumes one hundred and forty megabytes of storage; the resulting scans have a serene luminosity and depth of detail. I described to Warnock the Cornell project of digitizing and throwing away rare nineteenth-century math books and replacing them with black-and-white printouts at six hundred dots per inch. "I have no sympathy with that, I'm afraid," Warnock said.

At some point, maybe not so long from now, a company such as Octavo may want to scan a volume of newspapers, at high resolution, nondestructively, as if it were a fragile sixteenth-century folio. The president of the company will make inquiries at a library or historical society in his city. He will be led into a room that holds four hundred gray cabinets of microfilm. "But we need the originals," the company president will say. "Where are the originals?"

CHAPTER 36

Honest Disagreement

On September 29, 1999, President Clinton gave Patricia Battin a National Medal for the Humanities. "Patricia Battin is saving history," Clinton said at the ceremony. "The high acidic content of paper threatens to destroy millions of old books, but she has led the national campaign to raise awareness about this challenge and preserve the genius of the past." Clinton described Battin's efforts to "transfer information from so-called 'brittle books' to microfilm and optical disks." More than 770,000 books have "already been preserved," Clinton said. He ended: "Thank you for saving the knowledge of the past for the children of tomorrow."

Since Battin began campaigning for the cause in 1987, the National Endowment for the Humanities has given away more than $115 million to libraries for microfilming—seventy-some million dollars for books in addition to the forty-five million assigned to the participants in the U.S. Newspaper Program. "I think the NEH newspaper program is incredible," Battin said to me. "We have access to resources that we would never have if they had been left alone. I think we will have the same with the Brittle Books Program." The reason that the newspapers were thrown away after they were filmed, Battin explained to me, was that "they were crumbling during the process—I mean, they were breaking and everything during the process of filming them."

No. Even if things did instantly crumble after their final farewell wave of photographic transubstantiation—and they don't—that would explain only the discarding of those newspapers that were actually filmed, and not the practically universal dumpage of the same runs at other libraries. I suggested to her that microfilm also saves space.

"But I don't think that saving space was the issue," Battin remarkably replied. "Not ever in my experience. I would say we all went into microfilming with great reluctance."

When Battin was head of Columbia's libraries, one of her senior colleagues was Pamela Darling. Darling was a cheerfully unrepentant thrower-outer. "Think about space costs," she argued in *Microform Review:* if a library was to replace half of its volumes with microfilm, "existing shelf space would last almost twice as long." Darling advised readers of *Library Journal* to "keep re-examining your librarian's hoarding instinct." If you don't really want something enough to pay for its repair, then

> get rid of it! Give it to another library *if* it needs it and can care for it; sell it to a collector or dealer if there are enough pieces left to sell; or—horror of horrors—put it in the trash can.

If we don't start throwing things out, Darling insisted, "the central stacks of all major libraries will soon be condemned as unsanitary landfill—the world's intellectual garbage dumps." Darling was the head of Columbia's preservation department when she wrote these words. Later she was a special consultant for Peter Sparks's National Preservation Program Office; the National Endowment for the Humanities paid her to develop training programs and a self-study manual for preservation planning.

Battin herself was of the opinion that it "may well be cheaper to support access than large real estate holdings and service personnel to house and manage rapidly growing collections of artifacts." And yet to me she said, in the sincerest possible voice, "I don't think it's your librarians that have ever tried to miniaturize in order to save space. I think it hurt most of us as much as it did any scholar to have to make these decisions, but we had the responsibility." Later, however, when I asked her directly why a given book couldn't just resume its former place in a library's collection after it was "preserved," she said that "you have to look at the cost of maintaining this on the shelf." Then she seemed to sense a self-contradiction; she said: "And in that regard, space does become a factor in making the decision. But it is not the factor that led one to microfilm in the first place. I think that's very important, to make that distinction."

I asked her about Thomas Tanselle's proposal to store any post-preservational rejects in a publicly financed repository. "Tom has presented this to me in public meetings before," Battin said. "And I don't think the economics have been worked out." (She and her colleagues managed to work out the economics of a hundred million dollars' worth of microfilming; surely figuring out how to devote ten million dollars to the foundation of a national repository is not beyond their talents.) Tanselle, she said, "represents a fairly small group of scholars for whom this is a very passionate issue. I think the vast number of scholars would rather have the access that we were trying to provide."

And what access is that? How has the Brittle Books Program furthered access to anything? In the case of newspapers on film, you can mail around the spools, which is a convenience, since the newspaper volumes themselves (if they haven't been scrapped) must as a rule stay on site. But books are portable and parcel-postable. Columbia University, alone among world libraries, owns a microfilm copy of Francis de Croisset's memoir of Robert de Flers, which it once owned in the original. I now own the original, because Pamela Darling, or someone at Columbia's preservation department, gave it to Patricia Battin, who gave it to me. In 1985, everyone at Columbia had access to the original book; now I do. (Columbia can have the book back anytime.)

"Access," as employed by practicing retrievalists, does not mean physical access. The ability to summon words from distant, normally unreachable sources, which can be a fine thing for scholarship, is being linked to the compulsory removal of local physical access, which is a terrible thing for scholarship. Battin wrote once that "the value, in intellectual terms, of the proximity of the book to the user has never been satisfactorily established." No wonder scholars like Thomas Tanselle opposed her: she was determined to make it more difficult for them to do their work.

"We have differed from the very beginning," Battin says of Tanselle. "It's just an honest disagreement."

Speaking of honesty, late in our conversation I asked Battin what the thinking was behind the idea that books were "turning to dust."

She looked puzzled. "I guess I don't understand," she said. "They were. Are you thinking it's hyperbole?"

I said I didn't know quite what the phrase meant.

"Basically what we meant was they were crumbling," Battin explained. "I think we used 'crumbling.' 'Crumbling books' was what I remember much more that we used rather than 'turning to dust.' "

In 1995, in testimony offered to Congress on behalf of the Association of Research Libraries, the Commission on Preservation and Access, and the National Humanities Alliance, Battin said, without qualification, that before 1988 (that is, before "the massive salvation effort" of the full-scale brittle-books initiative) "millions of books were crumbling and turning to dust on shelves in libraries and archives. . . . Surveys confirmed that nearly 80 million books were threatened with such destruction."

I brought up Peter Waters and his question of whether any library anywhere had a substantial inventory of losses caused by brittle books crumbling to dust. In response, Battin patted the marbled boards of Croisset's memoir. "This was withdrawn," she explained. "That's what we did. That's our inventory—what's been withdrawn."

The book she had given me—its pages quite intact well over

a decade after the microfilming company disbound it—qualified as an example of a book that was crumbling to dust? Had she possibly exaggerated somewhat?

"I don't think the statistics were exaggerated," Battin answered carefully. She said that Sidney Yates, the congressman, used to call her up saying "I need to know this and I need to know that." Battin finally told him, "We've got the best information we can get. We can either wait ten years, and do careful counts, and lose more, or we can go on with these figures." In other words, it's an emergency because our statistics tell us so, and we have to go with the statistics that confirm that it is an emergency because since it is an emergency we have no time to waste gathering other statistics that might indicate that it isn't an emergency, so please give us seventeen million dollars right now.

Battin finally said to me: "You probably are quite right that 'turning to dust' may well be hyperbole, as a way to catch the imagination of people."

CHAPTER 37

We Just Kind of Keep Track

I, obviously, have a different view of the Brittle Books Program and the U.S. Newspaper Program than Patricia Battin does. The Newspaper Program, in particular, has, in my opinion, drained beauty and color and meaning from the landscape of the knowable past in ways that are reminiscent of what happened to the English countryside as a result of the government-financed destruction of the hedgerows in the fifties and sixties—and runs of daily newspapers, unlike rows of hawthorns, can't be replanted. But after more than a year of interviewing librarians, I am aware that many of them don't agree with me (although some do). I talked to Robert Dowd, who coordinates a subset of the Newspaper Program out of an office at the New York State Library in Albany. Dowd said: "There are cases of course when we are going to find the microfilm, it is not any good, and the papers from which the microfilm is produced are gone, because they were disposed of, and there's absolutely nothing you can do about that."

We have, I said to Dowd, lost intellectual content as a direct result of our massive effort to preserve it.

"I'm not going to disagree with you," Dowd replied. "It's

absolutely true, we have, and it's unfortunate. What's the other option, we don't try? That's obviously not the way to go."

But that *is* the way to go. When trying does far more harm than not trying, don't try. Go slow. Keep what you have.

"Unless someone sits down with the papers to be considered for disposal, and compares issue by issue, perhaps even page by page," there is no way to be sure that issues aren't being lost, Dowd said.

Since that isn't happening, I said, the conclusion we must draw, artifactuality aside, is that we have to hold on to the originals.

"Somewhere in the back of my mind I absolutely agree with you," Dowd replied. He told me about some of the New York State Library's volumes of a Buffalo paper that he has saved because, even though there is ostensibly complete microfilm, he happens to know that there are things in the volumes that the microfilm copy lacks.

And yet, though Dowd acknowledges the losses to history, his project cuts up almost all the newspaper volumes they film, for the usual reason: to get the "very, very best image we can" consistent with high-speed production. Were they forbidden to cut the volume, his filmers would have to take precious time moving it around under the camera: "You'd lay it down, then you'd move it over, then you'd flip it over, then you'd move it over—that kind of thing, so the handling becomes a factor." If the library that owns a particular run of newspapers wants them back, their loose leaves are returned; if not, they usually go in the trash. Even the ones that aren't thrown away are the worse for filming: once disbound, newspaper pages don't stay aligned and have less edgewise strength-in-numbers than pages within intact volumes—they are harder to keep safe.

Dennis Hardin supervised work on the U.S. Newspaper Program at the Indiana Historical Society, and he continues to film local papers. "If the library wants them back," Hardin says, "we wrap them up in kraft paper and send them back or take them back, but in a lot of cases, if they were looking to unload them to make more space, we make an agreement with them that we will just discard them." Of the volumes he photographs, "very, very few go back on the shelf."

But there are still runs of interesting Indiana papers—family-owned, small-town papers—that Hardin hasn't been able to get his hands on. "Many publishers do not want to turn over their bound volumes to us," he said. "For one thing, one of our policies here is that we have to take the bindings off. . . . Well, a lot of publishing offices, especially men and women who are elderly who have had the paper in their family all their lives, don't want to see their legacy just taken and torn apart that way." Hardin keeps his eye on these remaining caches of paper. "Having been at it for eighteen years, we are fairly aware of where certain unfilmed collections still reside. I'm still more than twenty years away from retirement, so some of these elderly publishers and county recorders and so forth, we just kind of keep track, and as we are able to gently prod them into doing the right thing with their newspapers before they retire, or maybe leaving their papers to someone who will take care of that for them after they're gone."

I pointed out to Hardin, as I had to others, that dealers make a living buying and selling ex-library wood-pulp newspapers volumes—many seemed to hold up surprisingly well. Hardin replied: "At any given moment, there's lots of it that's still in pretty good shape, but that's not to say that some day, eventually, every one of them will crumble. It is inevitable—it *is* inevitable. And though you may still find bound volumes of papers from the twenties or even earlier—you may find a bound volume from 1912 that still has the *Titanic* story in it in pretty good shape—but as inevitable as the sinking of that ship was, those papers will crumble."

In the summer of 1999, an ex-library bound volume of the New York *Sun* containing issues from April 1 through June 30, 1912, sold for three thousand dollars on eBay: it was in "immaculate" condition and contained weeks of news about the *Titanic* disaster. The sinking of the *Titanic* was not, of course, inevitable—other big ships sailed safely across the Atlantic before and afterward. The reason that ship sank was that human beings in positions of trust made horrible errors of judgment.

CHAPTER 38

In Good Faith

Which brings us back, finally, to the foreign-newspaper collection at the British Library. In August 1999, I got the list of the U.S. papers that the British Library was getting rid of. How could they be saved? In a rush, I formed the American Newspaper Repository, with my mother, my father, and my wife on the board of trustees—they were the only ones I felt I could ask to serve on such short notice. The repository's purpose was, as a lawyer phrased it for the IRS, "to acquire, preserve, and make available to the public, original newspapers of historic and scholarly interest that would otherwise be destroyed or dispersed into private ownership." (I took some satisfaction in seeing the word "preserve" used in its traditional sense.) Having faxed off letters of inquiry to the MacArthur Foundation, the Knight Foundation, and the Getty Foundation, I flew to London a week before the British Library's September 30, 1999, deadline for bids. About forty volumes were set out for inspection by potential purchasers, and I was given a tour of the shelves. I wasn't allowed to take pictures. I suddenly felt, turning the pages of a beautiful *Chicago Tribune* volume from 1909, as if I'd stumbled on a lost, jewel-encrusted city in the jungle, and that curio dealers were waiting for a sign to begin chiseling away at it.

Edmund King, the director of the Newspaper Library, gave me tea in his office. I described to him, at the point of tears, the historical importance of Joseph Pulitzer's *World,* and I asked if there was some way to convince the Library to call off its sale and keep the papers, or to act responsibly by transferring them to a non-profit entity such as the one I'd just started. I explained how the vintage-newspaper market worked in the States, and I told him that there were almost no duplicates of these papers left, and that the duplicates weren't duplicates in any case because of editional variations. The decision to dispose of the foreign papers was made by the board several years earlier, King said. "As things stand, because we have gone to dealers, perhaps the best thing to do is to act as if you are a dealer, and place a bid for the runs."

A few days later, on a Saturday, with the help of Nicolas Barker, editor of *The Book Collector* and a former head of preservation at the British Library, I got in touch with Brian Lang, the library's director, on his cellular phone. (He was waiting in line at a supermarket when I first reached him.) I asked him to call off the sale. "I don't have an answer for you now," Lang said, but he seemed somewhat taken aback and willing to give the problem thought.

Heartened, I got back to the States and faxed Lang a long follow-up letter that I thought would clinch it. "The very best thing for these papers would be for the Newspaper Library to reshelve them carefully, tightly control their use, and keep them safe," I wrote. I acknowledged the library's space difficulties—but perhaps there was a way to turn that problem around, I suggested, and use the present disposal emergency to inspire a major donor to endow a new rare-newspaper storage facility in Colindale. If the library's decision to dispose of the listed papers was firm, then I hoped they would consider donating the papers to the American Newspaper Repository. I listed the members of the repository's advisory board, thinking that some impressive names might help sway him. (Two of the advisers, who have since become trustees, are William Hart, Chairman of the National Trust for Historic Preservation, and Thomas Tanselle, an obvious choice.) I closed the letter by asking Lang again to suspend the September 30 sale, and to "take steps to ensure that this great surviving collection is kept intact for future scholarship."

Lang got the letter, cc'd to Edmund King, on Monday afternoon; Thursday was the deadline for bids. I heard nothing on Tuesday, and on Wednesday morning I started to get nervous. I called Lang's office, and then I faxed a letter to King requesting "that no irrevocable sales or other dispersals of any of the foreign newspapers listed take place at least until I have gotten a response to my letter to Brian Lang." At 5:30 P.M. British time, on the very eve of the deadline, Mike Crump, Director of Reader Services and Collection Development, e-mailed me. Brian Lang was in Estonia, he wrote. "We believe that at this stage we cannot stop the sale of material to dealers who have been examining it in good faith."

There was also the good faith of international (and intergenerational) scholarship to consider, but no matter. By then it was too late to lodge protests with upper-level luminaries. The only thing to do, I realized, if I wanted to save at least some of the papers, was, as Edmund King had suggested, to bid on them myself, on behalf of the American Newspaper Repository. At 1:30 A.M. on September 30, 1999, I faxed in over $50,000 worth of blind bids, distributing the money unequally over every lot that was for sale. (I kept it to around $50,000, because that's how much my wife and I figured we would clear if we liquidated one retirement account and paid taxes and early-withdrawal penalties. If no grant money came through, we planned to buy the papers with that money, and then pay for the shipping and storage of the collection by cashing out the other retirement account.) I bid £9,200 (about $15,000) for the *Herald Tribune* and the same amount for Pulitzer's *World;* £4,875 (about $8,000) for the *Chicago Tribune;* £300 apiece for the St. Louis *Globe-Democrat,* the New Orleans *Times-Picayune,* and the short run of Hearst's *American;* £2,875 for *The New York Times;* and £2,440 for the *San Francisco Chronicle.* And I bid three pounds each for a hundred or so other titles. I stressed that the bids didn't constitute a withdrawal of my plea that the British Library keep the collection or donate it as a whole to the repository, and I asked them to keep in mind, in the event that my bids were below what others offered, that the repository was committed, as dealers were not, to keeping the volumes whole. A day later, on the advice of William Hart, I submitted a second global "preservation bid" equal to the sum of all outstanding high bids received by the deadline plus one thousand pounds.

Mike Crump acknowledged my first bid letter as received, and then there was silence. I wrote to Prime Minister Tony Blair, and to Chris Smith, Britain's Heritage Secretary, and to John Ashworth, the chairman of the British Library's board, and again to Brian Lang. Thomas Tanselle wrote a letter urging the library to reverse its position. Nicolas Barker wrote John Ashworth to say that the sale of the newspapers, under conditions of secrecy, would cause an "international scandal." Barker observed that "no good has ever come from previous dispersals from the Library." (The last significant dispersals came early in the nineteenth century, Barker said: "The gain was temporary and soon forgotten; the loss is permanent and irremediable.") Lucy Caswell introduced a resolution at the annual meeting of the American Journalism Historians Association entreating the British Library to act responsibly; it passed unanimously and was sent by the association's president to Brian Lang.

These efforts got nowhere. Alan Howarth, the Minister of Culture, Media, and Sport, wrote me that he was "assured that the procedures for disposal were rigorously followed in this case," and he added that he had "no power to intervene in the Library's decision." Two weeks after the sale deadline, the library sent out its official notification: everything on the list was going to the highest bidder; no allowances were made for nondestructive intent. (The "preservation bid" was disallowed, as coming after the deadline.) My offers prevailed for the *World* and the *Herald Tribune,* and for ninety other titles, but failed for the *Chicago Tribune, The New York Times,* the New Orleans *Times-Picayune,* the Philadelphia *Public Ledger, Motion Picture Daily, The Christian*

Science Monitor, and about thirty others. The library required payment by March 31, 2000, which was, thankfully, five months away and allowed time for fund-raising. Their invoice said, "Deselection (Newspapers) £19,282.00."

Most or all of the titles I failed to get went to Timothy Hughes, the dealer in Williamsport, Pennsylvania. I was especially unhappy over the *Chicago Tribune* (my great-grandfather was a Chicago newspaperman), and I called around to libraries in Chicago to see how serious a loss the destruction of that title would be. A helpful cataloger at the Chicago Historical Society wrote: "I went through the online database that contains the holdings records of the U.S. Newspaper Program and found that no one has a good run of the *Trib* on paper. Many institutions have the full run on microfilm, but the hardcopy issues that exist are mostly scattered issues and short (under 5 year) runs."

Reading that, I found I couldn't tolerate the idea that the British Library's *Tribune* would be broken down. I asked Timothy Hughes to quote me a price. He wrote back that "its value to me is in selling the individual historic issues as well as the potential for birthday sales as I currently don't have any runs from the mid-West. Exploring its potential to me over the years I've decided that the very least I would have to sell the run for would be $63,000. Otherwise I will just keep the run as it would be more profitable to me in the long run." I told him he had a deal. The MacArthur Foundation came up with a grant of fifty thousand dollars, which covered much of the purchase price, and my mother and mother-in-law made contributions, as did Viscountess Eccles, a scholar-collector of Boswell and Johnson who with her late husband endowed the British Library's David and Mary Eccles Centre for American Studies. Later, the Knight Foundation made a one-hundred-thousand-dollar grant.

Sixty-three thousand dollars, or about fifty dollars a volume, may seem like a lot of money to pay for old news, but it's actually a bargain. To buy the equivalent microfilm run from Bell and Howell would cost about $177,000. We're at a bizarre moment in history, when you can have the real thing for considerably less than it would cost to buy a set of crummy black-and-white snapshots of it which you can't read without the help of machine.

The *San Francisco Chronicle*'s fate also bothered me, so I got in touch with Gray Brechin, author of *Imperial San Francisco,* who uses old newspapers a lot in his historical work; he and I made a case to the California State Library for buying the *Chronicle* directly from Timothy Hughes, which they did (seventy years for sixty thousand dollars), with the help of the Wells Fargo Foundation. "We're trying to keep a library here that doesn't go goofy—that pays attention to the immemorial challenges and trusts of libraries," Kevin Starr, the state librarian of California, told me.

And then there was *The New York Times* from 1915 to 1958. At first, Hughes was hesitant to sell it as a whole ("It sort of defeats my purpose," he said), but eventually we were able to agree on a price of fifty-six thousand dollars, which is, at a guess, five times more than he paid for it, but still a fair price. With the money he's making, Hughes plans to buy an electric lift to speed the retrieval of volumes on high shelves, and he is thinking of building another warehouse.

In February 2000, shortly after the lots, amounting to approximately 6,400 volumes, arrived at Hughes's warehouse from England—each volume dutifully stamped BRITISH LIBRARY DISCARD—I drove to Williamsport to make sure the *Chicago Tribune* volumes were properly wrapped and labeled, and I handed Hughes a certified check. Sixteen pallets, ten tons of major metropolitan history, were forklifted onto a truck which took them to a warehouse in New Hampshire, near where I live. On June 29, forty-seven hundred or so more volumes arrived direct from the British Library, in two large Hyundai shipping containers. I cut the bands of a five-foot-high pallet and tore away some of the transatlantic shipper's black plastic: there were the words THE WORLD repeated over and over on the stack of spines. Pulitzer's originals were safe. What I have to do now is buy shelves and put the collection in order.

Maybe someday a research library will want to take responsibility for these things, or maybe not—whatever happens, at least they aren't going to be cut up and sold as birthday presents. Sometimes I'm a little stunned to think that I've become a newspaper librarian, more or less, and have the job of watching over this majestic, pulp-begotten ancestral stockpile. And of course I worry about running out of money, and about devoting months and years of my life, and my wife's life, to this effort. But at the moment nobody else seems to want to do what must be done. Six thousand square feet of space near where I live, with room to shelve all the papers and to hold a small reading room, costs about twenty-six thousand dollars a year to rent—about the salary of one microfilm technician. That seems cheap to preserve more than a century's worth of inherent vice, and virtue.

EPILOGUE

Four Recommendations

Libraries that receive public money should as a condition of funding be required to publish monthly lists of discards on their websites, so that the public has some way of determining which of them are acting responsibly on behalf of their collections.

The Library of Congress should lease or build a large building near Washington, and in it they should put, in call-number order, everything that they are sent by publishers and can't or don't want to hold on site. If the library is unwilling to perform this basic function of a national repository, then Congress should designate and fund some other archive to do the job.

Several libraries around the country should begin to save the country's current newspaper output in bound form.

The National Endowment for the Humanities should either abolish the U.S. Newspaper Program and the Brittle Books Program entirely, or require as a condition of funding that (1) all microfilming and digital scanning be nondestructive and (2) all originals be saved afterward.

Notes

CHAPTER 1 – Overseas Disposal

Page

3 Ten thousand volumes: British Library Newspaper Library, *History: The British Library Newspaper Library,* www.bl.uk/collections/newspaper/history.html (viewed August 15, 2000). Edward Miller says that "30,000 volumes, mostly of nineteenth-century British provincial newspapers" were "lost irretrievably." Edward Miller, *That Noble Cabinet: A History of the British Museum* (Athens, Ohio: Ohio University Press, 1974). The British Library became an entity separate from the British Museum in 1973; several years ago, over much protest, the library moved its main quarters from the domed reading room in Bloomsbury (where Swinburne, Virginia Woolf, Karl Marx, and many others worked) to a building near St. Pancras station.

3 Pulitzer discovered that illustrations: "The *World*'s achievement consisted in using illustration not only as a marvel to be admired for its own sake, as in the case of the *Daily Graphic,* nor as an occasional fillip for an otherwise dull page, as in the case of the *Herald,* but rather as a major tool in the art of reporting the news." George Juergens, *Joseph Pulitzer and the* New York World (Princeton: Princeton University Press, 1966), pp. 96–97.

5 "Since the adoption": Charles Z. Case, "Photographing Newspapers," in *Microphotography for Libraries,* ed. M. Llewellyn Raney (Chicago: American Library Association, 1936), p. 53.

6 "Old wood-pulp files": A. F. Kuhlman, "Are We Ready to Preserve Newspapers on Films? A Symposium," *Library Quarterly,* April 1935, reprinted in *Studies in Micropublishing, 1853–1976: Documentary Sources,* ed. Allen B. Veaner (Westport, Conn.: Microform Review, 1976).

6 "total space requirements": Keyes DeWitt Metcalf, "Some Trends in Research Libraries," in *William Warner Bishop: A Tribute,* ed. Harry Miller Lydenberg and Andrew Keogh (New Haven: Yale University Press, 1941).

6 "All that it is necessary": New York *Sun,* June 1, 1837, quoted in Frank M. O'Brien, *The Story of the Sun* (New York: George H. Doran, 1918), p. 124.

6 brought prices way down: Alfred McClung Lee, *The Daily Newspaper in America* (New York: Macmillan, 1937), pp. 742–45.

7 interesting article: Detroit *Evening News,* January 10, 1892.

7 "the acidity of the paper alone": Klaus B. Hendriks, "Permanence of Paper in Light of Six Centuries of Papermaking in Europe," in *Environnement et conservation de l'écrit, de l'image, et du son* (Paris: Association pour la Recherche Scientifique sur les Arts Graphiques [ARSAG], 1994), p. 136. See also Otto Wächter, "Paper Strengthening: Mass Conservation of Unbound and Bound Newspapers," *Restaurator* 8 (1987).

7 scientists have been making this observation: Sally Roggia cites *Paper Makers Monthly Journal* (June 1920), which summarizes a work by Aribert and Bouvier: the "most frequent and most harmful chemicals remaining in the paper are free acids and free chlorine"; it is "important to avoid acidity in the alum." Sally Roggia, "William James Barrow: A Biographical Study of His Formative Years and His Role in the History of Library and Archives Conservation from 1931 to 1941," Ph.D. diss., Columbia University, 1999.

8 Wilson: William K. Wilson and E. J. Parks, "Comparison of Accelerated Aging of Book Papers in 1937 with 36 Years Natural Aging," *Restaurator* 4 (1980): "Unfortunately the papers were accidentally discarded several years ago." Elsewhere, Wilson and Parks write: "Very few organizations can maintain a project [such as testing naturally aging paper] that spans 25–50 years, especially when there is no pot of real gold at the end of the trail." "Historical Survey of Research at the National Bureau of Standards on Materials for Archival Records," *Restaurator* 5 (1983). In 1998, the American Society for Testing and Materials announced a one-hundred-year natural-aging experiment; books containing fifteen different kinds of test paper have gone into ten libraries in North America. The object is to develop an accelerated-aging test that better correlates with natural aging.

8 now viewed with skepticism: In *Artificial Aging as a Predictor of Paper's Future Useful Life,* an *Abbey Newsletter* Monograph Supplement, Helmut Bansa and Hans-H. Hofer find that "there may be at best an accidental agreement between the results of artificial aging at high temperatures and natural aging" (Provo, Utah: Abbey Newsletter, 1989). See also Wilson and Parks, "Comparison of Accelerated Aging," in which the data suggest that "either the number of samples is less than adequate to provide a valid statistical population or the accelerated aging method used in 1937 does not fully simulate natural aging, or both." Later (p. 47) Wilson writes: "Don't try to predict permanence in years." E. Ströfer-Hua, after an experiment that demonstrated the flaws of oven aging, concludes: "History can only happen; it cannot be simulated in advance." E. Ströfer-Hua, "Experimental Measurement: Interpreting Extrapolation and Prediction by Accelerated Aging," *Restaurator* 11 (1990).

8 "an interesting academic exercise": American Society for Testing and Materials, "Standard Test Method for Determination of Effect of Moist Heat (50% Relative Humidity and 90°C) on Properties of Paper and Board," *Annual Book of ASTM Standards, 1998,* vol. 15.09, D 4714, Appendix (Conshohocken, Pa.: American Society for Testing and Materials, 1998).

8 "naive hope": Tom Lindstrom, "Discussion Contribution: Slow Fires—It's Paper Chemistry, Physics, and Biology," in *Paper Preservation: Current Issues and Recent Developments,* ed. Philip Luner (Atlanta: Tappi, 1988). Glen G.

Gray writes: "Although several accelerated-aging procedures or chemical specifications have been proposed, carefully controlled experiments and many years of natural aging would be required to verify predictions." Glen G. Gray, "Determination and Significance of Activation Energy in Permanence Tests," in *Preservation of Paper and Textiles of Historic and Artistic Value,* ed. John C. Williams (Washington, D.C.: American Chemical Society, 1977). Wilson and Parks write: "An accelerated aging test does not tell what a paper will be like after 25 or 50 years of storage. It only provides information concerning the ranking of different samples with respect to storage properties." William K. Wilson and E. J. Parks, "An Analysis of the Aging of Paper," *Restaurator* 3 (1979): 56.

9 newspaper library's newsletter: British Library Newspaper Library, "Disposal of Overseas Newspapers," *Newspaper Library News* 22 (winter 1996–1997).

9 wire-service story: Associated Press, "British Library Giving Away Old Newspapers," January 29, 1997, Nexis.

9 library selected for discard: British Library Newspaper Library, "Disposal of Overseas Newspapers (Continued)," *Newspaper Library News* 24 (winter 1997–1998).

10 "overseas disposals project": British Library Newspaper Library, "Disposal of Overseas Newspapers: Eastern Europe, Latin America, and the USA," *Newspaper Library News* 25 (winter 1998–1999).

10 "Increasing pressure": British Library Newspaper Library, "Disposal of Overseas Newspapers."

11 "Material for which we cannot": British Library Newspaper Library, "Disposal of Overseas Newspapers."

CHAPTER 2 – Original Keepsakes

14 micro-madman: Herman H. Fussler's early how-to book is *Photographic Reproduction for Libraries* (Chicago: University of Chicago Press, 1942). Research libraries have been "duly grateful for the space saved through newspaper-salvaging operations," he writes, in "Photographic Reproduction of Research Materials," *Library Trends,* April 1954, reprinted in Veaner, *Studies in Micropublishing,* p. 26. Fussler's work at the Chicago branch of the Manhattan Project is briefly discussed in Burton W. Adkinson, *Two Centuries of Federal Information* (Stroudsburg, Pa.: Dowden, Hutchinson, and Ross, 1978), pp. 42–43. See also Fussler's obituary in the *Chicago Tribune,* March 7, 1997.

15 Shawn Godwin: Letter to author, July 30, 2000; Godwin would prefer that I not name the institution. Some years later, Godwin took a historical-research job in which he was supposed to make a catalog of the murals painted by two Hungarian-American artists. "Many of their murals had long been destroyed and the only documentary evidence, especially the only color evidence for them existed in a vertical file of real newspaper articles maintained by a major library. When the library moved into a new, much larger facility the vertical files were microfilmed in black and white and the originals destroyed according to apparently standard archival procedure. Fortunately on pain of death the reference librarian had previously allowed me to take the articles outside the building to a local copy shop to make color copies (the hoops I had to jump through to do this were in retrospect ironic given that the material was slated to be destroyed)."

15 U.S. Newspaper Program: See Robert P. Holley, "The Preservation

Microfilming Aspects of the United States Newspaper Program: A Preliminary Study," *Microform Review* 19:3 (summer 1990); and Larry E. Sullivan, "United States Newspaper Program: Progress and Prospects," *Microform Review* 15:3 (summer 1986); Nancy E. Gwinn, "The Rise and Fall of Cooperative Projects," *Library Resources and Technical Services* 29:1 (January/March 1985).

17 "part of the City's own heritage": Charles Longley, "Newspapers at the Boston Public Library," t.s., March 13, 1998, p. 3. "The paper collection should not be discarded," Longley writes, since "for many titles the Library has the only remaining original paper copy. As artifacts the original files provide a direct physical link with the past and are of interest as such."

19 "original keepsake newspaper": Hammacher Schlemmer, spring 1999 catalog (p. 58), late winter catalog (p. 17), etc.

19 its bookplates announce: The text is:

Gift of
MRS. OGDEN REID
(Helen Rogers Reid)
President,
NEW YORK HERALD TRIBUNE, INC.
January 2, 1951

Not all the *Tribune* volumes are bookplated, however.

20 $39.50 an issue: If you buy from Hammacher Schlemmer, you receive the newspaper "set in a hand-bound, leatherette-covered binder that is gold-embossed with the publication title, date, and the recipient's name," but that costs $129.95.

CHAPTER 3 – Destroying to Preserve

22 They often do: Canadian libraries do a better job of keeping the originals as well: "With regard to the preservation of originals, the Bibliothèque Nationale du Québec (BNQ) deserves special mention. Under the legal deposit regulation of its act, the BNQ receives two copies of every newspaper published in the province of Quebec. One copy is sent immediately to the conservation unit where it is filmed, and placed unfolded in an acid-free carton, in a climate-controlled storage area. Access to originals is strictly controlled." Mary Jane Starr, "The Preservation of Canadian Newspapers," *Microform Review* 15:3 (summer 1986).

23 "stock control": See, for example, J. A. Urquhart and N. C. Urquhart, *Relegation and Stock Control in Libraries* (Stocksfield, Northumberland: Oriel Press, 1976), which discusses something called a "weedability factor," defined as "the number of uses per working day per metre of shelving occupied." Circulation statistics are all-important: "Intuitively, books which were last borrowed a long time ago seem ripe for relegation, books which were recently borrowed are left alone."

25 "kissing through a pane of glass": Quoted in Stephen R. Salmon, "User Resistance to Microforms in the Research Library," *Microform Review* 3:3 (July 1974).

25 leave the bindings alone: "Poor binding also presents its own problems and although our cameras do cope well with tight binding we have unbound some

volumes to allow filming to proceed." John E. Lauder, "The Scottish Newspapers Microfilming Unit," *Microform Review* 24:2 (spring 1995).

25 Historical Records Survey: Clifton Dale Foster, "Microfilming Activities of the Historical Records Survey, 1935–42," *American Archivist* 48:1 (winter 1985). Foster writes that "the text of many filmed documents is almost illegible. One general complaint of those repositories housing copies of Historical Records Survey microfilm was that the film images are unreadable." Luther Evans was a disciple of Robert C. Binkley, whose *Manual on Methods of Reproducing Research Materials* (Ann Arbor: Edwards Brothers, 1931) influenced many. Binkley, who believed in microfilming newspapers and "letting the originals disappear" (*Manual on Methods,* p. 106), took an interest in the Historical Records Survey and "worked closely with Luther Evans in an advisory capacity and as a part-time field director in Ohio," writes Foster. "During the first few months of the Survey's existence, [Binkley] frequently urged Luther Evans to broaden the project's scope to include microfilming. Evans, although hesitant at first, was eventually convinced and implemented many of Binkley's suggestions." The Historical Records Survey supplied the camera and the labor; the owning institution paid for the negatives: Luther Evans, "Recent Microfilming Activities of the Historical Records Survey," *Journal of Documentary Reproduction* 2:1 (March 1939).

25 "The entire back of the binding": Luther Evans, "Reference Department," in Library of Congress, *Annual Report of the Librarian of Congress for the Fiscal Year Ended June 30, 1941* (Washington, D.C.: U.S. Government Printing Office, 1942), p. 133. Charles Case, at Recordak, led the way. "A rotary machine for photographing separate sheets is considerably more rapid than a machine for handling bound volumes. One machine can therefore turn out more work and so go further in its job of preserving evanescent material and saving valuable space than one machine of the other type. . . . The rotary machine can also be used for back files if they are cut out of the binding. This is the way we have photographed the 1914–1918 *New York Times*" (Case, "Photographing Newspapers," p. 57).

25 "This was a major decision": S. Branson Marley, Jr., "Newspapers and the Library of Congress," *Library of Congress Quarterly Journal* 32:3 (July 1975), reprinted in Veaner, *Studies in Micropublishing,* p. 425.

26 over a hundred and fifty dollars per volume: A price sheet distributed in 1998 by the Northeast Document Conservation Center, "Microfilm Department Hourly Standards and Price Per Frame," lists a price of twenty-three cents per frame for "good newspapers"; the cost is forty cents per frame for "poor newspapers." A typical volume—containing two weeks of a major newspaper from the first half of the twentieth century, say—might have two 150-page Sunday issues and thirteen thirty-page issues, or about 690 pages; that is, filming it would cost over $150 if the filmer classes it as good.

26 less than five dollars a volume: According to an Ohio State report, it cost $2.76 per volume to construct Berkeley's Northern Regional Library Facility; $3.36 per volume to build the Sixth Stack Addition at the University of Illinois; $1.30 per volume (including land and financing) to build the Harvard Depository. Ohio Board of Regents, *Academic Libraries in Ohio: Progress through Collaboration, Storage, and Technology,* Report of the Library Study Committee, September 1987, appendix E.

27 "condensing records": Case, "Photographing Newspapers," p. 53.

27 wall of volumes of *The New York Times:* Reproduced as plate 1 in Fussler, *Photographic Reproduction for Libraries.* The caption is "Twelve Years of the *New York Times* in Original and on Film." In those early years, Charles Puckette, the business manager of *The New York Times,* was less enthusiastic about replacing paper with film: "We recognize the need of the libraries to conserve space and when one is looking about for ways in which to save space, the large newspaper files naturally attract attention. But we are printers. We deal in the printed page just as librarians are primarily the custodians of the printed page. We think that the actual paper and ink as they appear in the form of the daily printed paper have inherent values in them which cannot be transmitted by film alone and which suffer, too, in reduction. An essential part of the record of today which you will preserve for the future will be the development of newspaper printing. And that part of the history of our times only the actual printed page will show." C. McD. Puckette, "Question of Filming the New York Times," in Raney, *Microphotography for Libraries,* p. 61.

27 who bought two microfilm readers: See Keyes Metcalf, *Random Recollections of an Anachronism* (New York: Readex Books, 1980), pp. 276–77. In 1935, "a film reproduction of the *New York Herald Tribune* replaced the Japanese-tissued bound file and since that time has been the only back file for the period available to readers," Metcalf proudly wrote at the time. Keyes Metcalf, "Microphotography in the New York Public Library," in Raney, *Microphotography for Libraries,* p. 85. (Semi-transparent Japanese tissue, applied with paste and pressed through a heated mangle, reinforced the pages.) See also Metcalf's "Newspapers and Microphotography," *The Journal of Documentary Reproduction* 2:3 (September 1939), which grants that the foreign-newspaper film that he is producing at Harvard "costs much more than the original," but when you take into account the cost of binding and storage things begin to even out.

27 "to help push microphotography": Quoted in David C. Weber, "The Foreign Newspaper Microfilm Project, 1938–1955," *Harvard Library Bulletin* (spring 1956), reprinted in Veaner, *Studies in Micropublishing.*

27 sprocket perforations: Thomas A. Bourke, "The Curse of Acetate; or, a Base Conundrum Confronted," *Microform Review* 23:1 (winter 1994); and Thomas A. Bourke, "Scholarly Micropublishing, Preservation Microfilming, and the National Preservation Effort in the Last Two Decades of the Twentieth Century: History and Prognosis," *Microform Review* 19:1 (winter 1990).

27 siege of Paris: See Ralph de Sola, *Microfilming* (New York: Essential Books, 1944), pp. 22–25.

28 Eugene Power: See Jack Rubin, *A History of Micrographics in the First Person* (Silver Spring, Md.: National Micrographics Association, 1980), pp. 69–70. In the OSS project, Power had help from Frederick Kilgour, who went on to glory as the founder of OCLC, the bibliographic database. See "Eugene Barnum Power" and "Frederick Gridley Kilgour" in American Society of Information Scientists (ASIS), *Pioneers of Information Science in North America,* www.asis.org/Features/Pioneers/isp.htm.

28 Neil MacKay: Neil MacKay, *The Hole in the Card: The Story of the Microfilm Aperture Card* (St. Paul: Minnesota Mining and Manufacturing, 1966), p. 5. See also Rubin, *History of Micrographics,* which quotes Langan's own *Notes on the Early History of Microfilm Aperture Cards;* and Robin W. Winks, *Cloak and Gown: Scholars in the Secret War, 1939–1961,* 2d ed. (New Haven: Yale University Press, 1987), p. 107.

28 Vernon D. Tate: See Rubin, *History of Micrographics,* pp. 57–58. In the thirties, as Herman Fussler wrote approvingly in *Photographic Reproduction for Libraries,* the National Archives, under Vernon Tate's direction, filmed bulky governmental records, which "are then destroyed except for a small percentage (e.g., 10 per cent) kept to illustrate the original format. The saving in space thus obtained is very great." Tate himself wrote: "Legislation was procured to enable the disposition under certain conditions of valuable records that have been microfilmed." Vernon D. Tate, "Microphotography in Wartime," *Journal of Documentary Reproduction* 5:3 (September 1942); 134–35.

28 "secret military weapon": Tate, "Microphotography in Wartime."

29 "We're going places Verner": Luther Evans to Verner Clapp, June 25, 1945, Clapp papers, Library of Congress.

29 narrowly missing the chieftaincy: Clapp probably missed being appointed librarian of Congress because a McCarthyite senator from Clapp's home state of Maryland, John Marshall Butler, had it in for him, according to a fascinating paper by Betty Milum, "Eisenhower, ALA, and the Selection of L. Quincy Mumford," *Libraries and Culture* 30:1 (winter 1995). Clapp gave permission for the Library of Congress to display (as part of a UNESCO exhibit entitled "The Library in a Free World") one of Butler's campaign photographs, in a display-panel entitled "Distortion of Information." (It was a cut-and-paste job, produced in 1951 by Butler's campaign office with the apparent aid of Joe McCarthy's money and staff, showing Butler's opponent, veteran senator and McCarthy opponent Millard Tydings, in what at a glance seemed to be close conference with Earl Browder, ex-head of the U.S. Communist Party.) Butler complained, and Clapp sent an apology and substituted a different composite photo from *Time.* But Butler wasn't appeased, and he and/or McCarthy seems to have set the FBI to work gathering dirt on Clapp, whose 1953 FBI report mentions an informant's letter from 1928 in which Clapp was said to have been arrested in 1922 in connection with some suspicious fires at Trinity College—this sounds like FBI smear-to-order work. By his own admission, however, Clapp had been detained in the twenties for "lurking in an alley." He wrote in his application form for the CIA: "I commenced action for false arrest, but was assured by my lawyer that the record was erased."

29 "Reduction in bulk": Council on Library Resources, *Meeting on the Problems of Microform in Libraries* (Washington, D.C.: Council on Library Resources, 1958). See also "Space Problems of Large (General) Research Libraries: Report of a Meeting," *College and Research Libraries,* May 1959, p. 219, in which is mentioned, as a "deferred" suggestion, a "proposal for a 'weeding authority,' which would roam through large research libraries and, endowed with authority derived from joint sponsorship, would recommend consolidation of collections, transfers of materials to central storage warehouses, etc." An institution designated as "University C" (Yale, probably; see pp. 88–89) was described as "meeting the storage problem" by cutting back on acquisitions and "working through its collections subject by subject so as to discard materials of less value, replace with microtext those materials for which this may be done effectively, and transfer to a compact storage collection those items which should be retained locally but which may be assigned to a location of inferior physical accessibility." "University D" planned to "reduce to microtext a significant segment (covering one field of study) in the library of one of the professional schools of the University" in order to test its financial feasibility and its "effects on consumers and consumer-reaction."

29 Minuteman missile: See "Contracts," *Missiles and Rockets,* January 15, 1962. AVCO also had $5.7 million for the development of nose cones for the Titan and Atlas missiles.

29 "A Good Beginning": Verner Clapp, "A Good Beginning," in *Proceedings of the Eighth Annual Meeting and Convention* (Washington, D.C.: National Microfilm Association, 1959), on microfiche. Vernon Tate was on the governing board of the National Microfilm Association that year, as were emissaries from Xerox Haloid and Bell Labs.

30 list of names: Verner Clapp, diary, November 4, 1951, Clapp papers, Library of Congress. Another who worked on the Library of Congress's CIA projects was Burton W. Adkinson, Director of the Reference Department. Burton, a map expert and former OSS analyst, worked for the National Science Foundation from 1957 to 1971; in 1978, he wrote *Two Centuries of Federal Information,* a book about the history of information science in the federal government that manages to edit the CIA out almost completely. One of the CIA projects mentioned in Clapp's notes was the "Mo. Russ. Acc. List"—the Monthly List of Russian Accessions, begun in 1951.

30 Cold War mania: The CIA's "Intellofax" aperture-card system was described in 1961: "The classified documents are received from scores of different major sources. . . . Since 1954 we have been miniaturizing the documents by microphotography and mounting them in apertures on IBM punched cards. Access to the document itself is indirect, through codes punched into the cards to indicate subject, area, source, security classification, date and number of each document." Senate Committee on Government Operations, *Documentation, Indexing, and Retrieval of Scientific Information,* 86th Cong. 2d sess., Document no. 113 (Washington, D.C.: U.S. Government Printing Office, 1961), pp. 63–64; quoted in Robert M. Hayes and Joseph Becker, *Information Storage and Retrieval: Tools, Elements, Theories* (New York: Wiley, 1963), p. 168.

30 BEST COPY AVAILABLE: The CIA's cover letter to me says: "We apologize for the poor quality of these pages, but there are no better copies available." According to C. P. Auger, other formulas are: "Reproduced from the best available copy" and "Copy available does not permit fully legible reproduction" and "This document has been reproduced from the best available copy furnished by the sponsoring agency. Although it is recognized that certain portions are illegible, it is being released in the interest of making available as much information as possible." C. P. Auger, "The Importance of Microforms," *Microform Review* 20:4 (fall 1991), reprinted from *Information Sources in Grey Literature,* 2d ed. (New York: Bowker-Saur, 1989).

31 AMERICA'S SPACE PROGRAM: *Microform Review* 5:3 (July 1976). Another Xerox/UMI ad, which ran in the January 1975 issue (4:1) of *Microform Review,* is headlined "The Beast and the Librarian." It tells the story of a librarian who adopted a serials collection that began to multiply and turned into "seemingly uncontrollable beasts": "As the swelling menagerie usurped more space, the librarian realized how many thousands of dollars the animals devoured—just sitting on the shelves. . . . The librarian was in distress, about to be swallowed up by the paper monster, when who should come to the rescue but MIGHTY MICROFILM!" In 1984, University Microfilms produced an ad headlined SPACE INVADERS: "Nobody knows where they came from. But suddenly, they were everywhere. In the stacks. In the aisles. And now, even advancing on the lobby" (*Microform Review* 13:4 [spring 1984]). Eugene Power, founder of

University Microfilms, sold the company to Xerox in 1962; in 1983, Xerox bought Microfilm Corporation of America from *The New York Times* and merged it with UMI; and then in 1985, Bell and Howell bought UMI from Xerox and in 1999 renamed it Bell and Howell Information and Learning. See Bourke, "Scholarly Micropublishing."

31 "files of American and foreign newspapers": William Warner Bishop, "Thirty Years in the Library of Congress, 1899 to 1929," in *Essays Offered to Herbert Putnam by His Colleagues and Friends on His Thirtieth Anniversary as Librarian of Congress, 5 April 1929,* ed. William Warner Bishop and Andrew Keogh (New Haven: Yale University Press, 1929), quoted in Paul M. Angle, *The Library of Congress: An Account, Historical and Descriptive* (Kingsport, Tenn.: Kingsport Press, 1958), p. 53.

31 "badly congested condition": Serials Division, Library of Congress, "Serials Division Report, 1949–1950" in *Annual Reports, Reference Department,* t.s., Library of Congress Manuscripts Division. Each department head submitted an annual report to the librarian of Congress; they are internal documents, not to be confused with the library's published annual reports, which are beautifully produced books. In the published annual reports, the decision to buy microfilm copies of newspapers from external sources (e.g., Recordak), and to give away or throw away the bound originals in order to conserve space, is not mentioned.

31 "merely more of the same": Verner Clapp, foreword to J. C. R. Licklider, *Libraries of the Future* (Cambridge, Mass.: MIT Press, 1965).

31 *steady space* model: Also known as the "static-capacity" model. Ann Okerson, once head of the Serials Division at Simon Fraser University Library, Burnaby, British Columbia (now a big gun in digitalism at Yale), wrote in 1985: "In anticipation of the space problem, the chief librarian had earlier proposed a 'steady space' policy which undertook to contain the Library's collections within the existing building until the year 2000 by various means, including microfilm alternatives to hardcopy, resource sharing, using online facilities, moving to high-density shelving for lower-use research materials, and weeding/discard." Okerson's library sold some of its more valuable backfiles to a dealer in Scarsdale, or swapped them for microfilm, an arrangement that "turned out to be very fruitful for the library." Ann Okerson, "Microform Conversion—A Case Study," *Microform Review* 14:3 (summer 1985). In the early nineties, Okerson advised William Bowen, president of the A. W. Mellon Foundation, as the Foundation planned its ambitious assault on paper. See Anthony M. Cummings et al., *University Libraries and Scholarly Communication: A Study Prepared for the Andrew W. Mellon Foundation,* Association of Research Libraries, November 1992, www.lib.virginia.edu/mellon/mellon.html.

32 "It is an art": Clapp, "Good Beginning."

32 "permitting the disposal": Marley, "Newspapers and the Library of Congress," in Veaner, pp. 429, 436n.

32 None of this epochal activity: The closest the library came at the time to publicly revealing what was afoot was the statement that "since 1939 the Library has been engaged in preserving its newspaper files by transferring them to microfilm," in a section describing the microfilming of foreign archives. Library of Congress, *Annual Report of the Librarian of Congress for the Fiscal Year Ending June 30, 1952* (Washington, D.C.: U.S. Government Printing Office), p. 62. Luther Evans makes no reference to the decision to substitute microfilm

(in-house or bought) for the library's originals in his "Current Microfilm Projects at the Library of Congress," *Das Antiquariat* (Vienna) 8 (August 15, 1952).

33 "The problem of deteriorating newspapers": Library of Congress, *Annual Report of the Librarian of Congress for the Fiscal Year Ending June 30, 1956* (Washington, D.C.: U.S. Government Printing Office, 1957), p. 25.

33 naval warehouse: In 1972, the library moved "some 50,000 volumes of bound domestic newspapers, which are gradually being microfilmed," to the Duke Street warehouse, "to provide space for the expansion of the overcrowded general collections." Bound foreign newspapers were stored in Alexandria beginning in 1968. Library of Congress, *Annual Report of the Librarian of Congress for the Fiscal Year Ending June 30, 1972* (Washington, D.C.: U.S. Government Printing Office, 1973), p. 36.

33 in its *Information Bulletin:* E.g., "From commercial sources, major titles being acquired on film to replace the Library's holdings include the Portland, Maine, *Press Herald* for January 1940–December 1944 and January 1947–May 1950, the Rochester, N.Y., *Democrat and Chronicle,* 1905–June 1955 [my hometown paper], the Concord, N.H., *Daily Monitor,* 1874–1923, the Leavenworth, Kans., *Times,* April 25, 1871–1950, the Topeka, Kans., *Daily Capitol,* 1890–June 1950, the Dallas, Texas, *Morning News,* 1900–April 1950, the Portland, Oreg., *Daily Journal,* March 11, 1902–1936, and the Milwaukee, Wis., *Journal,* 1891–1909 and 1921–August 1950." "Serial Division," *Library of Congress Information Bulletin* 35:2 (January 9, 1976). Six months later, there were new titles: "Major domestic titles being filmed at the Library during the past half year are the Sioux City (Iowa) *Journal* for 1871–1874 and 1894–1950, the New York City *Jewish Journal and Daily News* for 1910–1915 and 1929–March 1953 (films for 1916–1928 are already available), the Portland (Oreg.) *Oregonian* for July 1874–December 1945, and as a cooperative project with the Enoch Pratt Free Library, the Baltimore (Md.) *Post* for November 20, 1922–March 24, 1934." The list continues: "From commercial sources, major titles being acquired on film to replace the Library's holdings included the New Orleans (La.) *Item* for 1920–1958, and the *States* for January 1916–August 1933, the Lewiston (Maine) *Evening Journal* for 1880–1955, the Topeka (Kans.) *State Journal* for 1880–June 1934, the Philadelphia (Pa.) *Record* for 1877–August 1910, the Las Vegas (Nev.) *Sun* for 1951–1961, the San Francisco (Calif.) *Daily Alta California* for 1859–1891, the Norfolk (Va.) *Virginian-Pilot* for 1945–May 1955, and the Nashville (Tenn.) *American* for 1853–September 1910." "Newspaper Preservation Program," *Library of Congress Information Bulletin* 35:28 (July 9, 1976).

34 "Wood pulp paper" here just seems: It isn't true, of course, that newsprint suddenly became composed of wood pulp in 1870—paper manufacturers used some percentage of rag and straw for decades afterward, and they mixed chemically digested wood and mechanically ground wood together—but it is an appealing simplification if you want to clear shelf space. The *Albany Argus* of March 19, 1872, for example, contained "fifteen per cent. chemical woodpulp in addition to fifteen rag and seventy straw." Lee, *Daily Newspaper in America,* p. 102.

34 detailed inventory: Library of Congress, "19th and 20th Century U.S. Newspapers in Original Format: Inventory of Volumes Held in Remote Storage," 1998, www.loc.gov/rr/news/inventor.html.

34 ALL ON FILM: One of the cards for the *Chicago Daily Tribune* confides: "Vols. For 1900–1971 have been discarded."

35 "Generally we retain the inkprint": See also "Collections Policy Statements: U.S. Newspapers," November 1996, on the library's website, lcweb.loc.gov/acq/devpol/neu.html (viewed June 2, 2000): "The preferred format for permanent retention is silver-gelatin-on-polyester-base 35mm roll microfilm. . . . newspapers published prior to 1870 on 'rag' paper may be retained in original ink-print format if they have artifactual value."

35 rag-paper library editions: These titles are listed in the *Annual Report of the Librarian of Congress for the Fiscal Year Ended June 30, 1938* (Washington, D.C.: U.S. Government Printing Office, 1939), p. 193. See also Library of Congress, Serials Division, *Holdings of American Nineteenth and Twentieth Century Newspapers Printed on Wood Pulp Paper,* mimeograph, May 1950, in which a note below the listing for *The Detroit News* says: "Commencing July 8, 1929, the Library of Congress file of this title is printed on rag paper." The library owns no issues of *The Detroit News* now. Incidentally, in the 1941 annual report, the library announced its receipt of a gift of 221 volumes of the New York *Forward,* 1901–1927: "This extensive file of the early years of this important Jewish paper was received by gift from the *Jewish Daily Forward,* of New York. It supplements the later years of the file already on our shelves." All but a handful of these gift volumes are gone, according to the library's 1998 online inventory.

35 "Microfilming came at a propitious time": Charles G. La Hood, Jr., "Microfilm for the Library of Congress," *College and Research Libraries,* July 1973. La Hood writes: "Normally, the Library requires the supplier [of newspaper microfilm] to furnish sample rolls of each file for quality-control testing before ordering, so that the pulp files are not destroyed prematurely."

35 "crisis of space": Library of Congress, Working Group on Reference and Research, *Report to the Task Group on Shelving Arrangement* (July 8, 1997, updated October 30, 1997), p. 2.

36 James Billington: At the CIA's Office of National Estimates, a quasi-professorial group under the direction of historian Sherman Kent, Billington wrote research reports, known as intelligence estimates, for President Eisenhower and other advisers. Richard Nixon, who as vice president paid close attention to intelligence briefings, became an admirer: "James Billington is, of course—you mention intellectuals. Now, there's an intellectual—just to show you I have an open mind—who everybody ought to know better. He has a first-class geopolitical mind. He particularly is expert in Soviet affairs. I'd like to see him sometime—I'd like to see him ambassador to Russia. I think he would be a great ambassador" (Richard Nixon interview with Brian Lamb, part 2, *Booknotes,* C-SPAN, March 1, 1992). In 1956, while the CIA's MKULTRA drug experiments on unwitting Canadians were in full swing (formally approved by Allen Dulles on April 13, 1953), and not so long after the CIA's 1954 paramilitary invasion of Guatemala (micro-managed by Dulles), James Billington toured the intelligence capitals of the world as Dulles's personal assistant. See Peter Grose, *Gentleman Spy: The Life of Allen Dulles* (Boston: Houghton Mifflin, 1994), pp. 393, 429; and James Srodes, *Allen Dulles: Master of Spies* (Washington, D.C.: Regnery, 1999), pp. 489–92. Dulles had "this ability to make quite cold-blooded assessments while remaining warm and gracious that was quite remarkable," Billington told Srodes. "People

talk about the Cold War frenzy, but I admit I slept better after that trip knowing that some of these plans never got off the ground." The Library of Congress doesn't make too much of Billington's CIA years now; a website biography of him skips past that time: "A graduate of Princeton University, he attended Oxford University's Balliol College as a Rhodes Scholar, earning a doctorate in history. At Harvard University from 1957 to 1962, he taught history and was a research fellow at the Russian Research Center" (Library of Congress, "James H. Billington," www.loc.gov/bicentennial/bios_billington.html). But as late as 1959, while he was employed by Harvard's Russian Research Center, Billington apparently still had a consulting relationship of some kind with the agency: he wrote a CIA memorandum entitled "Sino-Soviet Relationship," dated September 18, 1959; it is footnoted in a paper published in the CIA's in-house historical journal, *Studies in Intelligence.* See Harold P. Ford, "The CIA and Double Demonology," *Studies in Intelligence,* winter 1998–1999, www.odci.gov/csi/studies/winter98–99/art05.html (viewed August 22, 2000). For the relationship between the CIA and Harvard's Russian Research Center, see Sigmund Diamond, *Compromised Campus: The Collaboration of Universities with the Intelligence Community, 1945–1955* (New York: Oxford University Press, 1992).

CHAPTER 4 – It Can Be Brutal

37 Richmond, Virginia, *Daily Dispatch:* The yellow address label reads:

A R Spofford 12mch80
Librarian of Congress

38 what looks to be a butcher's apron: Gene Gurney and Nick Apple, *The Library of Congress: A Picture Story of the World's Largest Library* (New York: Crown, 1981), p. 113.

39 Joseph Mitchell: See Ben Yagoda, *About Town:* The New Yorker *and the World It Made* (New York: Scribner, 2000), p. 139.

39 "The anarchist": New York *World-Telegram,* February 2, 1934, p. 1.

40 "people rarely browse": E. E. Duncan, "Microfiche Collections for the New York Times/Information Bank," *Microform Review,* October 1973.

41 "blind as lovers": Veaner, *Studies in Micropublishing,* p. 440.

41 the research was subsidized: Bourdon W. Scribner, "Summary Report of Research at the National Bureau of Standards on Materials for the Reproduction of Records," in *Transactions, International Federation for Documentation,* vol. 1, fourteenth conference (Oxford, 1938).

41 "cellulose acetate motion-picture film": John R. Hill and Charles G. Weber, "Stability of Motion-Picture Films as Determined by Accelerated Aging," *Journal of Research of the National Bureau of Standards* 17 (December 1936).

41 "in the same category of permanence": Quoted in Kuhlman, "Are We Ready to Preserve Newspapers on Films?" in Veaner, *Studies in Micropublishing,* p. 385.

41 shrink, buckle, bubble: See Bourke, "Curse of Acetate." Bourke writes: "Libraries with extensive collections of older silver gelatin and diazo microforms should realize that much of this may be at risk." According to Preservation Resources, a top-of-the-line modern microfilming company, "the only solution is reduplication onto polyester films before the acetate film

becomes so deteriorated that it compromises the legibility of the film image. If left for too long, even duplication becomes impossible." Preservation Resources, "Preserving Microfilm," www.oclc.org/oclc/promo/presres/9138.htm (viewed September 13, 2000).

41 "dreaded vinegar syndrome": Bourke, "Curse of Acetate."

41 by the mid-eighties: "NYPL did not abandon the use of cellulose acetate until about 1983 with the inception of the Research Libraries Group Cooperative Preservation Microfilming Project, which mandated the use of polyester base for all silver gelatin film made by the participants in the project." Bourke, "Curse of Acetate."

42 Corona spy satellites: "One serious problem was unanticipated breakage of the acetate film," according to F. Dow Smith, but "new polyester-based film from Eastman Kodak increased the reliability considerably." F. Dow Smith, "The Design and Engineering of Corona's Optics," in *Corona: Between the Sun and the Earth,* ed. Robert A. McDonald (Bethesda, Md.: American Society for Photogrammetry and Remote Sensing, 1997). In an article about the Corona project, Seth Shulman writes: "Help finally arrived when a research team at Eastman Kodak discovered how to adhere emulsion to a polyester-based film, which proved much more durable under harsh conditions." Seth Shulman, "Code Name Corona," *Technology Review,* October 1996.

42 Millions of rolls of acetate images: It wasn't cheap to produce that acetate: "From 1952 through 1966, the Library spent well over $1,000,000 putting 150,000 brittle books on microfilm." John P. Baker, "Preservation Programs of the New York Public Library. Part Two: From the 1930s to the '60s," *Microform Review* 11:1 (winter 1982). Bourke sums up the New York Public Library's predicament: "The physical condition of many reels of silver gelatin film on cellulose actate base at NYPL is not good." Bourke, "Curse of Acetate."

42 strange spots: Lawson B. Knott, Jr., "Aging Blemishes on Microfilm Negatives," General Services Administration Circular, no. 326, January 21, 1964. See also Ellen McCrady, "The History of Microfilm Blemishes," *Restaurator* 6 (1984). McCrady observes that microfilm's fineness of grain causes problems: "Silver, normally a stable material, becomes more reactive when finely divided. As a result, silver halide microfilm is more strongly affected by processing, humidity and various oxidizing gases and contaminants than many other types of film."

42 "attacked metal filing cabinets": Susan Cates Dodson, "Microfilm—Which Film Type, Which Application?" *Microform Review* 14:2 (spring 1985).

43 "complete image loss": Carl M. Spaulding, "Kicking the Silver Habit: Confessions of a Former Addict," *American Libraries,* December 1978.

43 Dodson measured the temperature: She also quotes Peter Adelstein of Kodak: "Examples of image loss have been observed after short exposures to 150°. . . . The essential fact to keep in mind about vesicular film stability in that even very short exposure times to elevated temperatures will destroy the image." Peter Z. Adelstein, "Preservation of Microfilm," *Journal of Micrographics* 11:6 (July/August 1978), quoted in Dodson, "Microfilm—Which Film Type."

43 serious light-damage: Mark Jones, *Fading of Diazo Microfilms in Readers,* NRCd Publication 10 (Hatfield, England: NRCd, 1978), cited in Dodson, "Microfilm—Which Film Type."

43 certain species of fungi: *Aspergillus, penicilium, alternaria,* and *cladosporium,* for example, can grow in the gelatin emulsion of film. See E. Czerwinska and

R. Kowalik, "Microbiodeterioration of Audiovisual Collections," *Restaurator* 3 (1979).

43 easily scratched: "Silver film is easily scratched and abraded. Small foreign particles and the sharp edge of a poorly designed or out-of-adjustment reading machine will both gouge away the thin, soft gelatin emulsion as roll film is wound back and forth in use. In the main, this type of damage happens to such frequently used film as recent years of major newspapers; but a pristine roll of film can be badly scratched in a single use, particularly in the hands of an unskilled person." Spaulding, "Kicking the Silver Habit."

43 "extreme susceptibility": Spaulding, "Kicking the Silver Habit." See also Philippe Rouyer, "Humidity Control and the Preservation of Silver Gelatin Microfilm," *Microform Review* 21:2 (1992); and Peter Adelstein, "Status of Permanence Standards of Imaging Materials," *Journal of Imaging Science and Technology* 36:1 (January/February 1992).

43 check of master negatives: Erich J. Kesse, "Condition Survey of Master Microfilm Negatives, University of Florida Libraries," *Abbey Newsletter* 15:3 (May 1991), palimpsest.stanford.edu/byorg/abbey/an/an15/an15-3/an15-313.html. Kesse writes, "Mold was the primary or partial cause of deterioration of 64% of cases." And the master negatives weren't always master negatives: "Further examination of the entire master negative collection revealed a distressing fact. 12% of master negatives were acetate- and polyester-based diazo copies. Another 40% of the masters, while silver-gelatin emulsion, were not first generation film." Some of the damage that Kesse describes sounds relatively minor; on the other hand, a bit of foxing that might on paper obscure a single letter may blot out a portion of a paragraph on film.

43 "there seems to be a much wider": James M. Reilly, et al., "Stability of Black-and-White Photographic Images, with Special Reference to Microfilm," *Abbey Newsletter* 12:5 (July 1988).

44 original draft: The draft title was "Are Your Microfilms Deteriorating Nicely, Librarian?" Clapp papers, Library of Congress. In 1957, Clapp correctly wrote that microfilm's "dangers of deterioration are even greater" than those of paper, because they are "less easily detectible and more devastating." Council on Library Resources, *First Annual Report,* 1957, p. 20. In the next year's report, he writes that "though microfilm is widely used to provide a permanent copy in place of the impermanent original form of the newspaper, it has been found that microcopies are themselves subject to deterioration. This is all the more dangerous for being much less easily detected" (p. 25). Eventually, though, Clapp stopped talking about the dangers of microfilm deterioration and stressed the dangers of paper deterioration instead.

44 "excessive residual hypo": Robert C. Sullivan, "The Acquisition of Library Microforms: Part 2," *Microform Review* 6:4 (July 1977), p. 210.

44 "in more than 50 percent": Sullivan, "Acquisition," p. 210. In fiscal year 1972, for example, 589 units were tested, and 356 were rejected; in fiscal year 1976, 639 units were tested, and 266 were rejected. "It must be *emphasized,*" Sullivan writes, "that rejection by the laboratory does not necessarily mean rejection for addition to the Library's collections. In fact, since the majority of microform units purchased for the Library are 35mm microfilm reels of newspaper files, and many of these are non-current files dating back fifty to one hundred years or more, many of the 'Rejections' noted by the laboratory are for reasons such as loss of text due to uncut bindings, original damaged or mutilated, leader

and/or trailer insufficient, or incompleteness. If, after consultation with the Recommending Officer, it is determined that the best or only file available was filmed, then the decision may be made to accept the film." Sullivan offers some reassurance, however, saying that the lab's recommendation to reject film is accepted when the flaw or combination of flaws is "considered fatal, such as excessive hypo content, pagination inverse, splice in positive film, non-silver emulsion film stock, or lack of clarity or readability." Buying flawed film is not in itself an act of irresponsibility; buying flawed film to replace originals is.

44 trance-inducing job: In the mid-sixties, the Library of Congress's Photoduplication Service, including the Newspaper Camera Room, had a "high rate of staff turnover, exceeding 40 percent overall, with correspondingly increased difficulty in recruiting qualified replacements." Library of Congress, "Administrative Department—Office of Collections Maintenance and Preservation," *Library of Congress Information Bulletin* 25:41 (October 13, 1966).

44 "invisible product": Allen B. Veaner, "Crisis in Micropublication," *Choice,* June 1968, pp. 448–53.

44 "Serious defects": Veaner, "Crisis in Micropublication." Carl Spaulding, in "Kicking the Silver Habit," says that "few libraries test their silver film acquisitions, few know for sure whether those micropublications have been processed according to archival standards." Because *The New York Times* is heavily used, librarians discovered the problems with its filmed copies, beginning in September 1967, almost immediately. There was, Veaner writes, a "precipitous drop in technical quality" after the *Times* bought Microfilm Corporation of America and ended its arrangement with University Microfilms; some pictures appeared as "unintelligible blotches of grey, black, and white"; "it was reliably reported that the newspaper's research staff was unable to utilize its own product." Eventually, the *Times* refilmed a stretch of months; now Bell and Howell/UMI, formerly University Microfilms, is producing the film. See Allen Veaner, "New York Times on Microfilm," *Choice,* December 1968.

45 about one third of her library's reels: Nancy Kraft, *Final Report, Iowa Newspaper Project: Microfilming,* State Historical Society of Iowa, 1992.

45 compelled some improvements in standards: The Kodak MRD line of microfilm cameras, whose basic design dates from the fifties and even earlier (they are no longer sold or serviced by Kodak) remain the pack mules of American newspaper work, despite the fact that there are now, and have been for at least a decade, computer-controlled camera systems that offer higher resolutions and better ways of monitoring and adjusting contrast and focus than Kodak's cameras offer. In the late eighties, C. Lee Jones, president of MAPS (now Preservation Resources, a microfilm bureau founded by the Council on Library Resources), began evaluating a German-designed Herrmann & Kraemer camera, which offered, he told me, "resolutions that had only been dreamed about prior to that." Within a month he was convinced that he had to "convert the whole shop to H&K cameras." Eventually they bought twelve more. Resolution, in the microfilm world, is measured in line-pairs per millimeter. A typical frame of Kodak-shot preservation microfilm can legibly record one hundred and twenty pairs of lines per millimeter on a test-pattern "target"; Herrmann and Kraemer cameras offered resolutions forty to sixty percent better than that (higher, by the way, than the six hundred dots-per-inch

resolution that is the benchmark in many current digitization projects)—a matter of considerable importance when you are shrinking large newspaper pages from the eighteen-eighties and eighteen-nineties filled with many columns of closely printed footnote-sized type onto a fixed width of thirty-five-millimeter film. The H&K cameras also had ways of automatically correcting for variations in contrast—another endemic problem in age-toned newsprint pages. "It's the subtle change in contrast that throws microfilmers most often," Jones explained. "Where they may have a perfectly fine setting at the beginning of a book, it may not be worth the powder to blow it up at the end." But the bulk of newspaper-microfilming work did not go to MAPS, but to places with less good equipment. "MAPS got very little of the U.S. Newspaper Project," says Jones, "because those were long established procedures often done by commercial shops, and examined by people who were not really trained to evaluate the quality of film." The NEH, which was paying the bills, demanded only that microfilming shops adhere to industry standards that, according to Jones, were written with the limitations of the Kodak camera in mind. "These were minimum standards," Jones says. "And if you're talking about producing preservation microfilm for the very long term future, I don't think you can afford to adhere to minimum standards." In 1993, Jones wrote: "To simply reformat endangered materials into a form resistant to scanning or one that complicates scanning is a serious disservice to scholars and researchers of the future." That, however, is what has happened. C. Lee Jones, "Preservation Film: Platform for Digital Access Systems," Commission on Preservation and Access, *Newsletter* 58 (July 1993). Jones now directs the Linda Hall Library of Science, Engineering and Technology in Kansas City.

46 "NORTHAM COLONISTS HOLD MEETING": *Foster's Weekly Democrat & Dover Enquirer,* January 16, 1914.

CHAPTER 5 – The Ace Comb Effect

49 "News is selected": G. C. Bastian, *Editing the Day's News,* 1923, quoted in Lee, *Daily Newspaper in America,* p. 279.

50 "Papers are torn apart": Joseph G. Herzberg, *Late City Edition* (New York: Henry Holt, 1947), p. 13.

51 "there will be many times": James F. Green, "Problems with NYT Eds. & Indexes," posting to Library Collection Development List, March 9, 1994.

51 Chicago *Sun-Times* published a story: The article, by Peter Lisagor, appeared in the *Sun-Times* on September 17, 1970. See Jeffrey P. Kimball, *Nixon's Vietnam War* (Lawrence, Kans.: University Press of Kansas, 1998), pp. 226–27. Some of what Nixon said was quoted by Henry Brandon in *The Retreat of American Power* (Garden City: Doubleday, 1973), p. 134; Kimball would like to see it all in its original form.

52 *Newspapers in Microform:* Various volumes (Washington, D.C.: Library of Congress, 1984 and earlier).

52 Bosse: David Bosse, *Civil War Newspaper Maps: A Cartobibliography of the Northern Daily Press* (Westport, Conn.: Greenwood Press, 1993).

52 "significant gaps": For example, fourteen days were missing from the Chicago *Daily Tribune* for 1862 and 1863, and January 2 through April 28, 1865, were missing from the Chicago *Post.* Bosse, *Civil War Newspaper Maps,* pp. 211–12.

53 Edwina Dumm: See Lucy Shelton Caswell, "Edwina Dumm: Pioneer Woman

Editorial Cartoonist, 1915–1917," *Journalism History* 15 (spring 1988). In another Ace comb variation, several libraries get rid of a particular title before anyone has microfilmed it, knowing, however, that another set exists; later, the single remaining copy available for microfilming turns out to have gaps. Matthew J. Bruccoli, working on a biography of John O'Hara, wanted to study a run of the Pottsville, Pennsylvania, *Journal,* in which O'Hara had published his earliest journalism. (O'Hara wrote a column for the *Journal* called "After Four O'Clock"—of which, according to Bruccoli, O'Hara was "intensely proud.") The *Journal*'s own backfile had gone to the Schuylkill County Historical Society when the paper went out of business, but Bruccoli discovered that this run lacked volumes for 1924 through 1926, the period of O'Hara's activity there. The other libraries in the area had, Bruccoli told me, donated their runs of the *Journal* to paper drives during the Second World War, "apparently with a certain amount of glee." In his foreword to *The O'Hara Concern* (New York: Popular Library, 1977), Bruccoli writes: "The disappearance of this material resulted in the most serious hole in my research."

CHAPTER 6 – Virgin Mummies

55 Dr. Isaiah Deck: "On a Supply of Paper Material from the Mummy Pits of Egypt, by Dr. Isaiah Deck, chemist, etc., New-York," in *Transactions of the American Institute of the City of New-York, for the Year 1854* (Albany: C. van Benthuysen, Printer to the Legislature, 1855), pp. 83–93.

55 113 Nassau Street: Deck, "On a Supply of Paper Material," p. 93. *The New York Times:* Elmer Davis, *History of the New York Times, 1851–1921* (New York: *The New York Times,* 1921), illus. f.p. 74. *Vanity Fair:* "The staff of 'Vanity Fair' met on Fridays in the old editorial rooms, 113 Nassau Street, and drank, and smoked, and discussed the next issue." Albert H. Smyth, *Bayard Taylor* (Detroit: Gale Research, 1970), pp. 137–38, quoted in n. 63 of a biography by Dave Gross of nineteenth-century American hashish-eater and journalist Fitz Hugh Ludlow (1836–1870), nepenthes.lycaeum.org/Ludlow/THE/Biography/foot63.html.

55 six thousand wagons: Joel Munsell, *Chronology of the Origin and Progress of Paper and Paper-Making* (New York: Garland, 1980; facsimile of 5th ed., Albany: J. Munsell, 1876), p. 146. Munsell derived this figure from "The Rag and Paper Business," New York *Tribune,* November 4, 1856, p. 3.

55 Mill women sorted: See Library of Congress, *Papermaking: Art and Craft* (Washington, D.C.: Library of Congress, 1968), illus. p. 67.

55 four-inch squares: "The woman stands so as to have the back of the blade opposite to her, while at her right hand on the floor is a large wooden box, with several divisions. Her business consists in examining the rags, opening the seams, removing dirt, pins, needles, and buttons of endless variety, which would be liable to injure the machinery, or damage the quality of the paper. She then cuts the rags into small pieces, not exceeding four inches square, by drawing them sharply across the edge of the knife, at the same time keeping each quality distinct in the several divisions of the box placed on her right hand. During this process, much of the dirt, sand, and so forth, passes through the wire cloth into a drawer underneath, which is occasionally cleaned out." Richard Herring, *Paper and Paper Making, Ancient and Modern,* 3d ed. (London: Longmans, Green, 1863), pp. 75–76.

55 cutting machine: O'Brien, *Story of the Sun;* Munsell, *Chronology,* p. 82.

55 black specks: Herring, *Paper and Paper Making,* p. 88. India rubber, writes Herring, "is a source of much greater annoyance to the paper maker than is readily conceived."

56 equal to England's and France's combined: Munsell, *Chronology,* p. 144.

56 Rag imports: Munsell, *Chronology,* pp. 126, 138.

56 "Complaints of the price and scarcity": Munsell, *Chronology,* p. 136.

56 "on account of the high price": Munsell, *Chronology,* p. 136.

56 Several generations of papermakers: See Munsell, *Chronology,* and Dard Hunter, *Papermaking: The History and Technique of an Ancient Craft* (New York: Alfred A. Knopf, 1943).

57 a paper made from horseradish: Munsell, *Chronology,* p. 137.

57 "seem to invite us": Quoted in Hunter, *Papermaking,* p. 233.

57 "reluctant to spare even a fragment": Hunter, *Papermaking,* p. 286n.

58 "flames would literally spout": Quoted in Bob Brier, *Egyptian Mummies* (New York: William Morrow, 1994), p. 318.

59 "locomotives of Egypt": Mummies were bought "by the ton or by the graveyard" as locomotive fuel, Mark Twain half-skeptically noted in his 1869 book of travels, *Innocents Abroad.* Mark Twain, *The Innocents Abroad; or, the New Pilgrims' Progress* (New York: Hippocrene Books, n.d.; facsimile of Hartford, Conn.: American Publishing Company, 1869), p. 632.

59 *Punch:* "Musings on Mummy-Paper," *Punch* 12 (May 29, 1847), p. 224.

60 twenty-three tons: Munsell, *Chronology,* p. 120.

61 "fairer (Pharaoh)": The pun is Deck's, not mine.

61 exactly contemporary with the publication: Deck's article is dated "March, 1855" at the end, although it appeared in the 1854 volume of the American Institute's *Transactions.*

61 J. Priestly bought 1,215 bales: Munsell, *Chronology,* p. 142.

61 "It is within": "The Rag and Paper Business," New York *Tribune,* November 4, 1856.

62 "made from the wrappages": "Paper from Egyptian Mummies," Syracuse *Daily Standard,* August 19, 1856 (undated editorial reprinted from *The Albany Journal*). See also Munsell, *Chronology,* p. 149.

62 "into the hopper": Munsell, *Chronology,* p. 198. The report appeared in an editorial in the *Bunker Hill Aurora,* sometime in 1866.

62 Dard Hunter was oddly hesitant: Hunter, *Papermaking,* pp. 287–91. Joseph Dane goes further. He believes mummy paper to be a "delusion" and a "myth," and he has no confidence in Hunter's sources for Syracuse, Broadalbin, and Gardiner; and he isn't at all sure about Deck's Swiftian proposal, either. But Dane hasn't read Deck's proposal, which, he says, is "untraceable"—Hunter gave no citation for it and called it a "manuscript," which makes Dane suspicious. I traced Deck by calling the helpful librarian at the Onondaga Historical Association, Judy Haven. Joseph A. Dane, "The Curse of the Mummy Paper," *Printing History* 18:2 (1995).

62 Horace Greeley: Greeley was an active member of the American Institute; he became its president in 1866. John Campbell, a paper merchant a few doors down from Dr. Deck on Nassau Street, was also a member of the Institute in 1855. I found them listed in a scarce pamphlet owned by Columbia University: *Catalogue of the Life and Annual Members of the American Institute of the City of New York* (New York: New York Printing Co., 1868).

62 Richard Hoe: Hoe's specialty was high-speed presses. Without plentiful, cheap paper, publishers would be less likely to convert to faster equipment; I speculate that Hoe may have had an interest in Deck's proposal for that reason. Hoe had served on the committee in 1852 that organized the Institute's popular fair at Castle Garden (now Battery Park), where novelties of science and engineering were awarded prizes. Morse's telegraph was first displayed at the 1842 fair; Walt Whitman delivered a "Song of the Exposition" to open the 1871 fair, announcing that America would build a cathedral of sacred industry that was "mightier than Egypt's tombs."

63 whiskey blenders: Nicolas Barker is the source of this image.

63 Hall and McChesney: Hendrix TenEyck, an executive of Hall and McChesney, was president of the American Microfilm Association when Verner Clapp gave his keynote address in 1959.

CHAPTER 7 – Already Worthless

65 "A Life-Cycle Cost Analysis": William Richard Lemberg, Ph.D. diss., School of Library and Information Studies, University of California at Berkeley, 1995, www.sims.berkeley.edu/research/publications/DigtlDoc.pdf. Michael Buckland, Lemberg's thesis supervisor at Berkeley, writes that "one of the principal expected benefits of the move from paper-based to digital libraries is in the massive cost-savings expected to result from an expected reduction in duplication." Michael Buckland, "Searching Multiple Digital Libraries: A Design Analysis" (Berkeley: University of California, 1995), www.sims.berkeley.edu/research/oasis/multisrch.html (viewed August 13, 2000).

65 "the most valuable fibre": Munsell, *Chronology.* Munsell is at first unfamiliar with esparto grass, calling it "spartum," "Exparto," and "waterbroom"—he attributes its initial use to a Parisian stationer named Jean A. Farina, in 1852. The material "at first encountered great opposition both from proprietors and their workmen, but finally assumed vast importance as a raw material" (p. 124). In 1866, *Lloyd's Newspaper* imported two hundred and sixty tons of esparto grass to London (p. 200); in 1870, there was an esparto shortage, and the price more than doubled (p. 213); in 1871, Lloyd, the newspaper publisher, owned 180,000 acres in Algeria, on which he raised his own esparto crop (p. 221); in 1872, English esparto imports had passed 130,000 tons, and Munsell writes that the *Times* "was printed on paper made more or less of this material, as was that of most of the other leading journals, periodicals and current publications generally" (p. 226). In its article "Paper," the 1911 *Encyclopaedia Britannica* has a large and handsome engraving of the "Sinclair Esparto Boiler," featuring recirculative "vomiting pipes," and no pictures of wood-pulping equipment. See also British Paper and Board Makers' Association, *Paper Making: A General Account of Its History, Processes, and Applications* (Kenley, Eng., 1950), pp. 31, 47, 101. The turn-of-the-century English book, then, is likely to have little or no wood pulp in it; American paper and English paper have different compositions and are likely to age differently.

66 Lesk: Michael Lesk, *Practical Digital Libraries: Books, Bytes, and Bucks* (San Francisco: Morgan Kaufmann, 1997). Lemberg's dissertation gets a paragraph on pp. 76–77.

68 "very high performance Backbone Network Service": E.g., a 1999 National Science Foundation grant of $422,000 to Harvard for a "High-Performance

Internet Connection" connecting Harvard to NYNEX and the NSF's vBNS, in order to support scientific projects and "Digital Library Applications." Of course Harvard should have high-speed Internet connections, if it needs them, but the federal government shouldn't be paying for them, and the money shouldn't come bundled in a plan to destroy traditional libraries.

68 routinely prepare for digitization: At a 1998 conference sponsored by the Research Libraries Group and Great Britain's National Preservation Office, John E. McIntyre, head of preservation of the National Library of Scotland, discussed the results of an informal survey of digitization practices in a paper called "Protecting the Physical Form." He wrote: "Returns from the Preparation Group's questionnaire suggest that disbinding in order to scan a volume is common, in most cases so that a flat bed scanner can be used." John E. McIntyre, "Protecting the Physical Form," in *Guidelines for Digital Imaging,* Joint RLG and NPO Preservation Conference, 1998, www.rlg.org/preserv/joint/mcintyre.html.

68 "knowing that the original will be disbound": Carla Montori, "Re: electronic/paper format & weeding," PADG (Preservation Administrators Discussion Group), December 15, 1997, archived on the CoOL (Conservation OnLine) website, palimpsest.stanford.edu/byform/mailing-lists/padg/1997/12/msg00011.html (viewed September 29, 2000).

68 *Making of America:* Michigan's *Making of America* books are to be found at moa.umdl.umich.edu.

69 "It is substantially cheaper": Michael Lesk, "Substituting Images for Books: The Economics for Libraries," Document Analysis and Information Retrieval (symposium), Las Vegas, April 1996, www.lesk.com/mlesk/unlv/unlv.html (viewed September 19, 2000).

70 "avaricious in [their] consumption": William G. Bowen, "JSTOR and the Economics of Scholarly Communication," the Andrew W. Mellon Foundation, October 4, 1995, www.mellon.org/jsesc.html. JSTOR's webpage background document states that the "basic idea" behind Bowen's JSTOR "was to convert the back issues of paper journals into electronic formats that would allow savings in space (and in capital costs associated with that space) while simultaneously improving access to the journal content." JSTOR, *Background,* www.umich.edu./~jstor/about/background.html (1996) (viewed September 15, 2000). A recent JSTOR brochure entitled "Electronic Archives of Core Mathematics Journals" says: "By making the complete runs of important journal backfiles available and searchable over the World Wide Web, JSTOR not only provides new research possibilities, it also helps librarians reduce longterm costs associated with storing these materials."

70 survey conducted by JSTOR: JSTOR, *Bound Volume Survey,* April 3, 2000, www.jstor.org/about/bvs.html (viewed September 19, 2000).

71 "modem life": "The third class of tendencies is easily identifiable with those impulses to disinterested benevolence which are so prominent in modern [OCR'd as modem] life." Henry Rutgers Marshall, "Emotions versus Pleasure-Pain," *Mind,* n.s. 4:14. (April 1895): 180–94. I also got multiple hits for "modemist" and "modemism," none having to do with data-communications.

CHAPTER 8 – A Chance to Begin Again

73 "application of the camera": Raney, "Introduction," in *Microphotography for Libraries,* p. v.

73 "a couple of curious librarians": M. Llewellyn Raney, "A Capital Truancy," *The Journal of Documentary Reproduction* 3:2 (June 1940). Possibly Keyes Metcalf was there, and the scout was probably from the Rockefeller Foundation; Charles Z. Case of Recordak helped out with the cost analysis.

74 "Every research library would": Fremont Rider (writing anonymously), "Microtext in the Management of Book Collections: A Symposium," *College and Research Libraries,* July 1953, reprinted in Veaner, *Studies in Micropublishing,* p. 206. Rider presented this proposal anonymously here, but in other settings he repeated it almost word for word under his own name.

74 James T. Babb: In the 1952–1953 annual report of the Yale University library, Babb announced that "our shelves are weighted down with many books and periodicals that we easily could do without." In the past, he said, Yale was "ambitious to be a library of record; that is, have one copy of every book of any importance." This was "a highly questionable ambition," Babb believed; and it was time to undo what his forebears had done. He proposed, and the Yale Corporation approved, a "drastic" plan to "1. Decatalogue and discard material which is considered to have no further scholarly value," and "2. Purchase or reproduce with our own equipment, in microtext form other books and periodicals, the original then being discarded." James T. Babb, *Report,* 1952–1953, quoted in John H. Ottemiller, "The Selective Book Retirement Program at Yale," *Yale University Library Gazette* 34:2 (October 1959).

75 "Roses, jasmine": Fremont Rider, *And Master of None: An Autobiography in the Third Person* (Middletown, Conn.: Godfrey Memorial Library, 1955), p. 46.

75 "converted to psychism": Fremont Rider, *Are the Dead Alive?* (New York: B. W. Dodge, 1909). Theodore Dreiser supplied the book's title; David Belasco based a play on it called "The Return of Peter Grimm."

76 "They are thoroughly disgusted": Fremont Rider (writing as Alfred Wayland), *Are Our Banks Betraying Us* (New York: Anvil Press, 1932), quoted in Rider, *And Master of None,* p. 98.

76 "astonishing flood": Rider, *And Master of None,* p. 99.

76 "You are right!": Roosevelt's letter (typewritten except for the last two sentences) reads: "Dear Mr. Rider: Thank you ever so much for your very nice letter and the pamphlet which you sent me. I have been much interested in reading it. You are right! Keep it up— Very sincerely yours, Franklin D. Roosevelt." The letter is dated "At Warm Springs, Georgia, May 6, 1932." Franklin D. Roosevelt, letter to Fremont Rider, Fremont Rider papers, Wesleyan University, Middletown, Conn. (Suzy Taraba, Wesleyan's university archivist and head of special collections, located it and sent me a copy.) Roosevelt gave his nomination speech at the Democratic National Convention on July 2, 1932: "I pledge you, I pledge myself, to a new deal for the American people."

76 He began a system: Rider, *And Master of None,* p. 152: "Wholesale methods of disposition do not bring the highest possible prices; but they enabled Wesleyan to dispose of its discards at very small handling cost"; after buying fifty thousand volumes and selling off thirty thousand, Rider was pleased to discover that "the additions to the Library actually cost it nothing."

76 "mathematical fact": Fremont Rider, *The Scholar and the Future of the Research Library* (New York: Hadham Press, 1944), p. 8.

76–77 "natural law": Rider, *The Scholar,* p. 16.

77 "veritable tidal wave": Rider, *The Scholar,* p. 13.

77 "It is a problem": Rider, *The Scholar,* p. 13.

77 "We absolutely *must*": Rider, *The Scholar,* p. 13. Rider's book predated by a year Vannevar Bush's famous article in the *Atlantic Monthly,* "As We May Think" (July 1945), which envisioned a scholar's workstation holding thousands of books on microfilm.

77 later students of library progress: Robert E. Molyneux, "What Did Rider Do? An Inquiry into the Methodology of Fremont Rider's *The Scholar and the Future of the Research Library,*" *Libraries and Culture* 29:1 (summer 1994); and Steven Leach, "The Growth Rates of Major Academic Libraries: Rider and Purdue Reviewed," *College and Research Libraries,* November 1976. Leach writes: "The Rider hypothesis cannot be used reliably to project library growth"; after reaching three million volumes, "an individual library can anticipate a deceleration in its rate of collection growth." On the other hand, Leach confirms "Rider's fundamental perception that library growth would become an increasingly perplexing problem for university libraries." Molyneux finds "serious flaws in Rider's analysis" and argues that Rider's law of exponential doubling "resulted from a miscalculation which was either not caught in the subsequent versions of these tables or caught and not reported." It is "troubling," writes Molyneux, that "Rider's analysis escaped criticism and was cited approvingly for so many years, especially given the fact that the theory so obviously contradicted common experience."

77 "tacit confession of past failure": Rider, *The Scholar,* p. 56.

77 "new expenses and fresh problems": Rider, *The Scholar,* p. 57.

78 "gratifyingly close": Fremont Rider, "Microcards vs. the Cost of Book Storage," *American Documentation* 2:1 (January 1951), reprinted in Veaner, *Studies in Micropublishing.* See also p. 203, where Rider (anonymously) says that the storage cost would come "gratifyingly close to 99%," and Rider, *The Scholar,* pp. 101–2. Rider had no qualms about clearing out existing card catalogs; his paper "The Possibility of Discarding the Card Catalog" appeared in *Library Quarterly* in July 1938.

78 "micro-reading machines": Fremont Rider, "Author's Statement," in Keyes Metcalf et al., "The Promise of Microprint: A Symposium Based on *The Scholar and the Future of the Research Library,*" *College and Research Libraries,* March 1945.

78 Microcard Foundation: Rider, *And Master of None,* pp. 204–5; Martin Jamison, "The Microcard: Fremont Rider's Precomputer Revolution," in *Libraries and Culture* 23:1 (winter 1988).

78 Atomic Energy Commission: See Adkinson, *Two Centuries of Federal Information,* p. 47. The Department of Defense and the weather bureau were also users of Microcards: Rider, *And Master of None,* p. 205.

78 "produces heat which": J. S. Parsonage, "The 'Scholar' and After: A Study of the Development of the Microcard," *Library Association Record,* November 1949, reprinted in Veaner, *Studies in Micropublishing.*

78 conventional microfilm: Microcards are hard on the eyes, but Readex Microprint, another opaque system that relies on reflected light, is worse, in my experience.

79 1,600 Microcard-viewing machines: Jamison, "The Microcard." In his autobiography, Rider claims that there were three thousand reading machines in use, but he often exaggerated. Rider, *And Master of None,* p. 205.

79 "To any one who has New England blood": Rider, *And Master of None,* p. 112.

79 "All that we have to do": Rider, *The Scholar,* p. 115.
80 "required reading": Metcalf et al., "The Promise of Microprint."
80 "it is difficult": Edward G. Freehafer, in Metcalf et al., "The Promise of Microprint." In the same symposium, Donald Coney of the University of Texas wrote: "Mr. Rider's proposal for the transfer of books to micro-cards is a genuinely epochal idea. If widely adopted, it would mark the first significant change in books since the substitution of the codex for the roll."
80 page full of praise: Rider, *And Master of None,* p. 202.

CHAPTER 9 – Dingy, Dreary, Dog-eared, and Dead

83 Rider's friend and ally: Rider wrote a letter of support endorsing Clapp for the position of librarian of Congress. Betty Milum, "Eisenhower, ALA, and the Selection of L. Quincy Mumford," *Libraries and Culture* 30:1 (winter 1995), n. 16. Clapp's diary records a breakfast with Rider (July 13, 1951) and a request from the Microcard Foundation to borrow material from the Library of Congress for copying (March 16, 1951). Verner Clapp papers, Library of Congress. Both Rider and Clapp were frustrated inventors—Rider developed the Wesleyan book truck ("astonishingly practical," he said in his autobiography), and he had "revolutionary" ideas for vertical-takeoff-and-landing propellers; Clapp became caught up in the inventions that the Council on Library Resources was paying for.
83 "full cropping": On books that had "inordinately wide margins and no more than nominal value," Rider had his staff "trim a *wide* slice off all three edges of the book, covers and all. . . . Our theory in treating them thus roughly is that it is expensive enough to store the *texts* of such materials: and that we have no very good reason to store forever a lot of accompanying waste paper" (*Compact Book Storage* [New York: Hadham Press, 1949], p. 60). Henry Petroski discusses (without, perhaps, the requisite incredulity) Rider's related attempts to store Wesleyan's books with their fore-edges down and their titles and call numbers hand-lettered on their cleanly guillotined bottom edges; Petroski says that "overall [Rider's] analyses were sound and truly space-saving, even if a bit extreme and labor intensive." Henry Petroski, *The Book on the Bookshelf* (New York: Alfred A. Knopf, 1999). On the jacket of *Compact Book Storage,* Rider prints blurbs from prominent librarians: Luther Evans at the Library of Congress was, predictably, "very much impressed" by the book's recommendations: "I entertain the serious possibility that we may adopt some of them." Harvard's Keyes Metcalf wrote, "We have been doing thinking along the same lines"; Yale's James T. Babb said the book was "tremendously interesting."
83 *Wildlife Disease:* See "Scientific Journal in Microfilm—An Experiment in Publishing," *Library Journal,* April 1, 1959.
83 "The Problem of Size": Council on Library Resources, *Third Annual Report* (1959), pp. 11ff. In 1961, Clapp wrote: "One of the most obvious advantages to be obtained by libraries from microcopying is in saving of storage space, but the cost of microcopying is so great as rarely to justify its use for space-saving alone. Additional justification is required, such as saving of binding costs, preservation against deterioration, ease of duplication, or adaptation to mechanized duplicating or information storage-and-retrieval devices." Council on Library Resources, *Fifth Annual Report* (1961), p. 23.

84 "baloney, baloney": Kathleen Molz, "Interview of Verner Clapp, Council on Library Resources, Inc. by Kathleen Molz, editor, *Wilson Library Bulletin,*" p. 17, Verner Clapp papers, Library of Congress. Later published as Kathleen Molz, "Interview with Verner Clapp," *Wilson Library Bulletin* 40:2 (1965). In this version, Clapp refers to the gap between scientists and humanists as "a bunch of sheer baloney."

84 "After numerous inquiries": Verner Clapp, "The Library: The Great Potential in Our Society?" Keynote address at the second annual Congress for Librarians, St. John's University, Jamaica, N.Y., February 22, 1960, *Wilson Library Bulletin,* December 1960.

84 "The world's population": Council on Library Resources, *Third Annual Report* (1959).

84 "Massive dissemination": Verner Clapp, *The Future of the Research Library* (Urbana: University of Illinois Press, 1964), p. 30.

84 "the storage library would": Clapp, *Future of the Research Library,* p. 25.

84 "lesser-used books": Clapp, *Future of the Research Library,* p. 25.

84 "loved gadgets": Deanna B. Marcum, "Reclaiming the Research Library: The Founding of the Council on Library Resources," *Libraries and Culture* 31:1 (winter 1996).

85 "solutions to the problems": Council on Library Resources, *First Annual Report* (1957).

85 Warren Weaver: Weaver was a guiding spirit at the Rand Corporation; at an early Rand gathering in June 1948, doing his best to recruit the finest war talent available, he said that Rand would occupy itself with problems of "military worth," investigating "to what extent it is possible to have useful quantitative indices for a gadget, a tactic or a strategy, so that one can compare it with available alternatives and guide decisions by analysis." Fred Kaplan, *The Wizards of Armageddon* (New York: Simon and Schuster, 1983), p. 72. See also Erik Peter Rau, "Combat Scientists: The Emergence of Operations Research in the United States during World War II," Ph.D. diss., University of Pennsylvania, 1999; Rau mentions, for example, Weaver's hope of recruiting architects, civil engineers, and construction engineers to aid the mathematical study of "aerial bombardment," p. 330.

85 "fire control": See Warren Weaver, *Scene of Change: A Lifetime in American Science* (New York: Scribner's, 1970), pp. 77ff.

85 Philip Morse: Morse's autobiography is *In at the Beginnings: A Physicist's Life* (Cambridge, Mass.: MIT Press, 1977). In 1946, Morse and another "polemologist" (warfare scientist; their coinage, from the Greek *polemos,* warfare) published a classified textbook covering damage coefficients, lethal areas, train bombardment, and gunnery statistics, but even then Morse was already thinking about using the same quantitative techniques to assist in urban planning. Philip M. Morse and George E. Kimball, *Methods of Operations Research* (Washington, D.C.: Operations Evaluation Group, U.S. Navy, 1946).

86 Morse wanted to computerize: Morse mentions a decision to move some books to the basement of the science library: "If circulation had been computerized at the time, the move could have been planned with greater knowledge of expected results, and also a wider variety of possible actions would have been available to choose from." Philip M. Morse, *Library Effectiveness: A Systems Approach* (Cambridge, Mass.: MIT Press, 1968), p. 166.

86 "cannot now be operated": Morse, *Library Effectiveness,* p. 1. "Books are still the

most convenient packages of information, but this may no longer be true in the future," Morse writes (p. 186).

86 secret OR analysis: "The broad purpose of Project AC-92 is the determination of optimum tactics for use in the employment of very heavy bombers in operations against Japan." Merrill M. Flood, *Aerial Bombing Tactics: General Considerations (A World War II Study)* (Santa Monica: Rand, 1952).

86 "poison gas": Flood, *Aerial Bombing Tactics,* p. 6. Flood was also one of the inventors of the Prisoner's Dilemma, a game-theoretic thought-experiment in which two criminals decide independently whether each will inform on the other. See William Poundstone, *Prisoner's Dilemma* (New York: Doubleday, 1992).

86 "very major steps": Merrill M. Flood, "New Operations Research Potentials," *Operations Research* 10:4 (July–August 1962): 436.

86 "many of the decisions normally": Flood, "New Operations Research Potentials," p. 429.

86 Verner Clapp hired Flood: I say "Clapp hired" because Clapp made all the decisions: "the choice of projects to be funded were," in the early years of the Council on Library Resources, "very much Clapp's." William Joseph Crowe, "Verner W. Clapp as Opinion Leader and Change Agent in the Preservation of Library Materials," Ph.D. diss., Indiana University, 1986, p. 70.

86 Gilbert W. King: Gilbert W. King et al., *Automation and the Library of Congress* (Washington, D.C.: Library of Congress, 1963). King was a follower of Warren Weaver and Philip Morse; "Operations research is meaningless unless it gets results quickly," he wrote in a paper on probabilistic techniques. Gilbert King, "The Monte Carlo Method as a Natural Mode of Expression in Operations Research," *Journal of the Operations Research Society of America* 1:2 (February 1953). King worked on projects for the Office of Naval Research, and he developed a translation machine at International Telemeter and IBM before moving to Itek. The others who worked on the King Report, as it came to be known, were: Harold P. Edmundson (of Planning Research Corporation, a Rand spin-off with large military and CIA contracts), Merrill M. Flood (formerly of Rand and later of the Mental Health Research Institute at the University of Michigan, a center that sponsored research in psychopharmacology and computer networks under the direction of wartime OSS psychologist James Grier Miller), Manfred Kochen (also of Rand and then of the Mental Health Research Institute; Kochen did the math behind the idea of "six degrees of separation"), Richard L. Libby (Air Force intelligence), Don R. Swanson (who worked at defense-and-intelligence contractor Thompson Ramo Wooldridge, soon to become TRW, and who eventually took charge of the library school at the University of Chicago); and Alexander Wylly, who had studied tank logistics for Planning Research Corporation in 1956.

86 Itek Corporation: Itek's role in the CIA's Corona satellite program is covered in Smith, "Design and Engineering of Corona's Optics"; and in Shulman, "Code Name Corona."

86 ex-CIA paramilitarist: Frank Lindsay was Itek's president beginning in 1962; Lindsay was deputy chief of the CIA's Office of Policy Coordination from 1949 to 1951. "He joined the Ford Foundation in 1953, served on several Presidential commissions, and, since 1962, has been president of the Itek Corporation. After the 1968 election, President-elect Nixon asked Lindsay to

head a secret task force on CIA reorganization." R. Harris Smith, *OSS: The Secret History of America's First Central Intelligence Agency* (Berkeley: University of California Press, 1972), p. 161.

87 the stacks would be closed: "The adoption of an automated system will require that the Library stacks be closed in order to insure the accuracy of the various recording functions. Closing the stacks will result in a reduced need for subject-related classification as a medium for stack arrangement, since the stacks will no longer serve as a single large browsing collection. As a result, new methods of efficient storage based on demand frequency or other criteria will become feasible." King et al., *Automation and the Library of Congress,* p. 43.

87 funded by the Department of Defense: King et al., *Automation and the Library of Congress,* p. 68.

87 Filesearch: *Automation and the Library of Congress,* pp. 47, 76. The Filesearch system was built by FMA, Inc.; the initials stood for Fenn, McPherson, and Arsenault—three engineers from Magnavox who developed this variation on Vannevar Bush's Rapid Selector microfilm machine. Robert M. Hayes, letter to author, September 1, 2000.

87 military used the Filesearch: "As with most early computer systems, FileSearch information can not be accessed as originally designed. FileSearch was used primarily by the defense and intelligence communities and was not adopted by the civilian sector in any numbers. Thus, there was no commercial commitment to maintain this particular system. Unable to make Filesearch work on current hardware, the National Archives re-filmed the Vietnamese documents on standard microfilm. Historians should resign themselves to facing similar frustrations with computer databases." Michael E. Unsworth, "A Lesson Not Learned: The MACV 'Answer Machine,' " abstract of a paper given at a symposium, "After the Cold War: Reassessing Vietnam" (April 1996), www.ttu.edu/~vietnam/96papers/macv.htm (viewed September 14, 2000).

87 wiry, energetic: Clapp is so described in Louise S. Robbins, "The Library of Congress and Federal Loyalty Programs, 1947–1956: No 'Communists or Cocksuckers,' " *Library Quarterly* 64:4 (October 1994). The title quotes Luther Evans, who informed poet Karl Shapiro that he didn't want either of them in the Library of Congress.

87 Lawrence F. Buckland: Interview with author, October 5, 2000.

88 Henriette Avram: Association for Library Collections and Technical Services, "Henriette Avram, Associate Librarian for Collections Services, to Retire from the Library of Congress," *ALCTS Network News,* 1:8 (June 25, 1991), www.ala.org/alcts/publications/an2/an2v1/an2.v1_no8.html.

88 Some of Verner Clapp's ideas: Library of Congress, *Verner Warren Clapp, 1901–1972: A Memorial Tribute* (Washington, D.C.: Library of Congress, 1973).

88 John H. Ottemiller: Yale's Ottemiller is described as "shrewd, tough, and crusty" in Robin W. Winks, *Cloak and Gown: Scholars in the Secret War, 1939–1961* (New Haven: Yale University Press, 1987), which mentions his wartime work for the Office of Strategic Services with Frederick Kilgour, later of OCLC.

88 "a possible need": Ottemiller quotes Fremont Rider's estimate that Yale would own two hundred million volumes by 2040 and says, "Panic, then, becomes a moderate word which no longer exaggerates the situation." The grant was for fifty thousand dollars, allowing the selective retirement program to increase its

throughput from twenty thousand to sixty thousand books a year (some moved to departmental libraries or storage, some microfilmed and then discarded, some discarded outright), "thereby providing a body of material large enough to validate statistical data as soon as possible." Ottemiller, "Selective Book Retirement Program," p. 72.

89 Arthur Carson: Interview with author, June 23, 2000. The National Security Agency was initially interested in Carson's crystal storage system, as was the FBI (they were thinking of using it for a visual database of fingerprints), but it was the Council on Library Resources that came through with a contract. Before starting Carson Laboratories, Carson says that he designed a small, stealthy, nuclear-powered submarine, to be made of fiberglass, that he very nearly convinced the English to build; however (according to Carson), Hyman Rickover, head of the U.S. nuclear fleet, didn't want the British admiralty to be operating nuclear subs and used his influence to have the project dropped.

89 Fiber optics?: Council on Library Resources, *Seventh Annual Report,* period ending June 30, 1963, p. 28. The Institute for Scientific Information, founded by Eugene Garfield, published *Current Contents* and the *Science Citation Index;* Garfield called Clapp a "great gadgeteer." Eugene Garfield, "Information Science and Technology: Looking Backward and Looking Forward," a lecture at the Catholic University of America, January 25, 1999, students.cua.edu/org/asis/jan99.htm; and Eugene Garfield, *Eugene Garfield, Ph.D.* (homepage), www.garfield.library.upenn.edu.

89 "reducing the required number": Council on Library Resources, *Fifth Annual Report* (1961), p. 25.

89 combine closed-circuit TV: Council on Library Resources, *Second Annual Report* (1958), p. 24.

89 de Florez Company: Council on Library Resources, *Second Annual Report* (1958), p. 24. Clapp also hired the Defense Electronic Products division of Radio Corporation of America to build a page-turner. RCA came up with a system of air blowers and "thumbs": "Once the top page is pulled from the stack, it is quickly blown by jets of air to the opposite side where another thumb catches it and pulls it tightly to the portion of the book on that side. This machine is endowed with four thumbs, not just two." Radio Corporation of America, Defense Electronic Products, "A Proposal for an Automatic Page Turner: Submitted to the Council on Library Resources in Response to 'An Automatic Page Turner—the Basic Requirements,' November 1, 1957."

89 radiological weapons: A memo to the chief of operations of the CIA's Directorate for Plans (DD/P), dated 28 October 1954, discusses the possibility of irradiating the Soviet Union "in conjunction with appropriate psychological warfare measures" and "paramilitary exploitation," possibly accompanied by radio broadcasts and leaflets emphasizing the "humanitarian concern of the United States" (as evidenced by the use of this "relatively benign" weapon), yet stressing, on the other hand, that "full recovery would depend upon complete inactivity, in the absence of which sterility, prolonged illness and possibly death would ensue." The proposal's attachment (dated June 6, 1952) discusses the "need of many special techniques and devices not commercially available or as yet undeveloped or unknown"; it proposes "to establish a research program under the over-all guidance of a CIA Research Board chaired by Admiral Luis De Flores [*sic*]" and to "continue the contract with his company." The document is one of thousands that have been scanned, OCR'd, and made

available on the Web as part of a federal investigation into human radiation experiments; see Argonne National Laboratory, Human Radiation Experiments Information Management System, record number c0030 ("CIA, Memorandum for DD/P from DC/SE, dated 28 October 1954, subject: same as above"), hrex.dis.anl.gov. When in 1954 a germ-warfare scientist jumped out a window following a CIA-sponsored drug-research session, de Florez sent a memo to CIA head Allen Dulles asking him not to issue reprimands to those in charge of the experimental program because it would interfere with "the spirit of initiative and enthusiasm so necessary in our work." John Marks, *The Search for the Manchurian Candidate* (New York: Times Books, 1979), chap. 5.

89 "not particularly suited": Charles La Hood, letter to Verner Clapp, June 26, 1970, de Florez files, Council on Library and Information Resources.

90 Joseph Becker: Before he left the CIA in 1968, Becker won the CIA's Intelligence Medal of Merit; in an obituary, *The New York Times* wrote that he "computerized the Central Intelligence Agency's records." "Joseph Becker, 72, Information Expert," *The New York Times,* July 27, 1995, p. D22.

90 "some of the realities": Council on Library Resources, *1962 Annual Report,* p. 9.

90 "Transceiving time": H. G. Morehouse, *Telefacsimile Services Between Libraries with the Xerox Magnavox Telecopier* (Reno: University of Reno Library, December 20, 1966).

90 white rats: J. C. R. Licklider's M.A. thesis at Washington University was "The Influence of a Severe Modification in Sleep Pattern on Growth and Learning Ability of White Rats" (1938); his experiments with sleepy rats at Harvard are described in J. C. R. Licklider and R. E. Bunch, "Effects of Enforced Wakefulness Upon the Growth and the Maze Learning Performance of White Rats," *Journal of Comparative Psychology* 39 (1946). In "The Computer as a Communication Device," *Science and Technology* (April 1968), Licklider writes that "life will be happier for the on-line individual because the people with whom one interacts most strongly will be selected more by commonality of interests and goals than by accidents of proximity."

91 *Libraries of the Future:* J. C. R. Licklider, *Libraries of the Future* (Cambridge, Mass.: MIT Press, 1965). Among the participants and committee members acknowledged by Licklider in his preface were Marvin Minsky and John McCarthy, both cyberneticists of distinction; Caryl P. Haskins, President of the Carnegie Institution of Washington; Gilbert King of Itek; Philip Morse, the OR pioneer; and John R. Pierce of Bell Labs, designer of Telstar 1 and coiner of the word "transistor." For background on Licklider, SAGE, DARPA, air defense, real-time computing, and man-machine symbiosis, see Paul N. Edwards, *The Closed World: Computers and the Politics of Discourse in Cold War America* (Cambridge, Mass.: MIT Press, 1996).

91 "special manifestations of library work": Council on Library Resources, *Fourth Annual Report* (1961; introductory essay by Verner Clapp), p. 10.

91 Air Force Librarian: CIA file, Verner Warren Clapp.

91 fired or allowed to resign: See Robbins, "Library of Congress and Federal Loyalty Programs"; Robbins cites one librarian's plaintive appeal to Clapp in October 1952: "Next month it will be one year since I received the first interrogatory, and needless to say this matter has weighed very heavily on me." Clapp answered that he was "anxious for settlement"; her case wasn't settled for another six months. The well-placed hints of informants could be career-

destroyers, as Clapp knew, and he was careful in his deliberations; his daily journal from the early fifties reveals the extraordinarily time-consuming work he performed as part of the Library of Congress's three-man loyalty-review board, manned by Clapp, Frederick Wagman, and Burton Adkinson. Only two employees were fired outright from the library for political disloyalty between 1947 and 1956; but, as Robbins writes, "some resigned during the investigation process; some, after charges but before a hearing," while others weren't hired because "the loyalty panel concluded that a full field investigation would just be too costly"; and "at least ten lost their jobs during the purge of 'perverts.' " When the American Library Association (rather bravely, considering the temper of the times) passed a resolution condemning loyalty oaths, Clapp stoutly defended their necessity; to oppose their use, he wrote, "is actually to aid and abet the hysteria which the tests are designed to counteract" (*Library Journal,* April 15, 1950).

91 Office of Censorship: See Steven M. Roth, *The Censorship of International Civilian Mail during World War II: The History, Structure, and Operation of the United States Office of Censorship* (Lake Oswego, Oreg.: La Posta Publications, 1991). Censors slit letters open neatly on the left side (so that the examiner's resealing label wouldn't cover the stamp); they read the contents, noted certain items (discussions of enemy troop movements, for instance); sometimes photographed the letter and placed its sender or addressee on a watch list; "condemned" some mail; and returned to sender mail that contained prohibited material—e.g., statements "indicating low morale of the United States or its allies" (p. 98).

91 Human Ecology Fund: See Marks, *Search for the Manchurian Candidate,* chap. 9, which mentions Keeney on p. 156n. And see Andrew Sommer and Marc Cheshire, "The Spy Who Came in from the Campus," *New Times,* October 30, 1978, p. 14, in which Keeney, interviewed in retirement, admitted that he had (according to the authors) "advised the Agency on ways of setting up covert funding operations" and said that he "was told by CIA officials that MKULTRA [one of the covert drug-testing programs] was designed to counter Soviet and Chinese brainwashing techniques, developed through the use of psych-chemicals and hypnosis." The authors mention Keeney's work at the National Endowment for the Humanities: "When questioned as to whether the NEH was ever used to cloak CIA operations, he [Keeney] asked incredulously, 'Do you know what would happen to an agent who used the NEH as a cover?' After a dramatic pause he answered, 'He would be killed.' He would not elaborate on this peculiar assertion."

92 Caryl Haskins: For Haskins's work on the Ad Hoc Committee on Biological Warfare, see Susan Wright, *Preventing a Biological Arms Race* (Cambridge, Mass.: MIT Press, 1990), pp. 29–30.

92 Project Artichoke: "Dr. Caryl Haskins was selected to head up the Panel and endeavored, in conjunction with OSI [the CIA's Office of Scientific Intelligence] to enlist the services of other qualified professional personnel." Memo to Assistant Director, Scientific Intelligence from Project Coordinator, Subject: Project Artichoke, April 26, 1952. See Argonne National Laboratory, Human Radiation Experiments Information Management System (HREX), record number c0022 ("CIA, Meeting Attendance") at rex.dis.anl.gov.

92 Haskins traveled to Canada: "The genesis for the mind-control research was

worked out at a top-secret meeting June 1, 1951, at the Ritz Carleton Hotel in Montreal. . . . an anonymous handwritten note found in the archives identifies Dr. Caryl Haskins and Commander R.J. Williams as the CIA representatives at the meeting." David Vienneau, "Ottawa Paid for '50s Brainwashing Experiments, Files Show," *The Toronto Star,* April 14, 1986, final edition, p. A1, Nexis. And see related articles in *The Toronto Star,* April 15–17, 1986, and April 20, 1986. Haskins did not return calls from the *Toronto Star* reporter. (Haskins didn't answer my letter, either, but his former assistant sent a polite note saying that Haskins was "in excellent health" but that I shouldn't be surprised if he didn't answer, as "1951 was such a long time ago.")

92 available to the CIA as a consultant: "Dr. Haskins indicated that the Panel had contributed about as much as it could for the present and until resources were built up in the agency to undertake the staff and field work necessary, the panel would hold itself ready (as individual consultants) to be of any further advisory assistance." Memorandum to Assistant Director, April 26, 1952, Argonne National Laboratory, Human Radiation Experiments Information Management System (HREX), record number c0022 ("CIA, Meeting Attendance"). Haskins was also (for over twenty years) an influential member of the executive committee of the Smithsonian Institution—and here's the strange part: in the sixties, under director Leonard Carmichael (also a board member, like Barnaby Keeney, of the CIA's Human Ecology Fund), the Smithsonian did germ-warfare research. After receiving a series of inoculations, Smithsonian researchers traveled to islands in the Pacific to study how birds transmit disease; avian blood samples were shipped, frozen, to the Army's biological-weapons lab at Fort Detrick. The disease data was turned over to the CIA, whose MKULTRA program was studying "Avian Vectors in the Transmission of Disease." The Smithsonian's germ-warfare studies, and the CIA's biological experiments for that period, are chronicled in two *Washington Post* investigations: Bill Richards, "Germ Testing by the CIA," *The Washington Post,* August 11, 1977, p. A1, Nexis, and Bill Richards, "CIA Involvement at Smithsonian Called Limited," *The Washington Post,* August 31, 1977, p. A12, Nexis; and Ted Gup, "The Smithsonian Secret: Why an Innocent Bird Study Went Straight to Biological Warfare Experts at Fort Detrick," *The Washington Post Magazine,* May 12, 1985, Nexis. See also Ed Regis, *The Biology of Doom: The History of America's Secret Germ Warfare Project* (New York: Henry Holt, 1999); and Stephen Endicott and Edward Hagerman, *The United States and Biological Warfare* (Bloomington: Indiana University Press, 1998). It occurs to me that the CIA's interest in the avian vectors of disease may possibly explain the otherwise puzzling choice of *Wildlife Disease* as the journal Verner Clapp published on Microcards.

92 gruff and likeable: For an account of Louis Wright's increasing doubts about the activities of the Council, see Deanna B. Marcum, "Reclaiming the Research Library: The Founding of the Council on Library Resources," *Libraries and Culture* 31:1 (winter 1996). Marcum confirmed Wright's doubts about Clapp in a phone interview.

93 "the most informed point of contact": Crowe, "Verner W. Clapp as Opinion Leader," p. 93.

93 "first library millionaire": Paul Wasserman, "Interview with Paul Wasserman Regarding the Early History of CLIS," Esther Herman (interviewer), January 11, 1995, College of Information Studies, University of Maryland,

www.clis.umd.edu/faculty/wasserman/pwinterview.html. In 1947, at the Library of Congress, Mortimer Taube was put in charge of a project paid for by the Office of Naval Research to index and abstract scientific research and reports of interest to Navy weapons designers; see Adkinson, *Two Centuries of Federal Information,* p. 149. Robert M. Hayes, former dean of the UCLA's School of Library and Information Science, wrote me that Taube was "among the librarians who helped the CIA." Having come up with his improved "Uniterm" method of indexing, Taube formed Documentation, Inc., and "received funding from the intelligence community, CIA included, to carry out the development of a variety of retrieval techniques based on that concept." Robert Hayes, e-mail to author, 29 August 2000.

93 didn't work either: In 1967, the annual report mentioned the Council's "continued but unsuccessful attempts to develop a hand-held portable inexpensive device for viewing microforms." Having no luck with hand-helds, the Council proceeded to commission the Taylor-Merchant Corporation to build a prototype *projector* for microfiche and microfilm, whose "portability and economy should prove attractive to graduate students and others." The microform projector never made it to market. Council on Library Resources, *Eleventh Annual Report* (1967), p. 28.

93 a conduit for CIA money: David Wise and Thomas B. Ross, *The Espionage Establishment* (New York: Bantam, 1967), p. 137; and Sol Stern, "A Short Account of International Student Politics and the Cold War with particular reference to the NSA, CIA, etc.," *Ramparts,* March 1967. The sponsorship of the Independence Foundation is recorded on the title page of Carl F. J. Overhage and R. Joyce Harman, eds., *Intrex: Report of a Planning Conference on Information Transfer Experiments* (Cambridge, Mass.: MIT Press, 1965).

93 "better and more economical systems for weeding": Overhage and Harman, *Intrex,* p. 14.

93 "digital storage of encoded full-text": Also "transmission of a scanned-image electrical signal over a communication network and display and/or reproduction in full size or microform for temporary and/or permanent retention by the user." Council on Library Resources, *Eleventh Annual Report* (1967), p. 15.

93 "Project INTREX fell very short": Colin Burke, "Librarians Go High-Tech, Perhaps: The Ford Foundation, the CLR, and INTREX," *Libraries and Culture* 31:1 (winter 1996).

94 traditionalist members of his board: Besides Louis Wright, there was Lyman Butterfield, of the Massachusetts Historical Society, editor of the Adams papers. But the scientists dominated: in addition to Caryl Haskins, Philip Morse, and Warren Weaver, there was Joseph C. Morris, a large cigar-smoking physicist from Tulane who had worked on submarine warfare and then on the Manhattan Project (where he got a radiation burn on one hand), described in a eulogy as "a notorious gadgeteer" and an "inveterate dial-twiddler" (College of Arts and Sciences, Tulane University, "Resolution on the Death of Professor Morris," Meeting Minutes, May 19, 1970, Tulane University Archives). And there was James S. Coles, president of Bowdoin College, where he built tall buildings and raised huge sums. Coles, a chemist, spent the war at the Underwater Explosives Research Laboratory at Wood's Hole; there, according to *The Boston Globe* (June 14, 1996, p. 49), he "conducted research to improve

[the] underwater ignition and explosive power of depth charges, depth bombs, and torpedo warheads." He joined the Council's board in 1960.

94 "rescued many millions of pages": Council on Library Resources, *Second Annual Report* (1958), pp. 25–26.

95 "the destruction of the text": Alan B. Pritsker and J. William Sadler, "An Evaluation of Microfilm as a Method of Book Storage," *College and Research Libraries* 18:4 (July 1957).

95 Crerar Library: Research Information Service, John Crerar Library, *Dissemination of Information for Scientific Research and Development* (Chicago: John Crerar Library, 1954).

95 The library was moving: See Council on Library Resources, *Seventh Annual Report* (1963), p. 24; and Edward J. Forbes and David P. Waite, *Costs and Material Handling Problems in Miniaturizing 100,000 Volumes of Bound Periodicals,* Lexington, Massachusetts: Forbes & Waite, 1961, held by the University of Michigan Libraries.

95 "Costs and Material Handling": The consultants were Forbes and Waite, who specialized, wrote Clapp vaguely, in "information systems design including photographic applications," for which imprecision one should perhaps substitute "defense and/or intelligence workers"; Clapp, normally a scrupulous bibliographer, doesn't supply the full names of the consultants in the annual report for several years—an indication of some concern over secrecy. Edward J. Forbes and David P. Waite, *Costs and Material Handling Problems in Miniaturizing 100,000 Volumes of Bound Periodicals* (Lexington, Mass.: Forbes and Waite, 1961), held by the University of Michigan Libraries; Verner Clapp and Robert T. Jordan, "Re-evaluation of Microfilm as a Method of Book Storage," *College and Research Libraries,* January 1963. Forbes and Waite write that the volumes under consideration are a collection of "older periodical issues (prior to 1920)."

95 "considerable labor saving": Clapp and Jordan, "Re-evaluation."

96 "except that of destruction": Clapp and Jordan, "Re-evaluation."

CHAPTER 10 – The Preservation Microfilming Office

97 twenty-four microfilm cameras: La Hood, "Microfilm for the Library of Congress."

97 "otherwise beyond redemption": Council on Library Resources, *Twelfth Annual Report* (1968), p. 28. See also Library of Congress, "National Preservation Program—First Phase," *Library of Congress Information Bulletin* 26:4 (January 26, 1967): "In its own preservation program, the Library of Congress has been segregating its brittle books for several years and microfilming thousands of publications too brittle to bind."

97 "Space was a key word": Library of Congress, "Administrative Department."

97–98 "arrangements for assuring the preservation": Council on Library Resources, *Eleventh Annual Report* (1967), p. 34. See also Norman J. Shaffer, "Library of Congress Pilot Preservation Project," *College and Research Libraries,* January 1969. Shaffer writes that the Library of Congress preferred to microfilm nonfiction, rather than fiction, since scholars interested in fiction "would probably want to use the physical volumes."

98 "safely discard": Gordon Williams, *The Preservation of Deteriorating Books: An Examination of the Problem with Recommendations for a Solution,* report of the

ARL Committee on the Preservation of Research Library Materials, September 1964, p. 17. In *Library Journal,* Williams compellingly wrote that "it will cost only about $2 more per volume to preserve the original for an indefinitely long future time and make a microfilm copy of it only when the book needs to be used, than it will cost to microfilm the original now and discard the original completely." But Williams also condoned heavy discarding: "It is not necessary that more than one example of most deteriorating books be preserved" if "another example is being preserved" and a "usable copy of the text is cheaply and readily available." Gordon Williams, "The Preservation of Deteriorating Books," *Library Journal,* January 1, 1966.

98 "varied greatly": Shaffer, "Library of Congress Pilot Preservation Project." Shaffer writes that "in nearly all cases the survey located at least one copy elsewhere which was, except for the brittleness of the paper, in excellent condition."

98 "the slums": Richard L. Williams, "The Library of Congress Can't Hold All of Man's Knowledge—But It Tries, As It Acquires a New $160-Million Annex," *Smithsonian* 11:1 (April 1980), p. 43.

98 Frazer G. Poole: Library of Congress, "Frazer G. Poole," *Library of Congress Information Bulletin* 26:10 (March 9, 1967).

98 at Clapp's suggestion: Crowe, "Verner W. Clapp as Opinion Leader," p. 86. Clapp rejected the traditional method of bookbinding, sewing through the fold, as too costly for most libraries (p. 88).

98 indiscriminate rebinding: See Linda J. White, *Packaging the American Word: A Survey of Nineteenth and Early Twentieth Century American Publishers' Bindings in the General Collections of the Library of Congress,* Library of Congress Preservation Directorate, 1997; formerly available at lcweb.loc.gov/preserv/survey. "It is alarming to find," White writes, "that of the general collections 93% of the sample items from the 1840s have been library bound; only 7% remain in original publisher's bindings." White's paper was also presented at a conference entitled "Getting Ready for the Nineteenth Century: Strategies and Solutions for Rare Book and Special Collections Librarians," sponsored by the Rare Books and Manuscripts Section, Association of College and Research Libraries, American Library Association, June 23–26, 1998, Washington, D.C.

98 three hundred thousand non-newspaper volumes: Lawrence S. Robinson, "Establishing a Preservation Microfilming Program: The Library of Congress Experience." *Microform Review* 13:4 (fall 1984).

99 "embrittled to the extent": Robinson, "Establishing a Preservation Microfilming Program."

99 "The volumes are cut": Robinson, "Establishing a Preservation Microfilming Program."

99 "running our cameras against the clock": William J. Welsh, "The Library of Congress: A More-Than-Equal Partner," *Library Resources and Technical Services* 29:1 (January/March 1985): 89.

99 Joanna Biggar: "Must the Library of Congress Destroy Books to Save Them?" *The Washington Post Magazine,* June 3, 1984.

100 not bound by the Freedom of Information Act: "Although the Library is not subject to the Freedom of Information Act, as amended (5 U.S.C. §552), this Regulation follows the spirit of that Act consistent with the Library's duties, functions, and responsibilities to the Congress. The application of that Act to the Library is not to be inferred, nor should this Regulation be considered as

conferring on any member of the public a right under that Act of access to or information from the records of the Library." Library of Congress Regulation 1917–3, September 18, 1997.

102 shelving everything: The library receives three free copies of a great many books—two under the copyright-deposit program and one under the Cataloging-in-Publication (CIP) program. "In fiscal year 1995, the Library obtained 49,201 books through the CIP program. These additional titles are either added to the collections or used as part of the Library's exchange program." They also receive the discards from other federal libraries; generally, they swap these for things they want, or they give them away. "In fiscal year 1995, the Library received more than two million items from Federal agencies, and, although only a very small number were selected for the collections, several thousand were used in exchanges with other libraries for materials needed by the Library of Congress. Many thousands of other Federal transfers were used in the Library's surplus books programs." In 1995, the estimated value of the books given to the library under the copyright deposits program was $20,158,594. General Accounting Office, *Financial Statement Audit for the Library of Congress for Fiscal Year 1995,* www.gao.gov/special.pubs/pw_loc.txt (viewed June 3, 2000). See also Linton Weeks, "Brave New Library," *The Washington Post Magazine,* May 26, 1991, which describes the work of the Selections Office, where books that aren't to be added to the collection are marked with a red X on the first page. Lolita Silva of that office told Weeks, "I think you develop a feel for the material. Sometimes with a book of poetry—how it's published, how it's presented to you—tells you it's worth keeping." Weeks writes that the library did not take elementary-school or high-school textbooks except those dealing with American history.

102 "I am happy to announce": The memo, dated September 13, 2000, is from the head of the Library of Congress's Processing and Reference Section to serials librarians; it refers to the library's new program of asking certain publishers to stop sending the library items for copyright deposit.

102 *Finnegans Wake:* This story came from a book dealer. Verner Clapp and Luther Evans authorized the disposal of duplicates in the fifties, during a space crunch. Clapp noted on March 19, 1951, that he had visited the annex, deck 7, north, with Frederick Wagman and Luther Evans. "Agreed: To dispose of stuff from Dupl. Coll. by weeding good stuff, advertising the remainder & pulping if no bids are recd." The library also throws away book jackets, except in rare instances, see lcweb.loc.gov/acq/devpol/bookjack.html, June 15, 1999 (viewed June 2, 2000).

102 misshelved: Side-by-side duplicates make shelvers' lives easier, and thus reduce shelving errors, because the copy remaining on the shelf offers a quick visual cue as to where a book is supposed to go.

102 A recent survey: White, *Packaging the American Word.* White created a random population of four hundred books sold by six American publishing houses between 1830 and 1914 to serve as a sample for her study of American bookbindings. She found that of these ("the rare books of tomorrow," she called them) twenty-six percent had received an "inappropriate" rebinding, and about six percent were missing in inventory or Not on Shelf, even after special additional searches. Thirty-seven books had already been reformatted, and, of those, thirty-three were found to be "Reformatted (original destroyed)" while four were "Reformatted (original retained)"—thus, in her sample nearly ninety

percent of the microfilmed books from these six American publishers had been destroyed. Nine books had been deacidified.

CHAPTER 11 – Thugs and Pansies

106 "Space is always a problem": Irene Schubert, "Re: Serials microfilming," PADG (Preservation Administrators Discussion Group), archived on the CoOL website (CoOL stands for Conservation OnLine), palimpsest.stanford.edu/byform/mailing-lists/padg/1997/10/msg00023.html, October 31, 1997. Paula De Stefano, head of preservation at New York University, also contributed to this thread: she wrote that generally she stopped at the copyright cutoff date, then 1922. (That's one reason so many older obscure things that libraries would otherwise have left alone were sliced open and expensively emulsioned—they're in the public domain.) Then De Stefano wrote: "Of course, any titles already available on film are bought and the hard copy is tossed to make room on shelves. Space is a huge issue here." PADG archives, CoOL website, October 31, 1997, palimpsest.stanford.edu/byform/mailing-lists/padg/1997/10/msg00022.html. The current textbook of preservation microfilming says that it's okay to throw out volumes that aren't yet brittle, if you gain lots of space in doing so—hardly a preservational argument: "The institution may decide that filming long runs of serials, theses, or other coherent collections will so significantly ease space constraints that these items should be filmed as a unit even if some individual pieces are less suitable. For example, even if a few issues of a serial title were not acidic or not yet brittle, there would still be advantages in filming the entire run"—and getting rid of the paper. Lisa L. Fox, ed., *Preservation Microfilming: A Guide for Librarians and Archivists,* 2d ed. (Chicago: American Library Association, 1996), pp. 105–6.

108 Scotch-taping of the Dead Sea Scrolls: Esther Boyd-Alkalay and Lena Libman, "The Conservation of the Dead Sea Scrolls in the Laboratories of the Israel Antiquities Authority in Jerusalem," *Restaurator* 18 (1997). The cellotaping, which caused "irreversible damage," began in the late fifties in the Rockefeller Archaeological Museum in East Jerusalem; later, some of the tape was removed with trichloroethylene, and then the fragments were reinforced with lens tissue glued on with polyvinyl acetate or Perspex in solution. "As a result, the parchment glitters like glass and becomes rigid and fragile."

108 "This cannot be emphasized": Nancy E. Gwinn, ed., *Preservation Microfilming: A Guide for Librarians and Archivists* (Chicago: American Library Association, 1987), chap. 2, p. 36. Wesley Boomgaarden originally drafted this chapter, according to the preface.

108 "It must be stressed": Gwinn, *Preservation Microfilming,* p. 37. The textbook asks: "With the enormous volume of paper-based materials that require reformatting to preserve primarily the intellectual content, can the institution justify microfilming as only an interim measure, and thus retain great quantities of printed materials after microfilming?"

108 book conservators generally report: See, for example, the organization chart published in Peter Sparks, "The Library of Congress Preservation Program," in *The Library Preservation Program: Models, Priorities, Possibilities,* ed. Jan Merrill-Oldham and Merrily Smith, proceedings of a conference, April 29, 1983 (Chicago: American Library Association, 1985), p. 71.

109 "With few exceptions": David H. Stam, "Finding Funds to Support

Preservation," in Merrill-Oldham and Smith, *Library Preservation Program.* The Rockefeller Foundation in 1940 made a grant to the New York Public Library that "would supply funding to make a master negative from which the income to be derived from future sales would amortize the original investment"—helping libraries to help themselves. Bourke, "Scholarly Micropublishing."

109 "a lot of material from the Jewish division": Phone interview with Wesley Boomgaarden, April 21, 2000.

110 "When my hard-working": Wesley Boomgaarden, "Preservation Microfilming: Elements and Interconnections," in *Preservation Microfilming: Planning and Production,* papers from the RTSD Preservation Microfilming Institute, New Haven, April 21, 23, 1988 (Chicago: Association for Library Collections and Technical Services, 1989), p. 8.

110 "most of the filmed volumes": Committee on Institutional Cooperation, "Coordinated Preservation Microfilming Project," *Annual Report 1995–1996,* nova.cic.uiuc.edu/CIC/annrpt/ar95-96/cpmp4.html (viewed September 25, 2000). This multiphase, NEH-funded enterprise was also called the Cooperative Preservation Microfilming Project.

CHAPTER 12 – Really Wicked Stuff

113 "licensing arrangements": The phrase appears in the testimony of Peter Sparks before the Subcommittee on Postsecondary Education, House of Representatives, *Oversight Hearing on the Problem of "Brittle Books" in Our Nation's Libraries,* March 3, 1987 (Washington, D.C.: Government Printing Office, 1987), p. 105.

113 "Oh, the odor": Scott Eidt, phone interview, April 25, 2000. Edward Frankland, the great nineteenth-century chemist who discovered diethyl zinc, wrote in his diary of his early experience with a related compound (dimethyl zinc) that when he exposed the new substance to air there was a "violent action" and a foot-long flame, followed by a "gas of a most insupportable odour." Colin A. Russell, *Edward Frankland: Chemistry, Controversy, and Conspiracy in Victorian England* (Cambridge: Cambridge University Press, 1996), p. 79.

113 Koski: Ahti A. Koski et al., "Studies of the Pyrolysis of Diethylzinc by the Toluene Carrier Method and of the Reaction of Ethyl Radicals with Toluene," *Canadian Journal of Chemistry* 54 (1976).

114 "In the late fifties": Richard D. Smith, whose Wei T'o process was slighted by the Library of Congress for years, published a thorough critique of diethyl zinc in *Restaurator,* in which he said that it had been tried as an ignition agent for Apollo-Saturn rocket, an assertion that some rocket scientists confirm. Smith's excellent study is, however, prefaced by several paragraphs of hoo-ha about "the history of modern civilization deteriorat[ing] into dust." "Deacidifying Library Collections: Myths and Realities," *Restaurator* 8 (1987).

114 Ballistic-missile engineers: John J. Rusek, Department of Aeronautical and Astronautical Engineering, Purdue University, phone interview. See also John D. Clark's entertaining *Ignition!: An Informal History of Liquid Rocket Propellants* (New Brunswick, N.J.: Rutgers University Press, 1972), pp. 9, 13. Also George P. Sutton, *Rocket Propulsion Elements: An Introduction to the Engineering of Rockets,* 3d ed. (New York: Wiley, 1963), p. 252.

114 hypergolic: The term "hypergolic" was first used by German rocket scientists. Clark, *Ignition,* p. 14.

114 "high-energy aircraft and missile fuel": *Hawley's Condensed Chemical Dictionary,* 12th ed. (New York: Van Nostrand Reinhold, 1993), p. 397.

115 "During the war": In 1944, the Army was considering the use of pyrophorics, but they had not yet proved "of practical value." "They are difficult to control and constitute a great storage hazard," wrote Brigadier General Alden H. Waitt of the Chemical Warfare Service. "However, there are a number of substances that ignite spontaneously on contact with the air, and methods may be devised for making practical use of them." *Gas Warfare: Smoke, Flame, and Gas in Modern War,* 2d ed., Fighting Forces ed. (Washington, D.C.: Infantry Journal, 1944), p. 52.

115 "encapsulated flamethrower": Interview with Allen Tulis, April 4, 2000. Later, the Air Force picked up on the idea of a pyrophoric flame weapon, adapting it for air-to-ground use, but they chose a slightly less reactive compound called triethyl aluminum in place of diethyl zinc. Triethyl aluminum also bursts into flame on contact with air, but it's cheaper. Tulis worked on chemical demining and fuel-air explosives, as well.

116 rupture eardrums: For a description of blast injuries related to fuel-air explosives, see United States Department of Defense, "Clinical Presentation of Primary Blast Injury," Virtual Naval Hospital, www.vnh.org/EWSurg/ch05/05ClinPresPrimBlast.html (viewed September 25, 2000).

116 its own voraciously combustive chemistry: See G. von Elbe and E. T. McHale, *Annual Interim Report: Chemical Initiation of FAE Clouds,* report by Atlantic Research Corporation to Bernard T. Wolfson, Bolling Air Force Base, Washington, D.C. contract no. F49620-77-C-0097 (Washington, D.C.: Air Force Office of Scientific Research, 1979). The report is marked "Approved for public release; distribution unlimited." Von Elbe was a bomb designer with a Ph.D. from Berlin; he wrote a paper on "The Problem of Ignition" in the *Fourth Symposium (International) on Combustion* (*Combustion and Detonation Waves*), held at MIT in 1952 (Baltimore: Williams and Wilkins, 1953).

116 Dr. John Lee: Much of the Air Force's FAE research is still restricted; Dr. Lee, however, holds a relevant unclassified patent. John H. Lee, "Chemical Initiation of Detonation in Fuel-Air Explosive Clouds," U.S. patent no. 6,168,123 (December 1, 1992), which lists diethyl zinc as one of the liquid initiators.

CHAPTER 13 – Getting the Champagne out of the Bottle

119 a grant from the Council: Nancy E. Gwinn, "CLR and Preservation," *College and Research Libraries* 42:2 (March 1981).

119 unhappy time at a pesticide company: Kelly told me that the plant would get a boatload of white arsenic from Europe and make a big pile of it in a warehouse. Then, in the heat of summer, managers would hire men off the street to shovel it into the reactor to make pesticides like calcium arsenate and lead arsenate. The men "were sweating like pigs, and they'd get arsenic dust all over them," Kelly said. "Inside of about two weeks, they'd be unable to work because of arsenic poisoning. The plant said, 'It's okay, just go ahead and work, you won't get hurt.' Finally they couldn't work any more so they just laid them off and got some more in." Kelly left the company after nine months.

120 thirty and seventy pounds of liquid DEZ: The DEZ was initially diluted with a solvent (which "provides increased safety in the handling of the agent," according to Williams and Kelly's patents) but later used in its undiluted,

neat form. John C. Williams and George B. Kelly, Jr., "Method of Deacidifying Paper," U.S. patent nos. 3,969,549 (July 13, 1976) and 4,051,276 (September 27, 1977).

120 "thoroughly acidified": John Williams, phone interview, April 2000.

120 General Electric was lukewarm: GE was "unwilling to take the risk of an incident with the chemical diethyl zinc." Carolyn Harris, "Preservation of Paper Based Materials: Mass Deacidification Methods and Projects," in *Conserving and Preserving Library Materials,* ed. Kathryn Luther Henderson and William T. Henderson (Urbana-Champaign: University of Illinois Press, 1983), p. 67.

120 "small air leaks": U.S. Congress, Office of Technology Assessment, *Book Preservation Technologies,* OTA-0-375 (Washington, D.C.: U.S. Government Printing Office, 1988), p. 30. One GE worker burned his arm when some diluted DEZ "dripped on his skin from piping that he was cleaning." The injury did not require hospitalization (p. 73).

120 "we have demonstrated": George B. Kelly, Jr., "Mass Deacidification," in *Preservation of Library Materials,* ed. Joyce R. Russell (New York: Special Libraries Association, 1980). In the discussion that followed this paper, Kelly was asked whether other conservation labs might adapt an existing vacuum-drying chamber to treat books using DEZ. "It is possible," Kelly wrote, "but you are going to have to have some extremely good engineers and extensive modifications of the chamber. You cannot afford one mistake. One mistake and you have a disaster on your hands. Proceed with caution."

121 "400 to 600 years": W. Dale Nelson, "Space Technology Used to Prolong Life of Books," Associated Press, May 23, 1982, Nexis.

121 "at least five million volumes": "Conquest of Brittleness, the Ruin of Old Books," *The New York Times,* August 8, 1984, sec. B, p. 8, late city final edition, on microfilm. In a 1990 *Times* article on deacidification, Malcolm Browne, the great war journalist, apparently divided 77,000 by 365 days in order to come up with a fresh-seeming number: "At a rate of more than 200 volumes a day, books in the Library of Congress, the largest library in the world, are turning to dust. But after a decade of research, accidents and administrative delays, the library reports that it is about to take a major step toward stopping the rot." Malcolm W. Browne, "Nation's Library Calls on Chemists to Stop Books from Turning to Dust," *The New York Times,* May 22, 1990, p. C1.

121 "handling of diethyl zinc": *Library of Congress Information Bulletin,* April 23, 1984; quoted in Karl Nyren, "The DEZ Process and the Library of Congress," *Library Journal,* September 15, 1986.

122 "no known safety risks": Daniel Boorstin, "Letter to the Honorable George M. O'Brien, Member of Congress [Transmitting] Statement on the Library of Congress's Diethyl Zinc Gas Phase Book Deacidification Process," July 10, 1984, quoted in a footnote to Smith, "Deacidifying Library Collections."

123 weapons procurers: The library's secretiveness and its unwillingness to document its experiments in peer-reviewed journals are discussed in Jack C. Thompson, "Mass Deacidification: Thoughts on the Cunha Report," *Restaurator* 9:4 (1988).

123 113 degrees: Glenn Garelik, "Saving Books with Science," *Discover,* March 1983.

123 "self-sustaining and uncontrollable": U.S. Congress, *Book Preservation Technologies,* p. 25.

123 The results were "mixed": U.S. Congress, *Book Preservation Technologies,* pp. 31, 42–43.

124 Thus many of the stacked books: U.S. Congress, *Book Preservation Technologies,* pp. 42–43.

124 "Cause of odor a mystery": Kenneth E. Harris and Chandru J. Shahani, *Mass Deacidification: An Initiative to Refine the Diethyl Zinc Process,* Library of Congress Preservation Directorate, October 1994, lcweb.loc.gov/preserv/deacid/proceval.html (viewed September 20, 2000).

124 "a Library of Congress representative": National Aeronautics and Space Administration, Goddard Space Flight Center, *Accident Investigation Board Report of Mishaps at the Deacidification Pilot Plant, Building 306 on December 5, 1985, and February 14, 1986,* James H. Robinson, Jr., Board Chairman (September 4, 1986), p. 96.

124 Later, Welsh admitted: Representative Vic Fazio "criticized the librarians for secretly diverting funds from other library programs to support the DEZ experiment," reported *The Washington Post.* " 'Specifically,' [Fazio] wrote Boorstin last Dec. 2, 'over $2.3 million of the $3,740,474 obligated since fiscal year 1981 has come from funding sources other than those approved by . . . Congress.' " Phil McCombs, "Library's Preservation Go-Ahead; Dangers of Book-Saving Process are Discounted," *The Washington Post,* February 11, 1987, p. C-1, final edition, Nexis. At the hearing, Fazio said, "You didn't realize you had gotten hooked on this approach." Welsh answered, "I realized I was hooked, but not that I was using that much money without your permission." Subcommittee on Legislative Branch Appropriations, U.S. House of Representatives, *Hearings before a Subcommittee of the Committee on Appropriations,* pt. 2, February 10, 1987 (Washington, D.C.: U.S. Government Printing Office, 1987), p. 417.

124 "The time drivers": See NASA, *Accident Investigation,* p. 79.

125 "Shortly after the water injection": NASA, *Accident Investigation,* p. 6.

125 "[Name whited out] has been applying pressure": NASA, *Accident Investigation,* p. 80. A memo of December 5, 1985, reporting the "Incident at Magnetic Test Quiet Lab 306" to a NASA manager ends thus: "Any inquiries concerning this incident should be referred to Dr. Peter Sparks, Library of Congress, 202-287-5213." NASA, *Accident Investigation,* p. 49.

125 Before NASA had completed its investigation: NASA had produced an interim report on the December 5 explosion, but not a final one, when the second explosion took place. "By February 14, 1986, Mr. Marriott's group was well into the investigation of the December 5, 1985, mishap and verbal reports had been provided to the Director of Engineering, and an interim written report was provided on January 17, 1986" (NASA, *Accident Investigation,* p. 15). One respondent stated that he was "upset that they were working out at building 306 before the report from the December 5, 1985, Accident Review Board was released" (p. 92). The Library of Congress asserted that the DEZ facility was shut down after the "fire" in December "pending a review of the cause of the fire." Cleanup began, the library claimed, "following completion of the review," whereupon the "second incident occurred." Library of Congress, "Library's Book Deacidification Program Moves Forward Following Review of Incidents and Pilot Plant," *Library of Congress Information Bulletin* 45:27 (July 7, 1986).

125 "disenchanted" electrician: There were, he said, "too many people giving orders

without following normal procedures." NASA, *Accident Investigation,* p. 91. "Before the December 5 fire," the electrician "had not known that DEZ could explode" (p. 92).

125 a substantial volume: "After the December 5, 1985 fire, it was general knowledge that DEZ was in the system," according to one interviewee. NASA, *Accident Investigation,* p. 95.

125 "black goop": NASA, *Accident Investigation,* pp. 9, 110.

125 copper elbow pipe: NASA, *Accident Investigation,* pp. 11, 93.

126 too hot to touch: NASA, *Accident Investigation,* p. 109.

126 Northrup did not inform NASA: NASA, *Accident Investigation,* pp. 25–26.

126 "the walls were blown apart": NASA, *Accident Investigation,* p. 14.

126 "The violence of the explosion": NASA, *Accident Investigation,* p. 36.

126 there were no relief valves: NASA, *Accident Investigation,* p. 28.

126 "We're going to blow it": Welsh, phone interview, March 25, 2000.

126 armored vehicles: Welsh, phone interview, March 25, 2000.

126 "vast and unprecedented cuts": Library of Congress, "The Librarian of Congress Testifies Before Appropriations Subcommittee," *Library of Congress Information Bulletin* 45:9 (March 3, 1986).

127 "disassembled by means of shaped": NASA, *Accident Investigation,* p. 16.

127 *whoomp:* Phone interview with an eyewitness who does not want to be named, April 2000.

127 "there has never been an important": Boorstin also formally said good-bye to the members of the house subcommittee during that meeting; he was retiring from the Library of Congress. Subcommittee on Legislative Branch Appropriations, *Hearings,* p. 394.

127 rats: "The study will expose rats to acute, subchronic, and chronic inhalation of zinc oxide particles at various concentrations in air. . . . An examination of sperm morphology and vaginal cytology will also be performed on specimens in the sub-chronic and chronic studies. Some specimens from the sub-chronic exposures will be mated to study the reproductive and teratogenic effects." U.S. Congress, *Book Preservation Technologies,* p. 79. The cost of the rat study, performed by the Battelle Memorial Institute, is given on p. 18.

127 The tests were "inconclusive": U.S. Congress, *Book Preservation Technologies,* p. 77. In another test, DEZ-treated paper was applied to the skin of guinea pigs and the eyes of rabbits.

127 optical-disk program: See, for example, William J. Welsh, "The Preservation Challenge," in Merrill-Oldham and Smith, *Library Preservation Program.* "In the area of preservation research, the Library of Congress is currently engaged in two promising projects of enormous potential value," Welsh writes, both of which apply "ultra-high technology to preservation": diethyl zinc and optical disk.

127 "On Friday, February 21": Library of Congress, "Engineering Problems Experienced at Deacidification Test Facility," *Library of Congress Information Bulletin* 45:11 (March 17, 1986).

128 "The Library's own review": Library of Congress, "Library's Book Deacidification Program." The DEZ technique "is a viable process that can be implemented and handled safely," according to the article.

128 "didn't have the chemical processing experience": Subcommittee on Legislative Branch Appropriations, *Hearings,* p. 435.

128 "Dump DEZ": Karl Nyren, "It's Time to Dump DEZ," *Library Journal,* September 15, 1986.

129 "danger and unmanageability of DEZ": Karl Nyren, "DEZ Process."

129 Welsh published a rebuttal: William J. Welsh, "In Defense of DEZ: LC's Perspective," *Library Journal,* January 1987.

129 when it does use DEZ: Scott Eidt told me: "Diethyl zinc wasn't used a great deal as a Ziegler-Natta catalyst. It was used, as far I remember, and is still used, in dilute hydrocarbon solution, to scavenge out water from the polymerization process—that is, it would react with the water in the solvent and knock it out." *Book Preservation Technologies* also resorts to vague language, perhaps in order to avoid mentioning the military uses: "Metal alkyls have been used for many years in a variety of applications. Their major use today is as an intermediate in the manufacturing of polyethylene and polypropylene" (p. 28).

129 neat and by the ton: "During the course of a year, Texas Alkyls will be trucking 15 to 20, 430-gallon tanks of neat liquid DEZ from their facility in Houston to the full-scale plant site," U.S. Congress, *Book Preservation Technologies,* p. 71. Stauffer Chemical wrote a letter to the Library of Congress dated April 18, 1985, in which it observed that the rate of gas generation is two orders of magnitude greater for neat diethyl zinc than for DEZ diluted fifty-fifty with a solvent. The letter is paraphrased in NASA, *Accident Investigation,* p. 144. The gas, mainly ethane, is flammable.

129 "DEZ is produced": Welsh, "In Defense of DEZ."

129 "DEZ is and always will be": Koski added, "The cylinder that DEZ is stored in is labelled as pyrophoric but these cylinders are not perpetually in flame either, although [their contents] certainly would be if the valve was cracked open."

129 $2.8 million: U.S. Congress, *Book Preservation Technologies,* p. 18.

130 "I think the safety questions": Boyce Rensenberger, "Acid Test: Stalling Self-Destruction in the Stacks," *The Washington Post,* August 29, 1988, p. A13, final edition, microfilm.

130 "were so startling": Robert J. Milevski, "Mass Deacidification: Effects of Treatment on Library Materials Deacidified by the DEZ and MG-3 Processes," in *The 1992 Book and Paper Group Annual,* vol. 11 (Washington, D.C.: American Institute for Conservation, 1992). Milevski became the preservation librarian at Princeton in 1992.

131 one-hundred-million-dollar twenty-year contracts: Rensenberger, "Acid Test."

131 thirty thousand books a week: Subcommittee on Postsecondary Education, *Oversight Hearing,* p. 111.

131 "And if you know Billington": Billington's occasional outbursts are described in Linton Weeks, "In a Stack of Troubles: The Librarian of Congress Has Raised Funds. And His Voice. And a Lot of Eyebrows," *The Washington Post,* December 27, 1995, p. F1, Nexis. "In August 1995, Billington learned that the U.S. attorney had written him a letter expressing concern about the way book damage was being reported. Someone on the library staff had answered the letter. 'Unsatisfactorily, and in my name,' says Billington. 'He went hysteric,' says one library official who asked not to be named. Billington remembers that he threw something. He says it may have been a book."

131 Alphamat: Nielsen Bainbridge, Alphamat Artcare, www.nielsen-bainbridge.com/bainbridge/html/sparks_testimonial.html (viewed September 20, 2000).

132 "strategic information reserve": Testimony of James Billington, April 19, 1994, before the Senate Subcommittee on Education, Arts, and Humanities. Billington disseminated several variations of this speech.

132 "substituting technology for paper": James Billington, *Library of Congress Information Bulletin,* June 15, 1992, excerpted in Commission on Preservation

and Access, *Newsletter,* September 1992. In 1999, Billington told Congress that one of the library's "key current overriding initiatives" is "providing massive digital access to information and, at the same time, streamlining and re-engineering our handling of access to books and other traditional containers of knowledge." Senate Subcommittee of the Committee on Appropriations, 106th Cong., 1st sess., 1999, p. 120.

132 Bhabha Atomic Research Center: See the capsule biography accompanying Chandru Shahani and William K. Wilson, "Preservation of Libraries and Archives," *American Scientist,* May–June 1987. Bhabha scientists began work on India's nuclear bomb in 1971, according to Nicholas Berry of the Center for Defense Information (e-mail to author). See also Center for Defense Information, "Building the Indian Bomb," May 19, 1998, www.cdi.org/issues/testing/inbombfct.html (viewed August 14, 2000).

132 "pathetically poor engineering": Kenneth E. Harris and Chandru J. Shahani, *Mass Deacidification: An Initiative to Refine the Diethyl Zinc Process,* Library of Congress Preservation Directorate (October 1994), lcweb.loc.gov/preserv/deacid/proceval.html.

135 If in fifty years: Jana Kolar notes that "while most treated papers degrade less rapidly, some results of accelerated ageing experiments show an increased degradation of papers whose pH has been changed from the acidic to the alkaline region using deacidification treatment." Accelerated-aging experiments can, however, supply only directional hints. Jana Kolar, "Mechanism of Autoxidative Degradation of Cellulose," *Restaurator* 18 (1997).

CHAPTER 14 – Bursting at the Seams

136 costs were bundled: Between 1984 and 1994, the Library of Congress spent $5.7 million of the $11.5 million congressional appropriation for the construction of a diethyl-zinc facility, according to General Accounting Office, *Financial Statement Audit for the Library of Congress for Fiscal Year 1995.* Although they are difficult to document, the overhead costs attributable to diethyl-zinc research and development must be added to that amount.

136 Landover: Library of Congress, *Library of Congress Information Bulletin* 35:22 (May 28, 1976).

137 long-frozen Everyman's Library edition: F. L. Hudson and C. J. Edwards, "Some Direct Observations on the Aging of Paper," *Paper Technology* 7 (1966); cited in Richard Smith, "Paper Impermanence as a Consequence of pH and Storage Conditions," *Library Quarterly* 39:2 (April 1969): 183.

137 Cold War librarians: See Library of Congress, "Welsh Named Deputy Librarian," *Library of Congress Information Bulletin* 35:4 (January 23, 1976).

137 "warehouses of little-used material": William J. Welsh, "Libraries and Librarians: Opportunities and Challenges," paper presented at the seventh international seminar, Kanazawa Institute of Technology, Library Center, Kanazawa, Japan, 1989, in *Research Libraries—Yesterday, Today, and Tomorrow,* ed. William J. Welsh (Westport, Conn.: Greenwood Press, 1993).

137 "vastly more than the microfilming": Welsh, "Library of Congress."

138 "Disk storage is attractive": Welsh, "Library of Congress."

138 "the extremely high resolution": Welsh, "Library of Congress."

138 "reproduce items with sufficient quality": Carl Fleischhauer, "Research Access and Use: The Key Facet of the Nonprint Optical Disk Experiment," *Library of*

Congress Information Bulletin 42:37 (September 12, 1983). Also quoted in Biggar, "Must the Library of Congress Destroy Books."

138 reduce the three Library of Congress buildings: The article describes the data-retrieval jukebox that is "humming away" in the basement of the Madison building: "Deputy librarian W.J. Welsh says the jukebox, part of a three-year, $2.1 million pilot program, is the face of the bibliographical future—one that could shrink the library's entire 80 million item collection into one of the library's three existing building[s]." Ken Ringle, "Card Catalogue to Be Filed Away; Library Turns to Computers," *The Washington Post,* November 13, 1984, p. A1, final edition. See also Ellen Z. Hahn, "The Library of Congress Optical Disk Pilot Program: A Report on the Print Project Activities," *Library of Congress Information Bulletin* 42:44 (October 31, 1983), which gives space and "compaction" as one of the justifications of the optical-disk program. Hahn writes that "miniaturization in some form" is essential because "the likelihood of building another Library building on Capitol Hill is at best remote." The scanning will be destructive: "In most cases, the print material, that is, periodicals, will be guillotined and then scanned automatically at a rate of one page every two seconds." One of the benefits of the optical-disk program, according to a later article, is "the elimination of the not-on-shelf or 'N.O.S.' problem": if you destroy the item in order to scan it, it is no longer part of the collection, and therefore won't be missing when you look for it. Library of Congress, "Library Announces Public Opening of Access to Optical Disk Technology," *Library of Congress Information Bulletin* 45:7 (February 17, 1986).

138 war propaganda: During the war, "a division for the study of propaganda analysis was established. What later became the Research and Analysis Branch of the Office of Strategic Services was first set up as the Division of Special Information in the Library of Congress. . . . A War Agencies Collection gave duly accredited representatives of the Government access to materials which, for reasons of security, had to be withheld from the public. . . . Exhibits, broadcasts, lectures were designed to reflect the war aims of the United States. . . . Mr. MacLeish was frequently absent, sometimes for extended periods, first as director of the Office of Facts and Figures, subsequently as assistant director of the Office of War Information." David C. Mearns, *The Story Up to Now: The Library of Congress, 1800–1946* (Washington, D.C.: Library of Congress, 1947), p. 214.

138 letter of agreement: The text of the agreement between MacLeish and Donovan is reproduced in William R. Corson, *The Armies of Ignorance* (New York: Dial, 1977), pp. 141–44n.

139 "bursting at the seams": Gurney and Apple, *Library of Congress,* p. 17.

139 marble-finned kitsch box: The building "reminds some critics of the monumental architecture of the Third Reich." Stephen Klaidman, "Cultural Center Problems Are Space, Money, Boredom," *The Washington Post,* June 12, 1977, p. B1.

139 "miniaturiz[ing] existing collections": Welsh, "Libraries and Librarians."

139 "Networking can and should": Welsh, "Libraries and Librarians."

CHAPTER 15 – The Road to Avernus

142 groundless guesswork: "Perhaps the most outrageous of Barrow's distortions of prior work was his equation of 25 years of natural age to 72 hours in a dry oven

at 100°C., with his use of multiples of 72 hours to represent multiples of 25 years. This must have been based on ruler measurement of freehand lines in charts in one NBS [National Bureau of Standards] study; yet this study, the only direct comparison of natural and accelerated aging available when Barrow introduced his equation, warned explicitly and repeatedly that the four data points on which the charts were based were insufficient for quantitative treatment. Later work has removed all credibility from Barrow's equation; yet it is apparently still used by some librarians and vendors." Thomas Conroy, "The Need for a Re-evaluation of the Use of Alum in Book Conservation and the Book Arts," *Book and Paper Group Annual* 8 (Washington, D.C.: Book and Paper Group of the American Institute for Conservation of Historic and Artistic Works, 1989), p. 14n.

142 three days in an artificial-aging oven: Barrow Research Laboratory, *Test Data of Naturally Aged Papers* (Richmond, Va.: Barrow Research Laboratory, 1964), p. 21. See also Verner Clapp, "The Story of Permanent/Durable Book Paper, 1115–1970 (part 2)," *Scholarly Publishing,* April 1971, and Smith, "Paper Impermanence," p. 186.

142 Barrow's results: *Deterioration of Book Stock, Causes and Remedies,* conducted by W. J. Barrow, ed. Randolph W. Church (Richmond: Virginia State Library, 1959), p. 15.

142 "The research carried out": Leon J. Stout et al. of the Preservation Committee of the Pennsylvania State University Libraries, "Guaranteeing a Library for the Future," *Restaurator* 8:4 (1987).

142 "Barrow startled the library world": Rutherford D. Rogers, "Library Preservation: Its Scope, History, and Importance," in Merrill-Oldham and Smith, *Library Preservation Program.*

143 Perhaps all those who, like Peter Sparks: "Library officials say that unless the destruction is stopped, 97 percent of the volumes in the federal government's premier library—also the world's largest information storage center—will eventually disintegrate. All other libraries are thought to face the same problem. 'It's a very serious problem but, fortunately, we think we're moving rapidly toward a solution that we think is very promising,' said Peter G. Sparks, director of the library's Mass Deacidification Program." Rensenberger, "Acid Test."

143 "From the investigations": Clapp, *Future of the Research Library,* p. 87.

143 hire some statisticians: Council on Library Resources, *Sixth Annual Report,* p. 22.

143 "these 1.75 billion pages": Clapp, *Future of the Research Library,* p. 27.

144 Robert N. DuPuis: DuPuis also worked at General Foods. At Philip Morris, he became chairman of the Industry Technical Group of TIRC, the Tobacco Industry Research Committee, stalwart funder of pro-cigarette scientific research. Another Philip Morris scientist, John D. Hind, served as a consultant to the Barrow lab; see Barrow Research Laboratory, *Permanence/Durability of the Book: A Two-Year Research Program* (Richmond: Barrow Research Laboratory, 1963).

144 DuPuis wrote memos: Richard Kluger writes that "Philip Morris's research director, Robert DuPuis, sent a memo dated July 20, 1956, from Richmond to the company's top officers in New York reporting in ventilated cigarettes 'a proved decrease in carbon monoxide and carbon dioxide plus an increase in oxygen content of the smoke'; the former, he explained, was 'related to decreased harm to the circulatory system as a result of smoking,' while the latter meant there would be less chance of depriving cells of oxygen 'and of starting a possible chain of events leading to the formation of a cancer cell.' " Richard

Kluger, *Ashes to Ashes: America's Hundred-Year Cigarette War, the Public Health, and the Unabashed Triumph of Philip Morris* (New York: Alfred A. Knopf, 1996), p. 184. See also Council on Library Resources, *Twelfth Annual Report* (1968), p. 29.

144 "If we do find any": Gene Borio, *Jones, Day, Reavis and Pogue Draft: Corporate Activity Project: Part 1,* undated, www.tobacco.org/Documents/jonesday1.html, p. 101. DuPuis appeared on the second of two *See It Now* programs on "Cigarettes and Lung Cancer," CBS TV, June 7, 1955.

144 Vacudyne: See Gwinn, "CLR and Preservation," and Gene Borio, "Secret Tobacco Document Quotes," www.tobacco.org; Kluger, *Ashes to Ashes,* discusses tobacco ammoniation.

144 Litton Bionetics: Gwinn, "CLR and Preservation." Litton also performed the DEZ tests on guinea pigs: the report is entitled *Guinea Pig Dermal Sensitization Study DEZ (Diethyl Zinc) Treated Paper and Untreated Paper, Final Report* (Rockville, Md.: Litton Bionetics), 1984.

145 caused headaches and nausea: U.S. Congress, *Book Preservation Technologies,* p. 27.

145 "comparatively expensive": Clapp, *Future of the Research Library,* p. 28.

145 "sensible solution": Clapp, *Future of the Research Library,* p. 29.

145 "storage, binding, and other maintenance costs": Clapp, *Future of the Research Library,* p. 28.

145 "already the standard method": Clapp, *Future of the Research Library,* p. 28.

146 long, multi-part essay: Clapp, "Story of Permanent/Durable Book Paper," *Scholarly Publishing,* January, April, and July 1971.

146 known and advised since 1948: Crowe, "Verner W. Clapp as Opinion Leader," p. 47.

146 "an essentially solitary worker": Clapp, "The Story of Permanent/Durable Book Paper" (July 1971), p. 362.

146 a formula developed by the S. D. Warren: S. D. Warren had a recipe that employed "lime mud," an alkaline substance; the paper performed better in accelerated-aging tests. See Richard D. Smith, "Deacidification Technologies: State of the Art," in Luner, *Paper Preservation.*

146 "treated his sources crudely": Thomas Conroy, "Methodology of Testing for Permanence of Paper—Progress Notes no. 2—Tentative Outline," quoted in Roggia, "William James Barrow," p. 7.

146 "aggressive promoter": Roggia, "William James Barrow," p. 177.

146 "widely, if incorrectly, credited": Roggia, "William James Barrow," p. 176.

146 "stop holding onto myths": Roggia, "William James Barrow," pp. 166–76.

146 "I have spent many hundreds of hours": Verner Clapp, letter to Bernard Barrow, August 19, 1968, in Crowe, "Verner W. Clapp as Opinion Leader," pp. 100–101.

147 "catastrophic decline": Clapp, "Story of Permanent/Durable Book Paper" (July 1971), p. 230.

147 "disastrous condition of paper": Clapp, "Story of Permanent/Durable Book Paper" (July 1971), p. 231.

147 "The Road to Avernus": Clapp, "Story of Permanent/Durable Book Paper" (January 1971), p. 114. The phrase alludes to Virgil's *Aeneid* 6:126. The Avernian Lake, near Vesuvius, whose sulphurous vapors supposedly killed any bird that flew over it, was an entrance to hell.

147 "librarian/archivist's worst enemy": Clapp, "Story of Permanent/Durable Book Paper" (January 1971), p. 115.

CHAPTER 16 – It's Not Working Out

148 "knew more about old papers": Clapp, "Story of Permanent/Durable Book Paper" (July 1971), p. 356.

148 He quit college: Sally Cruz Roggia, "William James Barrow," in *Dictionary of Virginia Biography* (Richmond: Library of Virginia, 1998).

149 "The Barrow laminating process": Clapp, "Story of Permanent/Durable Book Paper" (January 1971), p. 112.

149 same substance that microfilm: Barrow published an early description of his method, entitled "The Barrow Method of Laminating Documents," in the *Journal of Documentary Reproduction* 2:2 (June 1939), which in the thirties and forties was a center of microfilm theory. An experienced operator could laminate between 75 and 125 documents per hour, wrote Barrow.

149 Protectoid: James L. Gear, "Lamination after 30 Years: Record and Prospect," *American Archivist* 28:2 (April 1965).

149 The reason that Barrow knew: See Smith, "Deacidification Technologies."

149 New York Public Library: Five rare playbills from the NYPL's theater collection were the first to be treated to the Barrow process, in 1956. John Baker, "Preservation Programs of the New York Public Library."

149 the Library of Congress: Barrow demonstrated his lamination process at the Library of Congress in 1951, at a staff forum called "Techniques for the Preservation of the Collections," presided over by Verner Clapp and Luther Evans. "The acetate film seals up the document and makes it relatively resistant to acidic gases and other injurious elements in the air," reported the *Library of Congress Information Bulletin*. At the same forum, Barrow also previewed his experimental technique of ink-lifting: the "process of transferring print from a deteriorated paper to a good rag paper" by stripping off a layer of ink onto a sheet of acetate and then laminating the acetate to a sheet of rag paper. "Staff Forum," *Library of Congress Information Bulletin* 10:42 (October 15, 1951). In an obituary of Barrow published in the *Eleventh Annual Report* (1967) of the Council on Library Resources, the Library of Congress is said to have "availed itself of this technique for a number of important documents" (p. 46). In addition to a regular-size laminator, the Library of Congress also bought from Barrow a large laminator for maps. [William James Barrow], *Procedures and Equipment Used in the Barrow Method of Restoring Manuscripts and Documents* (Richmond: W. J. Barrow, 1961), p. 11.

149 "We have found": David H. Stam, "The Questions of Preservation," in Welsh, *Research Libraries—Yesterday, Today, and Tomorrow*, p. 313.

151 Zentrum für Bucherhaltung: Ann Olszewski, the Preservation Librarian at the Cleveland Public Library, sent a book from her library's local-history collection to ZFB for restoration. Olszewski's predecessor had sent the book to Booklab for photocopying, where it was disbound, but Olszewski didn't throw it away. Post paper-splitting, the repaired book is "nothing short of miraculous," she says.

CHAPTER 17 – Double Fold

152 MIT Fold Tester: Barrow used a slightly gentler device that oscillated through ninety degrees. It was built to his own specifications, making independent verification of his results impossible; later he used the MIT machine exclusively; in any case, the nature of the mechanical stress is the same.

152 "Changes in folding endurance": D. F. Caulfield and D. E. Gunderson, "Paper Testing and Strength Characteristics," in Luner, *Paper Preservation.* "It has long been known," writes Robert Feller, "that folding endurance decreases markedly in the early stages of thermal aging of paper, whereas tensile strength does not." Robert L. Feller, *Accelerated Aging* (Marina del Rey, Calif.: Getty Conservation Institute, 1994).

152 B. L. Browning: B. L. Browning, "The Nature of Paper," in *Deterioration and Preservation of Library Materials,* ed. Howard W. Winger and Richard D. Smith (Chicago: University of Chicago Press, 1970). Caulfield and Gunderson similarly note that the results of fold-endurance tests "vary widely even on presumably identical samples." See also Gerhard Banik and Werner K. Sobotka, "Deacidification and Strengthening of Bound Newspapers Through Aqueous Immersion," in Luner, *Paper Preservation:* "Although the folding endurance is a sensitive test procedure, it only leads to reasonable results when applied to new and strong paper samples."

153 "While folding endurance": Hendriks, "Permanence of Paper," p. 133, n. 2.

153 "None of the commonly used paper tests": Hendriks, "Permanence of Paper," p. 133.

153 "simulates the bending of a leaf": Barrow Research Laboratory, *Test Data of Naturally Aged Papers* (Richmond, Va.: Barrow Research Laboratory, 1964), p. 13.

153 one of the Barrow Laboratory's books: Barrow Research Laboratory, *Permanence/Durability of the Book.*

154 one of the last big experiments: Barrow Research Laboratory, *Permanence/Durability of the Book—V: Strength and Other Characteristics of Book Papers, 1800–1899* (Richmond: Barrow Research Laboratory, 1967).

154 Clapp's literary assistance: "Clapp's editorial aid to Barrow was of the most intensive kind—typically page-on-page of notes suggesting the clarification of meaning, restructuring and reordering of text, deletion of whole sections, and addition of fact and opinion. There is no evidence that Clapp provided such extensive and extended collaboration to any other person at any time." Crowe, "Verner W. Clapp as Opinion Leader," pp. 50–51.

154 including seven books: Frazer G. Poole, "William James Barrow," in *Encyclopedia of Library and Information Science* (New York: Dekker, 1969).

156 "An 'unusable' record": Williams, *Preservation of Deteriorating Books,* p. 15. Williams is following Barrow, who at one point defined as "unusable" a book having a fold endurance of between one tenth of a fold and one fold. "A leaf in a book of this strength should be turned with much care and is unsuitable for use unless restored." Barrow Research Laboratory, *Test Data of Naturally Aged Papers,* p. 41. (Barrow's fractional folds are scientifically meaningless, by the way.) Elsewhere, Barrow says that papers that fail to survive three folds on an MIT tester are "brittle papers needing restoration." Barrow Research Laboratory, *Permanence/Durability of the Book,* p. 10.

156 whose page "breaks off": Preservation Department, Indiana University Bloomington Libraries, *Preservation Department Manual,* www.indiana.edu/~libpres/Manual/prsmanual2.html, last revised March 16, 2000.

156 "four corner test": Mono Acquisitions and Rapid Cataloging (MARC), *MARC Procedures: Brittle Books,* Northwestern University, www.library.nwu.edu/marc/procedures/brittle.html, last revised March 10, 1999.

156 "when a lower corner": "Brittle Books Replacement Processing," Memorandum 95-1, Ohio State University Libraries Preservation

Office, www.lib.ohio-state.edu/OSU_profile/preweb/memo951.html, July 1995. Brittle books under this definition "are not able to be rebound or routinely repaired."

156 "very gentle tug": Preservation Department, University of Maryland Libraries, Brittle Materials and Reformatting Unit, www.lib.umd.edu/UMCP/TSD/PRES/checkrelated.html, last revised July 28, 1999.

156 "in jeopardy when anyone": Paul Koda, "The Condition of the University of Maryland Libraries' Collections," Technical Services Division, University of Maryland Libraries, www.lib.umd.edu/UMCP/TSD/PRES/surtext.html, last revised March 5, 1999.

156 Columbia University: In 1987, Columbia's method was as follows: "To TEST FOR PAPER STRENGTH fold the lower corner of page 50 back-and-forth three times. (For volumes less than 100 pages long, fold corner of page located about ⅓ of the way from title page.) If the paper withstands folding and a slight tug it is strong and can be sent for commercial treatment. If paper folds 2 or 3 times but then falls off it is borderline brittle and must be sent to the Conservation Lab for treatment. If the paper breaks easily it is brittle and can only be replaced, filmed, photocopied or boxed." Columbia University Libraries, Preservation Department, *The Preservation of Library Materials: A CUL Handbook,* 4th ed., March 1987, p. 2.

156 "A book is considered": "Definition of Brittleness," Reprographics Unit, Preservation Department, George A. Smathers Libraries, University of Florida, web.uflib.ufl.edu/preserve/repro/brittle/britdef.html, last revised December 3, 1996.

157 "planned deterioration": "Planned Deterioration: Guidelines for Withdrawal," Reprographics Unit, University of Florida, web.uflib.ufl.edu/preserve/repro/brittle/autowd_pd.html, 1998.

157 If and when: George A. Smathers Libraries, *Preservation Bulletin* 7.6, August 11, 1992, web.uflib.ufl.edu/cm/manual/CMManual7-6.html, part of *A Manual for Collection Managers.* This particular Florida document defines an item as brittle if it fails to survive a "double fold test measure less than six." Though the chapter is dated 1992, the *Manual* is listed as "Updated 5/17/99."

157 "one cannot qualify a book page": Hendriks, "Permanence of Paper," p. 133. See also David Erhardt, Charles S. Tumosa, and Marion F. Mecklenburg, "Material Consequences of the Aging of Paper," in *Preprints, ICOM Committee for Conservation,* vol. 2, twelfth triennial meeting, Lyon, 1999: "Even quite degraded paper retains most of its elasticity, and it is only 'abuse', such as folding over a corner, that results in damage. Careful handling is still safe."

CHAPTER 18 – A New Test

158 Edmund Gosse: A company called Archival Survival microfilmed *Questions at Issue* in 1991 for New York University's preservation department.

159 I turned the page: Really I should say "I turned the leaf": bibliographers make a distinction between leaves and pages, there being a page on either side of a leaf. But I'm speaking loosely here.

160 not have been creased in vain: Linda White, author of *Packaging the American Word,* the survey of book bindings at the Library of Congress (since suppressed by the library), tested all the books in her sample for brittleness in the approved Library of Congress manner by folding a corner until it broke. She found that

only fifteen books, out of 294 she tested (i.e., the 294 she was able to test out of the 400 she took from the catalog as her sample, some of which were missing or Not on Shelf or destroyed after filming), were classifiable (using Library of Congress definitions) as "Brittle Unusable." (Some of the other books from her sample that had been reformatted and destroyed would presumably have failed their fold tests, too, however.) White told me that in the first ten or so fold tests that she performed, she made fairly big corners, and then they got gradually smaller. "Toward the end they're just these tiny little things, because I started feeling so guilty about taking those corners off." She kept the broken-off folds in a Baggie in her desk.

160 Barrow once took a reporter: "The Paper Man," Richmond *News Leader,* June 8, 1963; quoted in Gwinn, "CLR and Preservation."

CHAPTER 19 – Great Magnitude

162 Stanford University: Sarah Buchanan and Sandra Coleman, *Deterioration Survey of the Stanford University Libraries Green Library Stack Collection,* June 1979. "When fold test of 6 folds employed at corner; breaking or tearing occurs when corner tugged *gently.*" I'm assuming (I hope correctly) that the six folds are single folds, convertible into three double folds.

162 "in the judgement of experienced": Robert R. V. Wiederkehr, *The Design and Analysis of a Sample Survey of the Condition of Books in the Library of Congress* (Rockville, Md.: King Research, 1984), p. 20. Wiederkehr writes that "if a book has paper so brittle that FOLD is 0 to 1, it should be preserved by microfilming rather than deacidification, and is assigned a value for FOLDC1 of 0."

162 "The Yale Survey": Gay Walker et al., "The Yale Survey: A Large-Scale Study of Book Deterioration in the Yale University Library," *College and Research Libraries,* March 1985.

163 "Water leaks occurred": Gay Walker, "The Evolution of Yale's Preservation Program," in Merrill-Oldham and Smith, *Library Preservation Program,* p. 53.

164 "To get a piece of the action": Peter Sparks, "Marketing for Preservation," in Merrill-Oldham and Smith, *Library Preservation Program,* p. 75.

164 Haas's undergraduate thesis: Warren James Haas, *English Book Censorship,* Thesis, Bachelor of Library Science, University of Wisconsin (Rochester, N.Y.: University of Rochester Press, for the Association of College and Reference Libraries, 1955), Microcard [microfiche]. Haas begins with a quotation from a 1664 pamphlet that he found in Bigmore and Wyman's *A Bibliography of Printing* (1884): "Printing is like a good dish of meat, which moderatly eaten of turns to the nourishment and health of the body; but immoderately, to surfeits and sickness." It looks as if the Library of Congress microfilmed and discarded an original three-volume Quaritch edition (250 copies printed, 1880–1886) of this work.

164 *Preparation of Detailed Specifications:* Warren J. Haas, *Preparation of Detailed Specifications for a National System for the Preservation of Library Materials* (Washington, D.C.: Association of Research Libraries, February 1972).

165 "much master negative microfilm": Haas, *Preparation,* p. 10. A master can be hard to find sometimes. One survey noted in 1992 that "many micropublishers currently listed in machine readable bibliographic records have moved, sold all or portions of their businesses, or are no longer supplying microfilm copies of

masters." Erich Kesse, "Survey of Micropublishers," A Report to the Commission on Preservation and Access, October 1992. Robert DeCandido says that "the master has to some extent become a public resource. Certainly a compelling argument can be made that the fate of that film is a matter of public concern and its destruction or loss is against the public interest. In the same way that historic and cultural landmarks are legally protected even if privately owned, so should preservation microfilm masters have some sort of restrictions on their use and disposal." True, and yet a "microfilm master" is in fact a copy: DeCandido, who ran the Shelf and Binding Preparation Office at the New York Public Library during a period when the library was destroying large numbers of books, fails to extend his analysis to cover the real master—not the film, but the original document. Robert DeCandido, "Considerations in Evaluating Searching for Microform Availability," *Microform Review* 19:3 (summer 1990).

165 "ultrafiche": See E. M. Grieder, "Ultrafiche Libraries: A Librarian's View," *Microform Review,* April 1972. "Two- and four-year colleges or emerging universities are most likely to be tempted by these collections. They may feel the lack of large foundation collections, and perhaps hunger for more impressive libraries." See also Mark R. Yerburgh and Rhoda Yerburgh, "Where Have All the Ultras Gone? The Rise and Demise of the Ultrafiche Library Collection, 1968–1973," *Microfilm Review* 13 (fall 1984). In 1968, a subsidiary of Encyclopaedia Britannica called Library Resources charged $21,500 for more than twelve thousand books, pamphlets, documents, and periodicals, reproduced on 12,474 ultrafiches. While acknowledging that ultrafiche collections ultimately failed, the Yerburghs contend that the "librarian must declare war on microform illiteracy and user resistance." They point out that a 1968 proposal by David Hays was the proximate cause of the ultrafiche fervor. In 1966, however, Clapp's Council on Library Resources had paid Republic Aviation, builder of fighter planes and photoreconnaissance aircraft, to investigate "an ultra-fiche storage and retrieval system." See David G. Hays, *A Billion Books for Education in America and the World; a Proposal* (Santa Monica: Rand Corporation, 1968); and Council on Library Resources, *Twelfth Annual Report* (1968).

165 "should weigh heavily": Haas, *Preparation,* p. 25.

165 "federal financial support": Haas, *Preparation,* p. 27.

165 even perhaps a film: Haas, *Preparation,* p. 14.

165 former OSS outpost chief in Paris: John Edward (Jack) Sawyer was head of the Mellon Foundation from 1975 to 1987. His career in the Office of Strategic Services is mentioned in Bradley F. Smith, *The Shadow Warriors* (New York: Basic Books, 1983), pp. 385–86.

165 "savvy, shrewdness": James M. Morris, "The Foundation Connection," in *Influencing Change in Research Librarianship: A Festschrift for Warren J. Haas,* ed. Martin M. Cummings (Washington, D.C.: Council on Library Resources, 1988), p. 73.

166 "Careful analytical work": [Warren Haas], *Brittle Books: Reports of the Committee on Preservation and Access* (Washington, D.C.: Council on Library Resources, 1986), p. 7.

CHAPTER 20 – Special Offer

168 "collection building": Veaner, "Crisis in Micropublication," pp. 448–53. In 1990, Susan Cady wrote that the "quality of a research library is still measured primarily by the size of its holdings. Microforms are counted within those holdings as items owned (film rolls, microfiche pieces, etc.) and titles held. Thus they enhance the status of the institution at a relatively low cost in terms of both purchase price and storage space." Cady herself has no regrets about the loss of the newspapers: she says that the "preservation of newspapers by microfilming has been one of the real success stories of this technology." Susan A. Cady, "The Electronic Revolution in Libraries: Microfilm Déjà Vu?" *College and Research Libraries,* July 1990.

168 accreditation: Bourke, "Scholarly Micropublishing."

169 shady entrepreneurs: Veaner, "Crisis in Micropublication."

169 "disposing easily and profitably": Murray S. Martin, "Matters Arising from the Minutes: A Further Consideration of Microform-Serials Exchange," *Microform Review* 2 (April 1973); and "New Microfilms for Old Books," *American Libraries,* February 1970. Martin points out that "a minimum sale of ten to fifteen copies is necessary for a micropublisher to reach a break-even point." When he was associate dean of libraries at Penn State, Martin wrote: "It may save money to buy microforms instead of holding on to bound volumes, *but* if the volumes were not used before, they are unlikely to be used in the new format in which case even more money would be saved by discarding them altogether." Murray Martin, "Promoting Microforms to Students and Faculty," *Microform Review* 8:2 (spring 1979).

169 "to cooperate with micropublishers": Pamela Darling, "Developing a Preservation Microfilming Program," *Library Journal,* November 1, 1974.

169 Iowa's NEH- and state-funded newspaper project: Prison inmates hired by the State Historical Society of Iowa prepped the pages. But the historical society didn't participate in Heritage's free filming offer, because they wanted to keep control of their master negatives.

170 "gilded age": Bourke, "Scholarly Micropublishing."

170 "Let's suppose that the user": Salmon, "User Resistance."

171 "an information burial system": Harold Wooster, *Microfiche 1969—a User Survey* (Arlington, Va.: Air Force Office of Scientific Research, 1969), quoted in Salmon, "User Resistance." Another librarian wrote Wooster: "Daily we have an experience which breaks my librarians' hearts. Our users come in or call up for information. We research and locate it. In those instances when they are told we have it only on microfiche, the reply is 'forget it' usually accompanied by an emphatic wave of a hand." Daniel Gore writes: "Underlying most decisions to purchase microcollections is, I believe, an instinctive realization that such things will, with few exceptions, get little or no use once they are acquired." Daniel Gore, "The View from the Tower of Babel," in *To Know a Library* (Westport, Conn.: Greenwood Press, 1978), originally published in *Library Journal,* September 15, 1975; quoted in John Swan, "Micropermanence and Electronic Evanescence," *Microform Review* 20:2 (spring 1991).

171 "the plain fact is that": Spaulding, "Kicking the Silver Habit."

172 "we need massive infusions": Margaret S. Child, "The Future of Cooperative Preservation Microfilming," *Library Resources and Technical Services* 29:1 (January/March 1985): 96.

172 "need to be targeted": Child, "Future," p. 100.
172 "the general public needs": Child, "Future," p. 100.
172 "universal panacea": Child, "Future," p. 96.

CHAPTER 21 – 3.3 Million Books, 358 Million Dollars

174 "Analysis of the Magnitude": Robert M. Hayes, "Analysis of the Magnitude, Costs, and Benefits of the Preservation of Research Library Books: A Working Paper Prepared for the Council on Library Resources," January 21, 1985. With further funding from the Council on Library Resources, Hayes followed this up with a longer report in 1987, which included a revealing survey of attitudes toward microfilm. ("Nearly half the respondents regarded microform, in general, as UNACCEPTABLE," Hayes writes, and he quotes responses such as "Film is the last resort; never use if we can get copy"; and "Personally abhor microfilm for use"; and "Intolerable for reading, especially hard technical reading"; and "Easier to see thing in newspaper in the original.") The second, expanded version was entitled "The Magnitude, Costs, and Benefits of the Preservation of Brittle Books," November 30, 1987; in it, the original 1985 working paper was reprinted, exactly as it was first published, as "Report #0." Robert M. Hayes, e-mail letter to author, June 21, 1999.

174 Hayes was a network consultant: Hayes's papers are at UCLA; the OCLC entry for them (accession no. 37992540) includes a biographical note. See also Anne Woodsworth and Barbara von Wahlde, eds., *Leadership for Research Libraries: A Festschrift for Robert M. Hayes* (Metuchen, N.J.: Scarecrow Press, 1988), which includes an incomplete biography and a bibliography—Hayes's work for the military is either unmentioned or shielded behind acronyms such as USAFBMD.

174 SWAC: The Standards Western Automatic Computer was designed by an Englishman, Harry Huskey, in 1950. Robert Hayes used it on problems of "matrix decomposition," but the SWAC was also employed to calculate Mersenne primes, useful for cryptography. Hayes wrote me: "Much of the work of staff at the Institute for Numerical Analysis at UCLA"—home of the SWAC—"was actually concerned with coding and decoding methods. I am sure that NSA funding was important. That wasn't the focus of my own work, so I cannot say for certain, but from all that I have learned since then, I am sure it was the case."

174 Magnavox: In the late fifties, Magnavox invented the Magnacard system of information storage, an unsuccessful product. Also, as subcontractors for Kodak, Magnavox's engineers worked on the electronics for the Minicard System, developed for the Air Force and the CIA.

174 Joseph Becker: Hayes had no consulting contracts with the CIA, he informs me; he took care not to discuss the CIA with Becker. Hayes would have been "delighted to have had such contracts for both financial and intellectual reasons," but they were not forthcoming.

175 "The most far-reaching solution": Robert M. Hayes and Joseph Becker, *Handbook of Data Processing for Libraries* (New York: Becker and Hayes, 1970), p. 69.

175 "effectively destroying": Hayes, "The Cost Analysis for the Preservation Project: Report # 3 on the Preservation Project," in his "The Magnitude," p. 27.

175 a 1984 "Preservation Plan": Hayes, "Analysis of the Magnitude," p. 15.

CHAPTER 22 – Six Thousand Bodies a Day

178 "many documents": Subcommittee on Postsecondary Education, *Oversight Hearing,* p. 1.
178 "dangerously brittle state": Subcommittee, *Oversight Hearing,* p. 40.
179 "Across the country": Subcommittee, *Oversight Hearing,* p. 39.
179 "facing extinction": Subcommittee, *Oversight Hearing,* p. 31.
179 "French generals": Subcommittee, *Oversight Hearing,* p. 35.
179 "almost a dead book": Subcommittee, *Oversight Hearing,* p. 23.
179 "A mind is a terrible": Subcommittee, *Oversight Hearing,* p. 24. Vartan Gregorian may not have written this speech himself and so perhaps should not be held responsible for all of it. Gregorian's remarks were repeated nearly verbatim a year later in a talk by the New York Public Library's Richard De Gennaro. Here is Gregorian, before Congress: "Anyone of us who uses books and paper is exposed to the problem of deteriorating paper. Looking at a four day old Washington Post, or a four year old paperback, they decay before our eyes." Here is De Gennaro: "Any one of us who uses books and paper is exposed to the problem of deteriorating paper. Look at a four-day-old newspaper or a four-year-old paperback. They decay before our eyes." Richard De Gennaro, "Research Libraries: Mankind's Memory at Risk," in Luner, *Paper Preservation.* De Gennaro went on to run Harvard's library system.
179 "Our thrust at the Endowment": Subcommittee, *Oversight Hearing,* p. 3.
179 "has only been in the forefront": Subcommittee, *Oversight Hearing,* p. 37.
179 "We are dependent upon people": Subcommittee, *Oversight Hearing,* p. 33.
180 "Our research houses": Subcommittee, *Oversight Hearing,* p. 44.
180 "join in the task": Subcommittee, *Oversight Hearing,* p. 61.
180 "a kind of giant step": Subcommittee, *Oversight Hearing,* p. 125.
180 "The purpose of the work": Subcommittee, *Oversight Hearing,* p. 60.
181 "The books themselves": Subcommittee, *Oversight Hearing,* p. 58.
181 "It is not unlikely": Subcommittee, *Oversight Hearing,* p. 109.

CHAPTER 23 – Burning Up

185 Haas himself (blue shirt): Terry Sanders, *Slow Fires,* written by Ben Maddow and narrated by Robert MacNeil, a presentation of the American Film Foundation (Washington, D.C.: Council on Library Resources, 1987). The film exists in an hour version and a half-hour version. The longer version was the original one; this account is based on it.

186 trying tendentiousness: For example, near the end of *Slow Fires,* we move slowly past an enormous computer, while Robert MacNeil says, "Stone, clay, canvas, paper, tape, and disk—a human diary, a chain of knowledge that connects everyone to everyone else. All our faith, passion, and skill—all the horror and beauty of the generations past—are left for us to ponder, unless we choose to let it wither, disintegrate, burn, and die, leaving us to stumble in the dark."

187 Grand Prize: The Commission on Preservation and Access, *Newsletter,* November–December 1989. Daniel Boorstin, however, says some excellent things in the film about the book as a technological achievement and, perhaps with diethyl zinc on his mind, calls the library "a laboratory of our memory and a catalyst of our expectations."

188 "do anything to help": Commission on Preservation and Access, " 'Slow Fires' Film Wins Award, is Widely Shown," *Newsletter* insert, February 1988.

188 "giant Brittle Books exhibit": See the photograph in the Commission on Preservation and Access, *Newsletter* 20 (February 1990). The exhibit included a leather-bound book, two feet by three feet, with some distressed bits of paper arranged in front of it, and a quotation from *Slow Fires* reproduced in large letters: "The great task of libraries, worldwide, is the preservation of the ordinary."

189 " 'slow fires,' triggered": Quoted in Merrily Taylor, "Paper—Why Friends Should Care About It!" *Among Friends of the Library of Brown University* 5:2 (March 1989).

CHAPTER 24 – Going, Going, Gone

191 "She will emerge": Billy E. Frye (provost of Emory University and chairman of Battin's Commission on Preservation and Access), speaking in *1996 CAUSE Elite Award Winner: Patricia Battin* (Washington, D.C.: CAUSE, 1996), videotape.

191 Booz, Allen and Hamilton: The grant was "sponsored by the Association of Research Libraries in cooperation with the American Council on Education under a grant from the Council on Library Resources." Warren Haas was president of the Association of Research Libraries when he got the grant for Columbia. Booz, Allen and Hamilton, *Organization and Staffing of the Libraries of Columbia University* (Washington, D.C.: Association of Research Libraries, 1972).

192 "the personal computer": Patricia Battin, "The Electronic Library—a Vision for the Future," *EDUCOM Bulletin,* summer 1984.

193 "The basic shape of our collections": Patricia Battin, "Preservation at the Columbia University Libraries," in Merrill-Oldham and Smith, *Library Preservation Program,* p. 37.

193 "active assault": Battin, "Preservation at the Columbia University Libraries," p. 37.

193 oversewing: W. Elmo Reavis invented the oversewing machine and began selling it in 1920. Like Barrow's process of lamination, oversewing was something that seemed fast and cheap and durable at the time, but it is irreversible, and it has worked out badly. You begin by milling off the back of the book. This destroys the serried integrity of its signatures, so that it can't from then on be repaired in the traditional way, by "sewing through the fold," and it removes about an eighth of an inch of inner margin. The oversewing needles stab obliquely into the paper from there, consuming more margin. If you then try, a decade later, to rebind an oversewn book, you have to mill off the back a second time, and you may end up with a book so tightly bound that you can barely get it open enough to read the inner text; the pages are likely to break and pull out at their puncture-points as you try to force them open, say, facedown on a photocopier. Between 1920 and 1986 (when specifications underwent modifications), countless books were oversewn that shouldn't have been, as libraries decommissioned or reduced their in-house binderies and sent books to commercial firms equipped with Elmo Reavis's angle-stabbing machines and their descendants. See Elmo Reavis's appendix to *Library Binding Manual: A Handbook of Useful Procedures for the Maintenance of Library Volumes,*

ed. Maurice F. Tauber (Boston: Library Binding Institute, 1972); and Jan Merrill-Oldham and Paul Parisi, *Guide to the Library Binding Institute Standard for Library Binding* (Chicago: American Library Association, 1990); and Robert DeCandido and Paul Parisi, eds., *ANSI/NISO/LBI Standard for Library Binding,* draft 7.3.1, June 12, 1998, sunsite.berkeley.edu/Binding/NISO7_4.txt.

193 "scraps of faded, rusted, brittle paper": New York Public Library, "When Did Newspapers Begin to Use Wood Pulp Stock?" *Bulletin of the New York Public Library* 33 (1929).

194 "we will not add to our collections": Battin, "Preservation at the Columbia University Libraries," pp. 38–39.

194 "old boy network": CAUSE, *1996 CAUSE Elite Award Winner.* The CAUSE Elite Award was sponsored by Systems and Computer Technology (now SCT), which sells database software and consulting services to universities and government agencies. CAUSE was a non-profit corporation devoted to furthering the "use and management of information systems in higher education" (Jane N. Ryland, "CAUSE: Notes on a History," September 1998, www.educause.edu/pub/chistory/chistory.html); in 1998, it merged with Educom, another non-profit advocate of educational networks and information systems; the new entity became EDUCAUSE. One of the founders of Educom in the sixties was James Grier Miller, former psychopharmacologist and OSS spy evaluator; Educom's acting president in 1970 was retired CIA man Joseph Becker. See Robert C. Herrick, "Educom: A Retrospective," *Educom Review* 33:5 (1998), www.educause.edu/pub/ehistory/ehistory.html; and EDUCAUSE, "EDUCAUSE is Official!" www.educause.edu/coninfo/educause_official.html (July 1, 1998) (viewed October 25, 2000). The current president of EDUCAUSE is Brian L. Hawkins, who was for a decade a computer administrator at Brown University and an adviser to companies such as IBM, Apple, NeXT, Sun Microsystems, and Microsoft; Hawkins and Patricia Battin together edited *The Mirage of Continuity: Reconfiguring Academic Information Resources for the Twenty-first Century* (Washington, D.C.: Council on Library and Information Resources, 1998). Hawkins believes in a thoroughgoing liquidation of research collections: "Not only would electronic storage be far cheaper, it would also eliminate the present duplication," he writes, in a chapter of *The Mirage of Continuity* entitled "The Unsustainability of the Traditional Library." EDUCAUSE is jointly funded by educational institutions and by large corporations; IBM, for instance, is currently a "Platinum Partner," meaning that in exchange for $100,000 or more in annual contributions, IBM receives "a guaranteed corporate presentation opportunity at the annual conference," plus free advertising, the best floor space at the conference, and other benefits. The president of a company called Word of Mouse, which sells advertising on mouse-pads at university libraries, said that "the people at EDUCAUSE know my customers and open the right doors." Word of Mouse is a Bronze Partner of EDUCAUSE. EDUCAUSE, "Corporate Partner Program," www.educause.edu/partners (viewed October 25, 2000).

194 piece by Eric Stange: Eric Stange, "Millions of Books Are Turning to Dust—Can They Be Saved?" *The New York Times Book Review,* March 29, 1987. Two months later, the *Chicago Tribune* published an article that began: "The book is a life's work condensed into 200 pages. It has survived for decades. The next time somebody looks at it, it will crumble to dust." *Chicago Tribune,* May 25,

1987, national edition, p. 3, Nexis. During a period of heavy bleaching in paper manufacture, John Murray, in 1824, instanced a Bible that was "CRUMBLING LITERALLY INTO DUST." John Murray, *Observations and Experiments on the Bad Composition of Modern Paper* (London: G. and W. B. Whitaker), quoted in Roggia, "William James Barrow."

195 "the estimated number of volumes": The Commission on Preservation and Access, *Newsletter* (June 1988). In an interview with *The Bottom Line,* Battin says that 3.3 million is "the estimated number of volumes that must be saved as representative of the 10 million that will turn to dust." "Preserving Our Crumbling Collections: An Interview with Patricia Battin, President, Commission on Preservation and Access," Betty J. Turock, interviewer, *The Bottom Line* 3:4 (1989).

195 "Have you seen a first edition": Michael Miller, *Ideas for Preservation Fund Raising: A Support Package for Libraries and Archives* (Washington, D.C.: Commission on Preservation and Access, 1990). The support package is the subject of a lead article in the Commission's *Newsletter* for September 1990.

196 "A slow fire is burning": Diane Ballard, "Goodness Gracious, Great Books Afire!" *Torchbearer,* fall 1990. The Commission distributed a typescript of the article, which omitted this title—perhaps it seemed too frivolous. The University of Oregon Library ran a money-raising ad in a house magazine that said, "Unless we act now, much of the collection in the largest research library in Oregon could disintegrate before our eyes." *Old Oregon* (magazine of the University of Oregon) 66:4 (summer 1987).

CHAPTER 25 – Absolute Nonsense

198 His experience began in Florence: These details come from Peter Waters, "From Florence to St. Petersburg: An Enlightening and Thought-Provoking Experience," paper read at the conference "Redefining Disasters: A Decade of Counter Disaster Planning," Library of New South Wales, September 1995.

199 "If swift and drastic action": Patricia Battin, "The Silent Books of the Future: Initiatives to Save Yesterday's Literature for Tomorrow," *Logos* (London) 2:1 (1991): 11.

201 When *Smithsonian* was doing a piece: Williams, "Library of Congress Can't Hold All of Man's Knowledge."

201 old boss Frazer Poole: Poole, by the way, worked with the Barrow Laboratory before he came to the Library of Congress (on durable catalog cards), as part of the ALA/Council on Library Resources Library Technology Project. He probably learned the trick of crumpling paper to bits in order to shock people from Barrow and DuPuis.

CHAPTER 26 – Drumbeat

203 "millions of rotting books": Battin uses this phrase twice, once in "Crumbling Books: A Call for Strategies to Preserve Our Cultural Memory," *Change,* September/October 1989, p. 56; and once in "Silent Books of the Future," p. 16. The continuation headline (not recorded in Nexis) for Malcolm Browne's 1990 article in *The New York Times* is "Nation's Library Calls on Chemists to Preserve Rotting Books." Carolyn Morrow, the preservation librarian at Harvard, backed Battin up, saying that her library is "literally rotting

from the inside out." Edward T. Hearn, "Self-Burning Books: Millions of Tomes Need Rescue from Their Acids," *Chicago Tribune,* November 19, 1989, Tempo, p. 2, final edition. Before Carolyn Morrow went to Harvard (as the first Malloy-Rabinowitz Preservation Librarian, an endowed chair), she worked for Peter Sparks; in the early eighties, Sparks hired her away from Southern Illinois University at Carbondale to staff a propaganda and fund-raising team at the Library of Congress which he called the National Preservation Program Office (NPPO). On Morrow, see *Abbey Newsletter* 8:6 (December 1984), copied on the CoOL website, palimpsest.stanford.edu/byorg/abbey/an/an08/an08-6/an08-603.html.

205 "will not embrittle to dust": See also Helmut Bansa, "Selection for Conservation," *Restaurator* 13:4 (1992), which offers "the scientifically correct fact that books do not 'literally crumble to dust.' "

CHAPTER 27 – Unparalleled Crisis

207 "comprehensive mass-production strategy": Commission on Preservation and Access, *1990 Annual Report.*

207 "major attack": Patricia Battin, "A Message from the President," Commission on Preservation and Access, *Newsletter* 3 (August 1988).

208 big day for acid-free paper: See "An End to the Yellowing Pages," *Newsweek,* March 20, 1989, p. 80, which says that about a quarter of the volumes in American research libraries are "crumbling into oblivion."

208 "35 out of the 88 miles": New York Public Library, "Authors and Publishers Sign Landmark Declaration for Book Preservation," news release (March 7, 1989), reprinted in Association of Research Libraries, *Preserving Knowledge: The Case for Alkaline Paper* (Washington, D.C.: Association of Research Libraries, 1990).

209 "There appears to be high user acceptance": Hayes, "Magnitude, Costs, and Benefits," p. 26.

209 "Making clear to scholars": Commission on Preservation and Access, *1992 Annual Report,* www.clir.org/pubs/annual/annrpt91.html.

210 "But if these original books": The brittle-book crisis should also be taught, Miller's report urged: "We should also begin at once to incorporate this awareness into graduate instruction in research methods." J. Hillis Miller, *Preserving the Literary Heritage: The Final Report of the Scholarly Advisory Committee on Modern Language and Literature of the Commission on Preservation and Access* (Washington, D.C.: Commission on Preservation and Access, July 1991), www.clir.org/pubs/reports/miller/miller.html.

211 "The Endowment could not have advanced": George F. Farr, Jr., "Preservation and the National Endowment for the Humanities," in Luner, *Paper Preservation.*

211 particular collection: Here is a representative brittle-books grant to Columbia University from the 1993 annual report of the NEH: "$2,298,320 To support preservation microfilming of 15,000 embrittled volumes on the development of the world's economy over the last two centuries and its impact on the formation of political and social institutions." $2.3 million divided by 15,000 is about $150 per volume.

212 "number of preservation operations": Battin, "Message from the President."

CHAPTER 28 – Microfix

213 He and Matthew Nickerson: Matthew Nickerson, "pH: Only a Piece of the Preservation Puzzle: A Comparison of the Preservation Studies at Brigham Young, Yale, and Syracuse Universities," *Library Resources and Technical Services* 36:1 (1992).

214 population of damaged or fragile books: Silverman tried to convince a former employer to accept several thousand post-microfilming discards that John Baker, head of preservation at the New York Public Library, was off-loading. (Baker is the one who in a voice of sorrow says, in *Slow Fires,* that many of the books "simply fall apart in your hands.") The NYPL was delighted by the idea that somebody wanted the books, but the administration at Silverman's library decided that there wasn't space.

214 Some of his colleagues had private misgivings: Critical voices are faintly audible in the report of a Review and Assessment Committee, chaired by David H. Stam, that evaluated the work of the Commission on Preservation and Access in 1991: "Some saw the microfilming program as 'anti-paper,' its hidden agenda designed to foster the eventuality of the electronic library, with digitized materials coming from microfilm or other sources. Some saw a lack of interest in preserving rare books or in preserving the original documents, regardless of condition or perceived importance, after filming has been completed." David H. Stam et al., *Review and Assessment Committee, Final Report* (Washington, D.C.: Commission on Preservation and Access, 1991), p. 18.

CHAPTER 29 – Slash and Burn

216 play by Robert de Flers: Francis de Croisset, *Le Souvenir de Robert de Flers, suivi de les précieuses de Genève par Robert de Flers et Francis de Croisset* (Paris: Editions des Portiques, 1929).

216 "Laying aside all malice": See the translation and explication of Columbia's seal in "The Mission of the University," *Columbia University Fact Book 1995–96,* www.columbia.edu/cu/udar/factbook/12.html.

216 "Cooperative Preservation Microfilming Project": For a history of the Research Library Group's microfilming projects, see Nancy Elkington, ed., *RLG Preservation Microfilming Handbook* (Mountain View, Calif.: Research Libraries Group, 1992), appendix 21.

217 "this kind of mass—": In 1992, Battin wrote that we must "change our focus from single-item salvation to a mass production process." "Substitution: The American Experience," typescript of lecture in Oxford Library Seminars, "Preserving Our Library Heritage," February 25, 1992, quoted in Abby Smith, "The Future of the Past: Preservation in American Research Libraries" (draft), Council on Library and Information Resources, January 1999.

218 George Farr . . . was on board: "The Endowment," Farr wrote in 1988, supports "the reformatting of knowledge on to a more stable medium, which at this time means microfilm produced and stored to national archival standards, in the absense of similar national standards for other media. The scale of the preservation problem, coupled with the fragility of most of these materials and the expense of item-by-item conservation, makes any other course of action impractical." Farr, "Preservation."

219 *"Slash and burn preservation":* Paul Conway, "Yale University Library's Project Open Book: Preliminary Research Findings," *D-Lib Magazine,* February 1996, www.dlib.org/dlib/february96/yale/02conway.html.

220 "approximately 7%": Harvard University, "History of Science: Preserving Collections for the Study of Culture and Society," proposal submitted to the National Endowment for the Humanities (Cambridge, Mass.: Harvard University, 1998), p. 27.

221 several thousand "pams": "Columbia University used $696,000 to microfilm 9,797 embrittled pamphlets on social and economic history published from 1880 to 1950," according to the NEH's website—$71.04 per pamphlet. National Endowment for the Humanities, "Brittle Books," www.neh.gov/preservation/brittlebooks.html (viewed October 4, 2000). (The page includes a picture—"Example of a brittle book"—of a book whose binding has failed, over which one of its pages has apparently been crumpled and sprinkled.) The New York Public Library's discard of approximately one hundred thousand pamphlets so troubled collector Michael Zinman that he distributed a poster in 1997 that reproduced some of the accessions stamps and gift bookplates from these lost collections; the headline was IT BECAME NECESSARY TO DESTROY THE TOWN IN ORDER TO SAVE IT—the words of an American officer who attacked a Vietnamese town in 1968. See Mark Singer's Talk of the Town article on Zinman and the pamphlets (which were microfilmed), *The New Yorker,* January 12, 1998.

CHAPTER 30 – A Swifter Conflagration

222 "Scarcely a day now passes": G. Thomas Tanselle, "Libraries, Museums, and Reading," in his *Literature and Artifacts* (Charlottesville: Bibliographical Society of the University of Virginia, 1998), p. 14.

223 "placed in the charge": G. Thomas Tanselle, "Statement on the Role of Books and Manuscripts in the Electronic Age," in his *Literature and Artifacts,* p. 334.

223 "The term 'preservation' ": G. Thomas Tanselle, "The Latest Forms of Book-Burning," in his *Literature and Artifacts,* p. 90.

224 "sizable portions": G. Thomas Tanselle, "Statement on the Significance of Primary Records," in his *Literature and Artifacts,* p. 335.

224 may qualify as objects: See, for instance, appendix 1 of Elkington, *RLG Preservation Microfilming Handbook,* "Considerations for Retaining Items in Original Format." Items that contain illustrations "not easily reproduced or meaningful only in the original color or original woodcuts, etchings, lithographs, etc." are possible candidates for retention, as is "ephemeral material likely to be scarce, such as a lettersheet, poster, songster, or broadside." Newspapers qualify under both these categories, but that hasn't helped them.

224 "Books of high market value": G. Thomas Tanselle, "Reproductions and Scholarship," in his *Literature and Artifacts,* p. 83.

224 "I think it is undeniable": Tanselle, "Libraries, Museums, and Reading," p. 17.

225 "approaching books as museum objects": Tanselle, "Libraries, Museums, and Reading," p. 5.

225 "Most books are not frequently used": Tanselle, "Libraries, Museums, and Reading," p. 16.

226 "A central repository": Tanselle, "Reproductions and Scholarship," p. 88.

226 "Although it is a pity": Tanselle, "Latest Forms of Book-Burning," p. 95.

CHAPTER 32 – A Figure We Did Not Collect

230 "We have not done so": George Farr, letter to the author, April 5, 1999.

230 "Analysis of 15 years": Montori, "Re: electronic/paper format & weeding."

231 staple-bound purple booklet: Martha Kyrillidou, Michael O'Connor, and Julia C. Blixrud, *ARL Preservation Statistics, 1996–97* (Washington, D.C.: Association of Research Libraries, 1998).

232 "dramatic reduction": Jutta R. Reed, "Cost Comparison of Periodicals in Hard Copy and on Microform," *Microform Review* 5:3 (July 1976).

232 as determined by the formulas: The formulas, Reed-Scott notes, are adapted from UMI founder Eugene Power's 1951 article "Microfilm as a Substitute for Binding"; Power was one of Verner Clapp's and Luther Evans's colleagues on the board of the microphilic American Documentation Institute, now the American Society for Information Science (ASIS).

233 save over *$145:* Ann Niles questions these figures in "Conversion of Serials from Paper to Microfilm," *Microform Review* 9:2 (spring 1980). She calculates that the cost of buying microfilm replacements of a collection of periodicals would be almost twice the cost of building new on-site space to house them, and to that must be added the maintenance and replacement of the microfilm readers, which have a life-span of five to ten years.

CHAPTER 33 – Leaf Masters

234 "a heavy proportion": Stam, "Questions of Preservation."

236 "Based on a non-scientific survey": Gay Walker, "One Step Beyond: The Future of Preservation Microfilming," in *Preservation Microfilming: Planning and Production.*

237 "Of all responding libraries": Jan Merrill-Oldham and Gay Walker, *Brittle Books Programs* (Washington, D.C.: Systems and Procedures Exchange Center [SPEC] Kit 152, Office of Management Services, Association of Research Libraries, 1989), introductory flyer and p. vi.

237 "have all ownership marks removed": Gay Walker, "Preservation Decision Making: A Descriptive Model," in Merrill-Oldham and Walker, *Brittle Books Programs,* p. 35.

237 "In the great majority of cases": Gay Walker, "Preservation Decision-Making and Archival Photocopying," *Restaurator* 8 (1987).

237 filmed another 150,000: At the congressional hearing in March 1987, William Welsh told committee members that the library had microfilmed four hundred thousand volumes between 1968 and 1987—about twenty thousand per year (Subcommittee on Postsecondary Education, *Oversight Hearing,* p. 123). The number may be lower than this, however; the Office of Technology Assessment's *Book Preservation Technologies* said in 1988 that the Library of Congress "microfilms between 10,000 and 20,000 brittle monographs and serials per year at a cost of about $40 per volume" (p. 14). On the other hand, in March 1983, Peter Sparks told a reporter from *Discover* magazine: "I can't microfilm them fast enough. We can manage about 23,000 books a year—and there are millions of them out there."

238 "A major concern about filming": Walker, "One Step Beyond," in *Preservation Microfilming: Planning and Production.*

239 "the highest quality film": Vickie Lockhart and Ann Swartzell, "Evaluation of

Microfilm Vendors," *Microform Review* 19:3 (summer 1990). In the study, the company that missed pages is given as "RP," which I assume stands for Research Publications.

239 "did not resolve to": Whitney S. Minkler, *Audit Procedures and Inspection Results from 1% of Microfilm Samples from Ohio State, Yale, and Harvard Universities* (Fairfax, Va.: MSTC, March 30, 1993). As part of her "NEH Medieval Institute Microfilming Project," Sophia Jordan, head of preservation at Notre Dame, made a database of microfilm vendors. Out of the available titles that her group checked, she recorded the percentage that did not "meet preservation standards," according to a somewhat stringent list of criteria (no master negative exists, etc.). Ninety-four percent of the titles available from University Microfilms did not meet preservation standards, fourteen percent of Columbia's titles did not, all of Cornell's did not, a quarter of Harvard's did not, forty-two percent of New York Public Library's did not, sixty percent of UC Berkeley's did not, and so on. Sophia Jordan and Dorothy Paul, *NEH Medieval Institute Microfilming Project: Database Report of Previously Filmed Titles Queried* (Notre Dame: University of Notre Dame Libraries, undated [circa 1990]). In providing this report, George Farr of the NEH wrote: "I would observe that the highly developed national standards and expectations for preservation filming that have been followed in NEH-funded projects might not have been in place when the volumes that were the focus of the Notre Dame survey were initially microfilmed." George Farr, letter to author, April 5, 1999.

CHAPTER 34 – Turn the Pages Once

240 "cost-effective buffer technology": Commission on Preservation and Access, *Newsletter* 21 (March 1990).

241 Technical Assessment Advisory Committee: The committee had a three-day retreat at the Coolfont Conference Center in September 1990, which the members judged "most productive." Commission on Preservation and Access, *Newsletter*, September 1990.

242 The relatively simple substitution: See my essay "Discards," in *The Size of Thoughts* (New York: Random House, 1996).

243 "Our biggest misjudgment was": William Welsh, "Can Bill Welsh Conquer Time and Space for Libraries?" interview with Arthur Plotnik, *American Libraries* 15:11 (December 1984).

245 "only a small increment": M. Stuart Lynn, "Digital Technologies, Preservation and Access," *The Commission on Preservation and Access Newsletter* 43 (March 1992), www.clir.org/pubs/cpanews/cpan143.html. Actually, Lynn's words here are "have our cake and eat it. too" because the OCR program interpreted the comma as a period. Michael Lesk is similarly recorded as estimating the number of "books per square fool" that a building can hold. Michael Lesk, *Preservation of New Technology,* a report of the Technology Assessment Advisory Committee to the Commission on Preservation and Access (Washington, D.C.: Commission on Preservation and Access, October 1992), www.clir.org/pubs/reports/lesk/lesk2.html. These are tiny errors that nonetheless demonstrate the importance of keeping the original printed report.

CHAPTER 35 – Suibtermanean Convumision

249 "anticipated resistance": Task Force on Collection Management, Systemwide Operations and Planning Group, "Action/Decision Minutes," February 26, 1999, *UCI's Information Page on UC Systemwide Library Planning,* sun3.lib.uci.edu/~staff/system_wide.htm (viewed September 25, 2000).

250 "digital collections can alleviate": Anne Kenney, "Digital Image Quality: From Conversion to Presentation and Beyond," paper presented at the Scholarly Communication and Technology conference, sponsored by the Andrew W. Mellon Foundation, Emory University, Atlanta, April 24–25, 1997, arl.cni.org/scomm/scat/kenney.html.

250 "rapidly self-destructing": Anne R. Kenney and Lynne K. Personius, *The Cornell/Xerox/Commission on Preservation and Access Joint Study in Digital Preservation. Report: Phase 1,* "Digital Capture, Paper Facsimiles, and Network Access" (December 1990).

250 extremely rare math books: Cornell University Library Math Book Collection, moa.cit.cornell.edu/dienst-data/cdl-math-browse.html. For instance, one of the books, Pierre Maurice Duhem's *Sur les déformations permanentes et l'hysteresis* (Brussels: Hayez, 1896), is listed on the OCLC database as existing in two places, at Princeton and at the Burndy Library of MIT. For an early work on hyperspace by Giuseppe Veronese entitled *Fondamenti di geometria a più dimensioni* (Padua: Tipografia del Seminario, 1891), there are six U.S. libraries on OCLC (and one in São Paulo) listed as owning the original book.

250 germ-free facsimiles: Kenney and Personius, *Cornell/Xerox/Commission on Preservation and Access Joint Study.*

250 Peruvian guano: Solon Robinson, *Guano: A Treatise of Practical Information for Farmers; Containing Plain Directions How to Apply Peruvian Guano to the Various Crops and Soils of America* (New York, 1853). If my count is correct, there are twelve original copies of *Guano* in the OCLC database (perhaps of two editions, perhaps of one edition differently cataloged), plus twelve microfiche copies made in 1985 by Lost Cause Press and one roll of microfilm produced by the Ohio Historical Society in 1985 and owned by Marietta College. See the Core Historical Literature of Agriculture, Albert R. Mann Library, Cornell University, cdl.library.cornell.edu/chla/. Solon Robinson writes: "With assurances to my friends that I have no other interest in the increased consumption of guano, I am most sincerely and respectfully, Your old Friend, Solon Robinson."

250 "There may also be opportunities": Kenney and Personius, *Cornell/Xerox/Commission on Preservation and Access Joint Study.*

250 "escalating cost of storage": "The Making of America: Creating Electronic Pathways to Our Heritage," Cornell University Library and Cornell Information Technologies, 1993. One of the aims of the Making of America project was to win over humanities scholars, who "lag behind their counterparts in the sciences and professions in making use of sources on-line." The proposal also mentions that Cornell "is committed to a policy of no new library building projects for central campus beyond the year 2000."

251 subterranean convulsion: "The Java Upheaval," *Manufacturer and Builder,* January 1883, p. 219, cdl.library.cornell.edu. The URL for the page is cdl.library.cornell.edu/cgi-bin/moa/pageviewer?frames=1&coll=moa&view=50&root=%2Fmoa%wFmanu%2Fmanu0015%2F&tif=00225.TIF&cite=http%

3A%2F%2Fcdl.library.cornell.edu%2Fcgi=bin%2Fmoa%2Fmoa-cgi%3Fnotisid %3DABS1821-0015-623; select "text" in the box next to "View as" to see the text that has been OCR'd from the image. I searched for the word "mmm" in Cornell's scan of the monumental and already fully microfilmed compendium of Civil War documents called *The War of the Rebellion* and found this from volume seven, p. 285, about the capture of Fort Donelson: "Timat evemming lime emmemv landed thirteen steamuboat loads of fresh troops. It was minov-mmm~mniP~st we could not homing maimmtain onr position agaumist smieli overwhnel maiming mmumbers. I xvas Satistie (1 that their last trool)s xvere ot (~mmeral Bimell's comninand. We felt time wammt of re-elminoreemminemints, bmmt did not ask for thenin, because we knew they were not to be had." The scanned image of this page is legible; the OCR text is, however, a wreck.

251 "OCR accuracy is high": I found this note by clicking on "A note on viewing the plain text of this volume" while browsing by title and year.

251 "to preserve the informational content": This production note appears on the first scanned page.

251 "due to the brittle nature": Cornell University Library, "The Conversion Process," *Making of America,* cdl.library.cornell.edu/moa/moa_conversion.html.

251 truffle hunting: Cornell's Making of America database helped me find the poem about mummy paper in *Punch,* because it was republished (with no date) in *Littell's Living Age* (which Cornell scanned and discarded), as well as the mummy item in *Scientific American.*

CHAPTER 36 – Honest Disagreement

255 "Think about space costs": Pamela W. Darling, "Microforms in Libraries: Preservation and Storage," *Microform Review* 5:2 (April 1976). Darling also points out that the "cost of the microform is almost always less than would be the cost of binding the original issues, and no one has to claim missing issues, replace lost covers, or give readers no service for months while last year's volumes are 'At Bindery.' Instead, the original issues can be held in the periodical reading area for as long as interest keeps them 'current,' and then sold, exchanged or discarded since the microform will be available for backfile reference." In a 1974 article in *Library Journal,* Darling said that microfilm was "a medium more stable than paper," which "takes up 90 percent less space to store." "Developing a Preservation Microfilming Program," p. 2803.

255 "keep re-examining": Pamela W. Darling, "A Local Preservation Program: Where to Start" (an article based on a paper presented at a "Books in Peril" conference), *Library Journal,* November 15, 1976. As a grande dame of the preservation movement, Darling later wrote the introduction to Nancy Gwinn's textbook, *Preservation Microfilming.*

255 special consultant: "National Preservation Program Office Expands," *Library of Congress Information Bulletin,* November 5, 1984.

255 self-study manual: Pamela Darling, ed., *Preservation Planning Program: An Assisted Self-Study Manual for Libraries* (Washington, D.C.: Association of Research Libraries, 1982).

255 "may well be cheaper": Patricia Battin, "The Management of Knowledge: Issues for the Twenty-first Century," paper presented at the seventh

international seminar, Kanazawa Institute of Technology, Library Center, Kanazawa, Japan, 1989, in Welsh, *Research Libraries,* p. 399. On the same page, Battin writes Byronically of the "tangled web of new interdependencies" brought about by our growing dependence upon technology.

257 "millions of books": Patricia Battin, *Written Statement of Patricia Battin, Past President, Commission on Preservation and Access, on the Fiscal Year 1996 Appropriations for the National Endowment for the Humanities,* March 31, 1995.

References

Adkinson, Burton W. *Two Centuries of Federal Information.* Stroudsburg, Pa.: Dowden, Hutchinson, and Ross, 1978.

American Institute of the City of New York. *Catalogue of the Life and Annual Members of the American Institute of the City of New York.* New York: New York Printing Co., 1868.

American Society for Testing and Materials. "Standard Test Method for Determination of Effect of Moist Heat (50% Relative Humidity and 90°C) on Properties of Paper and Board." *Annual Book of ASTM Standards, 1998.* Vol. 15.09, D4714. Conshohocken, Pa.: American Society for Testing and Materials, 1998.

American Society of Information Scientists (ASIS). *Pioneers of Information Science in North America,* www.asis.org/Features/Pioneers/isp.htm.

Angle, Paul M. *The Library of Congress: An Account, Historical and Descriptive.* Kingsport, Tenn.: Kingsport Press, 1958.

Associated Press. "British Library Giving Away Old Newspapers," January 29, 1997, Nexis.

Association of Research Libraries. *Preserving Knowledge: The Case for Alkaline Paper.* Washington, D.C.: Association of Research Libraries, 1990.

Auger, C. P. "The Importance of Microforms." *Microform Review* 20:4 (fall 1991). Reprinted from *Information Sources in Grey Literature,* 2d ed. New York: Bowker-Saur, 1989.

Bahr, Alice Harrison. *Microforms: The Librarians' View, 1978–79.* White Plains, N.Y.: Knowledge Industry Publications, 1978.

Baker, John P. "Preservation Programs of the New York Public Library. Part Two: From the 1930s to the '60s." *Microform Review* 11:1 (winter 1982).

Baker, Nicholson. "Books as Furniture." In *The Size of Thoughts.* New York: Random House, 1996.

———. "Discards." In *The Size of Thoughts.* New York: Random House, 1996.

———. "Weeds: A Talk at the Library." In *Reclaiming San Francisco,* ed. James Brooke et al. San Francisco: City Lights, 1997.

———. "Deadline." *The New Yorker,* July 24, 2000.

Ballard, Diane. "Goodness Gracious, Great Books Afire!" *Torchbearer,* University of Tennessee, fall 1990.

Bamford, James. *The Puzzle Palace.* New York: Penguin, 1983.

Banik, Gerhard, and Werner K. Sobotka. "Deacidification and Strengthening of Bound Newspapers Through Aqueous Immersion." In Luner, *Paper Preservation,* 1988.

Bansa, Helmut. "Selection for Conservation." *Restaurator* 13:4 (1992).

Bansa, Helmut, and Hans-H. Hofer. *Artificial Aging as a Predictor of Paper's Future Useful Life. Abbey Newsletter* Monograph Supplement. Provo, Utah: Abbey Newsletter, 1989.

Barrow, William James. "The Barrow Method of Laminating Documents." *Journal of Documentary Reproduction* 2:2 (June 1939).

[Barrow, William James]. *Deterioration of Book Stock, Causes and Remedies.* Conducted by W. J. Barrow. Ed. Randolph W. Church. Richmond: Virginia State Library, 1959.

———. *Procedures and Equipment Used in the Barrow Method of Restoring Manuscripts and Documents.* Richmond: W. J. Barrow, 1961.

Barrow Research Laboratory. *Permanence/Durability of the Book: A Two-Year Research Program.* Richmond: Barrow Research Laboratory, 1963.

———. *Test Data of Naturally Aged Papers.* Richmond: Barrow Research Laboratory, 1964.

———. *Permanence/Durability of the Book—V: Strength and Other Characteristics of Book Papers, 1800–1899.* Richmond: Barrow Research Laboratory, 1967.

Basbanes, Nicholas. *A Gentle Madness.* New York: Henry Holt, 1995.

Battin, Patricia. "The Electronic Library—a Vision for the Future." *EDUCOM Bulletin,* summer 1984.

———. "Preservation at the Columbia University Libraries." In Merrill-Oldham and Smith, *Library Preservation Program,* 1985.

———. *Preservation: Proposal for a National Approach.* [Speaking notes.] Sixth annual conference of Research Library Directors on OCLC. Dublin, Ohio, 1988.

———. "A Message from the President." Commission on Preservation and Access, *Newsletter* 3 (August 1988).

———. "Crumbling Books: A Call for Strategies to Preserve Our Cultural Memory." *Change,* September/October 1989.

[———]. "Preserving Our Crumbling Collections: An Interview with Patricia Battin, President, Commission on Preservation and Access." Betty J. Turock, interviewer. *The Bottom Line* 3:4 (1989).

———. "The Management of Knowledge: Issues for the Twenty-first Century." Paper presented at the seventh international seminar, Kanazawa Institute of Technology, Library Center, Kanazawa, Japan, 1989. In Welsh, *Research Libraries—Yesterday, Today, and Tomorrow.*

———. "The Silent Books of the Future: Initiatives to Save Yesterday's Literature for Tomorrow." *Logos* (London) 2:1 (1991).

———. *Written Statement of Patricia Battin, Past President, Commission on Preservation and Access, on the Fiscal Year 1996 Appropriations for the National Endowment for the Humanities,* March 31, 1995.

Bellardo, Lewis J. "National Archives Preservation Research Priorities: Summary and

Update." In *Preservation Research and Development: Round Table Proceedings, September 28–29, 1992,* ed. Carrie Beyer. Washington, D.C.: Library of Congress Preservation Directorate, June 1993.

Biggar, Joanna. "Must the Library of Congress Destroy Books to Save Them?" *The Washington Post Magazine,* June 3, 1984.

Billington, James. *Library of Congress Information Bulletin,* June 15, 1992. Excerpted in Commission on Preservation and Access, *Newsletter,* September 1992.

———. "The Historic Library and the Electronic Future." Universidade de São Paulo, March 18–25, 1999, www.usp.br/sibi/Billington_Lecture.html (viewed August 22, 2000).

Binkley, Robert C. *Manual on Methods of Reproducing Research Materials.* Ann Arbor: Edwards Brothers, 1931.

Boomgaarden, Wesley. "Preservation Microfilming: Elements and Interconnections." In *Preservation Microfilming: Planning and Production.* Papers from the RTSD Preservation Microfilming Institute, New Haven, April 21, 23, 1988. Chicago: Association for Library Collections and Technical Services, 1989.

Booz, Allen and Hamilton. *Organization and Staffing of the Libraries of Columbia University.* Washington, D.C.: Association of Research Libraries, 1972.

Borio, Gene. *Jones, Day, Reavis and Pogue Draft: Corporate Activity Project: Part 1,* undated, www.tobacco.org/Documents/jonesday1.html.

Bosse, David. *Civil War Newspaper Maps: A Cartobibliography of the Northern Daily Press.* Westport, Conn.: Greenwood Press, 1993.

Bourke, Thomas A. "The Curse of Acetate; or, a Base Conundrum Confronted," *Microform Review* 23:1 (winter 1994).

———. "Scholarly Micropublishing, Preservation Microfilming, and the National Preservation Effort in the Last Two Decades of the Twentieth Century: History and Prognosis." *Microform Review* 19:1 (winter 1990).

Bowen, William G. "JSTOR and the Economics of Scholarly Communication." The Andrew W. Mellon Foundation, October 4, 1995, www.mellon.org/jsesc.html.

Boyd-Alkalay, Esther, and Lena Libman. "The Conservation of the Dead Sea Scrolls in the Laboratories of the Israel Antiquities Authority in Jerusalem." *Restaurator* 18 (1997).

Brier, Bob. *Egyptian Mummies.* New York: William Morrow, 1994.

British Library Newspaper Library. "Disposal of Overseas Newspapers." *Newspaper Library News* 22 (winter 1996–1997).

———. "Disposal of Overseas Newspapers (Continued)." *Newspaper Library News* 24 (winter 1997–1998).

———. "Disposal of Overseas Newspapers: Eastern Europe, Latin America, and the USA." *Newspaper Library News* 25 (winter 1998–1999).

British Paper and Board Makers' Association. *Paper Making: A General Account of Its History, Processes, and Applications.* Kenley, Eng., 1950.

Browne, Malcolm W. "Nation's Library Calls on Chemists to Stop Books from Turning to Dust." *The New York Times,* May 22, 1990, p. C1.

Browning, B. L. "The Nature of Paper." In *Deterioration and Preservation of Library Materials,* ed. Howard W. Winger and Richard D. Smith. Chicago: University of Chicago Press, 1970.

Bruccoli, Matthew. *The O'Hara Concern.* New York: Popular Library, 1977.

Buchanan, Sarah, and Sandra Coleman. *Deterioration Survey of the Stanford University Libraries Green Library Stack Collection.* June 1979.

Buckland, Michael. "Searching Multiple Digital Libraries: A Design Analysis."

Berkeley: University of California, 1995, www.sims.berkeley.edu/research/oasis/multisrch.html (viewed August 13, 2000).

Burke, Colin. *Information and Secrecy: Vannevar Bush, Ultra, and the Other Memex.* Metuchen, N.J.: Scarecrow Press, 1994.

———. "Librarians Go High-Tech, Perhaps: The Ford Foundation, the CLR, and INTREX." *Libraries and Culture* 31:1 (winter 1996).

Bush, Vannevar. "As We May Think." *Atlantic Monthly,* July 1945.

Cady, Susan A. "The Electronic Revolution in Libraries: Microfilm Déjà Vu?" *College and Research Libraries,* July 1990.

Case, Charles Z. "Photographing Newspapers." In Raney, *Microphotography for Libraries,* 1936.

Casey, James P. *Pulp and Paper: Chemistry and Chemical Technology.* 2 vols. New York: Interscience Publishers, 1952.

Caswell, Lucy Shelton. "Edwina Dumm: Pioneer Woman Editorial Cartoonist, 1915–1917." *Journalism History* 15 (spring 1988).

Caulfield, D. F., and D. E. Gunderson. "Paper Testing and Strength Characteristics." In Luner, *Paper Preservation,* 1988.

CAUSE. *1996 CAUSE Elite Award Winner: Patricia Battin.* Washington, D.C.: CAUSE, 1996. Videotape.

Central Intelligence Agency. "SUBJECT: Project Artichoke," memo from Project Coordinator to Assistant Director, Scientific Intelligence, April 26, 1952. Reproduced in Argonne National Laboratory, *HREX: Human Radiation Experiments Information Management System,* record number c0022 ("CIA, Meeting Attendance") at hrex.dis.anl.gov (full URL: http://search.dis.anl.gov/plweb-cgi/mhrexpage.pl?c0022+032+75+_free_user_+1%2bminute+60+0+unix+22622+table+mhrex-user+query+doe%3adod%3ahhs%3acia%3ava%3anrc%3a+c.%20p.%20haskins).

Child, Margaret S. "The Future of Cooperative Preservation Microfilming." *Library Resources and Technical Services* 29:1 (January/March 1985).

Clapp, Verner. "A Good Beginning." In *Proceedings of the Eighth Annual Meeting and Convention.* Washington, D.C.: National Microfilm Association, 1959, on microfiche.

———. "The Library: The Great Potential in Our Society?" Keynote address at the second annual Congress for Librarians, St. John's University, Jamaica, N.Y., February 22, 1960. *Wilson Library Bulletin,* December 1960.

———. *The Future of the Research Library.* Urbana: University of Illinois Press, 1964.

———. "The Story of Permanent/Durable Book Paper, 1115–1970." *Scholarly Publishing,* January, April, and July 1971.

Clapp, Verner, Francis H. Henshaw, and Donald C. Holmes. "Are Your Microfilms Deteriorating Acceptably?" *Library Journal,* March 15, 1955.

Clapp, Verner, and Robert T. Jordan. "Re-evaluation of Microfilm as a Method of Book Storage." *College and Research Libraries,* January 1963.

Clark, John D. *Ignition!: An Informal History of Liquid Rocket Propellants.* New Brunswick, N.J.: Rutgers University Press, 1972.

Cole, John Y., ed. *Books in Our Future: Perspectives and Proposals.* Washington, D.C.: Library of Congress, 1987.

Columbia University Libraries, Preservation Department. *The Preservation of Library Materials: A CUL Handbook.* 4th ed. March 1987.

Commission on Preservation and Access. *Newsletter,* 1988–1997. www.clir.org/cpa/cpanews/cpanews.html.

———. " 'Slow Fires' Film Wins Award, Is Widely Shown." Insert to *Newsletter,* February 1988.

Committee on Preservation of Historical Records. *Preservation of Historical Records.* Washington, D.C.: National Academy Press, 1986.

Conroy, Thomas. "The Need for a Re-evaluation of the Use of Alum in Book Conservation and the Book Arts." *Book and Paper Group Annual* 8. Washington, D.C.: The Book and Paper Group of the American Institute for Conservation of Historic and Artistic Works, 1989.

"Contracts." *Missiles and Rockets,* January 15, 1962.

Conway, Paul. "Yale University Library's Project Open Book: Preliminary Research Findings." *D-Lib Magazine,* February 1996, www.dlib.org/dlib/february96/yale/02conway.html.

Corson, William R. *The Armies of Ignorance.* New York: Dial, 1977.

Council on Library Resources, annual reports. Washington, D.C.: Council on Library Resources, 1957–1972.

———. *Meeting on the Problems of Microform in Libraries.* Washington, D.C.: Council on Library Resources, 1958.

Crowe, William Joseph. "Verner W. Clapp as Opinion Leader and Change Agent in the Preservation of Library Materials." Ph.D. diss., Indiana University, 1986.

Cummings, Anthony M., et al. *University Libraries and Scholarly Communication: A Study Prepared for the Andrew W. Mellon Foundation.* Association of Research Libraries, November 1992, www.lib.virginia.edu/mellon/mellon.html.

Czerwinska, E., and R. Kowalik. "Microbiodeterioration of Audiovisual Collections." *Restaurator* 3 (1979).

Dane, Joseph A. "The Curse of the Mummy Paper." *Printing History* 18:2 (1995).

Darling, Pamela W. "Developing a Preservation Microfilming Program." *Library Journal,* November 1, 1974.

———. "Microforms in Libraries: Preservation and Storage." *Microform Review* 5:2 (April 1976).

———. "A Local Preservation Program: Where to Start." *Library Journal,* November 15, 1976.

Darling, Pamela, ed. *Preservation Planning Program: An Assisted Self-Study Manual for Libraries.* Washington, D.C.: Association of Research Libraries, 1982.

Davis, Elmer. *History of the New York Times, 1851–1921.* New York: Greenwood Press, 1969 (facsimile of 1921 ed.).

DeCandido, Robert. "Considerations in Evaluating Searching for Microform Availability." *Microform Review* 19:3 (summer 1990).

DeCandido, Robert, and Paul Parisi, eds. *ANSI/NISO/LBI Standard for Library Binding.* Draft 7.3.1, June 12, 1998, sunsite.berkeley.edu/Binding/NISO7_4.txt.

Deck, Isaiah. "On a Supply of Paper Material from the Mummy Pits of Egypt." In *Transactions of the American Institute of the City of New-York, for the Year 1854.* Albany: C. van Benthuysen, Printer to the Legislature, 1855.

de Croisset, Francis. *Le Souvenir de Robert de Flers, suivi de les précieuses de Genève par Robert de Flers et Francis de Croisset.* Paris: Editions des Portiques, 1929.

De Gennaro, Richard. "Research Libraries: Mankind's Memory at Risk." In Luner, *Paper Preservation,* 1988.

de Sola, Ralph. *Microfilming.* New York, Essential Books, 1944.

Diamond, Sigmund. *Compromised Campus: The Collaboration of Universities with the Intelligence Community, 1945–1955.* New York: Oxford University Press, 1992.

Dodson, Susan Cates. "Microfilm—Which Film Type, Which Application?" *Microform Review* 14:2 (spring 1985).

Donaldson, Scott. *Archibald MacLeish: An American Life.* Boston: Houghton Mifflin, 1992.

Duncan, E. E. "Microfiche Collections for the New York Times/Information Bank." *Microform Review,* October 1973.

Edwards, Paul N. *The Closed World: Computers and the Politics of Discourse in Cold War America.* Cambridge, Mass.: MIT Press, 1996.

Elkington, Nancy, ed. *RLG Preservation Microfilming Handbook.* Mountain View, Calif.: Research Libraries Group, 1992.

Endicott, Stephen, and Edward Hagerman. *The United States and Biological Warfare.* Bloomington: Indiana University Press, 1998.

"End to the Yellowing Pages, An." *Newsweek,* March 20, 1989.

Erhardt, David, Charles S. Tumosa, and Marion F. Mecklenburg. "Material Consequences of the Aging of Paper." In *Preprints, ICOM Committee for Conservation.* Vol. 2. Twelfth triennial meeting. Lyon, 1999.

Evans, Luther, "Recent Microfilming Activities of the Historical Records Survey." *Journal of Documentary Reproduction* 2:1 (March 1939).

———. "Current Microfilm Projects at the Library of Congress." *Das Antiquariat* (Vienna) 8 (August 15, 1952).

Farr, George F., Jr. "Preservation and the National Endowment for the Humanities." In Luner, *Paper Preservation,* 1988.

Feller, Robert L. *Accelerated Aging.* Marina del Rey, Calif.: Getty Conservation Institute, 1994.

Fleischhauer, Carl. "Research Access and Use: The Key Facet of the Nonprint Optical Disk Experiment." *Library of Congress Information Bulletin* 42:37 (September 12, 1983).

Flood, Merrill M. *Aerial Bombing Tactics: General Considerations (A World War II Study).* Santa Monica: Rand, 1952.

———. "New Operations Research Potentials." *Operations Research* 10:4 (July–August 1962).

Forbes, Edward J., and David P. Waite. *Costs and Material Handling Problems in Miniaturizing 100,000 Volumes of Bound Periodicals.* Lexington, Mass.: Forbes and Waite, 1961.

Foster, Clifton Dale. "Microfilming Activities of the Historical Records Survey, 1935–42." *American Archivist* 48:1 (winter 1985).

Fox, Lisa L., ed. *Preservation Microfilming: A Guide for Librarians and Archivists.* 2d ed. Chicago: American Library Association, 1996.

Fussler, Herman H. "Some Implications of Microphotography for Librarians." In *Journal of Documentary Reproduction* (September 1939). Reprinted in Veaner, *Studies in Micropublishing,* 1976.

———. *Photographic Reproduction for Libraries.* Chicago: University of Chicago Press, 1942.

———. "Photographic Reproduction of Research Materials." *Library Trends,* April 1954. Reprinted in Veaner, *Studies in Micropublishing,* 1976.

Garelik, Glenn. "Saving Books with Science." *Discover,* March 1983.

Gear, James L. "Lamination after 30 Years: Record and Prospect," *American Archivist* 28:2 (April 1965).

Gray, Glen G. "Determination and Significance of Activation Energy in Permanence Tests." In *Preservation of Paper and Textiles of Historic and Artistic Value,* ed. John C. Williams. Washington, D.C.: American Chemical Society, 1977.

Gregory, Winifred. *American Newspapers, 1821–1936: A Union List of Files Available in the United States and Canada.* New York, 1937 (New York: Kraus Reprint, 1967).

Grieder, E. M. "Ultrafiche Libraries: A Librarian's View." *Microform Review,* April 1972.

Grose, Peter. *Gentleman Spy: The Life of Allen Dulles.* Boston: Houghton Mifflin, 1994.

Gurney, Gene, and Nick Apple. *The Library of Congress: A Picture Story of the World's Largest Library.* New York: Crown, 1981.

Gwinn, Nancy E. "CLR and Preservation." *College and Research Libraries* 42:2 (March 1981).

———. "The Rise and Fall of Cooperative Projects." *Library Resources and Technical Services* 29:1 (January/March 1985).

Gwinn, Nancy E., ed. *Preservation Microfilming: A Guide for Librarians and Archivists.* Chicago: American Library Association, 1987.

Haas, Warren. *English Book Censorship.* Thesis, Bachelor of Library Science, University of Wisconsin. Rochester, N.Y.: University of Rochester Press for the Association of College and Reference Libraries, 1955. Microcard [microfiche].

———. *Preparation of Detailed Specifications for a National System for the Preservation of Library Materials.* Washington, D.C.: Association of Research Libraries, February 1972.

[———]. *Brittle Books: Reports of the Committee on Preservation and Access.* Washington, D.C.: Council on Library Resources, 1986.

Hahn, Ellen Z. "The Library of Congress Optical Disk Pilot Program: A Report on the Print Project Activities." *Library of Congress Information Bulletin* 42:44 (October 31, 1983).

Harris, Carolyn. "Preservation of Paper Based Materials: Mass Deacidification Methods and Projects." In *Conserving and Preserving Library Materials,* ed. Kathryn Luther Henderson and William T. Henderson. Urbana-Champaign: University of Illinois Press, 1983.

Harris, Kenneth E., and Chandru J. Shahani. *Mass Deacidification: An Initiative to Refine the Diethyl Zinc Process.* Library of Congress Preservation Directorate, October 1994, lcweb.loc.gov/preserv/deacid/proceva1.html (viewed September 20, 2000).

Harvard University. "History of Science: Preserving Collections for the Study of Culture and Society." Proposal submitted to the National Endowment for the Humanities. Cambridge, Mass.: Harvard University, 1998.

Hawkins, Brian L., and Patricia Battin, eds. *The Mirage of Continuity: Reconfiguring Academic Information Resources for the Twenty-first Century.* Washington, D.C.: Council on Library and Information Resources, 1998.

Hawley's Condensed Chemical Dictionary. 12th ed. New York: Van Nostrand Reinhold, 1993.

Hayes, Robert M. "Analysis of the Magnitude, Costs, and Benefits of the Preservation of Research Library Books: A Working Paper Prepared for the Council on Library Resources," January 21, 1985.

———. "The Magnitude, Costs, and Benefits of the Preservation of Brittle Books: Report #0 on the Preservation Project." Sherman Oaks, Calif., November 30, 1987. Typescript.

Hayes, Robert M., and Joseph Becker. *Information Storage and Retrieval: Tools, Elements, Theories.* New York: Wiley, 1963.

———. *Handbook of Data Processing for Libraries.* New York: Becker and Hayes, 1970.

Hearn, Edward T. "Self-Burning Books: Millions of Tomes Need Rescue from Their Acids." *Chicago Tribune,* November 19, 1989, final edition, Nexis.

Hendriks, Klaus B. "Permanence of Paper in Light of Six Centuries of Papermaking in Europe." In *Environnement et conservation de l'écrit, de l'image, et du son.* Paris: Association pour la Recherche Scientifique sur les Arts Graphiques (ARSAG), 1994.

Herring, Richard. *Paper and Paper Making, Ancient and Modern.* 3d ed. London: Longmans, Green, 1863.

Herzberg, Joseph G. *Late City Edition.* New York: Henry Holt, 1947.

Hill, John R., and Charles G. Weber. "Stability of Motion-Picture Films as Determined by Accelerated Aging." *Journal of Research of the National Bureau of Standards* 17 (December 1936).

Holley, Robert P. "The Preservation Microfilming Aspects of the United States Newspaper Program: A Preliminary Study." *Microform Review* 19:3 (summer 1990).

Hunter, Dard. *Papermaking: The History and Technique of an Ancient Craft.* New York: Alfred A. Knopf, 1943.

Jamison, Martin. "The Microcard: Fremont Rider's Precomputer Revolution." *Libraries and Culture* 23:1 (winter 1988).

Johnson, Eric. "Preserving the Printed Word." *United Technologies Magazine,* winter 1982.

Jones, C. Lee. "Preservation Film: Platform for Digital Access Systems." Commission on Preservation and Access, *Newsletter* 58 (July 1993).

Jordan, Sophia and Dorothy Paul. *NEH Medieval Institute Microfilming Project: Database Report of Previously Filmed Titles Queried.* Notre Dame: University of Notre Dame Libraries, undated [circa 1990].

JSTOR. *Background.* www.umich.edu/~jstor/about/background.html (1996) (viewed September 15, 2000).

———. *Bound Volume Survey,* April 3, 2000, www.jstor.org/about/bvs.html (viewed September 19, 2000).

Juergens, George. *Joseph Pulitzer and the* New York World. Princeton, N.J.: Princeton University Press, 1966.

Kaplan, Fred. *The Wizards of Armageddon.* New York: Simon and Schuster, 1983.

Kelly, George B., Jr. "Mass Deacidification." In *Preservation of Library Materials,* ed. Joyce R. Russell. New York: Special Libraries Association, 1980.

Kenney, Anne R. "Digital Image Quality: From Conversion to Presentation and Beyond." Paper presented at the Scholarly Communication and Technology conference, sponsored by the Andrew W. Mellon Foundation, Emory University, Atlanta, April 24–25, 1997, arl.cni.org/scomm/scat/kenney.html.

Kenney, Anne R., and Lynne K. Personius. *The Cornell/Xerox/Commission on Preservation and Access Joint Study in Digital Preservation. Report: Phase 1.* "Digital Capture, Paper Facsimiles, and Network Access." December 1990.

Kesse, Erich J. "Condition Survey of Master Microfilm Negatives, University of Florida Libraries." *Abbey Newsletter* 15:3 (May 1991), palimpsest.stanford.edu/byorg/abbey/an/an15/an15-3/an15-313.html.

———. "Survey of Micropublishers." A Report to the Commission on Preservation and Access, October 1992.

Kimball, Jeffrey P. *Nixon's Vietnam War.* Lawrence, Kans.: University Press of Kansas, 1998.

King, Gilbert. "The Monte Carlo Method as a Natural Mode of Expression in

Operations Research." *Journal of the Operations Research Society of America* 1:2 (February 1953).

King, Gilbert W., et al. *Automation and the Library of Congress.* Washington, D.C.: Library of Congress, 1963.

Klaidman, Stephen. "Cultural Center Problems Are Space, Money, Boredom." *The Washington Post,* June 12, 1977, p. B1.

Kluger, Richard. *The Paper: The Life and Death of the New York* Herald Tribune. New York: Alfred A. Knopf, 1986.

———. *Ashes to Ashes: America's Hundred-Year Cigarette War, the Public Health, and the Unabashed Triumph of Philip Morris.* New York: Alfred A. Knopf, 1996.

Knott, Lawson B., Jr. "Aging Blemishes on Microfilm Negatives," General Services Administration Circular, no. 326, January 21, 1964.

Kolar, Jana. "Mechanism of Autoxidative Degradation of Cellulose." *Restaurator* 18 (1997).

Koop, Theodore. *Weapon of Silence.* Chicago: University of Chicago Press, 1946.

Koski, Ahti A., et al. "Studies of the Pyrolysis of Diethylzinc by the Toluene Carrier Method and of the Reaction of Ethyl Radicals with Toluene." *Canadian Journal of Chemistry* 54 (1976).

Kraft, Nancy. *Final Report, Iowa Newspaper Project: Microfilming.* State Historical Society of Iowa, 1992.

Kuhlman, A. F. "Are We Ready to Preserve Newspapers on Films? A Symposium." *Library Quarterly,* April 1935. Reprinted in Veaner, *Studies in Micropublishing,* 1976.

Kyrillidou, Martha, Michael O'Connor, and Julia C. Blixrud. *ARL Preservation Statistics, 1996–97.* Washington, D.C.: Association of Research Libraries, 1998.

La Hood, Charles G., Jr. "Microfilm for the Library of Congress." *College and Research Libraries,* July 1973.

Lancaster, F. W. *Toward Paperless Information Systems.* New York: Academic Press, 1978.

Lauder, John E. "The Scottish Newspapers Microfilming Unit." *Microform Review* 24:2 (spring 1995).

Leach, Steven. "The Growth Rates of Major Academic Libraries: Rider and Purdue Reviewed." *College and Research Libraries,* November 1976.

Lee, Alfred McClung. *The Daily Newspaper in America.* New York: Macmillan, 1937.

Lee, John H. "Chemical Initiation of Detonation in Fuel-Air Explosive Clouds." U.S. patent no. 6,168,123 (December 1, 1992).

Lemberg, William Richard. "A Life-Cycle Cost Analysis for the Creation, Storage, and Dissemination of a Digitized Document Collection." Ph.D. diss., School of Library and Information Studies, University of California at Berkeley, 1995, www.sims.berkeley.edu/research/publications/DigtlDoc.pdf.

Lesk, Michael. "Image Formats for Preservation and Access: A Report of the Technology Assessment Advisory Committee to the Commission on Preservation and Access." Washington, D.C.: Commission on Preservation and Access, 1990. Republished in *Microform Review* 21:1 (1992).

———. *Preservation of New Technology.* A report of the Technology Assessment Advisory Committee to the Commission on Preservation and Access. Washington, D.C.: Commission on Preservation and Access, October 1992, www.clir.org/pubs/reports/lesk/lesk2.html.

———. "Substituting Images for Books: The Economics for Libraries." Document Analysis and Information Retrieval (symposium). Las Vegas, April 1996. www.lesk.com/mlesk/unlv/unlv.html (viewed September 19, 2000).

———. *Practical Digital Libraries: Books, Bytes, and Bucks.* San Francisco: Morgan Kaufmann, 1997.

Library of Congress. *Annual Report of the Librarian of Congress for the Fiscal Year Ended June 30, 1938.* Washington, D.C.: U.S. Government Printing Office, 1939.

———. *Annual Report of the Librarian of Congress for the Fiscal Year Ended June 30, 1941.* Washington, D.C.: U.S. Government Printing Office, 1942.

———. "Staff Forum." *Library of Congress Information Bulletin* 10:42 (October 15, 1951).

———. *Annual Report of the Librarian of Congress for the Fiscal Year Ending June 30, 1952.* Washington, D.C.: U.S. Government Printing Office, 1953.

———. *Annual Report of the Librarian of Congress for the Fiscal Year Ending June 30, 1956.* Washington, D.C.: U.S. Government Printing Office, 1957.

———. "Administrative Department—Office of Collections Maintenance and Preservation." *Library of Congress Information Bulletin* 25:41 (October 13, 1966).

———. "Administrative Department—Photoduplication Service." *Library of Congress Information Bulletin* 25:41 (October 13, 1966).

———. "National Preservation Program—First Phase." *Library of Congress Information Bulletin* 26:4 (January 26, 1967).

———. "Frazer G. Poole." *Library of Congress Information Bulletin* 26:10 (March 9, 1967).

———. *Papermaking: Art and Craft.* Washington, D.C.: Library of Congress, 1968.

———. *Annual Report of the Librarian of Congress for the Fiscal Year Ending June 30, 1972.* Washington, D.C.: U.S. Government Printing Office, 1973.

———. *Verner Warren Clapp, 1901–1972: A Memorial Tribute.* Washington, D.C., Library of Congress, 1973.

———. "Serial Division." *Library of Congress Information Bulletin* 35:2 (January 9, 1976).

———. "Welsh Named Deputy Librarian." *Library of Congress Information Bulletin* 35:4 (January 23, 1976).

———. "Newspaper Preservation Program." *Library of Congress Information Bulletin* 35:28 (July 9, 1976).

———. "National Preservation Program Office Expands." *Library of Congress Information Bulletin,* November 5, 1984.

———. "Library Announces Public Opening of Access to Optical Disk Technology." *Library of Congress Information Bulletin* 45:7 (February 17, 1986).

———. "The Librarian of Congress Testifies Before Appropriations Subcommittee." *Library of Congress Information Bulletin* 45:9 (March 3, 1986).

———. "Engineering Problems Experienced at Deacidification Test Facility." *Library of Congress Information Bulletin* 45:11 (March 17, 1986).

———. "Library's Book Deacidification Program Moves Forward Following Review of Incidents and Pilot Plant." *Library of Congress Information Bulletin* 45:27 (July 7, 1986).

———. "Collections Policy Statements: U.S. Newspapers." November 1996, lcweb.loc.gov/acq/devpol/neu.html (viewed June 2, 2000).

———. "19th and 20th Century U.S. Newspapers in Original Format: Inventory of Volumes Held in Remote Storage," 1998, lcweb.loc.gov/rr/news/inventor.html.

Library of Congress, Serials Division. *Holdings of American Nineteenth and Twentieth Century Newspapers Printed on Wood Pulp Paper.* Mimeograph. May 1950.

Library of Congress, Working Group on Reference and Research. *Report to the Task Group on Shelving Arrangement.* July 8, 1997, updated October 30, 1997.

Licklider, J. C. R. *Libraries of the Future.* Foreword by Verner Clapp. Cambridge, Mass.: MIT Press, 1965.

Licklider, J. C. R., and R. E. Bunch. "Effects of Enforced Wakefulness upon the Growth and the Maze Learning Performance of White Rats." *Journal of Comparative Psychology* 39 (1946).

Lindstrom, Tom. "Discussion Contribution: Slow Fires—It's Paper Chemistry, Physics, and Biology." In Luner, *Paper Preservation,* 1988.

Lockhart, Vickie, and Ann Swartzell. "Evaluation of Microfilm Vendors." *Microform Review* 19:3 (summer 1990).

Longley, Charles. "Newspapers at the Boston Public Library." T.s. March 13, 1998.

Luner, Philip, ed. *Paper Preservation: Current Issues and Recent Developments.* Atlanta: Tappi, 1988.

Lynn, M. Stuart. "Digital Technologies, Preservation and Access." *The Commission on Preservation and Access Newsletter* 43 (March 1992), www.clir.org/pubs/cpanews/cpan143.html.

McCrady, Ellen. "The History of Microfilm Blemishes." *Restaurator* 6 (1984).

McIntyre, John E. "Protecting the Physical Form." In *Guidelines for Digital Imaging.* Joint RLG and NPO Preservation Conference, 1998, www.rlg.org/preserv/joint/mcintyre.html.

MacKay, Neil. *The Hole in the Card: The Story of the Microfilm Aperture Card.* St. Paul: Minnesota Mining and Manufacturing, 1966.

Mann, Thomas. *The Height-Shelving Threat to the Nation's Libraries.* Washington, D.C.: AFSCME Local 2910 ("The Guild"), June 1999.

Marcum, Deanna B. "Reclaiming the Research Library: The Founding of the Council on Library Resources." *Libraries and Culture* 31:1 (winter 1996).

Marks, John. *The Search for the Manchurian Candidate.* New York: Times Books, 1979.

Marley, S. Branson, Jr. "Newspapers and the Library of Congress." *Library of Congress Quarterly Journal* 32:3 (July 1975). Reprinted in Veaner, *Studies in Micropublishing,* 1976.

Martin, Murray S. "New Microfilms for Old Books." *American Libraries,* February 1970.

———. "Matters Arising from the Minutes: A Further Consideration of Microform-Serials Exchange." *Microform Review* 2 (April 1973).

———. "Promoting Microforms to Students and Faculty." *Microform Review* 8:2 (spring 1979).

Mearns, David C. *The Story Up to Now: The Library of Congress, 1800–1946.* Washington, D.C.: Library of Congress, 1947.

Merrill-Oldham, Jan, and Merrily Smith, eds. *The Library Preservation Program: Models, Priorities, Possibilities.* Proceedings of a conference, April 29, 1983. Chicago: American Library Association, 1985.

Merrill-Oldham, Jan, and Paul Parisi. *Guide to the Library Binding Institute Standard for Library Binding.* Chicago: American Library Association, 1990.

Merrill-Oldham, Jan, and Gay Walker. *Brittle Books Programs.* Washington, D.C.: Systems and Procedures Exchange Center (SPEC) Kit 152, Office of Management Services, Association of Research Libraries, 1989. (Introductory flyer is bound in the book.)

Metcalf, Keyes D. "Microphotography in the New York Public Library." In Raney, *Microphotography for Libraries,* 1936.

———. "Newspapers and Microphotography." *The Journal of Documentary Reproduction* 2:3 (September 1939).

———. "Some Trends in Research Libraries." In *William Warner Bishop: A Tribute,* ed.

Harry Miller Lydenberg and Andrew Keogh. New Haven: Yale University Press, 1941.

———. *Random Recollections of an Anachronism.* New York: Readex Books, 1980.

Metcalf, Keyes, et al. "The Promise of Microprint: A Symposium Based on *The Scholar and the Future of the Research Library.*" *College and Research Libraries,* March 1945.

Milevski, Robert J. "Mass Deacidification: Effects of Treatment on Library Materials Deacidified by the DEZ and MG-3 Processes." In *The 1992 Book and Paper Group Annual,* vol. 11. Washington, D.C.: American Institute for Conservation, 1992.

Miller, Edward. *That Noble Cabinet: A History of the British Museum.* Athens, Ohio: Ohio University Press, 1974.

Miller, J. Hillis. *Preserving the Literary Heritage: The Final Report of the Scholarly Advisory Committee on Modern Language and Literature of the Commission on Preservation and Access.* Washington, D.C.: Commission on Preservation and Access, July 1991, www.clir.org/pubs/reports/miller/miller.html.

Miller, Michael. *Ideas for Preservation Fund Raising: A Support Package for Libraries and Archives.* Washington, D.C.: Commission on Preservation and Access, 1990.

Milum, Betty. "Eisenhower, ALA, and the Selection of L. Quincy Mumford." *Libraries and Culture* 30:1 (winter 1995).

Minkler, Whitney S. *Audit Procedures and Inspection Results from 1% of Microfilm Samples from Ohio State, Yale, and Harvard Universities.* Fairfax, Va.: MSTC, March 30, 1993.

Molz, Kathleen. "Interview of Verner Clapp, Council on Library Resources, Inc. by Kathleen Molz, editor, *Wilson Library Bulletin.*" Verner Clapp papers, Library of Congress. Later published as Kathleen Molz, "Interview with Verner Clapp," Wilson Library Bulletin 40:2 (1965).

Molyneux, Robert E. "What Did Rider Do? An Inquiry into the Methodology of Fremont Rider's *The Scholar and the Future of the Research Library.*" *Libraries and Culture* 29:1 (summer 1994).

Montori, Carla. "Re: electronic/paper format & weeding," PADG (Preservation Administrators Discussion Group), December 15, 1997. Archived on the CoOL website, palimpsest.stanford.edu/byform/mailing-lists/padg/1997/12/msg00011.html (viewed September 29, 2000).

Morehouse, H. G. *Telefacsimile Services Between Libraries with the Xerox Magnavox Telecopier.* Reno: University of Reno Library, December 20, 1966.

Morris, James M. "The Foundation Connection." In *Influencing Change in Research Librarianship: A Festschrift for Warren J. Haas,* ed. Martin M. Cummings. Washington, D.C.: Council on Library Resources, 1988.

Morse, Philip M. *Library Effectiveness: A Systems Approach.* Cambridge, Mass.: MIT Press, 1968.

———. *In at the Beginnings: A Physicist's Life.* Cambridge, Mass.: MIT Press, 1977.

Morse, Philip M., and George E. Kimball. *Methods of Operations Research.* Washington, D.C.: Operations Evaluation Group, U.S. Navy, 1946.

Mott, Frank Luther. *American Journalism.* New York: Macmillan, 1947.

Munsell, Joel. *Chronology of the Origin and Progress of Paper and Paper-Making.* New York: Garland, 1980. (Facsimile of 5th ed., Albany: J. Munsell, 1876.)

"Musings on Mummy-Paper." *Punch* 12 (May 29, 1847).

National Aeronautics and Space Administration, Goddard Space Flight Center. *Accident Investigation Board Report of Mishaps at the Deacidification Pilot Plant, Building 306 on December 5, 1985, and February 14, 1986.* James H. Robinson, Jr., Board Chairman. September 4, 1986.

National Endowment for the Humanities. "Brittle Books." www.neh.gov/preservation/brittlebooks.html (viewed October 4, 2000).

National Microfilm Association. *Proceedings of the Eighth Annual Meeting and Convention*. Washington, D.C., April 2–4, 1959, microfiche of disbound pamphlet.

Nelson, W. Dale. "Space Technology Used to Prolong Life of Books." Associated Press, May 23, 1982, Nexis.

New York Public Library. "When Did Newspapers Begin to Use Wood Pulp Stock?" *Bulletin of the New York Public Library* 33 (1929).

———. "Authors and Publishers Sign Landmark Declaration for Book Preservation." News release. March 7, 1989. Reprinted in Association of Research Libraries, *Preserving Knowledge*.

New York Times, The. "Conquest of Brittleness, the Ruin of Old Books." August 8, 1984, B8.

New York Times, The. "Joseph Becker, 72, Information Expert." July 27, 1995, D22.

Nickerson, Matthew. "pH: Only a Piece of the Preservation Puzzle: A Comparison of the Preservation Studies at Brigham Young, Yale, and Syracuse Universities." *Library Resources and Technical Services* 36:1 (1992).

Niles, Ann. "Conversion of Serials from Paper to Microfilm." *Microform Review* 9:2 (spring 1980).

Nyren, Karl. "The DEZ Process and the Library of Congress." *Library Journal*, September 15, 1986.

———. "It's Time to Dump DEZ." *Library Journal*, September 15, 1986.

O'Brien, Frank M. *The Story of the Sun*. New York: George H. Doran, 1918.

Ohio Board of Regents. *Academic Libraries in Ohio: Progress through Collaboration, Storage, and Technology*. Report of the Library Study Committee, September 1987.

Okerson, Ann. "Microform Conversion—A Case Study." *Microform Review* 14:3 (summer 1985).

Ottemiller, John H. "The Selective Book Retirement Program at Yale." *Yale University Library Gazette* 34:2 (October 1959).

Overhage, Carl F. J., and R. Joyce Harman, eds. *Intrex: Report of a Planning Conference on Information Transfer Experiments*. Cambridge, Mass.: MIT Press, 1965.

"Paper from Egyptian Mummies." Syracuse *Daily Standard*, August 19, 1856. Undated editorial reprinted from the *Albany Journal*.

Parsonage, J. S. "The 'Scholar' and After: A Study of the Development of the Microcard." *Library Association Record*, November 1949. Reprinted in Veaner, *Studies in Micropublishing*, 1976.

Petroski, Henry. *The Book on the Bookshelf*. New York: Alfred A. Knopf, 1999.

Poole, Frazer G. "William James Barrow." In *Encyclopedia of Library and Information Science*. New York: Dekker, 1969.

Poundstone, William. *Prisoner's Dilemma*. New York: Doubleday, 1992.

Preservation Microfilming: Planning and Production. Papers from the RTSD Preservation Microfilming Institute, New Haven, April 21, 23, 1988. Chicago: Association for Library Collections and Technical Services, American Library Association, 1989.

Preservation Resources, "Preserving Microfilm," www.oclc.org/oclc/promo/presres/9138.htm (viewed September 13, 2000).

Pritsker, Alan B., and J. William Sadler. "An Evaluation of Microfilm as a Method of Book Storage." *College and Research Libraries* 18:4 (July 1957).

Public Information Research. *NameBase* (database). www.pir.org.

Puckette, C. McD. "Question of Filming the New York Times." In Raney, *Microphotography for Libraries,* 1936.

Radio Corporation of America, Defense Electronic Products. "A Proposal for an Automatic Page Turner: Submitted to the Council on Library Resources in Response to 'An Automatic Page Turner—the Basic Requirements,' November 1, 1957."

"Rag and Paper Business, The," New York *Tribune,* November 4, 1856.

"Rags from Egypt." Syracuse *Daily Standard,* July 31, 1856.

Raney, M. Llewellyn. "A Capital Truancy." *The Journal of Documentary Reproduction* 3:2 (June 1940).

Raney, M. Llewellyn, ed. *Microphotography for Libraries.* Chicago: American Library Association, 1936.

Rau, Erik Peter. "Combat Scientists: The Emergence of Operations Research in the United States during World War II." Ph.D. diss., University of Pennsylvania, 1999.

Reed, Jutta R. "Cost Comparison of Periodicals in Hard Copy and on Microform." *Microform Review* 5:3 (July 1976).

Regis, Ed. *The Biology of Doom: The History of America's Secret Germ Warfare Project.* New York: Henry Holt, 1999.

Reilly, James M., et al. "Stability of Black-and-White Photographic Images, with Special Reference to Microfilm." *Abbey Newsletter* 12:5 (July 1988).

Rensenberger, Boyce. "Acid Test: Stalling Self-Destruction in the Stacks." *The Washington Post,* August 29, 1988.

Research Information Service, John Crerar Library. *Dissemination of Information for Scientific Research and Development.* Chicago: John Crerar Library, 1954.

Rider, Fremont. *Are the Dead Alive?* New York: B. W. Dodge, 1909.

———. *The Scholar and the Future of the Research Library.* New York: Hadham Press, 1944.

———. *Compact Book Storage.* New York: Hadham Press, 1949.

———. "Microcards vs. the Cost of Book Storage." *American Documentation* 2:1 (January 1951). Reprinted in Veaner, *Studies in Micropublishing,* 1976.

[———.] "Microtext in the Management of Book Collections: A Symposium." *College and Research Libraries,* July 1953.

———. *And Master of None: An Autobiography in the Third Person.* Middletown, Conn.: Godfrey Memorial Library, 1955.

Ringle, Ken. "Card Catalogue to Be Filed Away; Library Turns to Computers." *The Washington Post,* November 13, 1984, p. A1, final edition.

Robbins, Louise S. "The Library of Congress and Federal Loyalty Programs, 1947–1956: No 'Communists or Cocksuckers.' " *Library Quarterly* 64:4 (October 1994).

Robinson, Lawrence S. "Establishing a Preservation Microfilming Program: The Library of Congress Experience." *Microform Review* 13:4 (fall 1984).

Rogers, Rutherford. "Library Preservation: Its Scope, History, and Importance." In Merrill-Oldham and Smith, *Library Preservation Program,* 1985.

Roggia, Sally Cruz. "William James Barrow." In *Dictionary of Virginia Biography.* Richmond: Library of Virginia, 1998.

———. "William James Barrow: A Biographical Study of His Formative Years and His Role in the History of Library and Archives Conservation from 1931 to 1941." Ph.D. Diss., Columbia University, 1999.

Roth, Steven M. *The Censorship of International Civilian Mail during World War II: The*

History, Structure, and Operation of the United States Office of Censorship. Lake Oswego, Oreg.: La Posta Publications, 1991.

Rouyer, Philippe. "Humidity Control and the Preservation of Silver Gelatin Microfilm." *Microform Review* 21:2 (1992).

Rubin, Jack. *A History of Micrographics in the First Person.* Silver Spring, Md.: National Micrographics Association, 1980.

Russell, Colin A. *Edward Frankland: Chemistry, Controversy, and Conspiracy in Victorian England.* Cambridge: Cambridge University Press, 1996.

Salmon, Stephen R. "User Resistance to Microforms in the Research Library." *Microform Review* 3:3 (July 1974).

Sanders, Terry. *Slow Fires.* Written by Ben Maddow and narrated by Robert MacNeil. A presentation of the American Film Foundation. Washington, D.C.: Council on Library Resources, 1987. Motion picture.

Schubert, Irene. "Re: Serials microfilming," PADG (Preservation Administrators Discussion Group), archived on the CoOL website, palimpsest.stanford.edu, October 31, 1997.

Schudson, Michael. *Discovering the News: A Social History of American Newspapers.* New York: Basic Books, 1978.

"Scientific Journal in Microfilm—An Experiment in Publishing." *Library Journal,* April 1, 1959.

Scribner, Bourdon W. "Summary Report of Research at the National Bureau of Standards on Materials for the Reproduction of Records." In *Transactions, International Federation for Documentation.* Vol. 1. Fourteenth conference. Oxford, 1938.

Shaffer, Norman J. "Library of Congress Pilot Preservation Project." *College and Research Libraries,* January 1969.

Shahani, Chandru. *Accelerated Aging of Paper: Can It Really Foretell the Permanence of Paper.* Library of Congress Preservation Directorate, November 1995, lcweb.loc.gov/preserv/rt/age/age.html (viewed September 14, 2000).

Shahani, Chandru, and William K. Wilson. "Preservation of Libraries and Archives." *American Scientist,* May–June 1987.

Shulman, Seth. "Code Name: Corona." *Technology Review,* October 1996.

Singer, Mark. "Missed Opportunities Dept.: Did the New York Public Library Let Some History Slip Through Its Fingers?" Talk of the Town. *The New Yorker,* January 12, 1998.

Slauson, Allan B. *A Check List of American Newspapers in the Library of Congress.* Washington, D.C.: U.S. Government Printing Office, 1901.

Smith, Abby. "The Future of the Past: Preservation in American Research Libraries" (draft). Council on Library and Information Resources, January 1999.

Smith, Bradley F. *The Shadow Warriors.* New York: Basic Books, 1983.

Smith, F. Dow. "The Design and Engineering of Corona's Optics." In *Corona: Between the Sun and the Earth,* ed. Robert A. McDonald. Bethesda, Md.: American Society for Photogrammetry and Remote Sensing, 1997.

Smith, R. Harris. *OSS: The Secret History of America's First Central Intelligence Agency.* Berkeley: University of California Press, 1972.

Smith, Richard D. "Paper Impermanence as a Consequence of pH and Storage Conditions." *Library Quarterly* 39:2 (April 1969).

———. "Deacidifying Library Collections: Myths and Realities." *Restaurator* 8 (1987).

———. "Deacidification Technologies: State of the Art." In Luner, *Paper Preservation,* 1988.

"Space Problems of Large (General) Research Libraries: Report of a Meeting." *College and Research Libraries,* May 1959.

Sparks, Peter. "The Library of Congress Preservation Program." In Merrill-Oldham and Smith, *Library Preservation Program,* 1985.

———. "Marketing for Preservation." In Merrill-Oldham and Smith, *Library Preservation Program,* 1985.

———. "Mass Deacidification at the Library of Congress." *Restaurator* 8 (1987).

Spaulding, Carl M. "Kicking the Silver Habit: Confessions of a Former Addict." *American Libraries,* December 1978.

Srodes, James. *Allen Dulles: Master of Spies.* Washington, D.C.: Regnery, 1999.

Stam, David H. "Finding Funds to Support Preservation." In Merrill-Oldham and Smith, *Library Preservation Program,* 1985.

Stam, David H., et al. *Review and Assessment Committee, Final Report.* Washington, D.C.: Commission on Preservation and Access, 1991.

———. "The Questions of Preservation." In Welsh, *Research Libraries—Yesterday, Today, and Tomorrow,* 1993.

Stange, Eric. "Millions of Books Are Turning to Dust—Can They Be Saved?" *The New York Times Book Review,* March 29, 1987.

Starr, Mary Jane. "The Preservation of Canadian Newspapers." *Microform Review* 15:3 (summer 1986).

Stille, Alexander. "Overload." *The New Yorker,* March 8, 1999.

Stout, Leon J., et al. "Guaranteeing a Library for the Future." *Restaurator* 8:4 (1987)

Ströfer-Hua, E. "Experimental Measurement: Interpreting Extrapolation and Prediction by Accelerated Aging." *Restaurator* 11 (1990).

Subcommittee on Legislative Branch Appropriations, U.S. House of Representatives. *Hearings before a Subcommittee of the Committee on Appropriations,* pt. 2, February 10, 1987. Washington, D.C.: U.S. Government Printing Office, 1987.

Subcommittee on Postsecondary Education, U.S. House of Representatives. *Oversight Hearing on the Problem of "Brittle Books" in Our Nation's Libraries,* March 3, 1987. Washington, D.C.: U.S. Government Printing Office, 1987.

Sullivan, Larry E. "United States Newspaper Program: Progress and Prospects." *Microform Review* 15:3 (summer 1986).

Sullivan, Robert C. "The Acquisition of Library Microforms: Part 2." *Microform Review* 6:4 (July 1977).

Sutton, George P. *Rocket Propulsion Elements: An Introduction to the Engineering of Rockets.* 3d ed. New York: Wiley, 1963.

Swan, John. "Micropermanence and Electronic Evanescence." *Microform Review* 20:2 (spring 1991).

Swanberg, W. A. *Citizen Hearst.* New York: Scribner's, 1961.

Tanselle, G. Thomas. "The Latest Forms of Book-Burning." In his *Literature and Artifacts,* 1998.

———. "Libraries, Museums, and Reading." In his *Literature and Artifacts,* 1998.

———. *Literature and Artifacts.* Charlottesville: Bibliographical Society of the University of Virginia, 1998.

———. "Reproductions and Scholarship." In his *Literature and Artifacts,* 1998.

———. "Statement on the Role of Books and Manuscripts in the Electronic Age." In his *Literature and Artifacts,* 1998.

———. "Statement on the Significance of Primary Records." In his *Literature and Artifacts,* 1998.

Tate, Vernon D. "Microphotography in Wartime." *Journal of Documentary Reproduction* 5:3 (September 1942).

Tauber, Maurice F., ed. *Library Binding Manual: A Handbook of Useful Procedures for the Maintenance of Library Volumes.* Boston: Library Binding Institute, 1972.

Thompson, Jack C. "Mass Deacidification: Thoughts on the Cunha Report." *Restaurator* 9:4 (1988).

Twain, Mark. *The Innocents Abroad; or, the New Pilgrims' Progress.* New York: Hippocrene Books, n.d. (facsimile of Hartford, Conn.: American Publishing Company, 1869).

U.S. Congress, Office of Technology Assessment. *Book Preservation Technologies.* OTA-0-375. Washington, D.C.: U.S. Government Printing Office, 1988.

University of California, Systemwide Operations and Planning Group (SOPAG). "Action/Decision Minutes," February 26, 1999. *UCI's Information Page on UC Systemwide Library Planning,* sun3.lib.uci.edu/~staff/system_wide.htm.

Unsworth, Michael E. "A Lesson Not Learned: The MACV 'Answer Machine.' " Abstract of a paper given at a symposium, "After the Cold War: Reassessing Vietnam," April 1996. The Vietnam Center at Texas Tech University, www.ttu.edu/~vietnam/96papers/macv.htm (viewed September 14, 2000).

Urquhart, J. A., and N. C. Urquhart. *Relegation and Stock Control in Libraries.* Stocksfield, Northumberland: Oriel Press, 1976.

Veaner, Allen B. "The Crisis in Micropublication." *Choice,* June 1968.

———. "New York Times on Microfilm." *Choice,* December 1968.

Veaner, Allen B., ed. *Studies in Micropublishing, 1853–1976: Documentary Sources.* Westport, Conn.: Microform Review, 1976.

Vienneau, David. "Ottawa Paid for '50s Brainwashing Experiments, Files Show." *The Toronto Star,* April 14, 1986, final edition, p. A1, Nexis. Related articles April 15–17 and 20, 1986.

von Elbe, G., and E. T. McHale. *Annual Interim Report: Chemical Initiation of FAE Clouds.* Report by Atlantic Research Corporation to Bernard T. Wolfson, Bolling Air Force Base, Washington, D.C., contract no. F49620-77-C-0097. Washington, D.C.: Air Force Office of Scientific Research, 1979.

Wächter, Otto. "Paper Strengthening: Mass Conservation of Unbound and Bound Newspapers." *Restaurator* 8 (1987).

Waitt, Alden H. *Gas Warfare: Smoke, Flame, and Gas in Modern War.* 2d ed. Fighting Forces ed. Washington, D.C.: Infantry Journal, 1944.

Walker, Gay. "The Evolution of Yale's Preservation Program." In Merrill-Oldham and Smith, *Library Preservation Program,* 1985.

———. "Preservation Decision Making: A Descriptive Model" (1986). In Merrill-Oldham and Walker, *Brittle Books Programs,* 1989.

———. "Preservation Decision-Making and Archival Photocopying." *Restaurator* 8 (1987).

———. "One Step Beyond: The Future of Preservation Microfilming." In *Preservation Microfilming: Planning and Production,* 1988.

Walker, Gay, et al. "The Yale Survey: A Large-Scale Study of Book Deterioration in the Yale University Library." *College and Research Libraries,* March 1985.

Wasserman, Paul. "Interview with Paul Wasserman Regarding the Early History of CLIS." Esther Herman, interviewer. College of Information Studies, University of Maryland. www.clis.umd.edu/faculty/wasserman/pwinterview.html. January 11, 1995.

Waters, Peter. "The Deterioration of Library Materials: A Doomsday Inevitability or a Manageable Preservation Challenge?" Lecture, Columbus Discovers Calligraphy Conference, August 1, 1992. Typescript.

———. "From Florence to St. Petersburg: An Enlightening and Thought-Provoking Experience." Paper read at the conference "Redefining Disasters: A Decade of Counter Disaster Planning," Library of New South Wales, September 1995.

Weaver, Warren. *Scene of Change: A Lifetime in American Science.* New York: Scribner's, 1970.

Weber, David C. "The Foreign Newspaper Microfilm Project, 1938–1955." *Harvard Library Bulletin* (spring 1956). In Veaner, *Studies in Micropublishing,* 1976.

Weeks, Linton. "Brave New Library." *The Washington Post Magazine,* May 26, 1991.

———. "In a Stack of Troubles: The Librarian of Congress Has Raised Funds. And His Voice. And a Lot of Eyebrows." *The Washington Post,* December 27, 1995, p. F1, Nexis.

Welsh, William J. "Can Bill Welsh Conquer Time and Space for Libraries?" Interview with Arthur Plotnik. *American Libraries* 15:11 (December 1984).

———. "The Library of Congress: A More-Than-Equal Partner." *Library Resources and Technical Services* 29:1 (January/March 1985).

———. "The Preservation Challenge." In Merrill-Oldham and Smith, *Library Preservation Program,* 1985.

———. "In Defense of DEZ: LC's Perspective." *Library Journal,* January 1987.

———. "Libraries and Librarians: Opportunities and Challenges," paper presented at the seventh international seminar, Kanazawa Institute of Technology, Library Center, Kanazawa, Japan, 1989. In Welsh, *Research Libraries—Yesterday, Today, and Tomorrow,* 1993.

Welsh, William J., ed. *Research Libraries—Yesterday, Today, and Tomorrow.* Westport, Conn.: Greenwood Press, 1993.

White, Linda J. *Packaging the American Word: A Survey of Nineteenth and Early Twentieth Century American Publishers' Bindings in the General Collections of the Library of Congress.* Library of Congress Preservation Directorate, 1997. No longer available on the Library of Congress's website (or anywhere else); formerly at lcweb.loc.gov/preserv/survey.

Wiederkehr, Robert R. V. *The Design and Analysis of a Sample Survey of the Condition of Books in the Library of Congress.* Rockville, Md.: King Research, 1984.

Williams, Gordon. *The Preservation of Deteriorating Books: An Examination of the Problem with Recommendations for a Solution.* Report of the ARL Committee on the Preservation of Research Library Materials, September 1964.

———. "The Preservation of Deteriorating Books." *Library Journal,* January 1, 1966.

Williams, John C., and George B. Kelly, Jr. "Method of Deacidifying Paper." U.S. patent nos. 3,969,549 (July 13, 1976) and 4,051,276 (September 27, 1977).

Williams, Richard L. "The Library of Congress Can't Hold All of Man's Knowledge—But It Tries, As It Acquires a New $160-Million Annex." *Smithsonian* 11:1 (April 1980).

Wilson, William K., and E. J. Parks. "An Analysis of the Aging of Paper." *Restaurator* 3 (1979).

———. "Comparison of Accelerated Aging of Book Papers in 1937 with 36 Years Natural Aging." *Restaurator* 4 (1980).

———. "Historical Survey of Research at the National Bureau of Standards on Materials for Archival Records." *Restaurator* 5 (1983).

Winks, Robin W. *Cloak and Gown: Scholars in the Secret War, 1939–1961.* 2d ed. New Haven: Yale University Press, 1987.

Wise, David, and Thomas B. Ross. *The Espionage Establishment.* New York: Bantam, 1967.

Woodsworth, Anne, and Barbara von Wahlde, eds. *Leadership for Research Libraries: A Festschrift for Robert M. Hayes.* Metuchen, N.J.: Scarecrow Press, 1988.

Wright, Susan. *Preventing a Biological Arms Race.* Cambridge, Mass.: MIT Press, 1990.

Yagoda, Ben. *About Town:* The New Yorker *and the World It Made.* New York: Scribner, 2000.

Yerburgh, Mark R., and Rhoda Yerburgh. "Where Have All the Ultras Gone? The Rise and Demise of the Ultrafiche Library Collection, 1968–1973." *Microfilm Review* 13 (fall 1984).

Zinman, Michael. *It Became Necessary to Destroy the Town in Order to Save It.* Privately printed, December 1997. Poster.

Index

About the Author

NICHOLSON BAKER was born in 1957 and attended the Eastman School of Music and Haverford College. He has published five novels—*The Mezzanine* (1988), *Room Temperature* (1990), *Vox* (1992), *The Fermata* (1994), and *The Everlasting Story of Nory* (1998)—and two works of nonfiction, *U and I* (1991) and *The Size of Thoughts* (1996). His work has appeared in *The New Yorker, The Atlantic, The New York Review of Books,* the *London Review of Books, American Libraries, Best American Short Stories,* and *Best American Essays.* He lives in Maine with his wife and two children.